RELIGIOUS MEN AND WOMEN
IN CHURCH LAW

Authorized translation of
Religieux et Religieuses d'après le
Droit Ecclésiastique
septième edition
corrigée et augementée
MUSEUM LESSIANUM
1957

RELIGIOUS MEN AND WOMEN IN CHURCH LAW

by

JOSEPH CREUSEN, S.J.

PROFESSOR OF CANON LAW
PONTIFICAL GREGORIAN UNIVERSITY
CONSULTOR TO THE HOLY OFFICE AND TO THE
SACRED CONGREGATION OF RELIGIOUS

SIXTH ENGLISH EDITION
REVISED AND EDITED TO CONFORM WITH THE
SEVENTH FRENCH EDITION

by

ADAM C. ELLIS, S.J.

PROFESSOR EMERITUS OF CANON LAW

CONSULTOR TO THE SACRED CONGREGATION
OF RELIGIOUS

THE BRUCE PUBLISHING COMPANY
MILWAUKEE

IMPRIMI POTEST:

JOSEPH P. FISHER, S.J.
Superior Provincialis

NIHIL OBSTAT:

JOANNES A. SCHULIEN, S.T.D.
Censor librorum

IMPRIMATUR:

✝ ALBERTUS G. MEYER
Archiepiscopus Milwauchiensis
Die 18ª Aprilis, 1958

(SIXTH ENGLISH EDITION)

Library of Congress Catalog Card Number: 58–11569

(8/58)

Author's Preface to the
Seventh Edition

For more than a year requests have been coming to us for a new edition of *Religieux et Religieuses d'après le Droit Ecclésiastique*. The last edition appeared in 1950.

From 1951–1956 interest in the religious life continued to intensify. Evidence of this from the legislative angle was the publication of important documents about nuns, about the formation of clerical religious, and about other matters. Fortunately, we have also been able to use the recent instruction (March 25, 1956) concerning the pontifical cloister of nuns.

No change was necessary in the method of presentation adopted thirty years ago. We have tried to make this commentary as useful as possible by giving references to articles or opinions which have been published within recent years in *Revue des Communautés Religieuses,* and by bringing the doctrinal bibliography up-to-date.

A new appendix provides an accurate though succinct idea of *Secular Institutes* which, without being religious institutes, constitute nevertheless a state of perfection approved by the Church.

For their fraternal help in the revision of our text, we owe thanks to Fathers Bergh and de Bonhome, S.J.; also to Mr. Roger Demortier, secretary of the *Museum Lessianum,* who kindly undertook the task of seeing the work through the press.

May the Immaculate Virgin, Queen of all religious families, deign to accept the homage which we offer her by this work, so dear to our heart.

Rome, Feast of the Immaculate Conception, December 8, 1956.

Extracts From Author's Preface
to the Second Edition

The Code of Canon Law was promulgated on May 27, 1917. In its second book, all the laws of the Church regarding religious were methodically arranged for the first time.

In June 1918 we made a brief summary of this special legislation, insisting only upon its modifications of the former law.

Today, by reason of official or private responses of the Holy
See, of the numerous publications of canonists, of controversies
arising from appplications of the Code, a more complete statement and a more authoritative and practical commentary of the
new legislation are possible. That is our purpose in the present
work.

We have followed the order of the Code (Book II, Part 2),
and we have frequently cited the text itself.

Ideas and prescriptions borrowed from other sources are inserted in this commentary in large print. Preceding the alpha-
betical index is a vocabulary of more-frequently-used and harder-
to-understand juridical terms.

This book is intended particularly for the members of lay
orders and congregations, for their superiors and directors. However, in the part dealing with the laws governing clerical religious, everything of general interest for a knowledge of the
religious state may be found.

The idea of the religious life which the reader will be able to
formulate from this book, no less than the Code itself, will be
far from complete. Religious life is nourished by deeper and richer
sources than mere legislative formulas. Nevertheless, by her
Code, the Church, spurred on by the spirit of Jesus Christ, In-
spirer and supreme Lawgiver of all perfect life, has pencilled a
sketch by which we can infer, as from the canvas of a great
master, the beautiful and sublime ideal which religious strive
to attain.

Let no one, therefore, rest satisfied with the letter of the
formulas and of seeming minutiae. Strive rather to discern the
spirit of this legislation. Then one will behold ennobling con-
cepts emerge from it.

Would one be surprised, for instance, to find the Holy See
imposing very stringent penalties for the violation of some of
her prescriptions? Not unless he fails to realize that the government of every social activity is under the same compulsion.

To understand what the Church expects of those of her children who are bound by vow to strive for perfection, it is sufficient to consider the formation which she guarantees them, the
obligations which she fearlessly imposes upon them or repeals.
Besides, how many items in this part of the Code have as their

purpose to prevent the mistakes of an excessive generosity which would forget that prudence and moderation so imperative for projects undertaken and worked out in common.

To shed light constantly upon these features of the Church law would go beyond the scope of this present book. May our pages help to make ever better known and appreciated the solicitude of the Holy See for this choice portion of the flock which Christ has confided to its care.

Louvain, Feast of the Purification, February 2, 1921.

Editor's Preface to the Sixth English Edition

The first English edition of Father Creusen's work appeared in 1931 under the title "Religious Men and Women in Church Law." This translation had been made by Father Edward F. Garesche, S.J., and was edited by the present writer. Later a new translation was made from the original French, and a new English edition was prepared for each subsequent French edition. During the war years several reprints of the English text were issued in order to keep the book in circulation.

On September 23, 1957, Father Joseph Creusen completed sixty years as a member of the Society of Jesus. Shortly after, because of declining health, he resigned his professorship of canon law at the Pontifical Gregorian University, as well as his active duties as a consultor to several Roman Congregations. Early in November he left Rome to take up residence at St. Albert's Jesuit Faculty of Theology at Eegenhofen-Louvain, where he continues his work of preparing new editions of his books.

In his *seventh* edition of *Religieux et Religieuses d'après le Droit Ecclésiastique,* Father Creusen has made every effort to bring his text up to date with the latest Roman documents, and to introduce much useful information regarding the present "style and practice" of the Sacred Congregation of Religious. The bibliography has been enlarged to include all worthwhile recent European continental literature on the canon law for religious. Finally, a new chapter was added on *Secular Institutes,* a canonical creation of modern times.

Special effort has been made to bring this *sixth* English edition into complete conformity with the *seventh* French edition, which came from the press in May, 1957. Some few paragraphs of the text have been changed to conform with recent decrees which appeared after the French text went to press, for instance, the news laws regarding the Eucharistic fast for the sick, military service and religious, a few modifications in the Holy Week services to be held in religious community chapels, and the like. Some very recent decrees and instructions of the Holy See have been added to the appendices of this book.

We take this occasion to thank Fathers Francis N. Korth, S.J., and Clarence R. McAuliffe, S.J., for their generous assistance in reading the entire manuscript carefully and for the numerous valuable corrections and suggestions made by them.

We also thank Father T. L. Bouscaren, S.J., for permitting us to use his translation of the documents contained in Appendices IV, V, VI, prepared for use in the *Canon Law Digest,* as well as to its publishers, The Bruce Publishing Company.

Finally, those of our readers who are especially interested in the more recent English articles written about religious, may find them in Bouscaren-Ellis: *Canon Law: a Text and Commentary,* 3rd edition, 1957, in the *Readings* at the end of Chapters VI, VII, VIII, and IX.

ADAM C. ELLIS, S.J.

Saint Joseph Hall
Decatur, Illinois
February 11, 1958

Bibliography

Acta Apostolicae Sedis, official organ of the Holy See *(A.A.S.).*

*Acta et Documenta Congressus Generalis de Statibus Perfectionis Romae
1950.* Sacra Congregatio de Religiosis, Series "Congressus et cursus
speciales." Rome, 1952.

BASTIEN, DOM P., O.S.B., *Directoire canonique à l'usage des Congrégations
à vœux simples,* 5th Ed., Maredsous, 1951 *(D.C.).*

BATTANDIER, MSGR. A., *Guide canonique pour les constitutions des Instituts
à vœux simples,* 6th Ed., Paris, 1923 *(G.C.).*

BERUTTI, C., O.P., *Institutiones iuris canonici,* Vol. III, *De religiosis,*
Turin, 1936.

BEYER, J., S.J., *Les Instituts séculiers,* Paris-Brussels, 1954.

BIEDERLACK-FUEHRICH, S.J., *De religiosis,* Innsbruck, 1919.

BOUSCAREN-ELLIS, S.J., *Canon Law. A Text and Commentary,* 3rd Ed.,
Milwaukee, 1957.

BRANDYS, M., O.F.M., *Kirchliches Rechtsbuch für die religiösen Laien-
genossenschaften der Brüder und Schwestern,* Paderborn, 1920.

BRYS, J., *Iuris Canonici Compendium,* Vol. I, 10th Ed., Bruges, 1947.

Canonical Legislation Concerning Religious, authorized English translation,
Vatican City, 1949.

CARPENTER, R., S.J., *Témoins de la Cité de Dieu.* Réédition entièrement
refondue du Catéchisme des Voeux des PP. Cotel et Jombert, 3ᵉ édit.,
Museum Lessianum, Paris-Bruges, 1956.

CHOUPIN, L., S.J., *Nature et obligations de l'état religieux,* 4th Ed.,
Paris, 1929.

Collectanea S. Congr. de Propaganda Fide, 2nd Ed. *(Coll. P.F.),* con-
tinuées par *Sylloge,* 1939.

COTEL-JOMBART, S.J., *Catechism of the Vows,* authorized English translation by W. MCCABE, S.J., 2nd Ed., New York, 1945.

DE CARLO, C., M.I., *Ius religiosorum,* Paris-Tournai-Rome, 1950.

*Enchiridion de Statibus perfectionis. I. Documenta Ecclesiae sodalibus
instituendis,* Rome, 1949.

ESCOBAR, MARIO, *Ordini e Congregazioni religiose,* t. I e II, Turin, 1951
and 1952.

ESCUDERO, GERARDO, C.M.F., *Los Istitutos seculares,* Madrid, 1954.

FANFANI, L., O.P., *Le "Droit des Religieuses,"* Rome-Turin, 1924.

FANAFANI, L., O.P., *De iure religiosorum ad normam C.I.C.,* 3rd Ed.,
Rovigo, 1949.

FANFANI, L., O.P., *Catechism on the Religious State,* St. Louis, 1956.

FERRERES, J. B., S.J., *Las religiosas según la disciplina vigente,* 5th Ed.,
Barcelona, 1920.

FUEHRICH, M., S.J., see BIEDERLACK, S.J.

GOYENECHE, S., C.M.F., *Iuris canonici summa principia*, Vol. II, *De religiosis*, Rome, 1938.

GOYENECHE, S., C.M.F., *Quaestiones canonicae de iure religiosorum*, 2. vol., Naples, 1954.

HEIMBUCHER, M., *Die Orden und Kongregationen der katholischen Kirche*, Band I–II, Ed. 3, Paderborn, 1933–34.

JOMBART, E., S.J., *Manuel de droit canon*, Paris, 1949.

JONE, H., O.F.M.CAP., *Commentarium in Codicem Iuris Canonici*, Vol. I, Paderborn, 1950.

LEITNER, M., *Handbuch des kath. Kirchenrechts*, Vol. III, *Das Ordensrecht*, 2nd Ed., Regensburg, 1922.

LEMOINE, R., O.S.B., *Le droit des religieux du concile de Trente aux Instituts séculiers*, Museum Lessianum, Paris-Bruges, 1956.

MATTHAEUS CONTE A CORONATA, O.F.M.CAP., *Institutiones Iuris Canonici*, Vol. I, 3rd Ed., Turin, 1947.

NAZ, R., *Traité de droit canonique*, Vol. I (JOMBART, S.J., *Des Religieux*), Paris, 1947.

PALOMBO, J., C.SS.R., *De dimissione religiosorum*, Turin, 1931.

REGATILLO, E. F., S.J., *Institutiones Iuris Canonici*, Vol. I, *Pars de personis*, 4th Ed., Santander, 1951.

SCHAEFER, T., O.F.M.CAP., *De religiosis ad normam C.I.C.*, 4th Ed., Rome, 1947.

TABERA, A., C.M.F., *Derecho de los Religiosos*, Madrid, 1948.

VERMEERSCH, A., S.J., *De religiosis institutis et personis, tractatus canonico-moralis*, Vol. I, 2nd Ed., 1907; Vol. II, 4th Ed., Bruges, 1910 (*De relig.* I, II).

VERMEERSCH-CREUSEN, S.J., *Epitome iuris canonici cum commentariis*, Vol. I, 7th Ed., Malines, 1949 (*Epitome*).

WERNZ-VIDAL, S.J., *Ius canonicum*, Vol. III, *De religiosis*, Rome, 1933.

PERIODICALS

Ami du clergé, Langres.

Collationes: Brugenses, Gandavenses, Namurcenses, Tornacenses (*Coll. Brug., Gand., Nam., Torn.*).

Collectanea Mechliniensia, Malines (*Coll. Mechl.*).

Commentarium pro religiosis, Rome, 1920 sq. (*Comm. pro rel.*).

Ephemerides theologicae Lovanienses, Louvain, 1924 sq. (*Ephem. th. Lov.*).

Il Monitore Ecclesiastico, Rome (*Monit. eccl.*).

Monitor Ecclesiasticus (ME).

Nouvelle Revue théologique, Paris-Tournai (*N.R. Th.*).

Periodica de re morali, canonica, liturgica, Rome (*Per.*).

Review for Religious, St. Marys, Kans., 1942 sq. (*RfR.*).

Revue des communautés religieuses, Louvain (*R.C.R.*).

Revue ecclésiastique de Liége (*Rev. eccl. Liége*).

CONTENTS

Author's Preface to the Seventh French Edition . . v
Extracts From Author's Preface to the Second Edition . v
Editor's Preface to the Sixth English Edition . . . vii
Bibliography ix
Introduction 3

PART ONE

THE CONSTITUTION OF RELIGIOUS INSTITUTES

Chapter I. General Ideas 9
    § 1. The Religious State 9
    § 2. Forms of the Religious Life 15
    § 3. Application of the Laws 25
    § 4. The Law of Precedence 26

Chapter II. Erection or Suppression of a Religious In-
              stitute, of a Province, or of a House . . 29
    § 1. Erection and Suppression of a Religious Institute 29
        A. Erection of a Religious Institute . . . 29
        B. Suppression of a Religious Institute . . 33
    § 2. Erection, Suppression, or Division of Provinces 34
    § 3. Erection or Suppression of a Religious House . 35
        A. Erection of a Religious House . . . 35
        B. Suppression of a Religious House . . . 38

Chapter III. Government of Religious 40

    Article 1. Superiors and Chapters 40
    § 1. Preliminary Notions 40
    § 2. Exterior Hierarchy 45

§ 3. Interior Hierarchy 48
  I. Chapters 48
  II. Religious Superiors 50
    A. Nature and Extent of the Power of
      Superiors 50
    B. Requirements for the Election of
      Superiors 54
    C. Duration of Office 55
    D. Choice of Superiors 57
      a) *Convocation of the Chapter for*
        Election 58
      b) *Electors or Members of the Chapter* 59
      c) *Form of Election* 60
      d) *Postulation* 66
    E. Obligations of Superiors . . . 68
      a) *Canonical Visitation of Religious*
        Superiors 73
      b) *Canonical Visitation of the Local*
        Ordinary 74
    F. Honorary Titles 77
    G. Cessation of Office 78
  III. Counsellors, Bursars, and Procurators . . 78

Article 2. Spiritual Government 81
§ 1. Confessors of Religious Men and Women . . 82
  A. Confessors of Religious Men . . . 82
  B. Confessors of Religious Women . . . 84
    a) *Ordinary Confessors* . . . 87
    b) *Extraordinary Confessors and Supplementary Confessors* 88
    c) *The "Occasional" Confessor* . . 90
  C. Appointment of Confessors — Their Duties . 96
§ 2. The Account of Conscience 99

Article 3. Divine Service 104
§ 1. General Notions 104
§ 2. Divine Worship 106
  A. Churches and Oratories 106
  B. Eucharistic Worship 109
    a) *Holy Mass* 109
    b) *Reservation of the Blessed Sacrament* . 112

§ 3. Preaching 114
§ 4. Administration of the Sacraments . . . 115
   A. Baptism 115
   B. Holy Communion 115
   C. Viaticum and Extreme Unction . . . 116
   D. Sacrament of Orders 117
§ 5. Funerals 117

Article 4. Temporal Goods and Their Administration 119
§ 1. General Notions 119
§ 2. Acquisition and Administration of Temporal
   Goods 122
§ 3. Alienation of Property 125
§ 4. Special Sanctions and Penalties 127
§ 5. Rendering of Accounts to the Ordinary . . 128
§ 6. Alms and Gifts 129

PART TWO

THE RELIGIOUS LIFE

SECTION I. ADMISSION INTO RELIGION

Chapter IV. The Postulancy 133

Chapter V. The Novitiate 137

Article 1. Conditions of Admission 137
§ 1. Impediments 137
   A. Impediments to Valid Admission . . . 137
   B. Impediments to Licit Admission . . . 140
§ 2. The Competent Superior 142
§ 3. Testimonial Letters 143
§ 4. Dowry 146
§ 5. Canonical Examination 150

Article 2. Formation of Novices 151

Chapter VI. Religious Profession 173

Article 1. General Ideas 173
Article 2. Conditions Required for the Different Kinds
   of Profession 175

Article 3.   Effects of Religious Profession   .   .   .   183

§ 1. Temporary Profession   184
§ 2. Perpetual Profession   185
§ 3. Simple Profession   185
§ 4. Solemn Profession   188

Article 4.   Validation of an Invalid Profession   .   .   190

SECTION II.   OBLIGATIONS AND PRIVILEGES OF RELIGIOUS

Chapter VII.   Obligations of Religious   192

Article 1.   Obligations in Common With Clerics .   .   192
§ 1. A Life of Perfection   192
§ 2. Exercises of Piety   194
§ 3. Studies   198
§ 4. The Religious Habit   202
§ 5. Offices, Occupations, Recreation   202

Article 2.   Particular Obligations of Religious   .   .   204
§ 1. Observance of the Rules and Constitutions   .   204
§ 2. Obligations of Vows   207
§ 3. Cloister and Relations With the Outside World   212
    A. PAPAL CLOISTER   213
      I. *Cloister of Regulars*   213
      II. *Cloister of Nuns*   214
        A. MAJOR PAPAL CLOISTER   .   .   .   214
        B. MINOR PAPAL CLOISTER   .   .   .   221
        C. PAPAL CLOISTER AND FEDERATIONS   .   224
      III. *Establishing Papal Cloister*   .   .   .   225
    B. COMMON OR EPISCOPAL CLOISTER .   226
    C. VISITORS, PARLORS, LEAVING THE
      HOUSE   227
    D. CORRESPONDENCE   228
§ 4. Divine Office and Conventual Mass .   .   .   230
§ 5. Relations With the Diocesan Clergy .   .   .   232

Chapter VIII.   Privileges of Religious   234

Article 1.   General Ideas   234

Article 2.   Privileges Common to Religious and Clerics   236

Article 3. Exemption 237
   § 1. General Ideas 237
   § 2. Exemption of Regulars 239
   § 3. Exemption in Religious Congregations . . 241
   § 4. General Exceptions to All Exemption . . . 242

Article 4. The Privilege of Mendicants and the Right
         to Beg 244

Article 5. Privileges of Regular Abbots . . . 246

Chapter IX. Religious Promoted to Ecclesiastical
         Dignities or to Parishes 247

PART THREE

SEPARATION FROM THE INSTITUTE

Chapter X. On Passing to Another Institute . . . 251

Chapter XI. On Abandoning Religion 253
   § 1. Legitimate Leaving of Religious 253
   § 2. Unlawful Leaving 263

Chapter XII. Dismissal of Religious 266

  Article 1. Dismissal in General and by the Law . 266

  Article 2. Dismissal of Religious Who Have Taken
          Temporary Vows 269

  Article 3. Dismissal of Religious With Perpetual Vows,
          in an Institute of Nonexempt Clerics or of
          Lay Religious 272
   § 1. Dismissal of Religious Men 272
   § 2. Dismissal of Religious Women 274
   § 3. General Requirements for the Dismissal of
       Religious Men and Women 275

  Article 4. Dismissal of Religious With Perpetual Vows
          in an Institute of Exempt Clerics . . . 275
      The Process 276
      A. Preliminary Conditions 276

B. The Instruction 277

C. The Sentence 278

Article 5. The Condition of Dismissed Religious Who
Have Taken Perpetual Vows . . . 278

Appendix I. A Summary of the Law Regarding Diocesan
Congregations of Religious Women 281

Appendix II. Instruction to the Superiors General of Religious Institutes and of Societies of Clerics Concerning the Clerical and Religious Training of Subjects Destined for the Priesthood, and of the Investigation which Must Precede the Reception of Orders . . 286

Appendix III. The List of Questions Which Are to Be Answered by Religious Institutes and Societies in the Report to Be Sent to the Holy See Every Five Years According to the Decree *Cum Transactis* . . . 296

Appendix IV. Papal Instruction on the Cloister of Nuns 335

Appendix V. Apostolic Constitution *Sedes Sapientiae* . 353

Appendix VI. Decree of the Sacred Congregation of Religious Regarding Religious Who Are Obliged to Military Service 366

Appendix VII. Letter of the S. C. of Religious to the Superiors General of the Institutes of Perfection Regarding the Use of Radio and Television . . . 370

Index 375

RELIGIOUS MEN AND WOMEN
IN CHURCH LAW

RELIGIOUS MEN AND WOMEN
IN CHURCH LAW

Introduction

1. The Code of canon law is the official collection of the disciplinary laws of the Latin Church. It is true that some dogmatic principles are also set forth therein, but it contains hardly any liturgical prescriptions.

2. 1. From the first centuries the word "canon" or "rule" served to distinguish the laws of the Church from the civil laws. In their canons the councils formulated the rules of faith, of morals, or of discipline, imposed on the faithful. Thus, there are dogmatic canons, moral canons, and disciplinary canons.

Discipline which is necessary for the preservation and prosperity of any society, is the good order resulting from the uprightness of exterior actions. When these actions are in conformity with the laws, they are just and honest in the eyes of the human legislator from whom a person's conscience is necessarily hidden. This discipline is the subject matter of civil and ecclesiastical or canon law. In the sight of God, on the contrary, it is the uprightness of the will which makes one just, and the laws whose observance begets this justice are the subject matter of the moral law. Since God wishes that man should obey all rightly constituted authority, human laws give rise, in those who are subject to them, to an obligation in conscience the gravity of which will vary according to the nature, the purpose, and importance of the law.

2. The Church has received from her divine Founder the organization and the powers necessary for her existence and her development. Hand in hand with her extension throughout the world, the purely human element of her organization naturally developed little by little. As the relations of the faithful among themselves and toward their ecclesiastical superiors grew more complex and numerous, it was necessary that the ecclesiastical law should constantly grow and *be adapted* to their needs. For this reason it has been necessary, from time to time, to revise and codify the laws of the Church so as to keep them adapted to the times and give them coherence and unity.

This work of codification had not been undertaken since the beginning of the fourteenth century. Many of the laws of the Church were difficult to find and to know because they were scattered in different collections and documents. In 1870, the Fathers of the Vatican Council urged very strongly that a new and complete revision of the canon law should be made so as to unify the laws of the Church and group them together in an official collection.[1]

3. Pius X resolved from the very beginning of his pontificate to accomplish this work. It was an "arduous task,"[1] but he carried it on with exceptional energy. He named a commission of cardinals to work at the codification and gave them counsellors selected from the entire world. After the example of his predecessors, and to a greater extent than they, he prepared for this authoritative codification by a series of special reforms. In the constitutions and decrees which announced these reforms, one finds clear and concise statements after the manner of the modern civil codes. When Pius X died, the work was almost completed. Hence, when Benedict XV published the Code, he ascribed to his predecessor and his personal helpers all the merit and the glory of the work.

The new Code was promulgated on Pentecost Day, May 27, 1917, and went in force on Pentecost, May 19, 1918.

4. The Code of canon law is divided into five books.[2] In the first book we find the general principles of ecclesiastical law. The second book treats of the persons who make up the Church; the third deals with ecclesiastical "things," that is to say, with sacraments, sacred places and times, divine worship, the teaching power of the Church, and church property. The fourth book deals with procedure and gives the laws which are to be observed in ecclesiastical trials. In the fifth book we find an account of canonical crimes and penalties.

All the books except the first are divided into parts with subdivisions into titles, chapters, and articles. The numbering of the titles runs continuously from the first to the last of each book. The reader will find the greater number of the laws explained here in Book II, part 2, titles IX to XVII, canons 487 to 681.

---

[1] The edition of F. Santis, *Clementis Papae VIII Decretales* (Friburgi Brisg.: 1870), never received authentic approval.

[2] Motu proprio *Arduum sane munus* (March 19, 1904), *A.S.S.*, XXXVI, 549.

3. During the past century the conditions of existence of the religious state like those of many other ecclesiastical institutions have been greatly changed. This explains the large number of new laws which have to do with them. In this field also, Pius X showed an unusual activity. It is only right, however, to note that his predecessors had already prepared the way for him.

1. Pius IX wished that in all religious orders of men a simple profession of perpetual vows[3] should precede the solemn profession. This regulation was afterwards extended by Leo XIII to orders of women also.[4]

Meanwhile, the new needs of the times had caused an extraordinary growth of congregations with simple vows devoted to teaching and to works of mercy. Some of these were purely diocesan, others had obtained from the Holy See a more or less complete and definite approbation. By the constitution *Conditae a Christo*, on the 8th of December, 1900, Leo XIII carefully settled the relations of both the former and the latter to the diocesan Ordinaries.

An increasing number of institutes at this time were asking approbation from Rome. To guide their founders and the bishops in the preparation of their constitutions, the Sacred Congregation of Bishops and Regulars published a set of regulations entitled "Norms (rules) usually followed by the Sacred Congregation of Bishops and Regulars in the approval of new institutes with simple vows" (June 28, 1901).[5] These regulations were merely directive. The second part contained an outline of a model religious congregation according to the concept of the Holy See at that time.[6]

2. Pius X took up again and finished the reforms of his predecessors. One may say that all the different parts of the laws concerning religious underwent a revision. An experience of some years has shown the wisdom of these new laws. The greater part

---

[3] Letter *Neminem latet* (March 19, 1857).

[4] Decree *Perpensis* (May 3, 1902).

[5] We shall cite quotations by using the first word of the title: *Normae,* Ed. 1. The abbreviations Ed. 1, Ed. 2, etc., signify first edition, second edition, etc.

[6] The list and the text of all the documents concerning Religious Institutes will be found in Vermeersch, *De religiosis,* Vol. II (1910), which work is continued in the review entitled *Periodica.* Most of the documents from which we quote have also appeared in the *Nouvelle revue théologique.* Since 1925 all the documents which are of interest to lay religious communities are published with a commentary in the *Revue des Communautés Religieuses* (*R.C.R.*).

of them are inserted, with some modifications, in the Code; the tendency of some of them is still more emphasized; only a few of them, and this again is a proof of prudent moderation, are definitely discarded.

3. Since the promulgation of the Code the declarations and answers given by the Holy See have determined the exact meaning of certain articles or have solved the doubts which arose about the sense of this or that canon. A new edition of the *Normae* is in preparation. The structure of the present-day discipline has been completed by the *Instructions* of the Sacred Congregation of Religious, such as that regarding the second year of novitiate (November 3, 1921), and those of the S. Congregation for the Propagation of the Faith, for example, regarding the establishment of native congregations (March 19, 1937), and the like. In connection with the movement for renewal and adaptation which was the subject matter of the General Congress for the States of Perfection held in Rome in 1950,[7] most important documents have been promulgated: the constitution *Sponsa Christi* of November 21, 1950, and the general statutes for nuns re-establishing solemn vows and setting up a twofold papal cloister and recommending federations. This constitution was completed by two Instructions of the S. Congregation (November 23, 1950, and March 25, 1956). The constitution *Sedes Sapientiae* of May 31, 1956, and the general statutes attached to it have crystallized the procedure for the formation of clerics in the states of perfection. In a word, the legislative activity regarding the religious life has during recent years equaled or even surpassed the most productive preceding past periods in this field.

---

[7] See the address of His Holiness, Pius XII (December 8, 1950) in *RfR*, 14, 1955, 170–180.

PART ONE

THE CONSTITUTION OF
RELIGIOUS INSTITUTES

CHAPTER I

General Ideas

(cc. 487–491)

The detailed account of the legislation concerning religious is preceded in the Code by a short introduction. We find there the definition of the religious state (c. 487); an exact determination of the legal meaning of the terms employed in this legislation (c. 488); the principles to be used in applying the laws of the Code to religious (cc. 489–490); the conditions which govern the right of precedence of religious both among themselves and with regard to the secular clergy (c. 491).

§ 1. THE RELIGIOUS STATE

4. *Definition.*

"**The religious state,** that is, the firmly established manner of living in community, by which the faithful undertake to observe not only the ordinary precepts but also the evangelical counsels, by means of the vows of obedience, chastity, and poverty, must be held in honor by all" (c. 487).

1. Like every *state of life,* the religious state comprises three essential elements: a group of *obligations,* which have a *permanent* and *public* character. This state, therefore, results from the public profession of the three vows, taken with the intention of persevering in their practice.

The Church, however, recognizes the rights attached to the religious state only in persons grouped under the authority of a superior. By the will of the Church, *common life* is, therefore, in fact, a fourth essential of religious life.

2. The religious state is called the state of perfection because by binding themselves forever[1] to the practice of the evangelical counsels, religious by their state of life undertake to avoid with constancy the principal obstacles to Christian perfection, that is to say, to the perfect love of God.

This permanent obligation of practicing the evangelical counsels is sufficient to place those who have assumed it in a state of perfection,

---

[1] We say "forever" because perpetuity, though not demanded by the Code, is intended by the religious and is provided for by the legislator.

according to the moral meaning of the word. The three vows of religion, duly observed, greatly foster in every religious the perfect love of God and of one's neighbor by reason of the spirit which inspires them, because of the removal of the principal obstacles to the perfection of charity, and finally on account of the great number of acts which they demand. Hence those authors are mistaken who see or seem to see in the religious life a simple canonical state, a kind of life specially regulated by the Church, but which of itself is not superior to the life led by persons who have taken just a vow of chastity.[2]

The religious life is praised with great accord by Christian tradition and by the teachings of the Doctors of the Church from St. Thomas to St. Alphonsus de Liguori. The esteem which the Church has today for the religious state is amply shown by the privileges she gives to religious, the liberty offered to secular clerics to enter religion, and her prohibition against the giving of ecclesiastical offices of special honor and importance to priests who, after having passed a certain time in religion, leave it, even with a lawful dispensation, etc.

5. 1. The constitution *Provida Mater* of February 2, 1947, entitled: "On the Canonical States and on Secular Institutes directed to the attainment of Christian perfection" had drawn in grand outline the history of the evolution of the religious state under the maternal watchfulness of the Church. This text seems to us to be so important that it should be repeated here in its entirety:

In the course of the Centuries, the Church, ever faithful to Christ her Spouse, and true to herself, under the guidance of the Holy Spirit, with continuous and unhesitating progress up to the establishment of the present Code of Canon Law, gradually developed the discipline of the state of perfection. With a peculiar motherly affection for those who freely, under various forms, made external and public profession of a life of perfection, she constantly gave them every encouragement in their pursuit of so holy a purpose, and that under two distinct heads. In the first place, the individual profession of the life of perfection, always, however, to be made publicly and before the Church — such as the ancient and venerable liturgical blessing and consecration of virgins — was not only admitted and recognized, but the Church herself wisely sanctioned and strongly defended it, and attached to it a number of canonical effects. But the principal favor and more diligent care of the Church, from the earliest times after the peace of Constantine, were rightly and properly directed toward and exercised in favor of that

---

[2] See concerning this doctrine: De Guibert, S.J., *Revue d'ascetique et de mystique,* I (1920), 280 sq.; Dom Lottin, O.S.B., *La doctrine de S. Thomas sur l'état religieux,* in *La vie spirituelle* (1923), 385 sq.

complete and more strictly public profession of the life of perfection, which was made in societies and organized groups erected with her permission or approval or by her positive authority.

It is common knowledge that the history of the holiness of the Church and of the Catholic apostolate is most closely and intimately connected with the history and records of the canonical religious life, as, under the constant vivifying grace of the Holy Spirit, it continued from day to day to exhibit a wonderful variety and at the same time to grow into a new and even deeper and stronger unity. It is not to be wondered at that the Church, even in the field of law, faithfully following the direction which the provident Wisdom of God clearly indicated, purposely cultivated and regulated the canonical state of perfection in such wise that she rightly and properly designed to build the edifice of ecclesiastical discipline upon this as upon one of its cornerstones. Hence, in the first place, the public state of perfection was counted as one of the three principal ecclesiastical states, and in it alone the Church found the second order and grade of canonical persons (c. 107). Here is something surely worthy of attentive consideration: while the other two orders of canonical persons, namely clerics and the laity, are found in the Church by divine law, to which the ecclesiastical institution is superadded (cc. 107, 108, § 3), inasmuch as the Church is established and organized as a hierarchical society, this class, namely that of religious, intermediate between clerics and the laity and capable of being participated in by both clerics and the laity (c. 107), is entirely derived from the close and very special relationship which it has to the end of the Church, that is, to the efficacious pursuit of perfection by adequate means.

Nor was this all. Lest the public and solemn profession of holiness should be frustrated and come to nothing, the Church with ever increasing strictness was willing to recognize this canonical state of perfection only in societies which were erected and governed by herself, that is, in religious Institutes (c. 488, 1°), whose general form and purpose she had approved by her *magisterium* after a slow and careful examination, and whose institute and rules she had in every case not only scrutinized more than once doctrinally and in the abstract, but had also tested by actual trial. These requirements are laid down so strictly and absolutely in the Code of Canon Law, that in no case, not even by way of exception, is the canonical state of perfection recognized, unless its profession is made in a religious Institute approved by the Church. Finally, the canonical discipline of the state of perfection as a public state was so wisely regulated by the Church that, in the case of clerical Religious Institutes, in all those matters in general which concern the clerical life of the religious, the Institutes took the place of dioceses, and membership in a religious society was equivalent to the incardination of a cleric in a diocese (cc. 111, § 1; 116; 585).

After the Code of Pius and Benedict, in the second Part of Book II, which is devoted to religious, had diligently collected, revised, and carefully improved the legislation regarding religious and had thus in many ways confirmed the canonical state of perfection also in its public aspect, and, wisely perfecting the work begun by Leo XIII of happy memory in his immortal Constitution *Conditae a Christo,* had admitted Congregations of simple vows among religious Institutes in the strict sense, it seemed that nothing remained to be added in the discipline of the canonical state of perfection. Yet the Church, with her great breadth of mind and vision and with true maternal solicitude, decided to add to the legislation on religious, a brief title as an appropriate supplement. In this title (Title XVII of Book II), the Church declares as in a fairly complete sense equivalent to the canonical state of perfection, certain societies, of great value to herself and frequently also to the State, which, though they lacked some of the requirements which are necessary for the complete state of perfection, such as public vows (cc. 488, 1°; 487), yet in other respects which are regarded as essentials of the life of perfection, bear a close similarity to religious Institutes and are almost necessarily connected with them.[3]

2. The address of His Holiness, Pius XII, given on December 8, 1950, at the General Congress of the States of Perfection partially repeated the same ideas and gave a refutation of various errors regarding the religious state. The Pope declared that the clerical state as such is not to be counted among the states of perfection since it does not impose upon its members the practice of the three evangelical counsels. He also pointed out that the regular clergy is no less attached to the hierarchy than is the secular clergy, and that, like the latter, it is qualified for apostolic works. The Pope likewise proved to be false objections directed against the religious that they live apart from the world and destroy their personality by absolute obedience.[4]

3. Besides the two canonical states of perfection approved by the Code, namely, the religious state and the societies of common life without public vows (cf. n. 18), the constitution *Provida Mater* recognizes a third, *secular institutes,* whose members pledge themselves likewise in a stable manner to the practice of the three evangelical counsels, while they remain entirely in the world and generally without common life (see 5 bis). Henceforth canonical legislation speaks of the *states of perfection* or else of the *state of evangelical perfection* and its various juridical decrees.[5]

---

[3] *A.A.S.,* 39, 1947, 114 sq.; *Digest,* III, 135 sq.

[4] *A.A.S.,* 43, 1951, 26 ss; *Digest,* III, 119 sq.

[5] For the elements common to these states of perfection read article by Guttierez in CpR., 1950, 60–120.

5 bis. SECULAR INSTITUTES

Although secular institutes are not religious institutes and their members are not religious, requests have been made for some information about them. We shall try to satisfy these requests, but, for more detailed information, we shall refer to official documents and commentaries.[6]

1. Secular institutes are associations of clerics or lay persons whose members intend to strive for Christian perfection and to devote themselves entirely to the apostolate. Hence, though living in the world, they make profession of practicing the evangelical counsels. Since the kind of life which they impose on their members is in substance analogous to that of religious institutes and of societies of common life without public vows, secular institutes constitute a juridical state of perfection.

The intention to remain in the world is a special apostolic vocation. Formerly the law gave cognizance only to associations of the faithful, like pious unions, confraternities, third orders. These, however, suppose neither a total consecration of life to perfection nor ties of dependence between different local groups of the same kind.

2. The essential characteristics of secular institutes are as follows:

a) A *total consecration* to God by way of a voluntary and in itself definitive espousal of the practice of the evangelical counsels within a group approved by the Church for this purpose.

The form of commitment to the three counsels of poverty, chastity, and obedience varies according to the constitutions (vows, consecration, promise, oath). In every case there must be a stable, mutual, and full bond between the institute and the member, a bond which involves moral obligations on both sides.

b) The *secular character* of this state of perfection.

The pontifical documents are very clear on this point. They go so far as to say that the members should sanctify themselves *in* and *by* the world. The least this can mean is that they can retain their secular

---

[6] Consult the text and commentary of the Constitution *Provida Mater* of February 2, 1947, the *Motu proprio, Primo feliciter* of March 12, 1948, and the Instruction of the S. Congregation of Religious of March 19, 1948 in *Canon Law Digest*, 3, pp. 146, 147, 151, also J. Beyer, S.J., *Les Instituts Séculiers*, Paris-Bruxelles, 1954; C. Escudero, C.M.F., *Los Istitutos Seculares*, Madrid, 1951; F. Korth, S.J., three articles in *RfR*, 13, 1954.

occupations, live with their families, wear no distinctive garb. In short, they are not bound to common life in the same way as this is organized for religious. But the requirements of formation, of government, and of some forms of the apostolate can actually entail a certain common life.

c) Exercise of the apostolate.

"The entire life of the members of secular institutes is consecrated to God by the fact of their profession of perfection and should be directed to the apostolate. This apostolate should be actuated by purity of intention, by close union with God, by courageous self-denial and generous forgetfulness of self. It should be exercised unremittingly and holily so that it not only manifests the interior spirit inspiring it, but also constantly nourishes and renews this spirit" (*Motu proprio* of March 12, 1948).

3. *The promise of chastity* and of celibacy will nearly always be undertaken by vow. No further explanation of this is necessary, since the matter of the vow is the same as that of the virtue.

The members are obliged to observe the constitutions. Of themselves, however, these do not oblige under pain of sin. Yet, the occasions will not be wanting to practice *obedience* by submitting to superiors without waiting for a formal precept "in the name of our Lord Jesus Christ," which is the proper object of the vow.

The promise or the vow of *poverty* is the one which may at times offer the greatest difficulty. This will be owing to the fact that, while it is somewhat similar to the vow of religious, it is made under different circumstances. The members retain the bare ownership and the administration of their temporal goods. They may not dispose of anything having a money value without authorization of their superior (or director). At the beginning of the year the members with their superior decide upon a budget for their regular expenses, taking into consideration their social condition, their relations to, or the needs of their apostolate.

4. Secular institutes are *not religious institutes*. They are not regulated by the laws for religious, although these laws can, on many points be adapted to them. Generally speaking, the members are not authorized to take vows whose acceptance is guaranteed by ecclesiastical authority. Moreover, these vows

are not public but "social." In most instances the members do not lead a common life. Hence priests of the diocesan clergy can form secular institutes.

5. The constitutions often envision two classes of members, members in the strict sense and members in the broad sense. The secular institute itself can be affiliated with a stronger organization from which it may derive its spirituality, but not its superiors. The latter must be proper to the institute.

6. The establishment of a secular institute is fairly similar to that of a religious congregation. It is reserved to the local Ordinary. After the *nihil obstat* has been obtained from the Holy See, the Sacred Congregation gives this Ordinary for a period of ten years the power to organize the institute and to betow certain rights on those members who have already given proof of their fidelity and suitability.

7. Secular institutes can be either diocesan or pontifical, depending upon the degree of approval obtained. Ordinarily all of them pass through the first stage.

Today a secular institute is not approved if it cannot present its constitutions to the Sacred Congregation. The law about this has become more rigorous, lest institutes of a similar pattern be multiplied without notable benefit for the Church.

§ 2. FORMS OF THE RELIGIOUS LIFE (c. 488)

Many terms, the sense of which was in dispute in jurisprudence and in the authorities, are here given an exact meaning, to which writers and commentators must henceforth hold.

6. "An **institute** (*religio*) is every society, approved by legitimate ecclesiastical authority, the members of which tend to evangelical perfection, according to the laws proper to their society, by the profession of public vows, whether perpetual or temporary, the latter renewable after the lapse of a fixed time."

The Latin term *RELIGIO* was heretofore reserved in Canon Law for orders in which solemn vows were taken; now, beginning with the Code of Canon Law, it is used in a very general sense. Its English equivalent is rarely used except in certain expressions as "the vows of religion," to "enter religion." We shall substitute the term *INSTITUTE* which, though not used in the Code, has been applied to religious congregations up to the present, and is still used in that sense in several documents issued by the Holy See since the promulgation of the Code.[7] The term *INSTITUTE* is also used to translate *RELIGIO* in the authorized English translation of the canons concerning religious. In reading books written before 1918 and pontifical documents of even more recent date, we must remember that the term *RELIGIO* has, up to the present, not been applied to religious congregations.

7. An **order** is an institute whose members make profession of solemn vows. A **religious congregation** is an institute whose members make profession of simple vows only, whether perpetual or temporary; an **exempt institute** is an institute, with either solemn or simple vows, not subject to the jurisdiction of the local Ordinary.

The fact that some religious of an institute take simple vows only, does not keep the institute from being an order in the strict sense, e.g., the Society of Jesus. After all, the religious of all orders, since the Code, begin by making a simple and even temporary profession of vows.

All the religious orders of clerics are exempt. The Redemptorists, the Passionists, and the Salesians may be cited as examples of clerical congregations which are exempt.

8. 1. By a **monastic congregation** is understood the union of several independent (*sui iuris*) monasteries under one and the same Superior, for example, the Benedictines of Monte-Cassino, of Beuron, of Solesmes.

A monastic congregation differs from a religious congregation in the relative independence of the houses which make it up. The fact that there is one superior gives rise only to a very loose bond between the houses by reason of the very restricted powers which are ordinarily conferred on the superior of such a congregation.

2. **A federation of nuns** is a group of several monasteries belonging to the same order which, while preserving their autonomy, are united according to particular Statutes, under one and the same major superioress, for the purpose of mutual aid and collaboration regarding spiritual, disciplinary, and economic affairs.

---

[7] See the *Normae*, Ed. 2 (1921), n. 6; Congregation of Religious, Decree on Diocesan Institutes, November 30, 1922, nn. II, III, etc. After the Constitution *Provida Mater* on secular institutes, care should be taken to add the adjective "religious" to the word "institute," unless the context makes it superfluous.

This bond in no wise impedes the dependence of the various monasteries with regard to their regular superior or to the local Ordinary.

1. The advantages to be derived from such a federation are of such importance that the legislator, without forcing anyone, nevertheless eagerly wishes that all monasteries so unite among themselves. Among these advantages the following may be mentioned: to act as a moral entity for the defense of certain rights, and the like; the establishment of a common novitiate for those monasteries that so desire; to facilitate the exchange of a religious; material aid in case of need, and the like.

2. At the head of a federation there is a *president general* with her council. Even though the title of superior be given her, the president general does not have the powers possessed by a superior general of a congregation of religious women. She is merely the executive agent of the decisions taken by the *federal assembly* of superiors and delegates of autonomous monasteries.

3. To facilitate the execution of duties incumbent either on the federal council or on the communities, and to accomplish more perfectly the desires or the prescriptions of ecclesiastical authority, and in particular of the Holy See, each federation will be given an *assistant,* delegated by the S. Congregation of Religious. This assistant, to whose care several federations may be entrusted, exercises above all the role of counselor.

4. Several federations may unite among themselves to form a "confederation."

The growing number of federations already provides for the development of a real jurisprudence for this most recent institution.

Besides federations of autonomous monasteries, quite common in our day, one may envision possible federations of congregations by reason of spiritual or similar aims, for the same purpose of mutual help.

3. A **province** is the union of several religious houses under one and the same superior, and constituting part of the same institute.

These administrative divisions are also called vicariates, districts, etc. The very great dependence of local superiors and of all the inferiors in the province on the provincial superior gives rise to a close bond of union between the communities and all the members, which is almost totally lacking among the monasteries of a monastic congregation. A second difference is that the province is never more than a part of a larger group which it presupposes, the order or the religious congregation itself, while monastic congregations are composed of monasteries which enjoyed complete autonomy.

9. A pontifical religious institute (*religio iuris pontificii*) is one which has obtained from the Apostolic See either approbation or at least the decree of commendation (*decretum laudis*); a **diocesan institute** is one governed by Ordinaries (bishops, vicars apostolic, etc.), which has not yet obtained this decree of commendation.

In the case of congregations approved before 1900, the mere fact of their having received equivalently the decrees of praise, or even a certain amount of approval of the constitutions, does not constitute an absolute proof that they are no longer diocesan congregations. The presumption, however, is in their favor, and without morally certain proofs to the contrary, viz., that the Holy See has not withdrawn them from the complete episcopal jurisdiction, they must be considered as being approved by the Holy See. This conclusion follows (1) from the fact that after the Holy See has once intervened, diocesan Ordinaries can no longer change that which has been approved; (2) from the general law of the Code prescribing that a contrary privilege must be proved; (3) from the broad scope of an answer of the Congregation of Religious in favor of the Sisters of Mercy.

An indult which authorizes the bishop to approve the foundation of a religious congregation does not make it an institute approved by the Holy See, even if it praises the purpose of the founder and of the new institute. An explanation of the meaning of these decrees of praise and of approbation will be found in n. **27.**

10. A clerical institute is one the majority of whose members are destined for the order of priesthood; otherwise it is a **lay institute.**

The mere number of religious clerics or of laymen is not sufficient to determine the legal character of the institute. The institute would remain clerical even though it admitted lay brothers in greater number than that of the clerics, provided that the former remained subordinate to the latter in the constitution and the government of the institute.[8] One may give as an example the Brothers of St. Vincent de Paul, and the clerics of St. Viator.

11. 1. The term **religious house** is absolutely general and includes every house of any institute whatever; a *house of regulars* designates the house of an order; a formal house, every house in which dwell at least six professed religious, at least four of whom must be priests if it is a house of a clerical institute.

---

[8] See Vermeersch, *Epitome,* I[r], n. 590.

In the case of brothers or religious women the Code does not demand that the majority of the six professed belong to the class of those capable of governing the institute. Three professed choir sisters and three professed lay sisters will constitute a formal house.

2. The word **monastery** is used in the Code to designate convents of monks, or of regular canons, or convents of nuns, whether they take solemn vows or not (cf. cc. 497, § 1; 512, § 1, n. 1; § 2, n. 1; 494, § 1, etc.).

This term is reserved to the houses of a religious order and may not be used to designate the houses of a religious congregation; it must not be used, therefore, in the official publications of these Institutes. This prohibition is repeated in the new edition of the "Normae."[9]

12. The term **"filial house"** or **"dependent house"** is used in a strict sense[10] of a house which has no legal existence independent of another community to which it is attached. This absolute dependence may be recognized from the following circumstances: the absence of a chapter or of a council of its own and of separate financial responsibilities; complete submission of the religious to the superior of the principal house. In some orders this is the status of the farms established on the property of the abbey where three or four religious live to take care of the goods of the monastery; the same may be said of the schools, workshops, dispensaries, etc., of some congregations, in which a few religious live permanently or whither they go each day or each week from the house to which they are attached. These dependent houses are governed in the name of the superior of the principal community by a religious designated by the superior and whom he may change as he wishes. This religious is sometimes called the minister, the vice-superior, or even the superior.

Major superiors are not free to declare those communities to be dependent houses which can fulfill the conditions required for an independent house. For the presence of a local superior with his councillors and a certain financial independence are the common right of all religious communities. According to Father Vermeersch, the Congregation of Religious has ordered the fol-

---

[9] *Normae*, Ed. 2, a. 22, h.
[10] Congregation of Religious, response of February 1, 1924. *A.A.S.*, XVI (1924), 25; *N.R. Th.* (1924), 298; *Per.*, XIII, 53.

lowing conditions for a dependent house in the strict sense to be inserted in some constitutions:

a) it must not consist of more than three religious;

b) it must depend, for purposes of government, upon a formal house designated by the general council;

c) the superior of this formal house must appoint, with the approval of the superior general, a religious authorized to govern the dependent house in his name;

d) this religious may be removed from office at the pleasure of superiors, and may not remain in office for more than nine years without the consent of the Holy See.

These conditions are valuable indications of the present mind of the Holy See and contain the probable answer to questions which may arise in regard to dependent houses. In Father Vermeersch's opinion[11] the superior general or the provincial himself may exercise authority directly over these houses even though they are attached to a formal house in financial matters, e.g., if the personal relations between the dependent house and the formal house should become strained.

13. An **independent monastery** or an **independent house** (*sui iuris*) is a religious house whose interior government is autonomous, for example, in admitting candidates to the novitiate or to profession, in the election of the superior, in the administration of temporal goods, etc. This autonomy means that there is no provincial superior who exercises ordinary power over the monastic or religious congregation. It is not incompatible with the immediate dependence on a superior general even though he has very extensive powers as is the case among the Carthusians or the monks of Camaldoli.[12]

Although the monasteries of nuns are for the most part independent, the authority of the abbess or of the prioress is very limited in some points by the powers accorded to the Ordinaries and to the regular superiors on whom the nuns depend.[13]

14. "**Religious** are all those who have made profession of vows in any institute; religious with simple vows, those who have made profession of vows in a religious congregation; regulars, those who have made profession of vows in an order; **sisters,** religious women with simple vows" (c. 488, § 7).

[11] See Vermeersch, *Per.,* XIII, 55.

[12] See Creusen, *Autonomie et Centralization, R.C.R.,* (1934), 122 ss., 146.

[13] See Larraona, in *Comm. pro rel.,* III (1922), 133.

Formerly the term "religious" in the strict sense was synonymous with "regular." As all the regulars made solemn vows, some persons disputed whether scholastics and coadjutors of the Society of Jesus, who made simple vows, were regulars, but Gregory XIII solemnly ascribed that quality to them.

When Pius IX obliged the members of all orders to pronounce simple perpetual vows before the profession of the solemn vows (March 19, 1857), the same doubt was raised in their regard. But now it is certain that even those who have only taken simple vows in an order are regulars. The term "religious" now has a much wider sense and includes without distinction all those who have made their profession in a religious institute. When it is employed without distinction, it takes in the regulars and the professed of religious congregations, both exempt and not exempt.

The Code marks a third step in the history of these expressions and even in the history of simple vows, for henceforth the first profession, even in the orders, will be temporary, and in more than one regard the professed of simple perpetual vows become more like to the professed of solemn vows. (See the chapter on Dismissal.)

Hereafter when an official document speaks of religious women, we must understand all religious women without exception, both nuns and sisters. The use of one of these latter terms will show that there is question only of one of these two groups of religious.

15. "**Nuns** are religious women with solemn vows or, unless it appears otherwise from the nature of the case or from the context, religious women whose vows are normally solemn but which by a disposition of the Holy See are simple in certain regions" (c. 488 § 7).

1. Before the Code the term *nuns* meant religious with solemn vows; but it was employed also in a very wide sense to indicate every sort of religious women. The Code has declared that only those religious women shall be classed as nuns whose Rule or constitutions call for solemn vows, even though, as a matter of fact, they are unable to take them.

Among these nuns are the Benedictines, the Poor Clares, certain canonesses of St. Augustine, the Carmelites, the Dominicans (of the second order), the Ursulines (who belong to the Roman Union), Visitandines, etc. The great number of the women religious who are called tertiaries of St. Francis or of St. Dominic are not nuns, neither are the members of those Congregations which have adopted in part some ancient rule, for instance, the Franciscans of the Holy Family, of the Sacred Heart; the Dominicans of the Sacred Heart; the Ursulines who belong to diocesan congregations, etc.

Since the beginning of the nineteenth century until the decree of the Sacred Congregation for Religious of June 23, 1923, the nuns in France (with the exception of those in Nice and Savoy) and in Belgium could not make the solemn profession, but only the simple profession.

2. The constitution *Sponsa Christi* of November 21, 1950, intended to restore all its splendor to the status of nuns, defines them as follows: "In addition to religious women with solemn vows, [are included] those who have pronounced simple vows, perpetual or temporary, in monasteries where solemn vows are actually taken or should be taken according to the constitutions, unless the contrary is certain from the context or from the nature of the case" (*General Statutes for Nuns,* art. 1, § 1).

Thus all controversy is removed about the lawfulness of applying the term nun to religious women with simple temporary vows in a monastery of solemn vows.

As to the final restrictions "unless the contrary is certain . . . ," it should be admitted that they have now hardly any substance since the juridical character of nuns involves at least minor papal cloister.

3. The form of life proper to nuns, which is *canonical contemplative life,* is defined as follows by the constitution *Sponsa Christi:*

"The external profession of religious life which, by reason of cloister, or by reason of exercises of piety, prayer, and mortification, or finally by reason of work which the nuns are obliged to undertake, is so directed to interior contemplation that the entire scope of their life and activity easily can and efficaciously should be imbued with zeal for it" (art. 2, § 2).

4. The constitution *Sponsa Christi* strongly encourages the taking of solemn vows by all nuns, even by those who are engaged in certain apostolic works and as a consequence can observe only the minor papal cloister (art. III, § 2).

The request to reassume the taking of solemn profession, since it gravely affects the juridical condition of each religious, must be submitted to the chapter. Even though the vote is not unanimous, the Holy See can impose solemn profession. The simple vows, consequently, are the result of a merely temporary state of affairs and are in partial conflict with the Rule or the constitutions. If the Holy See takes into account the wish expressed by the majority, it apparently does not want to force any individual to change from the profession of simple vows to that of solemn.

5. Even though the nuns are subject to the local Ordinary, they all nonetheless are religious of *pontifical* right.

The Code indicates several matters in which nuns are subject to the local Ordinaries (for example: cc. 506, § 2; 512, § 2, 1°; 534, § 1; 603; 647, § 1). The constitution *Sponsa Christi* has not altered these prescriptions (art. VI, § 3).

6. After the publication of the Code and before the rather general resumption of solemn vows, "the nature of the case or the context" made it possible to realize that certain prescriptions enjoined upon nuns did not affect those with simple vows. Thus, by reason of the *nature of things* the excommunication of c. 2342 was incurred only by violations of the cloister of nuns having solemn vows.

16. *Outdoor Sisters.*

In a large number of monasteries, and even in the houses of certain congregations, in which enclosure is very strictly observed, the religious, in their relations with the outside world, have recourse to persons who are commonly called outdoor sisters. The juridical condition of these persons varies according to the different institutes. In some they are simply secular persons, even though they may take private vows and enjoy a share in the merits of the institute. In others they make an oblation which binds them to the Order more closely. In certain monasteries these outdoor sisters pronounce public vows which make them real religious.[14]

The status of these extern helpers will be determined either by the constitutions which have been approved by the Holy See or by a particular indult granted by the same. Outdoor sisters in the strict sense of the term may be found in the Visitation Order, and in the monasteries of the Poor Clares, the Benedictines, Carmelites, Good Shepherds, etc.

By a decree of July 16, 1931,[15] the Sacred Congregation of Religious has approved "Statutes to be observed by the outdoor sisters of monasteries of nuns of all orders." These statutes are of obligation in all monasteries of nuns who have outdoor sisters by reason of a special approbation of the Holy See. Furthermore, hereafter any monastery of nuns may establish a group of outdoor sisters subject to the above-mentioned statutes. In those cases in which the Holy See had already approved other

---

14 See Jombart, *Les Soeurs Tourieres*, R.C.R., (1926), 166.
15 *A.A.S.,* XXIII (1931), 380. — R.C.R., (1931), 180.

statutes for outdoor sisters by special indult, these may still be kept.[16]

17. "The **major** or **higher superiors** are the abbot primate, the abbot superior of a monastic congregation, the abbot of an independent monastery even though it forms part of a monastic congregation, the superior-general of the whole institute, the provincial superior, their vicars and all others who have powers equivalent to those of provincials" (c. 488, § 8).

Among the major superiors should be included the vicar general of an institute, the visitors of men religious, the vice-provincial; also the superiors of nuns in independent monasteries like those of the Benedictines, Poor Clares, Carmelites, etc.

In many institutes the first assistant or the first councillor of the superior general exercises supreme authority "when the superior general is absent or impeded," or has resigned, as also during the interval between the death of the superior general and the election of his successor. Does it necessarily follow that the first assistant or first councillor is a major superior? A distinction must be made here. When he actually takes the place of the superior general he has the powers of a major superior; outside such times his office does not carry any authority with it unless the constitutions or the superior general entrusts him with the care of certain persons or of certain matters of business.

The term *vicar* is employed instead of "provincial" in certain institutes better to indicate dependence upon the superior general and unity of government (e.g., Religious of the Sacred Heart, Helpers of Holy Souls).

18. Besides the religious institutes, properly so called, there exist **societies** whether of men or women, whose members imitate the manner of life of religious by living in a community under the government of superiors according to approved constitutions, but without being bound by the usual three vows (c. 673).

These societies are not religious institutes in the proper sense, nor are their members religious. They are often grouped with religious by the Code as we shall see in the following pages. Generally, their members

---

[16] See La Puma, in *Comm. pro. rel.*, 1931, 426 sq.; 1932, 245 sq. — Creusen, in *R.C.R.* (1931), 180 sq.

enjoy greater liberty in the disposition of temporal goods and a greater independence.[17]

Such a society is clerical or lay, pontifical or diocesan, according to the terms of canon 488, nn. 3 and 4. (See n. **9.**)

Among these societies are the Oratorians, the Sulpicians, the White Fathers, the Paulists, the Maryknoll Missionaries, etc.

§ 3. APPLICATION OF THE LAWS

19. 1. Rules and particular constitutions of religious institutes which are contrary to the Code are abrogated (c. 489), hence they may no longer be observed,[18] since by this canon the Sovereign Pontiff has formally revoked the approbation given to these parts of the constitutions. These provisions apply to directories and custom books as well.

2. Those articles of constitutions which add to the obligations of the Code without contradicting it may be kept. Such would be special conditions for the admission of candidates, for example, a greater age, legitimate birth, etc.

3. Sometimes the Code lays down a method of procedure at least for cases in which the particular law or the constitutions have no provision to the contrary. Such is the case in canon 101, regarding the relative or absolute majority of votes required in a ballot, as well as the number of ballots to be taken; similarly canons 161, 162, and 163 regarding elections; canon 531 relative to the juridical capacity of provinces and of particular houses; canon 569 with reference to the disposal of goods, etc.

In such cases: (*a*) one may follow the articles of the constitutions which depart from the rule laid down by the Code; (*b*) if new constitutions are to be edited, one may freely choose the norm to be followed; (*c*) if the Code allows an exception for a particular law, the legitimate custom of an institute or province may be retained.

20. Privileges and papal indults remain in force, unless the Code formally declares them revoked (c. 4).

If *by chance* an article contrary to the Code should remain in the text of constitutions which have been revised after the Code and submitted to the Holy See for approval, we believe that the ordinary approbation granted by the Sacred Congregation would not suffice to give such an article the character of a privilege, and it would not exempt one from the obligation of following the common law of the Code. The "style," that is to say, the habitual method of procedure of the Sacred Congregation will help to distinguish a case of clear oversight from a case in which a particular privilege is granted.

---

[17] We shall call them hereafter "religious societies." See Creusen, *Sociétés religieuses,* in *Ephem. the. Lov.,* 1934, 778 ss.

[18] The statement to the contrary in the posthumous edition of Battandier, *G.C.,* p. XXI, note 1, is evidently erroneous. See *N.R. Th.* (1923), 447.

21. It is important to notice that the new legislation has in some cases changed the conditions for the validity of important actions like elections, vows, the disposal of property, etc. These cases will be carefully noted in the following pages, since invalidating and disqualifying laws take effect even when one is ignorant of them (c. 16, § 1).

22. The dispositions concerning religious, even when expressed in the masculine gender, apply equally to religious women, except it appears otherwise from the context or from the nature of the case (c. 490).

What is said of the master of novices, of the superior, etc., applies equally to the mistresses of novices or to the women superiors, etc. Sometimes, however, doubts will occur. In c. 491, the Code seems to refer only to precedence among the members of institutes of men. Nevertheless, a certain application of this canon may be made to decide precedence at least by analogy in processions in which all the faithful are represented.

What is said of women religious, however, is never to be applied to men, and this principle is directly opposed to that of the ancient *Normae*.[19]

23. *Diocesan Congregations.*

According to a very probable opinion the constitutions and pontifical decrees concerning the religious life were formerly addressed only to religious institutes approved by the Holy See, unless express mention was made of the diocesan congregations, but since 1918 these latter are certainly included in all the regulations of the common law which speak of religious in general.

The decree of the Sacred Congregation of Religious, November 30, 1922,[20] on the necessity of establishing by a formal decree of erection the canonical existence of diocesan institutes, confirms an opinion which we believe good authors have ceased to question.

§ 4. THE LAW OF PRECEDENCE

24. 1. Precedence is the right in virtue of which a person, whether physical or moral, occupies a more honorable place, during ceremonies or in an assembly, or is the first to cast his vote. This external mark of respect is an acknowledgment of

---

[19] See Vermeersch, *De religiosis*, II, 130.
[20] *A.A.S., XIV* (1922), 644; *Per.,* XI, 173.

the dignity or of the authority of him who is called to precede others in this manner.

2. "Religious take **precedence** over the laity; clerical institutes over lay institutes; canons regular over monks; monks over other regulars; regulars over religious congregations; congregations approved by the Holy See over diocesan congregations; for those in the same species, the disposition of canon 106, n. 5, is to be observed."

"But the secular clergy precede the laity and the religious outside their own churches and, in the case of a lay institute, even in their own churches; the cathedral or collegiate chapter, however, precedes them everywhere" (c. 491).

Canon 106, n. 5, declares: "Between different corporate entities of the same species or of the same degree, precedence belongs to that which is in peaceful quasi-possession, and if quasi-possession cannot be proved, then to that which has been the first established in the place where the question arises; but among members of any college, the right of precedence shall be determined according to its own legitimate statutes; otherwise by lawful custom; or failing this, by the prescriptions of the universal law."

3. The first phrase (which is in quasi-possession) means that in the different corporate bodies (chapters of canons, religious institutes, etc.) that body will have precedence which has always enjoyed it and has habitually exercised the right of precedence without dispute. If now one body, now another, has obtained the precedence, it is necessary to have recourse to other titles to decide to which one it belongs.

4. *Canons Regular* are religious who have taken solemn vows and who are principally devoted to maintaining the splendor of the divine worship. Such are in order of antiquity, the canons regular of the Lateran, the Premonstratensians, the Crosier Fathers. Those are called *monks* (hermits) who, although they have lived in common (cenobites) for centuries, follow the rules composed by the first patriarchs of the religious life for the direction of the hermits of Egypt and of Syria. Translated into Latin, co-ordinated and modified, these rules serve as the rules of the convents of Europe. We mention as example the Benedictines, the Trappists, the monks of Camaldoli, the Cistercians who follow the rule of St. Benedict, the Carthusians,[21] etc. The

---

[21] The Carthusians are sometimes identified with the Benedictine family. As a matter of fact, St. Bruno did not give his monks a rule. Later on their customs were codified into a primitive rule which combined certain elements of the Benedictine Rule with other regulations which are quite distinct from the latter. See Heimbucher, *Die Orden und Kongregationen der K. Kirche*, I, p. 376 ss., *Dict. de Theol.* (Vacant-Mangenot), see Chartreux, II (S. Auctore).

28 CONSTITUTION OF RELIGIOUS INSTITUTES

other Regulars include the *mendicant orders,* like the Carmelites, Franciscans, the Dominicans, Augustinians, and the *Clerics Regular,* like the Theatines, the Jesuits, etc., whose principal aim is the apostolic ministry. The first religious congregations in the modern sense of the word date only from the sixteenth century.[22]

5. Besides the *external* precedence regulated by canon 491, the constitutions determine the habitual *internal* precedence, that is to say within the family of the order or congregation, in terms of the general principle: "One who has authority over physical or moral persons has also the right of precedence over them" (c. 106, § 2). Precedence, which as such does not confer any authority, may serve as a norm when there is question of taking the place of a superior who is absent, or when a group of religious are away from the religious house.

---

[22] Regarding orders and congregations, the following works may be consulted: *Les grands Ordres monastiques,* Grasset, Paris; *Les Ordres religieux,* Letouzey, Paris; Code, *Great American Foundresses,* Macmillan, New York, 1929; Heimbucher, *Die Orden und Kongregationen der Katholischen Kirche,* 3rd Ed., Paderborn, 1932; Creusen, *Les Congrégations religieuses,* in *Dict. dr. can.,* s.v. *Congrégations;* and *R.C.R.* (1940), 52, and (1945), 34.

CHAPTER II

Erection or Suppression of a Religious Institute, of a Province, or of a House

(Title IX, cc. 492–498)

§ 1. ERECTION AND SUPPRESSION OF A RELIGIOUS INSTITUTE

A. Erection of a Religious Institute

25. Bishops, but not the Vicar Capitular or the Vicar General, can establish religious Congregations; but they must not establish them or permit them to be established without consulting the Apostolic See; when it is a question of tertiaries living in community, it is required, besides, that they be affiliated to his Institute by the Superior-General of the first Order (c. 492, § 1).

Action by the ecclesiastical authority has always been necessary for the establishment of an order or a religious congregation. From the thirteenth century on, the sovereign pontiffs have reserved to themselves the right to authorize these foundations. While it was opposed to the multiplication, sometimes excessive, of new forms of religious life, the Holy See has tolerated, especially since the eighteenth century, that Congregations should be founded with the approbation of the bishops only. Now this right has been expressly recognized once more.

In 1906, Pius X by his *Motu Proprio Dei Providentia* (July 16) made the exercise of this right depend on the consent of the Holy See. The Code confirms this legislation.

26. The *Normae*[1] stated definitely the steps to be taken before the foundation of a religious Institute, the ordinary conditions, and the measures to secure its eventual approval by the Roman Curia. We shall content ourselves with indicating here the essential elements of this legislation. When there is question of founding a native congregation, the special prescriptions of the

---

[1] *A.A.S.,* XIII (1921), 312; *N.R. Th.* (1921), 424, 493; *Per.,* X, 295.

Sacred Congregation for the Propagation of the Faith must be observed.[2]

1. The authorization, or *Nihil obstat,* of the Holy See must precede any organization properly so called of the religious life (*re adhuc integra*). If some of the pious faithful unite to exercise themselves in the obligations of the religious life, without pronouncing public vows, without a common uniform habit, without giving the name of a religious institute to their group, that pious enterprise does not yet require the action of the Holy See. This action, however, will be needed before they may adopt the regular forms of the religious life.

For a still stronger reason, the Ordinary cannot, without having consulted the Holy See, take some members from an existing congregation, give them a different name and a different habit, and authorize them, even conditionally, to engage in new works, whether these works be like those of their institute or different from them. Moreover, the S. Congregation does not authorize such a separation except for grave motives, from which it excludes national aspirations.

2. The following information is required by the Sacred Congregation of Religious about proposed foundations: the name and the qualities of the founder; the end which he intends; the name or title of the congregation; the form, color, and material of the habit of the novices and of the professed; the number and kind of the works to which the community will devote itself; the origin and nature of the material means which are necessary; the existence or absence of similar institutes in the diocese (*Normae,* Ed. 2, n. 4). "Neither the name nor the habit of any institute already established can be assumed by those who do not legitimately belong to it, or by a new institute" (c. 492, § 3).

In mission territories, the local Ordinary is usually the founder of the new congregation. Accordingly the Sacred Congregation does not demand that he send in the name and qualities of the founder, although it does ask for the motives which prompted the Ordinary to make the foundation (*Instruction,* March 19, 1937, art. 7).

If the Ordinary was influenced by the plans or the request of a founder or foundress, it would be proper to give the name and qualities of this person.

3. If the Sacred Congregation declares that it is not opposed,

---

[2] Instruction, March 19, 1937, *A.A.S.,* XXIX (1937), 275 sq. *R.C.R.* (1937), 129 sq., 164 sq.; (1938), 2 sq.

the bishop may establish the new institute in the form of a congregation or of a religious society by a formal decree of erection. This decree is necessary, according to a special prescription of the Holy See, to give the new association a juridical personality.[3]

The decree of November 30, 1922, directs that the Ordinaries shall make sure that all diocesan institutes whose motherhouse is in their diocese, possess this formal decree. Where it is wanting, they must see that it is provided, unless they judge it preferable to suppress the institute. If the congregation has spread into other dioceses, the decree of erection cannot be issued except with the consent of all the Ordinaries of those dioceses.[4]

4. In the writing of the constitutions account must be taken of the prescriptions of the Code and of the *Normae*. No modifications may be introduced in the articles, which have been submitted to the Holy See.

When there is question of a native congregation in a mission territory, the local Ordinary must submit the constitutions to the Sacred Congregation for the Propagation of the Faith before approving them. The Sacred Congregation examines the text, makes corrections where needed, and adds suitable observations. It is evident, however, that there is no positive approbation given.[5]

27. When the new institute shall have developed sufficiently and shall have shown by the test of time the value of its religious spirit and its unity, it may ask of the Holy See a positive approbation. Practically the steps of approbation in the Roman Curia are the following: Decree of commendation of the institute;[6] decree of approbation of the new congregation;[7] approba-

[3] Decree of the Congregation of Religious, November 30, 1922, VII.

[4] See *Per.* XI, 173.

[5] See *R.C.R.*, (1937), p. 129 sq.

[6] The formula of the *decree of praise* is as follows: "Our most Holy Father N. . . ., being informed of the letters of recommendation of the bishops of the dioceses in which exist houses of the institute in question, highly praises and recommends, by the tenor of the present decree, the institute itself as a religious congregation under the authority of a superior general . . . without prejudice to the jurisdiction of the Ordinaries, according to the sacred canons" (*Normae,* Ed. 2, n. 6).

[7] The text of the *decree of approbation* of the institute: "Our most Holy Father N. . . ., in view of the abundance of the fruits of salvation which have been brought forth by the religious congregation N. . . ., having considered . . . approves and confirms it under the authority of a superior general without prejudice to the jurisdiction of the Ordinaries, according to the sacred canons" (*Normae,* Ed. 2, n. 11).

tion of the constitutions, first provisional, then final. Frequently the temporary approval of the constitutions is given together with the decree of praise. As soon as the decree of commendation is obtained, the institute becomes an institute approved by the Holy See. From this moment no article of the constitutions can be modified without the consent of the Holy See (c. 618, §2, 1).

28. "A diocesan Congregation, although it extends in the course of time into several dioceses, nevertheless, remains diocesan as long as it is without pontifical approval or the decree of commendation, and is entirely subject to the jurisdiction of the Ordinaries according to law" (c. 492, § 2).

According to numerous pontifical documents, the meaning of this article is as follows:

1. Each bishop exercises, to the exclusion of every other, his jurisdiction over the houses situated in his diocese.

Confessors are appointed by the Ordinary of the place; the visitation is made by the diocesan visitor; when the law requires the permission of the Ordinary for certain acts, it is the bishop of the diocese from whom this authorization is to be asked; it is he who grants an indult of secularization, etc.

2. The Ordinary of the motherhouse has not the authority of a superior general; except in the cases expressly mentioned by the Code, his power does not exceed that of other Ordinaries.

Before approving constitutions, the Sacred Congregation of Bishops and Regulars has often ordered stricken out whatever seemed to confer on the Ordinary of the motherhouse the powers of the superior general. Especially he has not been authorized to name a director general of the institute.[8]

Exceptions: to establish a first house in another diocese, it is always necessary to have the authorization of the Ordinary of the motherhouse (c. 495, § 1); the communications of the Holy See concerning several houses or the entire institute will usually be addressed to him, etc.

3. The measures which concern the whole congregation are, according to their character, freely decided on by the superior general with his council, or are submitted to all the Ordinaries of the dioceses where the congregation is established.

---

[8] Bizzarri, *Collectanea S.C. Ep. et Reg.*, 1885, p. 778 sqq.

Examples: Every change of the constitution requires the approbation of all the Ordinaries. The removal of local superiors and of simple religious are freely decided on by the superior general.[9] If the constitutions do not determine the place of the general chapter, the superior general may freely do so and the election is presided over and ratified or disapproved by the Ordinary of the place where the chapter is held.[10]

4. The jurisdiction of the Ordinaries ought to be exercised "according to the law." We have said in the foregoing (n. 23) that diocesan congregations are entirely subject to the common law as given in the Code. Thus, by virtue of numerous articles of the Code, diocesan congregations enjoy a real independence in their life and their interior government; the occasions and the measure of interference of the Ordinaries are here definitely specified.[11]

5. As a matter of fact, the Ordinary of the motherhouse will have a preponderating influence over the whole congregation because he is the Ordinary of the superior general. It is hardly necessary to add that very often gratitude will require that special consideration be shown him.

B. Suppression of a Religious Institute

29. "Every institute, even if only diocesan, once legitimately established even if it possesses only one house, cannot be suppressed except by the Holy See, to which is reserved in this case the disposition of the property, always, however, without prejudice to the wishes of the donors of the property" (c. 493).

The suppression of religious orders has always been reserved to the supreme authority in the Church. In its decree of November 30, 1922, concerning diocesan institutes, the Holy See provides for the suppression of congregations which have not been legitimately established or approved and whose interior state makes their discontinuance desirable. If only one religious should remain, the rights of all are concentrated in his person (c. 102, § 2).

The fusion of congregations occurs more frequently in our day than formerly. The lessening of efficiency due to the shortage of vocations and the usefulness of uniting two institutes having the same spirit and the same apostolate provoke such unions. They also assume different forms: an extinctive union whereby a congregation is absorbed by a

---

[9] *S.C. Ep. et Reg.* Response, April 9, 1895. Bastien, *D.C.,* n. 295.

[10] Congregation of Religious, Response, July 2, 1921; *A.A.S.,* XIII (1921), 481; *N.R. Th.* (1922), 44.

[11] See *Comm. pro rel.,* II (1921), 329, XIII.

more important one; the establishment of a new institute which unites two or more congregations of the same kind. In all such cases recourse must be had to the Holy See.[12]

In Belgium a great number of religious institutes are established as "Societies not for profit." The act of incorporation of such societies provides for the disposal of the property in case of the suppression or extinction of the society; this wish of the founders will, therefore, always be respected by the Holy See.

§ 2. ERECTION, SUPPRESSION, OR DIVISION OF PROVINCES

30. "It pertains exclusively to the Apostolic See: to divide into provinces an institute approved by the Holy See, to unite existing provinces or otherwise modify their boundaries, to establish new provinces or to suppress existing ones, to separate independent monasteries from one monastic congregation and to unite them to another" (c. 494, § 1).

The causes which justify a division into provinces are: the difficulty of a single administration, the necessity of having several novitiates on account of the wide extension of the institute. It is an advantage to gather all the subjects for some time in a central novitiate where they can imbibe the true spirit and gain a more lasting affection for all the members of the institute. The jurisprudence of the S. Congregation requires that the first division be made into at least three provinces, each of which shall include not less than three formal houses and a total of fifty professed religious.

The Code does not provide for the establishment of provinces in a purely diocesan institute. Such a possibility is, nevertheless, not ruled out (see question 9 of the quinquennial report for diocesan congregations in the Appendix, III, p. 300). But as a general rule when the congregation has gained such importance, it will be advisable to ask the Holy See for an approval which will give more autonomy to its life and its government.

31. "When a province becomes extinct, the right of disposing of its property, while safeguarding the laws of justice (payment of debts, the discharge of mortgages, etc.) and the wishes of the founders, belongs, unless the constitutions ordain otherwise, to the General Chapter or, outside the time of the Chapter, to the superior general with his council" (c. 494, § 2).

The Code does not require that the council shall have a deliberative voice — *cum suo concilio* (cf. c. 105).

---

[12] See Bergh, *Fusion de Congregations, R.C.R.,* 1955, 164–170.

§ 3. ERECTION OR SUPPRESSION OF A RELIGIOUS HOUSE

A. Erection of a Religious House

32. In this matter of establishing a religious house, the Code treats of diocesan institutes and of other institutes in separate canons. Since diocesan institutes are so greatly dependent upon their Ordinaries, it would be rather idle to define, for example, just what the permission to found a house may imply. The Holy See, on the other hand, has approved in detail whatever pertains to the interior government and external activity of other institutes; hence it is important to determine the extent of the rights contained in the episcopal authorization to establish a house.

33. *Necessary Authorization.*

"A diocesan religious congregation cannot establish houses in another diocese without the consent of both Ordinaries, namely: the Ordinary of the place where the motherhouse is situated, and the Ordinary of the place where it is desired to make the new foundation; but the Ordinary of the place of departure shall not without a grave reason refuse his consent" (c. 495, § 1).

To found a new house in a diocese where one is already established, the authorization of the Ordinary of the place is sufficient. The Ordinary of the motherhouse need approve, therefore, only the first establishment in another diocese.

This explanation follows: (1) from the constitution *Conditae a Christo*, article IV, which has inspired c. 495; (2) from the very terms of c. 495. When a congregation founds a new house in a diocese where it is already established, it does not transfer itself elsewhere (*loci quo velit commigrare*); it does not leave a diocese (*loci unde excedit*). Besides the authorization mentioned above, it is necessary to have recourse to the Congregation of the Propaganda for the erection of a community in mission territory, even though the community is merely diocesan (c. 497, § 1).

When a diocesan congregation establishes houses in other dioceses, no change may be made in its laws without the consent of all the Ordinaries in whose dioceses its houses exist (c. 495, § 2).

We have said above that the articles submitted for the examination of the Holy See before the foundation cannot be changed without its authorization.

34. "For the erection of an exempt religious house, whether formal or not, or a monastery of nuns, or, in places subject to the Sacred Congregation of Propaganda, any religious house whatever, the approval of the Apostolic See and the written consent of the local Ordinary are necessary" (c. 497, § 1).

To found a monastery of nuns of simple vows in France, in Belgium, or in the United States, it is probable that the authorization of the Holy See is not required. This opinion, which is shared by good canonists[13] rests on the repeated declarations of the Holy See that nothing is changed in the dependence of these nuns in regard to the bishops.

In the missions, a rather large number of religious priests do not live in a religious house. Their dwelling can be called a "quasi-presbytery," if such a station forms a quasi-parish. These houses are evidently established by authority of the vicar or prefect apostolic alone. If the number of religious who live together is large enough, a community ought to be established, and the religious house should be canonically erected. Otherwise the religious would not be complying with a formal prescription of law (c. 606, § 2) and could not enjoy their privileges.

35. To establish a nonexempt religious house of a Congregation approved by the Holy See in a territory subject to the common law of the Church, it is sufficient to have the approval of the Ordinary of the place (c. 497, § 1).

No special authorization is needed to change the dwelling of a religious house in the same locality; or to re-establish a community which has been unjustly deprived of its dwelling or to reconstruct a religious house which has been destroyed by fire, by an earthquake, etc.

The Ordinary must give his authorization in writing.

C. 497, § 1, after having spoken of the written approbation of the Holy See and of the Ordinary, continues by stating when the approbation of the Ordinary alone suffices, but it does not thereby withdraw the obligation of a written authorization. Why does § 3 require that the authorization for erecting a school or hospital be given in writing, if it be not required for the more important case of the establishing of a religious community?

36. "To build and open a school, a hospice, or any other such edifice separated from the house, even exempt, the special

---

[13] See E. Jombart, *Les Moniales à vœux simples; N.R. Th.* (1924), p. 197.

written permission of the Ordinary is necessary and sufficient" (c. 497, § 3).

In this case there is not a foundation of a new religious community, but rather an extension of its works. On the other hand, this is a new establishment and one not foreseen in the foundation, because it is separated from the religious house itself.

To add to an establishment within the precincts of a convent already approved does not require any particular authorization, if the bishop did not fix limits to the first foundation.

37. "To convert to other uses a house already established, the same solemnities as in § 1 are required (see preceding numbers **34, 35**); except the alteration be of such a nature that without prejudice to the laws of the foundation, it affect only the internal régime and religious discipline" (c. 497, § 4).

Changes which would require a special authorization are: the addition of a boarding school to a day school; the transformation of an apostolic school into a college open to all students; changing of a boarding school into a surgical clinic, etc. Changes which would concern only the interior management are: to change a juniorate into a theological scholasticate; to add to a novitiate a house of retirement for sick and infirm religious.

38. *Further Conditions for the Erection of a Religious House.*

1. "No religious house may be erected unless it can be prudently estimated that it will be able to provide suitably for the habitation and maintenance of its members from its own resources, or from habitual alms, or otherwise" (c. 496).

Serious faults in religious discipline and notable relaxation often come from the lack of suitable resources to support the number of subjects and the kinds of works which the institute prescribes. This lack of means leaves both superiors and inferiors exposed to the danger of employing means which compromise the observance of rules and religious recollection, the free exercise of their holy ministry or of the interior government. These facts explain the severity of the ecclesiastical laws in regard to the dowry of nuns, the administration of temporal affairs, loans, mortgages, etc., in religious institutes.

2. The old law for a long time forbade the establishment of a new house of religious within a determined distance of another monastery. Nothing of this kind remains in the Code. The spirit, however, from which this ancient prescription arose will suggest even today the exercise of a charitable discretion.

By thus keeping at a suitable distance communities will avoid rivalries which would be very disedifying, and a real harm which would be caused to religious who have merited highly by the services they have already rendered to the locality or to the diocese.

39. *Consequences of Authorization.*

The granting of permission to establish a new house implies the authorization:

1. For clerical institutes:

a) to have a church or public oratory annexed to the house; but its location must be especially approved by the Ordinary of the place;

b) to celebrate the sacred functions in conformity with the requirements of law.

2. For all institutes, to carry on works of piety proper to each institute according to the conditions contained in the permission (c. 497, § 2).

The Ordinary could, for example, in his concession, limit the number of pupils or boarders who are to be received; require that the establishment be restricted to certain nationalities, etc.

B. Suppression of a Religious House

40. 1. "No religious house, whether formal or not, belonging to an exempt institute, can be suppressed without Apostolic authority; a house belonging to a nonexempt congregation approved or commended by the Holy See, can be suppressed by the Superior-General, with the consent of the local Ordinary; if it belongs to a diocesan congregation, it can be suppressed by the mere authority of the local Ordinary after consultation with the Superior of the Congregation" (c. 498).

It is always taken for granted that the house to be suppressed does not make up the whole institute.

In saying "a house belonging, etc.," the Code evidently speaks of a religious community regularly established. The fact that the house occupied by this community is only rented changes nothing from the point of view of the suppression.

2. The suppression of separate establishments such as we have spoken of in n. 36 belongs entirely to the religious superior. But since this suppression may cause a serious damage to the

faithful of the neighborhood, it is only just to consult the bishop before taking action. On the other hand, the Ordinary cannot suppress such separate establishments without previous understanding with the religious superiors. By reason of the authorized erection, the institute or community has acquired a right which cannot be extinguished without the consent of both parties. By the abuse of their right the religious can forfeit it. In case of conflict either of the two parties can always have recourse to Rome.

In certain cases the authorization to open these establishments supposes an agreement, at least tacit, not to suppress them without the authorization of the Ordinary. If the Bishop should have refrained from the establishment of a school himself so as to allow religious to add such a school to their other works, it is hard to see how they could later on suppress the school without the bishop's authorization; otherwise very serious conflicts may arise afterwards from the divergent interests of the diocese or of the parish, and of the institute.

41. All the rules laid down in this chapter are applicable also to "religious societies" (see n. **18**).

CHAPTER III

Government of Religious
(Title X, cc. 499–537)

42. Under this title the Code has three chapters. The first two have to do with exterior government, discipline, with persons and their spiritual direction; the third chapter takes up the management of temporal goods. Since it is necessary to round out the discussion of these questions by referring to other titles of the code, we shall add an article on divine service, since this naturally comes under the heading of the government of religious.

Article 1. Superiors and Chapters
§ 1. PRELIMINARY NOTIONS

43. The two forms of authority which are exercised over religious are *jurisdiction and dominative power*. To understand the nature of these, some explanations are in order about the source and the manner of exercise of this authority.

Both the Church and State are societies which are perfect in their own order, independent of any other societies in the pursuit of their proper end. Other societies subordinated to them either arise from natural bonds (such, for example, are families), or else they come from an agreement made, as do commercial and industrial associations, etc.

44. 1. A perfect society is ruled by one or several persons who have authority in it. These persons prescribe for the members of the society all the acts which are necessary to attain their end, and for the well-being and maintenance of the community. This public power, called **jurisdiction,** includes the right to make laws, to establish courts, and to declare penalties against those who violate the laws. It exists in the Church as well as in the State.

2. Ecclesiastical jurisdiction is exercised in the **external forum** (tribunal) or in the **internal forum.**

In the external forum, jurisdiction has for its principal and main purpose the securing of the common good, the safeguarding of the social obligations and rights of the faithful; in the internal forum this jurisdiction concerns their personal obligations of conscience and their individual good. Thus, for example, it is an act of jurisdiction in the external forum to grant a dispensation from the vows of religion; on the other hand a confessor employs his power of jurisdiction in the internal forum when, by reason of special faculties granted to him, he dispenses a penitent from a private vow or from some hidden impediment to matrimony.

3. The Pope and the bishops can, to a certain extent, communicate to others of the faithful their power of jurisdiction. The ecclesiastical law forbids them to delegate it to simple laymen. By the common law of the Church jurisdiction is attached to certain offices; for example, all the superiors of exempt clerics have the power of jurisdiction even in the external forum over their subjects. Jurisdiction attached by law to a charge or an office in the strict sense is called *ORDINARY;* when a superior or the law grants it to a determined individual, it is said to be *DELEGATED.*

Ordinary jurisdiction is proper or vicarious: proper, when the person who possesses it may exercise it in his own name; vicarious, when he exercises it in the name of another. A vicar general has ordinary vicarious jurisdiction.

45. In ecclesiastical law the word **"Ordinary"** is used to designate, unless some special exception is made, the Sovereign Pontiff, the residential bishop for his territory, the vicars and prefects apostolic, certain other prelates, vicars general and, "for their subordinates, the higher superiors in the institutes of exempt clerics." All these, with the exception of religious superiors, are comprised under the name of Ordinaries of the place.

In legal language the word "bishop" is by no means synonymous with Ordinary of the place, because it may also be applied to titular bishops. In current phrase, however, the word "bishop" or "Ordinary" is quite often used to designate the diocesan Ordinary. We shall follow this usage, but shall take care to inform the reader whenever the term applies also to the higher superior of exempt clerics.

46. 1. In every particular society there is also an authority, but it is private. In order to determine the character of this authority we must inquire into its origin, that is to say, the fact, whether natural and necessary, or free, which has given it existence. Its extent and its exercise will vary with the end and the nature of the association itself.

Authority may directly govern the person subject to it in all his free actions, hence *practically* rule over his will, or it may have only a more or less extensive control over his activities.

By the natural law children are entirely subject to the authority of their father and mother, in everything that is necessary for their education; positive law (the ecclesiastical and civil law) fixes the duration of the legal exercise of this parental authority. It is generally recognized that the wife is, by the necessary consequences of the marriage contract, subject in the same manner, although within very much more narrow limits, to the authority of her husband. Finally, the professed religious in all religious institutes have, by their act of profession, given to superiors the free disposal of their person; they have fully submitted their will to their superiors.

All those who freely enter into a social group must submit themselves in a certain degree to the authority which directs it. Superiors have the right to demand whatever is necessary for the maintenance and the progress of the society. Their power does not extend directly to the person of their subordinates, but to a certain number of their actions, to the degree indicated above. Such, for example, is the dependence of domestic servants in regard to their master, of workmen in regard to their employer, of novices and postulants in regard to religious superiors.

2. When this personal authority is brought to bear directly on the will of the subjects, and when the persons themselves depend entirely on the superiors, this authority is called **dominative power.** The Code does not use any definite expression to designate the second form of private authority, that of a superior over the members of his community (cf. c. 1312). But the greater number of theologians or canonists call this authority *domestic power.*[1]

3. The power invested in superiors of societies which receive their juridical personality from, and are founded by, the Church is somewhat analogous to jurisdiction. This power is not of a private nature.

Its being acquired validly is linked up with conditions which are determined by the supreme authority. The Church also makes the validity of very important juridical acts depend upon the exercise of this power, for example, the admission or dismissal of novices or professed religious; the validity of certain acts dealing with the administration of temporal goods (borrowing, alienation, acquisition of property).

---

[1] See Raus, C.SS.R., *De sacrae oboedientiae virtute et voto,* n. 39 sq; Brandys, *Kirchliches Rechtsbuch,* n. 177.

Due to this analogy, one may apply to acts proceeding from this power the principle of canon 209. To illustrate, the Church supplies this power in case of common error. Accordingly, all acts of this nature will be valid if they have been placed by a person whom all believed to be the superior general, but whose election was invalid on account of some defect unknown to all, or to the majority, of the members of the institute, for example, illegitimate birth.

An interesting paper on this subject, entitled *Pouvoir dominitif et erreur commun*, was read at the International Juridical Congress held in Rome, November 12–17, 1934, by the Rev. Joseph Creusen, S.J. It was published in the Acts of the Congress, Vol. IV, 181 sq.

To avoid confusing this power with jurisdiction or with a power which is of a private nature, it has been suggested to call it *ecclesiastical power*. Lay superiors have this power when they cannot possess the power of jurisdiction.

47. Judicial power is exercised by the Church through ecclesiastical courts established at the Roman Curia and in each diocese.

In these courts are decided all the cases which have to do with ecclesiastical superiors and whose solution, because of the wish or the authority of the parties, requires the strict forms of judicial procedure. Instances are the decision as to the validity or nullity of the matrimonial bond, of ordination, of religious profession; the settling of the right of ownership in certain material possessions, rights, privileges, etc.

Superiors of *exempt clerics* likewise have the power of establishing a court.

The Roman Tribunals (*in foro externo*) are the tribunal of the *Rota* and that of the *Apostolic Segnatura*.

The first named of these deals almost exclusively with appeals which are made in the second or third instance (court of appeal); the second is chiefly a court of cassation, pronouncing on the validity of Rotal decisions on points of law or procedure.

The **Sacred Penitentiary** is a tribunal established by the Holy See for matters which concern only the internal forum or the court of conscience.

48. *Canonical Penalties*.

The Church exercises its power of coercion by means of what are called **canonical penalties.**

1. A canonical or ecclesiastical penalty is the deprivation of a spiritual or temporal good inflicted by legitimate authority for the correction of the culprit and the expiation of his crime.

Only the Sovereign Pontiff and the bishops may, by reason of the powers they receive from our Lord Jesus Christ, deprive one of the faithful of goods whose distribution is confided to the Church. This power is communicated to superiors of exempt clerics together with jurisdiction in the external forum of which it forms a part.

2. Certain penalties are incurred **ipso facto,** that is to say, by the mere fact that the crime is committed; others must be imposed by sentence by the legitimate superior before they take effect.

To incur an ecclesiastical penalty two things are required: first, to have committed a crime and second, to have known that the crime was punishable by an ecclesiastical penalty.

A crime in the strict sense,[2] is an external, gravely culpable transgression of a law or a precept whose violation is punishable by a canonical penalty, determined or undetermined (c. 2195). Every Christian is supposed to know the laws of the Church which concern him; if he violates them publicly, he can only avoid the penalty by proving that he was ignorant of the law, and that this ignorance did not come from his own inexcusable negligence. In the external forum the culpability of the action is measured principally by the seriousness of the law which has been violated, though the Code carefully enumerates causes which will diminish the liability to punishment. Ignorance directly willed (or *affected* ignorance, as it is called) regarding the penalty never excuses from it; ignorance which comes from a very culpable or crass negligence is seldom reason for escaping punishment.

49. Among ecclesiastical penalties the most grave is excommunication, which deprives the faithful almost entirely of the spiritual goods which the Church bestows on us, such as public prayers, indulgences, the lawful use of the sacraments, and participation in religious worship.

The Holy See sometimes reserves to itself the power of granting absolution from the excommunication, or it reserves this to the bishops or to confessors who have special powers.

As examples of crimes to which is attached the penalty of excommunication we may mention the following: to force a person to enter a religious institute (c. 2352); to inflict abusive treatment on a simple cleric or on a religious, or to make an attempt on their life or their liberty (c. 2343, § 4); to leave one's convent without authorization, with the intention of not returning

---

[2] We shall see that the word "crime" is not rigorously taken in this sense when there is question of the dismissal of religious. (See n. 353.)

to it (c. 2385, § 2); to enter on a contract of marriage without having been dispensed of one's simple perpetual profession (c. 2388, § 2); knowingly to fail to ask the authorization of the Holy See to alienate (sell, rent for a long time, mortgage) religious property of a value of more than $6,000 (c. 2347, 3).

50. *The Exterior and Interior Hierarchy.*

Since they are members both of the Church and of a particular society, religious are subject to a double *HIERARCHY.* The one is exterior to their institute, as such, and it is made up of the superiors of the Church; the other is interior, and is made up of the religious superiors. Within the institute the authority is held collectively by chapters or congregations and individually by superiors. Superiors themselves have their councils whose advice they must frequently ask and sometimes are bound to follow.

Though the government of those societies which imitate the religious life (see n. 18) is determined by their constitutions, they must all observe, with due proportion, canons 499–530 (c. 675).

§ 2. EXTERIOR HIERARCHY

51. 1. All religious are subject to the **Sovereign Pontiff,** as to their highest superior, by virtue of their very vow of obedience (c. 499, § 1).

The number and the difficulty of the affairs submitted to the Holy Father make it necessary that he should employ the aid of colleges or groups of Cardinals in the government of the Church, and these make up the different Roman Congregations. Each Congregation has at its head a prefect and a secretary, and each makes use of the advice of consultors and is assisted by subordinate officials in the transaction of business. The particular jurisdiction of each congregation is well determined.[3]

2. Since the Sovereign Pontiff employs the **Sacred Congregation of Religious** to make most of the laws which concern them, religious also owe obedience to this congregation. It can impose obligations on them in virtue of their vow of obedience.

The dispensations from the common law which are necessary for religious must nearly always be sought from the Sacred Congregation of Religious. All the questions which concern religious and whose solution requires the intervention of the Holy See must also be submitted to this congregation.

---

[3] See Jombart's excellent series of articles entitled, *La Curie romaine,* in *R.C.R.* (1934), 4 sq.

The document (petition) should give clearly and briefly the name and quality of the petitioners, the object of the petition, the reasons which justify it. When recourse is had to the Holy See to defend a right or a privilege which is thought to be unjustly violated, care should be taken not to give any mere impressions or conjectures; the petitioner should confine himself to giving documents and facts and should indicate sincerely and briefly their degree of probability or certainty. The petition is to be sent to His Eminence, the Cardinal Prefect of Sacred Congregation of Religious, Palace of the Congregations (Piazza S. Callisto), Rome. Although a petitioner can send his petition personally if he wishes, direct to the Sacred Congregation, still, if the petition does not require absolute secrecy, it is usually sent through the Ordinary of the place, the Papal Nuncio, or the Cardinal Protector of the institute. Unless there are special reasons to the contrary, religious who have a procurator general at Rome will naturally send their petitions through him. The proceedings require the payment of a fee which is due to the Sacred Congregation, to cover the expenses of the chancery (for copying, postage, etc.) and a fee for the drawing up and execution of the document. (This is paid to the Ordinary.)

To diminish the number of appeals to Rome, the Holy See accords to its Legates (Nuncios, Internuncios, and Delegates) and to the Ordinary of the place special powers, authorizing them to grant dispensations in a certain number of cases. These faculties deal with such matters as the alienation of property, loans, dowries required by the constitutions, leaving the cloister, celebration of certain offices such as those of Holy Week, etc. It would be well, therefore, to consult the Ordinary before sending petitions to Rome, to find out whether he can grant the desired dispensation.

52. 1. All religious orders, with the exception of the Society of Jesus, have a **Cardinal Protector.** The Holy See likewise appoints one for the congregations which it approves.

Any congregation may ask for a Cardinal Protector. This request should be sent by the superior general to the Cardinal Secretary of State. The name of the Cardinal desired may be indicated and it may be added that the Cardinal is prepared to accept if that be the case. The Secretariate of State will give notification that the favor is granted, and will instruct the department of Briefs to draw up the brief of nomination. The next step will be to send a fee proportionate to the expenses incurred in the drawing up of the brief. As this fee is very high, poor institutes may ask for a reduction before making their deposit. Once the money is received, the Secretariate will draw up and present the brief. In case the congregation has no house in Rome, the business should be transacted through a Roman agent. The agent of the bishop in whose diocese the motherhouse is located is usually recommended.

2. The Cardinal Protector of any institute whatever, except it be otherwise expressly provided in particular cases, possesses no jurisdiction over the institute or over any of its members, his only concern is to promote the good of the institute by his counsel and his patronage (c. 499, § 2).

53. Religious depend also in different degrees on the **Ordinary of the diocese.**

1. Exempt religious and nuns who by their constitutions are subject to the jurisdiction of regular superiors (of the first order) are subject to the Ordinary of the place only in the cases expressly defined by the law (c. 500).

In France and Belgium and in the United States, nuns, except in the rare case of an indult, do not enjoy any exemption in regard to the Ordinaries and do not depend on the superiors of regular orders. In other countries these latter intervene in the elections, the administration of property, the choice of confessors, etc.

2. The members of nonexempt institutes approved by the Holy See are subject to him as clerics or as members of the faithful, but not as religious; they depend entirely on their superiors for everything which has to do with religious discipline properly so called. In diocesan institutes, on the contrary, the religious, as such, depend upon the bishops whom they have made a vow to obey.

3. This dependence, nevertheless, is also limited by common law and by the approved constitutions. A diocesan institute is a moral person, directed by its own superiors conformably to the law. The Ordinary may not interfere with acts that deal with internal government and which are reserved by law or the constitutions to superiors. He may not, for example, admit or dismiss either postulants, novices, or professed religious; or command that a house be established; or assign duties to subjects; neither may he appoint local superiors nor remove them from office.

See nn. **308–318** for details concerning the privilege of exemption.

4. It sometimes happens that the superiors of lay congregations, especially those of women, ask of the Ordinary or of the Visitor dispensations

which they cannot grant. To avoid certain deceptions and to do away with needless requests and also to prevent certain regrettable concessions, it would be well for them to recall the tenor of c. 81; "The Ordinaries, being subject to the Sovereign Pontiff, cannot dispense from the general laws of the Church even in a particular case, unless this power has been explicitly or implicitly given them, or unless it is difficult to have recourse to the Holy See and in cases when a delay would cause grave harm, and finally, when there is question of a dispensation which the Holy See usually grants." It would, of course, be an abuse to wait to ask for a necessary dispensation until it would have become impossible to have recourse to the Holy See. No one should ask to be dispensed from obligations which the Holy See imposes as strict obligations, such as: the avoidance of exterior works and ministries during the canonical year of the novitiate, the strict probation even during the second year, certain prescriptions about the cloister, etc.

54. "No male institute can, without a special Apostolic indult, have religious congregations of women subject to it, or retain, as specially confided to it, the care and direction of such religious" (c. 500, § 3).

By privilege, the Lazarists have the exclusive direction of the Daughters of Charity of St. Vincent de Paul. These latter by reason of a particular grant are exempt from the authority of the local Ordinary. (See *R.C.R.* [1947], 155 sq.)

§ 3. INTERIOR HIERARCHY

I. CHAPTERS

55. A **chapter** is an assembly made up of at least three religious, lawfully convened to treat of the interests either of their institute or of some part of it.

The constitution of the chapter is determined by the rules of each institute.

In institutes composed of autonomous houses (for example, Benedictine monasteries, those of nearly all nuns), each has its *local chapter;* all institutes which have a superior general, even though he enjoy only limited power, have a *general chapter;* in orders and congregations which are entirely centralized, as are orders of clerics regular and most modern congregations, there are no local chapters, but *provincial chapters* are often found, whose function usually consists in choosing deputies to a general chapter.

Chapters for elections are distinguished from the chapters for the transaction of affairs. The first named have for their purpose the election of superiors and of their assistants; the second are for the discussion of the interests of the institute.

The *chapter of faults* is that assembly of a community in which the members accuse themselves of exterior faults for which the superior imposes certain penances. It has preserved this name even in communities which have no chapter in the strict sense.

56. The general chapters and a certain number of provincial chapters have dominative power over the religious. They can command in virtue of holy obedience. In institutes of exempt clerics, the chapters have also the power of jurisdiction (c. 501, § 1). One must consult the constitutions to find out the powers of the local chapter.

The right to change the constitutions with the approval of the Holy See and to issue general and perpetual prescriptions, is almost always reserved to the general chapter.

57. In chapters decisions are taken by an *absolute majority;* that is, by a half plus one of the lawful votes, unless the common law or particular law has established another manner of determination (c. 101, § 1).

An *absolute majority* of votes is any number which exceeds one half the number of members having the right to vote. Thus, 13 is an absolute majority when there are 24 qualified voters, 9 in the case of 17, etc. Any number of votes exceeding those obtained by the other individual candidates or other propositions is termed a *relative majority* (plurality).

After two ballots have been taken without decision, on the third ballot a relative majority will decide; that is, the largest number of votes actually cast. If after the third ballot there is still a tie, the presiding officer will decide by casting his vote; in elections if the presiding officer does not wish to use this right, that candidate will be declared elected who is the oldest in the point of time of ordination, of first profession, or in age (c. 101, § 1, n. 1).

In spite of the text of canon 101, the Holy See generally prescribes in constitutions of congregations that at the election of the chapter, after *three* ineffectual ballots, a fourth confine itself to the two candidates having the larger number of votes in the third ballot.

For detailed information on chapters read: Ellis "General Chapters of Elections" and "General Chapters of Affairs," *RfR.,* I, 146; 253.

II. Religious Superiors

A. Nature and Extent of the Power of Superiors

58. Superiors have over their subordinates a dominative power determined by the constitutions and the common law of the Church (c. 501, § 1).

1. Superiors, even lay superiors, may give formal commands which oblige in virtue of the vow of obedience if they declare expressly that they wish so to oblige. The *Normae* advised superiors to impose these precepts only rarely and for a grave reason either in writing or before two witnesses. Local superiors of small communities will do well never to impose them.[4]

2. Dominative power can never be exercised judicially; a court properly so called supposes that the judge has public authority. Still the power of demanding obedience evidently includes the power of imposing penances proportionate to the fault committed.

The penance will be lawful if it corresponds to the number and seriousness of the exterior culpable acts. But usually the degree of weakness or of malice of the will is unknown to a human superior. The superior should seek as much as possible in imposing the penance to bring about the amendment of the wrongdoer; if, which God forbid, the wrongdoer does not wish to acknowledge or repair his faults, then sufficient motives for punishing him exist in the religious spirit and discipline which is to be upheld and in the reparation which is to be made for the scandal given. The exterior conditions of the penance ought always to be determined carefully. In his manner of giving punishments, the superior ought not to forget that the power he exercises is, above all things, though not exclusively, a paternal power.

Here are some examples of penances that are laid down in certain constitutions and which do not exceed the authority of a local superior even in a lay congregation: the saying of vocal prayers more or less lengthy; the practice of some exterior mortification in the refectory or in the chapter; the saying of the culpa; the taking of a discipline; a reprimand given before two witnesses or even before the whole community; fasting; the order not to leave the convent during a certain time; exclusion from certain exercises of the community.

The superior may not forbid going to Communion as a penance. The most that the Code authorizes, is that confession shall precede the reception of the Eucharist so that the scandal may be repaired when a grave exterior fault has been committed (see n. **256**). The

---

[4] See Battandier, *G.C.*, n. 240.

right of voting (active voice) or of being voted for (passive voice), given by the constitutions, may not be taken away from a religious except in the cases determined by the common law of the Church or by the constitutions themselves.

3. "It is strictly forbidden to all superiors to interfere in causes pertaining to the Holy Office" (c. 501, § 2).

Such causes are: the crimes of heresy, of schism; certain very grave abuses of the sacraments, and the like. Should such a case ever occur and be referred to the Holy Office, the superior shall rest content to take such disciplinary measures as are intended to prevent scandal or at least to diminish it.

59. Though they are higher superiors, the abbot primate and the abbot superior of a monastic congregation have not all the powers which usually belong to higher superiors, but they possess only those which are explicitly mentioned in the constitutions of the congregation and in the special orders of the Holy See (c. 501, § 3).

Mention must also be made of power given a superior general to dismiss a professed of perpetual vows in an exempt institute (c. 655) and the right of judging an appeal from the sentences given by local abbots (c. 1594, § 4).

60. In an institute of exempt clerics the superiors have jurisdiction both in the external and in the internal forum (c. 501, § 1).

They may exercise their jurisdiction in the internal forum and in certain cases in the external forum in the case of those who live in the house, even though they are not religious.

Before the Code, servants properly so called and students who board in the house during their sojourn at college were included under this denomination "of those who live in the house."[5]

In several canons the new canon law seems to include among them other persons dwelling day and night in the religious house by reason of hospitality or because of sickness (cc. 514, § 1; 875, 1245, 1313, 1320).

Such persons are: oblates of certain orders, parents who are given hospitality in the convents while they are visiting their children, people who board in a religious house while they are attending the spiritual exercises, men or women who are lodgers in the house, even visitors who stay at a guest house within the convent.

In certain religious houses, the superiors have given shelter to

---

[5] Vermeersch, *De relig.,* I, n. 518.

"refugees" without any other place to go. These refugees are not members of the household or guests, if they live in places independent of the house, like renters who are allowed to go without paying; if they have been received into the religious house itself, they belong to the category of members of the household in virtue of c. 514, § 1.

61. In institutes of exempt clerics, superiors, even local superiors, have the following powers over their religious, the novices, and the members of the household in the sense explained in the foregoing:

a) They may grant to any priest delegated jurisdiction to hear their confessions (c. 875).

b) They may give them the last sacraments (c. 514, § 1).

Should a professed religious or novice become seriously ill outside a religious house, his own superior has the right to administer viaticum and extreme unction to him; as regards postulants and others, this right belongs to the parish priest (*Commission of Interpretation.* Response June 16, 1931. — *A.A.S.,* XXIII [1931], 353. — *N.R. Th.* [1931], 824. — *R.C.R.* [1931], 177).

c) They may dispense them from the observation of holydays, from fast, and from abstinence (c. 1245).

The Code declares that they can exercise this power "like parish priests." The power of parish priests, which is limited to special cases, extends not only to individuals but to families. Hence Father Vermeersch (*Epitome,* I, n. 556) thought that superiors could dispense groups "which resemble a family" because there is some common reason for dispensing them (such would be the novices) or where giving some a dispensation would make observance more difficult for others.

d) They can dispense for a just reason from vows which are not reserved, providing that no right already acquired shall be violated (c. 1313), and on the same condition they can dispense from a promise made under oath (c. 1320).

e) Higher superiors may give to their subjects (not to those who are merely members of the household) the permission to read books prohibited by church law or by the decree of the Holy See, but only for each book in particular and in urgent cases (c. 1402).

This limited power, however, is not given ordinarily to minor local superiors. The powers of higher superiors are usually more extended because of privileges or of special indults.

62. In every institute superiors by reason of their dominative power can annul the private vows of the professed. They can also suspend the vows of the novices if they or their superiors find these vows an obstacle to the performance of present duties. Vows taken before profession are suspended by the common law of the Church, certainly after the profession and probably from the beginning of the novitiate, as long as the subject remains in religion (see c. 1315, Vermeersch, *Summa*, n. 518). Even if the superior had approved the private vow made in religion, he could later on annul it or suspend its obligation.

63. 1. "The superior general has authority over all the provinces and houses and over all the members of the institute; but he must exercise it as prescribed by the constitutions; the other superiors have authority within the limits of their charge" (c. 502).

The perfect observance of this principle regarding the authority of superiors requires that religious should not have recourse to the higher superior for matters which pertain to the local superiors. In most institutes the rule requires that one shall not appeal to the higher superior from a decision given by his subordinate without having examined during prayer whether such an appeal is well founded and without honestly declaring the motives given by the lower superior to justify his decision. St. Ignatius of Loyola who held obedience in such high esteem also recommended to the higher superiors not to intervene without grave reason in the affairs which belong to their subordinates.

2. What authority has the assistant general (or first assistant or first consultor) who is deputed to take the place of the superior general when the latter is absent or incapacitated? During the time and in the measure in which the superior general is able to fulfill his office, the assistant has no authority over the institute as a whole. If the superior general is certainly and completely incapable of exercising his authority (e.g., in case of death or serious illness) the assistant governs the entire institute. Even then he will avoid taking grave measures of a permanent character except in case of urgent necessity. Such is the meaning of the maxim of the law, "During the vacancy of the See, nothing is to be changed" (R. I. in VI). Sometimes the constitutions define the length of the absence or the nature of the impediments which transfer a part of the superior general's authority to the assistant. We said "a part"; for when he

is capable, and in the measure in which he is capable, the superior general continues to rule with supreme authority. The assistant, then, should avoid taking any important measures which normally are decided only by the superior general, and in regard to which it is impossible to consult the latter. The same rule holds for the religious who takes the place of the provincial who is absent or incapacitated.

64. "Higher superiors in religious institutes of exempt clerics may appoint notaries, but only for the ecclesiastical affairs of their institute" (c. 503).

A notary is a functionary whose duty it is to draw up authentic acts and whose signature is taken as evidence for the documents which come within his sphere.

B. Requirements for the Election of Superiors

65. 1. The valid choice of a superior supposes that the candidate possesses those qualities which the common law of the Church and the constitutions of each institute require under pain of nullity; all the other prescriptions of the Code and special regulations of each institute are required for licit action.

Where the wise laws of the Church about the choice and especially about the election of superiors are neglected or violated, regrettable dissensions arise, respect for authority is weakened, and sometimes disaffection arises towards the institute. It is evident, therefore, how carefully these laws ought to be observed. Besides, they indicate the providential way in which God wishes to choose those to whom He desires at the time to entrust the government of the institute.

2. Independent of the conditions laid down by the constitutions, the qualities required by the common law of the Church for the valid choice of a higher superior are:

a) At least ten years of religious profession since the first profession in the institute.

These words "in the institute" (*eandem religionem professi*) are not repeated elsewhere, for example, where there is question of the appointment of the master of novices (c. 558, § 1). They ought to be attended to if there is question of naming as higher superior a religious who comes from another institute where he made his profession.

This condition forms a marked return to the discipline preceding the *Normae* which had reduced the time of profession demanded from eight to five years.

b) Legitimate birth.

Legitimation by the subsequent marriage of the parents, or granted by a general rescript for the reception of Holy Orders is sufficient (see c. 991).

Solemn profession exempts from the irregularity of illegitimacy, but not from the incapacity of being appointed a major superior (see c. 504)

c) Forty years of age for the superior general or the superior of a monastery of nuns, and thirty years for other major superiors (c. 504).

For all institutes the Holy See alone can dispense from this requirement. Inasmuch as the assistant general (first consultor, etc.) is not a major superior except when he temporarily exercises supreme power, it follows that a candidate for this office need not meet the requirements demanded for a major superior.

3. The Code does not contain any special provision regarding the qualities (age, length of profession, etc.) required for the minor local superiors. However, any provisions on this subject contained in the constitutions must be observed.

C. Duration of Office

66. 1. "The major superiors cannot be named for life unless the constitutions determine otherwise" (c. 505).

This prohibition applies even to the founders of congregations.[6]

It is possible to obtain a dispensation from the Holy See. Thus the priests of the Sacred Heart obtained permission for their venerated founder to retain for life the government of the congregation (Sacred Congregation of Religious, July 11, 1922).

2. When the term of office of higher superiors is limited, the constitutions determine the length of time the office shall endure. It is not *contrary* to the Code if the constitutions authorize the indefinite re-election of the same superior, but such a clause will hardly be approved by the Holy See. If they forbid a first or second re-election or provide that it shall not be valid without a dispensation from the Holy See, the superior is not eligible for re-election, but he can be asked for (postulated) (see n. 81). The Holy See does not favor a second re-election; it grants this only for grave reasons; such reasons more frequently exist in inde-

---

[6] Congregation of Religious, Response March 6, 1922. — *A.A.S.*, XIV (1922), 153; *N.R. Th.* (1922); *Per.*, XI, 31,

pendent communities when there is question of choosing a superior general of women.[7]

67. 1. "Minor local superiors are not to hold office for more than three years; on the expiration of this term they may be reappointed to the same office if the constitutions permit it, but not immediately for a third term in the same religious house" (c. 505).

Minor local superiors are so termed in opposition to the local superiors of houses which are entirely independent, such as the abbots and superiors of autonomous monasteries who are higher superiors.

If a superior general, by virtue of the constitutions, governs a motherhouse immediately, she does not come under this law about the local minor superiors. Hence, during her entire term as general she may remain superior of that house.

2. C. 505 applies to the religious superiors of schools, hospices, asylums, etc., who also have the government of the religious community.[8] When the nomination of the superior of a school, asylum, etc., is subject to the approval of the civil authority, it is better to entrust this office to some religious other than the superior of the community. In this way the difficulty will be obviated which would rise from the fact that the Code requires the removal of the superior of the community after a certain term of years. If this arrangement is not possible, application may be made to the Holy See which can give a general dispensation.

The Holy See does not seem to be disposed to allow very readily the prolongation of the term of office for minor local superiors. When His Eminence, the Cardinal Archbishop of Malines asked for a general indult which would allow him to dispense in certain cases, the Sacred Congregation answered: *non expedire* (that is to say: it is not expedient).[9]

The following reasons may be given for this provision of the law of the Church: serious inconveniences sometimes result from keeping the same local superior too long in office in the same place; the com-

---

[7] Letter of the Sacred Congregation of Religious, March 9, 1920. — *A.A.S.,* XII (1920), 365.

[8] Declaration of the Commission of Interpretation, June 2–3, 1918. — *A.A.S.,* X (1918), 344.

[9] See *La Vie Diocésaine* (1920), 533.

munity is directed according to his personal views and preferences, while certain points of religious discipline which are also important are in danger of being neglected; to have one person too long in power in the same community makes it difficult for some of the subjects to obey, or gives rise to sympathies not devoid of partiality on the part of the superior; when a superior grows used to commanding, he sometimes loses his sense of dependence. This regulation of the Code provides a way in which a superior who is not as capable as he might be, may be removed without discredit. Good superiors are thus soon free to help a new community or to enrich other good works with their personal qualities and their experience. Such are some of the motives which make one willing to put up with the disadvantages equally real which arise in practice because of frequent changes of government.[10]

3. In dependent houses strictly so called, the religious who exercises authority is not a real local superior and therefore need not be changed every three years.[11]

The Congregation of Religious has not seen fit to allow the superior of a dependent house to remain in office for more than nine years.

Nothing in the Code indicates that the local superior loses all his power at the expiration of three years. Hence we believe that he continues to exercise his authority validly until the naming or the installation of a successor.[12] Without doubt the major superior will make it a point to name the successor or to confirm the former superior on the anniversary of his entrance into office, but any serious reason would justify a delay of several days.

D. Choice of Superiors

68. Religious superiors are chosen in two ways: (1) by appointment by the higher superior after consultation with, or by the consent of, his council (this is the usual method of naming local superiors of dependent houses); (2) by election on the part of the chapter, with or without confirmation from the religious or secular superior.

The superior general and the superiors of independent monasteries are regularly chosen in this way.

---

[10] See *N.R. Th.* (1924), 205.

[11] See n. 12 Sacred Congregation of Religious, Response February 1, 1924. — *A.A.S.*, XVI (1924), 25; *N.R. Th.* (1924), 289.

[12] We cannot admit, on this point, the opposite opinion of Dom Bastien, *D.C.*, n. 537. — See Vermeersch-Creusen, *Epitome*, I⁷, n. 301, 3.

When the choice of the chapter falls on a candidate who does not fulfill the conditions required by the law, the superior is not elected, but postulated (asked for).

69. "In elections which are made by chapters, the universal law as set forth in canons 160–182 shall be observed, as well as the constitutions of the institute which are not contrary to the universal law" (c. 507, § 1).

The Code speaks here only of elections made in *chapter,* not of those held by a council, even when the members of the same have a deliberative vote. These latter are governed by cc. 101 and 105. Although the Code employs other terms also when speaking of the elections in congregations of religious women, there can be no doubt that the chapter held for the election of a superioress general, or of the superioress of an independent monastery, is a chapter in the canonical sense as used here.

Since these directions are general laws of the Church, the Ordinary cannot dispense from them unless he has a special indult or in the very unusual cases where there is an urgent necessity and in which the Holy See usually grants the same dispensation. To omit or change a particular direction of the constitutions of a particular institute, either the chapter, or the superior general with his council, or the Ordinary, or the Holy See must intervene.

We shall give briefly the directions of the common law of the Church in this matter.

a) Convocation of the Chapter for Election

70. 1. The president of the future chapter has the right and the duty of convoking it according to the manner prescribed by the constitutions, in the place and at the time which are suitable. The constitutions or the customs may bestow this right on another person (c. 162, § 1).

The president of whom there is question is either the superior general or the provincial or the local superior (in independent monasteries) or the person who exercises the powers of a deceased superior, or of one who is seriously sick or absent, etc. In congregations of women it is, therefore, not the Ordinary of the motherhouse. When an institute, even one of diocesan right, has houses in several dioceses, if the constitutions do not determine the place where the chapter is to meet, this is freely decided by the superior general who thus indirectly determines also the Ordinary who is appointed by law to preside over the election (c. 506).[13]

The Ordinary of the place is not the president of the chapter; he merely presides at the election of the superior general (or of the abbess, prior, etc.).

If the office of superior becomes vacant, the chapter must be held within the next three months, counting from the moment when the vacancy became known. Should an insurmountable obstacle to holding the chapter arise, the time during which it exists would not be counted in the three months (c. 161).

2. If an elector has not taken part in the election because he was not summoned, he may demand from the superior in charge the annulling of the election even though it has been already confirmed, but only on condition that he sends his demand within three days at the latest from the time when he receives knowledge of the election (c. 162, § 2).

An error in convoking the chapter does not render the election invalid unless one third of those who ought to attend the election have not been summoned and by reason of this irregularity, have not taken part in the voting (c. 162, §§ 3, 4).

3. The religious appointed members of the chapter may give up their right; in fact, they are morally obliged to do so if age or infirmity make the exercise of this right harmful.

b) Electors or Members of the Chapter

71. 1. All the members of the chapter present at the time and the place fixed for the election have a right to vote unless they are deprived of this right by the general law of the Church or by some particular law (c. 163).

May one send one's vote by letter or have someone else cast it for one (by proxy)?

The Code formally excludes these two kinds of votes, unless some particular law, that is to say, the constitutions or special privilege granted by the Holy See, authorize one to employ them (c. 163). Votes sent by letter or by proxy contrary to the law are invalid.

If the constitutions authorize the casting of votes by letter, they

---

[13] Congregation of Religious, Response July 2, 1921. — *A.A.S.*, XIII (1921), 481; *N.R. Th.* (1922), 44.

ought also carefully to lay down the formalities which will assure the identification and the secrecy of the votes given in this way. These letters may not be opened except before the president and the counters of the votes at the moment of the voting.

2. No one may cast several votes in his own name by reason of different titles (c. 164).

Constitutions may decree that some superior has, by reason of his office, the power to cast two votes. Where it is allowed to vote by proxy, one is not forbidden to cast two votes, one in his own name and the other as proxy in the name of another. This double vote is usually forbidden in assemblies of the common law, for example, in an ecumenical council (c. 224), in plenary and provincial councils (c. 287).

3. No one may validly vote for himself (c. 170).
4. "All must abstain from seeking votes either directly or indirectly for themselves or for others" (c. 507, § 2).

To seek votes for oneself would be an unfailing sign that one was unworthy of the office sought; to try to get votes for others is often an act of imprudence and in any case it is a violation of the law of the Church. Where there is question of choosing the members of the chapter, when the election is made to two grades, or of choosing the candidates for the office of superior, it will be sufficient to acquaint oneself with the qualities of this or that religious. A fervent religious who is prudent and sufficiently informed of the laws of the institute is always a good member of the chapter. During the chapter he will gather information and will vote according to his conscience thus enlightened. It is not necessary for anyone to secure at all costs the election of the person who is thought to be the most worthy, thus forcing the dispositions of Providence.

5. The vote of an elector who is declared by law to be unworthy or incapable is void, but this by itself does not render the election invalid, unless it is evident that the person elected would not have had the requisite number of votes without this invalid vote, or unless among the electors someone has been allowed to vote who is known to be under a formal sentence of excommunication (c. 167).

c) Form of Election

72. General remarks. 1. "Before proceeding to the election of the higher superiors in the institutes of men, all and each of the members of the chapter shall promise on oath to

elect those whom he deems before God should be elected"
(c. 506, § 1).

The omission of this formality will not render invalid either the vote
of one of the members of the chapter or the election itself. This oath
has sometimes been forbidden in congregations of women.[14]

2. Any conditions imposed on the future superior are null and
void (c. 169, § 2).

73. The casting of the votes. The President. In chapters
convoked for elections the presidency at the election itself is
sometimes given to another superior than the one who presided
over the chapter of affairs.

1. In the monasteries of nuns who are not exempt, the election of a superior (abbess, prioress) is presided over by the
Ordinary of the place or his delegate.

In the monasteries of nuns subject to a regular superior, the
regular superior ought to preside at the election, unless the
Ordinary wishes also to assist either in person or by a delegate.
In this latter case the Ordinary or his delegate has precedence
and should preside at the election (c. 506, § 2).[15]

If the Ordinary has not been informed, or if the time designated has not been observed, he can demand the annulment
of the election. When the Ordinary presides together with the
superior regular, the former has not only the precedence of
honor, but also real power of jurisdiction[16] and the rights of
president, e.g., that of determining a tie vote by his own ballot.
The Holy See, however, generally inserts in the constitutions
a prescription demanding a fourth ballot on those persons only
who have received the same number of votes.

2. In congregations of women the election of a superior general is presided over by the Ordinary of the place where the
chapter is held. He may send a delegate in his place (c. 506, § 4).

The delegate is often a vicar general, or a visitor of the religious communities.

According to the common law, the Ordinary presides only

---

[14] Battandier, *G.C.,* n. 368.
[15] See Commission of Interpretation, Response November 24, 1920. —
A.A.S., XII (1920), 575; *N.R. Th.* (1921), 154.
[16] See Commission of Interpretation, Response July 30, 1934. — *A.A.S.,*
XXVI (1934), 494; — *R.C.R.* (1934), 178 sq.

at the election of the superior general, to whom falls the right of presiding at the election of the councillors, etc. The constitutions of a certain number of institutes, however, allow the Ordinary likewise the right of presiding at the election of the members of the general council.

74. Scrutators (tellers). 1. Before each election scrutators ought to be appointed. It is their office to see that everything is carried on rightly and they are witnesses of this. It is their duty to count the votes and to verify the result together with the president. They will give the chapter and the institute their guarantee that the results of the election have been lawfully reached and are such as they are announced to be (c. 171, § 1).

2. There shall be at least two scrutators elected by an absolute majority of the chapter unless the constitutions should direct otherwise.

The constitutions may declare that the scrutators shall be the two oldest members or the two youngest members of the chapter.

3. In case of elections in the communities of nuns the counters of the votes shall be two priests appointed by the person who presides over the election. The Code forbids this office to be given to the ordinary confessors of the monastery (c. 506, § 3).

If it be necessary to go to get the vote of a sick religious, the chapter may employ two religious to do so; they may also be designated by the president of the election.

4. In the congregations of religious women the counters of the votes must be chosen from among the members of the chapter. This is the law of the Church; and the constitutions cannot change it, nor can the Ordinary dispense from it without a special indult. It is not necessary that the president should be accompanied by a priest as counter of the votes (c. 171, § 1).

5. Before the election the counters of the votes must take an oath to fulfill their office faithfully and to observe secrecy, even after the election, regarding what shall have been done (c. 171, § 1).

This obligation to secrecy has to do only with acts which are secret by their nature. Thus, for example, the counters of the votes are not allowed to reveal the names of those who have voted for or against anyone; nor to discuss the votes obtained by a candidate who has not been elected; nor to say who has cast an invalid vote, etc.

75. The manner of taking the vote. 1. The election should be carried on by secret votes (c. 169).

A written ballot, though it is not ordered, is the most common form, the most convenient one, and, it seems, the only one which is contemplated by the Code. Nevertheless, if one of the members of the chapter cannot write, he may declare before the president and the counters of the votes which candidate he chooses. Members of the chapter who are sick and who dwell in the same house will secretly write their vote and give it, in a sealed envelope, to the counters of the votes, who are delegated by law to come and take it (c. 168).

The Ordinary may not enter the enclosure of nuns in order to preside at an election (c. 506, § 2). He should receive the ballots at the grille.

A vote which is made public is by that very fact invalid (c. 169).

A vote will be invalid if the ballot on which it is written is sent unsealed, at least if it is sent to a person other than to the counters of the votes and the president; or if a member of the chapter declares for whom he has voted before the election is finished, etc.

2. The vote must be freely given. It is invalid if it has been extorted directly or indirectly by grave fear or by fraud, that is to say, by unjustly deceiving a member of the chapter regarding the conditions of the vote.

3. The vote must be certain, absolute, and determined (c. 169, § 1, n. 2).

A vote which is doubtful, conditional, or gives an alternative choice, is invalid. For example, it would be invalid to say: "I vote for either this one or that one"; "I vote for such a one if he is forty-five years of age," etc.

76. 1. The counting of the votes is to be made by the scrutators, together with the president.

The sealed votes are first counted. If their number exceeds that of the members of the chapter, they are destroyed and a new vote is taken (c. 171, § 3). If they do correspond, they are opened one by one, read by one of the scrutators and given to the president, and noted down by the secretary (c. 171, § 2).

The inspection of the ballots need not necessarily be made in the presence of the whole chapter. On this point the constitutions and customs of the institute should be observed.

2. The Code says explicitly that the presiding officer should

announce the number of votes obtained by each of the candidates (c. 171, § 2). Is this formality required for the validity of the election? The authors agree in affirming that the publication of the number of votes received by the elected candidates is an essential element of the election. Should one say the same with regard to the number of votes received by the others? This also certainly seems to be the opinion of the same authors.

Since the publication of the Code, many are nevertheless silent regarding this point. Others insist on the fact that here the Code does but reproduce the former law and hence should be interpreted in the same way.

One may not deny that this prescription does at times encounter a serious difficulty: when a superior general is elected unanimously, with his own vote excepted, his vote by the very nature of things becomes public, a thing absolutely prohibited by the Code. One way of avoiding the difficulty would be to substitute a blank vote.

3. An absolute majority is required on the two first ballots; on the third a relative majority is sufficient. If on the third ballot the votes are equal, the president may determine which shall have the majority by casting his own vote, but never in his own favor (c. 101, § 1).

It has already been stated above that the *absolute majority* is constituted by any number exceeding one half the number of valid votes, e.g., 9 out of 16, 8 out of 15, etc.

In fact, the Constitutions approved at Rome usually state that a fourth voting shall take place in regard to candidates who have received the majority of votes on the third ballot; in case of a tie after the fourth scrutiny, the deadlock will be broken by the ordinary norms (priority of profession, then of age). On this fourth ballot the candidates themselves may not vote.

77. Acceptance and confirmation of the election. 1. The notification of the election to the person who has been elected is made by the announcement of the result itself, if he is present; if he is not present, the result should be officially communicated to him as soon as possible.

---

[17] See Goyeneche, *Comm. pro rel.*, 1930, 353. Vidal, *Ius canonicum*, II, n. 257, IV does not say with the same clarity as Wernz, *Ius Decretalium*, II, n. 271, III, that the announcing of the votes is required for the validity of the election. The formula of the Code does not declare the invalidity; but this argument is not conclusive, for the Code takes up exactly the former law.

2. Unless some special law exists to the contrary, the person elected is not obliged to accept the choice. He has eight days in which to announce his acceptance, and these days are to be counted from the time of the receipt of the official notification (c. 175).

Quite a number of constitutions oblige the person elected to accept the office confided to him. It may be said that in most cases there exists a moral obligation of accepting the office thus imposed unless there be evident reasons for refusing. In our opinion the offices of assistant, councillor, etc., may always be imposed by the chapter.

3. By common law the Ordinary of the place has the power of confirming the election in diocesan congregations of religious women only (c. 506, § 4). The Code adds that he is to exercise this right according to his conscience. Some canonists have inferred from this that, even though the election took place according to the norms laid down in the law, the Ordinary may still refuse to confirm the choice made if he thinks that it is seriously detrimental to the congregation. This interpretation is quite probable.

Even if the Ordinary must for grave reasons annul the election, he is not allowed to name the superioress. The right of naming the superioress belongs in two cases to the Ordinary who is to confirm the election: (1) if the chapter has not carried out the elections within the time laid down; (2) if the chapter has been deprived of the right of election in punishment of a fault. This canonical punishment supposes the violation of an ecclesiastical law to which such a sanction is annexed, or the grave violation of a precept after a warning has been given that this punishment may be inflicted. It may be imposed without previous warning only when the fault committed was exceptionally grave and has given rise to much scandal (see cc. 178, 2222, 2265, § 1; 2291, n. 11).

Should the president, contrary to the Code or the constitutions, interfere with the freedom of the chapter in carrying on the elections, the latter will always have the right, and almost always the duty, to have recourse to higher authority, viz., to the Ordinary or to the Holy See. The chapter represents in this matter the entire community or the entire institute, and it has the duty of safeguarding the rights of the same. We may add that such regrettable interference imperils the interior peace and the good government of the community.

78. After the election, the person not belonging to the chapter who presided during the election gives up the presidency, and the superioress general, the abbess or the prioress resumes the presidency of the chapter for the transaction of business.

79. Compromise. 1. Compromise is an act by which the members of the chapter transfer their right of election for that occasion to one or several persons.

This form of election was forbidden by the former *Normae,* 229, but it is not forbidden to religious by the Code. The individual constitutions, however, may forbid it.

2. To be valid the compromise must have the formal and unanimous consent of the members of the chapter. In institutes of clerics those who are given the power to elect must be priests; if the electors have laid down conditions, these must be strictly observed (c. 172).

When there is question of an office properly so called which is to be conferred by the votes of the chapter, for example, the office of superior general, the constitutions may not declare that an absolute majority or two thirds of the votes can compel a compromise.

80. The law formerly recognized election by quasi-inspiration. This supposed that all the electors without any previous agreement and by a spontaneous and unanimous movement, would elect the same candidate for superior by acclamation. The new law only makes mention of this for the election of the Sovereign Pontiff (Constitution *Vacantis Apostolicae Sedis,* n. 66) and indirectly forbids it for elections by the chapter. In fact, it requires that the votes shall be secret under pain of nullity (c. 169, § 1, n. 2).

d) *Postulation*

81. 1. **Postulation** is an act which proposes to the competent superior the choice of a candidate who is able and worthy to fill an office, but is excluded by the requirement of some law from which the superior can and usually is willing to dispense (c. 179).

"Postulation can be admitted only in an extraordinary case, provided that the constitutions do not forbid it" (c. 507, § 3).

Such extraordinary cases are the absence of any candidate who is at the same time eligible and capable of worthily filling the office which is to be conferred; the presence of a subject who has exceptional qualities when the eligible candidates are really mediocre; a particularly difficult situation which makes it necessary or very desirable that a candidate who is not eligible by law should receive or should keep the government of the institute or the monastery. The most frequent cases are those where the candidate has not the age required by law to be a superior, or where a superior has already governed for the full length of time allowed by the law.

Canon 507, § 3, shows that the Holy See is not very favorably disposed to postulation. This severity tends to stimulate the training of subjects who have aptitude for government and administration.

2. Postulation, like election, is carried on by ballot. The votes are couched in these words: "I postulate N.N." If there is a doubt as to whether the person voted for is eligible or not, the voter may write: "I elect or postulate N.N." This vote will then be valid, according to the circumstances, for either election or postulation.

82. To be validly postulated the candidate must have at least a majority of the votes cast. If his opponent is an eligible candidate, the candidate who is postulated must at least receive two thirds of the votes. On the third ballot the eligible candidate who has obtained the relative majority will definitely prevail over the candidate who is postulated by less than two thirds of the valid votes (c. 180).[18]

Let us give some examples. For the sake of simplicity we will suppose that in the chapter there are 36 voters and that all the votes are valid:

First case. X is postulated by 19 votes, N by 17. The postulation becomes a fact, and X may be proposed to the superior who is competent to dispense from his impediment;

Second case. X is postulated by 23 votes, N is voted for by 10, and M by 3. A new vote is necessary. If X obtains 24 votes in the second or third taking of votes, he will be validly postulated;

Third case. In the third taking of votes X is postulated by 22 votes, N is voted for by 11, and M by 3. N is validly elected.

However, to avoid the drawbacks of such a settlement, which seems to run counter to the will of a very considerable part of the chapter, the jurisprudence of the S. Congregation has, for some years now, adopted the following rule: the superior who has already governed for two periods of six years each, has passive voice for postulation on the first two ballots only. If she does not obtain the necessary two thirds on the second ballot, she loses her passive voice, while retaining active voice. The preceding rounds are considered as having no effect, and the elections are resumed with their usual sundry ballots.

83. The constitutions may forbid postulation; they may also

---

[18] Commission of Interpretation, Response July 1, 1922. — *A.A.S.,* XVI (1922), 406; *N.R. Th.* (1923), 42.

require that even on the third ballot a candidate cannot be elected unless he has an absolute majority. In this case it would still seem admissible either to postulate or to proceed to another ballot; it would be preferable, however, to vote only for eligible candidates.

84. The postulation must be presented to the superior competent to dispense from the quality required by law.

If there is question, for example, of the age required by the Code, or if a second election is forbidden without the approval of the Holy See, recourse must be had to Rome. In diocesan congregations the Ordinary of the place may dispense from a condition required merely by the constitutions.

The Holy See does not readily grant the postulation of a superior who has completed the full term of government which is allowed in the constitution (cf. n. 66 sq.).

The S. Congregation points out that it is not much in favor of postulations, and it will confirm a superior in her office for example, for three years only, and "ad nutum S. Sedis." Sometimes it will require the members of the chapter to indicate by a ballot whose annulment is reserved to the Holy See, the name of a religious who will eventually succeed until the next chapter of elections, the superior who has been kept in office and whose new term is interrupted by death or by decision of the Holy See. It should be noted that in the case of a superior who has already had a first extension of term, a new possible postulation of the same superior will require not merely two thirds but a moral unanimity of the votes cast by the chapter of elections.

E. Obligations of Superiors

85. The general, local, and provincial superiors **must habitually reside** in a house which is assigned to them and must not absent themselves except for the reasons and for the time allowed by the constitutions (see c. 508).

86. 1. Even after the promulgation of the Code the Holy See has published several decrees which are of interest to religious. Every superior ought to acquaint his subjects with them and to see that they are carried out (c. 509, § 1).

If the superiors are in possession of the official text or of an authorized translation, they need not wait for a special communication to be made to them. The fact that the diocesan curia unwillingly forgets to make this communication does not dispense them from a duty which is directly made known to them. Obedience, charity, and often justice demand that religious, both subjects and superiors, be made acquainted not only with the obligations which the Holy See imposes on them, but also with the rights which it deems well to give them. This is a guarantee against those abuses which are always possible due to human weakness.

The decrees which deal with the obligations of the religious life are not the only ones the knowledge of which is useful and sometimes necessary to the members of religious institutes, even those for women. Among the responses or instructions given by the Sacred Congregations concerning pious associations, indulgences, liturgy, etc., are to be found decisions which have immediate interest for religious men and women. If superiors observe the directions of c. 509, § 1, they can, on occasion, correct false ideas, do away with open violation of liturgical laws, suppress abuses or superstitious practices, etc.

2. "Local superiors shall take care **to have read publicly** at least once a year on fixed days the constitutions of the institute, as well as the decrees ordered by the Holy See to be read in public" (c. 509, § 2, n. 1).

The custom of reading only the summary of the constitutions where those articles are set forth which are of interest to all the religious, may be continued.

The second part of the text has reference to those decrees the reading of which has been made obligatory since May 19, 1918.[19] It is certain that there is no longer any need to read the decrees publicly about the account of conscience (*Quemadmodum*), or about the confession of religious (*Cum de sacramentalibus*), or about frequent Communion (*Sacra Tridentina Synodus*).

Mention of these decrees has been omitted in the new *Normae;* for the rest, the Sacred Congregation has caused them to be left out of the constitutions which have been submitted for its approval since the Code. Moreover, it is not allowed to read them as existing laws of the Holy See because their contents have been modified by the Code. What is contained in them may still be useful to superiors to indicate what ought to be their line of conduct in matters contained in them and which have not been changed by the Code. But no superior is allowed to correct their text according to the Code and then have the corrected version read in public.

87. At least twice a month a **catechetical instruction** should be given to the lay brothers and to domestic servants; besides,

---

[19] Up to the present there is no decree, the reading of which is prescribed for all institutes. By order of Pope Pius XI, the Instruction *Quantum Religiones* issued by the Congregation of Religious on December 1, 1931, must be read in its entirety at the beginning of each year to the clerical students of all clerical institutes and societies. An English translation of this Instruction will be found in Appendix II, p. 268.

especially in lay institutes, a pious **exhortation** must be given
to all the members of the household (c. 509, § 2, n. 2).

Domestics, in the strict sense, are the persons who are in the service
of the master of the house and live at his expense and under his roof.
As contrasted with the members of the family, they comprise the
domestic servants. Even before the Code good authors were of the
opinion that the jurisdiction of the Holy See allowed us to extend a
little the meaning of this word, and that the two elements sufficient
to constitute a person a domestic were: a real dependence on the head
of the house and the fact that they were boarded in the household.
From this they concluded that boarding students could be considered as
domestics. The extension of the powers accorded by the Code to
exempt superiors over the guests of the community (see c. 514)
certainly confirms this viewpoint. In monastic language "the family"
signifies the community, and more especially the professed. Oblates who
are fully incorporated into the monastery, attendants, children who are
being reared in the hope that they will one day wish to enter the
order, may all be considered as members of the religious family.[20]

All the authors do not interpret the prescriptions of this c. 509, § 2,
n. 2, in the same way. The sources indicated in the Code do not give us
a clear solution. The instruction of July 9, 1947, on the quinquennial report [for pontifical religious institutes and societies] expresses the idea
as follows: "86. Do Superiors see to it that, according to the Constitutions
and the common law, there be spiritual and catechetical instructions for
the entire house (*familia*) (c. 509, § 2, 2°), for the novices (c. 565, § 2),
for the scholastics (c. 588, § 1), for the *conversi,* for the domestics and
servants (c. 509, § 2, 2°)."[21]

According to the strict sense, the Code prescribes that a
catechetical instruction be given to lay religious and "domestics,"
that is to say, to servants and employees who live habitually
within the religious house; a pious exhortation should be given
to all the members of the community.

Such is the opinion defended by Father Vermeersch;[22] it has,
among canonists, many more defenders[23] than the interpretation
according to which those of the household (*familiares, omnes de
familia*) would include also boarding students and guests of the
community.

---

[20] See *N.R. Th.* (1924), 483.

[21] The questionnaire for diocesan congregations and societies has the same
text under n. 74 (see Appendix III, p. 278).

[22] *Epitome,* I[7], n. 629.

[23] Goyeneche, *De religiosis,* n. 21, I; Berutti, *Inst. iuris can.,* vol. III, p. 67;
Larraona, *Comm. pro rel.,* VIII (1927), 172.

If need be, the parish clergy may be asked to give the catechetical instruction. If the convent has no chaplain who can give exhortations, the domestics of the house ought to be sent, whenever possible, to the parochial Mass. The exhortations to the community may be given by the superior; in lay congregations an effort should be made to have some priest give exhortations, at least from time to time. This canon, like the others, does not oblige anyone to attempt what is impossible; the fact that priests are not available will excuse superiors for omitting a certain number of instructions.

88. "The abbot primate, the superior of every monastic congregation, and the superior general of every institute approved by the Holy See must, every five years or oftener, if the constitutions prescribe it, send to the Holy See a written account of the state of the institute, signed by themselves and by the members of their council, and in the case of a congregation of women, also by the Ordinary of the place where the superior general with her council resides" (c. 510).

This account, given every three years before the Code, is now to be given every five years, and the Sacred Congregation wishes that it should not be sent oftener. The obligations for superiors of religious women to submit the report to the Ordinary, which was done away with in the decree of July 16, 1906, is once more restored in conformity with the former *Normae*, n. 262.

The obligation imposed by the Code has been considerably extended by reason of a decree of the Sacred Congregation for Religious dated July 9, 1947.[24]

---

[24] *A.A.S.*, XL (1948), 378–381. [The new questionnaires have not been published in the *Acta Apostolicae Sedis,* but may be obtained from "The Archivist, S. Congregation for Religious, Palazzo delle Congregazioni, Piazza S. Callisto, Rome, Italy." There are three editions of the Latin text of the *Elenchus Quaestionum:* (1) for *pontifical* institutes — 342 questions; (2) for *diocesan* institutes — 322 questions; (3) for *autonomous* monasteries and religious houses — 171 questions. Official translations in English, French, German, Italian, and Spanish of questionnaire n. 1 (for pontifical institutes) are available at the address given above. The *ten Latin* forms (not translated) for the *annual report* are to be obtained from the same source. The English translation of questionnaire n. 2 (for diocesan institutes) will be found in Appendix III of this book; that of n. 3 (for autonomous institutes) in *Review for Religious,* 251 sq.

Institutes directly subject to the Sacred Congregation for the Propagation of the Faith will be guided by the instructions and the questionnaire published by that Sacred Congregation on June 29, 1937 (*Sylloge* — S.C. de Prop. Fide, Rome, 1939, n. 225; pp. 656–667. — Ed.]

1. The following are bound to make the quinquennial report: the superiors general of all religious institutes, of all societies of common life, and of all secular institutes, **even those which are diocesan;** likewise all superiors of independent monasteries or houses (of men or of women) which do not belong to any confederation.

2. At the *end of each year* all the superiors mentioned above must send to the Sacred Congregation a brief statistical report on the ten official forms provided for this purpose.

Diocesan congregations, societies, and institutes must send their quinquennial report to the Holy See through the local Ordinary of the motherhouse. If the organization is spread through several dioceses, the Ordinary of the motherhouse must likewise send a copy of the report to all the local Ordinaries in whose territory the organization has one or more houses.

The year in which the report should be sent has been determined once for all by the Holy See, according to the nature of the institute in the case of institutes of men, and according to the country where the general motherhouse is established in the case of religious women.

1) The report is to be sent as follows:
   a) in 1958, 1963, etc., by the canons regular, monks, and the military orders;
   b) in 1959, 1964, etc., by the mendicant orders, clerics regular, and other regulars;
   c) in 1960, 1965, etc., by clerical congregations;
   d) in 1961, 1966, etc., by lay congregations;
   e) in 1957, 1962, etc., by societies of common life, secular institutes, and confederations.

2) The times for the religious institutes of women are as follows:
   a) in 1958, 1963, etc., from Italy, Portugal, and Spain;
   b) in 1959, 1964, etc., from France, Belgium, Holland, England, and Ireland;
   c) in 1960, 1965, etc., from the other countries of Europe;
   d) in 1961, 1966, etc., from North and South America;
   e) in 1957, 1962, etc., from the other countries of the world.

The superioresses general of societies of common life, of secular institutes, and of confederations throughout the world will discharge this obligation in 1957, 1962, etc.

The ordinaries and the superiors will find in the formula definite indications as to ideas of the Holy See about the government, the administration, and the principal obligations of religious. Nevertheless, each question is not to be taken as an obligation strictly imposed by the Code.

a. Canonical Visitation of Religious Superiors

89. 1. "In every institute, the higher superiors designated to this office by the constitutions **shall visit,** either in person or by others, if they themselves are legitimately impeded from doing so, and at the times appointed by the constitutions, all the houses subject to their jurisdiction" (c. 511).

The higher superiors of diocesan institutes are likewise subject to this prescription.

An extraordinary visitation may be ordered either by the superior general or by the general council, according to the constitutions. In this case the powers of the visitor are determined both by the constitutions and by his letters of delegation. According to the *Normae* the general may freely choose the visitor of a province or of a house. If he wishes to choose a visitor for the entire institute, he must take him from among his council or obtain the approval of the council for making another choice.[25]

In institutes which are divided into provinces, the visit is made by the provincial superior. According to the former *Normae,* § 255, the visit was to be made at least every three years.

2. The visitation has a double purpose: to assure oneself on the spot that the house is well governed both spiritually and temporally; to become better acquainted with the subjects, and to give them, as well as the local superiors, an opportunity of manifesting more freely their desires, their needs, their opinions about the administration and the good works of the community, etc.

3. In both the ordinary or extraordinary visit:

1) All the religious are obliged to answer with sincerity any question which has to do: (*a*) with their own exterior conduct; (*b*) with public occurrences having to do with the affairs or members of the community.

2) Charity may impose a grave duty of manifesting on one's own accord to the superior or his delegate exterior actions

---

[25] Battandier, *G.C.,* n. 408.

which may cause grave harm to individuals, to the community, or to the institute.

It is not allowed, however, to tell superiors a fault, even one which is grave and exterior, which one has learned only in confidence from the one who has committed the fault, unless the culpable person has abused this silence to cause a grave and unjust harm to some third person. There is hardly any need to add that a confessor cannot reveal any fault told in sacramental confession.

b. Canonical Visitation of the Local Ordinary[26]

90. When we speak of the Ordinary's right of visitation, we must distinguish between the religious communities (the members and the places where the religious dwell) and the works of the religious, the schools, hospitals, refuges, etc. The Code speaks here only of the visitation of the community; we shall deal afterwards (n. **94**) with the other canons which have to do with the visitation of schools, etc.

91. Regulars, that is to say, members of religious orders of men, are exempt from the episcopal visitation. The local Ordinary must make a visitation every five years, personally or through his delegate, to all other religious men. The extent of this right varies with the juridical condition of the institute (c. 512, § 1).

92. *Object of the Canonical Visit.*

1. In congregations of clerics approved by the Holy See, whether exempt or not, the visit has to do solely with what concerns the church, the sacristy, the public oratory, and the confessionals.

2. Among nuns who take solemn vows, some are directly under the Holy See, others depend on religious men of the first order, others, but these are few in number, are subject to the jurisdiction of the Ordinary of the place. Save in very exceptional cases, nuns who have simple vows are fully subjected to the episcopal jurisdiction.

In the case of nuns who are subject to orders of men, the required object of the visit is to see that the canonical prescriptions on the cloister are carried out. If, however, the superior of the regular order of men has neglected to visit the monastery for at least five years, the duty of making the visitation falls entirely on the Ordinary (c. 512, § 2, n. 1).

---

[26] See Jombart, *La visite canonique de l'Ordinaire du lieu*, R.C.R., 164 sq., 184 sq.

The Ordinary makes, alone and in entirety, the visitation of those monasteries which are under his jurisdiction or immediately under the jurisdiction of the Holy See.

3. In the houses of all congregations approved by the Holy See:

a) The Ordinary will look into what concerns the church, the sacristy, the public oratory, and the confessionals.

b) He ought to inform himself as to whether religious discipline is observed according to the constitutions; whether sound doctrine and correctness of conduct have suffered any harm; whether the cloister is well kept; whether the sacraments are received as frequently as is proper and is prescribed (see cc. 512, 618).

In the monasteries of nuns which immediately depend upon the Holy See, the Ordinary has the same powers. If the monastery is under a superior of an order of men, the bishop's right of visitation extends only to the observance of the cloister, except in the case where the superior has not made any visit for five years.

4. Since the diocesan congregations are fully under the jurisdiction of the Ordinary, his right of visitation has no limit except that put by the constitutions which have been freely approved by him.

93. *The Rights and Duties of the Visitor.*

1. "The visitor has the right and the obligation of interrogating the religious whom he deems it well to hear, and of informing himself on those matters that pertain to the visitation; all the religious, however, are under the obligation of replying according to the truth, and it is not lawful for superiors to divert them in any way from this obligation, or otherwise impede the scope of the visitation" (c. 513, § 1).

2. When the visit includes the members of the community and does not extend only to the places consecrated to sacred worship or to pious works confided to the institute, then it is strictly forbidden to the superiors to transfer the religious to another house without the consent of the visitor after the visit has been announced (c. 2413, § 1). This would often be an indirect means of preventing certain manifestations which are useful and necessary. The Code also makes it an offense to attempt any intimidation or to inflict any vexations on religious

because of reports made to the visitor, and this holds especially true for religious women.

The visitor ought to deprive of their office those superiors who violate these prescriptions and to declare the religious who are guilty of this fault unfit for any office which involves the government of others (c. 2413).

3. As a general rule, the visitor should proceed in a paternal way and should only have recourse to judiciary forms in circumstances of exceptional gravity. In the latter case, his decisions, like those of any other judge, will be subject to appeal which suspends their execution. In every other circumstance an appeal which is made to the higher superior or to the Ordinary against the decrees of the visitor does not dispense one from the duty of submitting to them. In other words, the appeal is devolutive, not suspensive (c. 513, § 2).

An appeal is said to be *suspensive* (*in suspensivo*) when the decree of the superior or judge against which the appeal is made is suspended, i.e., need not be observed until a final decision is given by the higher superior or judge to whom the appeal is made; it is said to be *devolutive* (*in devolutivo*) when the decree must be observed even during the appeal itself.

In institutes approved by the Holy See, the visitor can in no way interfere with internal government or discipline, except in those cases expressly determined by the law (c. 618, § 2, 2).

94. *Visits to schools, charitable works, etc.*

1. The Ordinary of the place has the right and the duty to see to it that in the schools of his diocese nothing is done which is against faith or good morals (c. 1381, § 1). The Code also recognizes his right to visit schools, social centers, institutes, etc., directed by religious, regarding everything which concerns religious instruction and education (c. 1382).

In this matter the authority of the Ordinary is very broad. He can demand the recall of both men and women teachers and can reserve to himself their approbation, but he cannot assume the right of naming or choosing them. He has also the right to forbid this or that book harmful to faith, to piety, or to good morals. The methods of teaching are not directly his affair.

As the visitation is not the necessary means of exercising this vigilance, the Ordinary is not obliged to make it. Usually the Ordinary leaves a great latitude to important congregations that have merited this mark of confidence.

In mission territory the secondary and higher schools which are directed by regulars are exempt from all visits of the Ordinary of the place by virtue of the privileges which Leo XIII granted in his Constitution *Romanos Pontifices,* n. 20;[27] in many countries where the general laws of the Church are in force this privilege has been acquired by legitimate custom or by prescription.[28]

2. **Hospitals, orphanages,** and other pious institutions which have been erected by ecclesiastical authority are fully subject to the episcopal visitation.

The good works which have not been made a moral person and which are directed by religious are entirely subject to the Ordinary of the place in the case of diocesan congregations; in the institutes approved by the Holy See the Ordinary has the right to watch over everything that concerns the teaching of religion, the correctness of morals, the exercise of piety, and the administration of the sacraments (c. 1491).

Even when a good work of this kind is fully exempt by privilege, prescription, etc., the Ordinary has always the right to demand that an account be given him of the way in which the funds have been expended that have been left as a legacy for the carrying on of the pious works (c. 1492). There is question here evidently of foundations properly so called.

A **foundation** is a sum of money entrusted to a moral person to be devoted to a determined use over a lengthy period of time. A pious foundation is one which is assigned to the support of a pious work (like the celebration of Masses, the upkeep of the church, a burse for clerical studies, a hospital, etc.), and which consists of a certain amount of personal or real property.

The Ordinaries have the right to demand that an account be given to them of the administration of this property; should the founder insert a clause to the contrary in the foundation charter, the foundation itself may not be accepted (c. 1492, § 2).

F. Honorary Titles

95. "Merely **honorary titles** of dignity or of office are forbidden; the titles of the higher offices, which the religious in their own institute have actually discharged, are alone tolerated if the constitutions permit it" (c. 515).

---

[27] Vermeersch, *De relig.,* II, 589.
[28] See Goyeneche, *Comm. pro rel.* (1923), 225.

This canon does not suppress the privileges to the contrary which have been granted; it does not forbid the titles of former mother, one time definitor, etc., but, for example, it does forbid the title of honorary abbot of a monastery which has been suppressed.

G. Cessation of Office

96. The powers of the superior cease by death, by the completion of his term of office, by transfer to other duties, by resignation or removal from office, or by a simple penal suspension.

1. The determining of the moment of death could have a certain importance in regard to the effects of acts placed by the dead superior or in regard to the legitimacy of the acts of the vicar, vice-superior, etc., who replace him. The difficulties involved are too rare to justify our delaying here.

2. In the chapter, one may not elect a new superior general before the completion of the time determined by the constitutions for the tenure of office of his predecessor: that would be equivalent to deposing the former superior. Nevertheless, a legitimate custom could allow the years to be calculated, not rigorously from day to day, but with a leeway of a few days. During the vacancy of the office, if this happens, the superior general going out of office retains the government of the institute under the title of vicar, even though the constitutions do not expressly say this.

3. The three-year term of office of local superiors need not be reckoned mathematically; they retain, then, their power up to the time of the installation of their successor. The constitutions, and especially custom, determine the precise moment when the transfer of power is to be made.

4. A religious superior is not free to resign his office; however, he may ask the proper superiors to relieve him of his office, or he may refer the matter to the Holy See. His resignation will not go into effect until he has been informed that the superior has accepted it.

5. As it is difficult to depose a major superior and as he rarely offers to resign at an opportune time, the members of the chapter ought always to ask themselves whether the candidate of their choice will be able to govern as he should until the day determined for a new chapter of election.

III. Counsellors, Bursars, and Procurators

97. "The superior general of every institute or monastic congregation, also every provincial superior and local superior, at least of every formal house, shall have their **counsellors** whose consent or counsel they must seek according to the terms of the constitutions and the sacred canons" (c. 516).

1. The counsellors or consultors are not commissioned with the government of the institute, province, or house. In virtue of their office, they have no authority. The right of initiative belongs to them only in the degree in which the constitutions may grant it to them. Their true role — a very important one — is to give the advice freely requested by superiors or that which should be requested by them. It is likewise the duty of consultors to approve or to reject measures which the Holy See or the constitutions submit to their deliberative vote.

They can, evidently, especially the first counsellor who is nearly always the assistant of the superior general, modestly suggest to the superior those measures which seem to them opportune. Some constitutions grant to all members of the institute the right to correspond freely with the general consultors: the Code, without itself granting this right, offers no opposition thereto.

2. The office of counsellor to the superior general is not incompatible with that of a local superior, or that of a master of novices. However, when the institute is of considerable size, there is not sufficient time to discharge rightly this double office; even in the case of institutes that are small it sometimes happens that such a counsellor ought not to take part in the council, so as not to be at the same time judge and party to the suit.

3. The Congregation of Religious requires that the assistants or consultors of the superior general should live in the same house with him. In case of necessity it will allow two of them to live elsewhere, provided they can easily be present at council meetings.

The answers of the Sacred Congregation of Bishops and Regulars were severe on this point. The *Normae* permitted two general counsellors to dwell outside the motherhouse. This provision is found in a large number of constitutions approved by Rome. Facility and speed of modern travel explain the change in policy.[29]

It is useful to have the constitutions determine how the absence of a consultor of the general or provincial superior may be supplied. The Congregation of Religious allows the oldest professed in the house, or the religious holding the next highest office, to be called into the council meeting, for example, the local superior.

98. 1. The vote of the council (or of the chapter) may be either *deliberative* or simply *consultative*. The vote is deliberative when the superior is obliged to follow it in order to act validly; it is consultative when it suffices for him to ask the advice of his council although he is not obliged to follow it.

The Code and the constitutions state precisely and rigorously

---

[29] See *Normae*, Ed. 1, pars. 277–300; Battandier, *G.C.*, nn. 462, 463, is too severe. Larraona inclines to the opposite opinion (*Comm. pro rel.* [1928], 420).

the cases in which the vote of the council (or of the chapter) is deliberative; when this is not stated expressly or equivalently, the vote is merely consultative.

When the Code says that the superior should act "with his council," he must consult the same, but he need not submit the matter in question to a deliberative vote. Even in that case he should not forget the recommendation of c. 105, § 1, i.e., that he should make much account of their unanimous opinion, and not differ from them without what seems to him a preponderating reason.

The consent of the council is required, for instance, to alienate goods or to contract a debt, even when the sum involved is less than $6,000 (c. 534, § 1; for present day monetary values see n. 157); to admit to first vows (c. 575, § 2); to dismiss a professed member, even one having only temporary vows (c. 647, § 1).

Sometimes the Code demands that the consent be given by secret ballot; e.g., for alienation of property or the contracting of debts amounting to less than $6,000 (c. 534).

2. When the Code says that superiors must "hear" their council, they must call them together for consultation, and it does not suffice to ask each individual separately.

3. The secret imposed on the counsellors (c. 105, n. 2) does not prevent them from asking the advice of a prudent person and one who is by his very office obliged to great prudence. The Sacred Congregation makes this remark in the case of a confessor or of an ecclesiastical delegate (for example, the visitor).

99. 1. All the institutes must have a **general bursar** as well as provincial and local bursars. A superior may not himself discharge the office of general bursar or provincial bursar; he may, however, discharge the office of local bursar if necessity requires it, though it would be better to keep this office distinct from that of superior (c. 516, §§ 2, 3).

The bursars are to be named according to the constitutions. If the constitutions have nothing to say on this subject, they are designated by the higher superior with the consent of his council (c. 516, § 4).

The vote of the council in this case is deliberative. The

constitutions can decide that the bursar shall be named without the consent of the council. But if there is question of a provincial or general bursar, would such action be prudent and conform to the intention of the legislator?

2. The Code explicitly demands "that all the bursars exercise their office under the direction of the superior" (c. 516, § 2).

Neither the constitutions nor custom can accordingly exempt the bursar from this supervision and dependence. If it be necessary to allow him a reasonable degree of initiative and liberty, he is still obliged to keep his superior informed of his transactions.

100. The institutes of men approved by the Holy See must appoint one of their members as **procurator general** to carry on the business of the institute with the Holy See. He should habitually dwell at Rome,[30] but a dispensation from this requirement will readily be granted to those institutes which are not widespread, which seldom have occasion to have recourse to the Holy See, and which have no house in Rome.

The procurator general must be a religious of the institute, the affairs of which he is to care for. The Code forbids him to give up his office before the time fixed by the constitutions has expired, without informing the Holy See, that is, the Congregation of Religious or the Congregation *de Propaganda Fide,* as the case may be.

The institutes of women ordinarily transact their affairs through the Ordinaries, and the more important matters through the cardinal protector. Nothing prevents the superiors from addressing the Holy See directly when the case requires or through someone who is known to the Roman Curia.

Article 2. Spiritual Government

101. In this article we shall explain the legislation on the confessors of religious men (cc. 518, 519, 528) and those of religious women (cc. 520–527). Then comes the account of conscience which is so closely connected with the spiritual government (c. 530). We shall reserve for the following article the provision of the Code regarding the administration of the sacraments and the powers of the chaplain.

---

[30] S. Cong. of Rel., decree June 4, 1920; *A.A.S.,* XII (1920), 301.

§ 1. CONFESSORS OF RELIGIOUS
MEN AND WOMEN

102. *Preliminary Remarks.*

The new legislation shows clearly a double purpose; on the one hand, it wishes to have religious seek from a permanent and experienced confessor that direction which is so necessary for spiritual progress; on the other, it wishes to guarantee in all circumstances a liberty of conscience which will allow the most entire sincerity and will insure the tranquillity of souls.

Liberty of conscience is safeguarded by the possibility of going to different confessors in case of need. An effective spiritual direction will be the necessary result of going habitually to one of the confessors designated by the superiors or by the Ordinary.

103. There is question here only of the professed. The special regulations for novices will be treated under n. **212.** As to postulants, the following articles do not pertain to them directly; however, absolute or relative cloister to which they are bound may make them, in practice, go to confession to the ordinary confessors of the house. If they have the lawful opportunity, they can go to confession even habitually to other priests.

104. Cardinals have the power to hear everywhere the confessions of all the faithful, even of religious of both sexes, and to absolve from reserved sins and penalties, except in four or five special cases, for example, certain profanations of the sacramental species (c. 239, § 1, n. 1).

A. Confessors of Religious Men

105. *Appointment of Confessors.*

In institutes of exempt clerics the confessors are appointed by the superiors; in lay institutes which are exempt, and in the case of clerics who are not exempt, the confessors are proposed by the superiors to the bishop so that he may give them jurisdiction. The Ordinary himself freely appoints the confessors of lay religious who are not exempt.

The same rules apply to religious societies (see c. 675).

106. 1. "In the houses of every clerical institute there shall be deputed, in proportion to the number of subjects, several legitimately approved confessors with power, if it be question of an exempt institute, to absolve also from the cases reserved in the institute" (c. 518, § 1).

2. "In lay institutes of men the bishop will appoint an ordinary and extraordinary confessor; and should any religious petition for a special confessor, the superior shall grant the petition and in no way seek the reason for or manifest displeasure at it" (c. 528).

107. *Religious Men May Confess Validly and Licitly:*

1. To their superiors (exempt or approved) (c. 518).

These superiors may hear the confessions of those subordinates who apply to them of their own accord. They shall not do this habitually, however, without a grave reason (c. 518, § 2).

They are strictly forbidden to influence in any manner whatsoever the liberty of their inferiors on this point (c. 518, § 3).

The term *superior* must be taken in the strict sense of the word. Hence it would not be contrary to the letter of the Code to appoint as confessor a religious who, without being a superior properly so called, exercises real authority over his penitents to be, e.g., a subprior, a minister of junior professed, etc. If such be the case, it will be all the more necessary to see to it that liberty in regard to confession be safeguarded. It certainly would not be conformable to the spirit of the Code for such priests regularly to hear the confessions of those religious who are subject to them in matters of discipline, unless a truly grave reason exists for doing so.

2. To the priests, whether regular or secular, who are delegated by their exempt superiors or by the Ordinary of the place, as the case may be (c. 875).

The limits of this jurisdiction evidently depend on the person who delegates the confessor.

In exempt clerical institutes only the superior general and the abbots of independent monasteries can reserve the sins of their inferiors; they must seek the advice of their council and they cannot in any way limit the exceptional faculties given by the law in cc. 518, 519 (see c. 896).

3. ". . . for the peace of their consciences, to any confessor approved by the local Ordinary. This confessor may absolve the religious even from sins and censures reserved in the institute. Every contrary privilege is revoked" (c. 519).

We may observe that every confession which is sincere and earnest "is made for peace of conscience."

4. A fortiori, to the local Ordinary, since he has at least the same powers to hear, within the limits of his territory, the confessions of all religious who have a domicile therein, or who are passing through the diocese.

108. 1. At the same time the Code formally declares to be still in force "the constitutions which prescribe confession to be made at stated times, or counsel that it be made" (c. 519). Since nothing is added here to the obligation of the rule, a reasonable motive is sufficient for going to confession in special cases to a confessor other than designated priests. To do this habitually, however, requires the permission of the superior.

If the religious, whether exempt or not, had committed a sin reserved to the Ordinary by diocesan law, a confessor who had no special powers could not absolve him from it without having recourse to the Ordinary, except in the case provided for by c. 900. We may recall here that an exempt religious does not incur censures imposed by the diocesan law alone, unless he is living unrightfully outside of his monastery.

2. To make use of the right here conferred a religious has no need of any permission whether he is in the convent or outside of it, and neither he nor his companion, if there be one, is bound to inform the superior that he has been to confession.

Canon 519, however, does not authorize any religious to leave his convent without permission or to interrupt the order of daily occupations.

B. Confessors of Religious Women

109. "§ 1. Every contrary particular law or privilege being revoked, all priests, whether secular or regular, no matter what may be their dignity or office, must have special jurisdiction to hear validly and licitly the confessions of any religious women and novices, safeguarding, however, the prescriptions of cc. 239, § 1, n. 1; 522, 523."

"§ 2. This jurisdiction is conferred by the Ordinary of the place in which the house of the religious is, according to the norm of c. 525" (c. 876).

C. 239, § 1, n. 1, gives to cardinals the privilege of hearing the confessions of any religious and in any ecclesiastical territory. C. 522 has to do with the case of religious who of their own accord seek to go to confession to a priest who has no special faculties; c. 523, concerns religious who are seriously ill.

110. 1. The exact meaning of c. 876 may be learned both from its text and its history.[31] It may be summed up as follows:

With the exception of the cardinals (c. 239), no one can validly exercise the office of ordinary or extraordinary confessor of religious women without having received the power to do so from the Ordinary of the diocese.

To hear the confession of any religious or novice *validly*, any other priest must have received of the Ordinary at least the jurisdiction for hearing the confessions of women. If he has no *special* jurisdiction, the priest can validly give sacramental absolution to religious women only in a place approved for hearing the confessions of women (c. 522). The prescriptions of the Code in regard to the motives and circumstances laid down in cc. 522 and 523 concern only the licit reception of the sacrament of penance.

This law is absolute and no reason for making exception is of value against it, such as: the fact that a regular is of the same order as the penitent; the fact that one has jurisdiction *in foro externo* over nuns; the episcopal dignity; the office of the director of the entire institute or of the motherhouse; any immemorial customs; special privileges conceded directly by the Holy See, etc. The text of c. 876 sums up or completes in an explicit way legislation already in use, and it is designed to put an end to the claims of some regulars, especially in this matter.

2. For very wise reasons the Church does not allow to religious women the same liberty given to the simple faithful in the choice of a confessor. The preservation of the cloister, the necessity of more experienced and enlightened directors, the ordinary advantages of direction easily explain this legislation. The Holy See has always endeavored to guard against the disadvantages which it might bring by safeguarding

---

[31] Decree *Cum de sacramentalibus,* February 3, 1913. Concerning this decree, see Vermeersch, *Per.,* VII, pp. 86 sqq.; (Father Salsmans, S.J.); pp. 49 sqq.; (Father Vermeersch) *Coll. Brug.,* XVIII (1913), p. 262; *Revue eccl. de Liége,* IX, p. 127, *Canon. Contemp.,* t. 36 (1913), pp. 267 sqq., 306, 409; *N.R. Th.,* t. 45 (1913); pp. 267 sqq.; Hizette, *Les confessions de religieuses,* Namur (1914); Mothon, O.P., *Traité de la confession sacramentelle à l'usage des communautés de religieuses,* Lille (1913). The history of this legislation is given by Father Vermeersch in his *Periodica,* t. V, 1 sq., and by R. E. McCormick, *Confessors of Religious,* Washington, D. C. (1926); De Sobradillo, O.M.C., *Tractatus de religiosarum confessariis,* Turin, 1932.

through special measures the liberty of conscience which is so desirable. The development of the laws on this subject show a marked inclination to grant larger concessions. This is explained first by the increasing number of congregations whose works bring the religious in continual contact with the outside world. If their activity is extended more widely, they themselves are also exposed to more dangers. On the other hand, in such surroundings a less uniform method of direction is not such a great disadvantage as in a monastery and, indeed, sometimes it may be an advantage. Finally, many of these religious women have sometimes, or even often, to leave the convent, and so without the least harm to the cloister they can easily go to confession to priests other than the ordinary confessor. But, above all, the increase of frequent and daily Communion has made it desirable that they should have greater facilities of access to the holy tribunal of penance.

There is no doubt that the Code upholds the principle that there should be one ordinary confessor for each community. But it confirms the right to summon other confessors from time to time, and it greatly extends the permission to go occasionally to confession to any priest who is approved for the hearing of confessions of women.

3. The Code, summing up and completing previous legislation, distinguishes several kinds of confessors for religious women; the ordinary confessors of a community or of one religious in particular (c. 520); the extraordinary confessors of the community (c. 521, § 1); the priests who have special jurisdiction and who can occasionally be called in to hear confessions without recourse to the bishop (assistant confessors) (c. 521, § 2). In special cases a religious may also, following the conditions of c. 522, present herself to any priest who has permission to hear the confessions of women; for this reason these priests are called occasional confessors. Finally, a religious who is seriously ill, can, during the entire time of her sickness, go to confession to any priest approved to hear the confessions of women, without the restrictions set down by c. 522 (c. 523).

111. The pontifical documents on this subject lead to the following conclusions: The Church wishes that religious should go to confession habitually to the confessor of the community, unless, by way of exception, they have obtained from the Ordinary a particular confessor; she wishes that all should present themselves at least four times a year to the extraordinary confessor of the community; she desires that religious who are seriously ill may have the greatest liberty in the choice of their confessor; and that others may, for a supernatural motive, go to confession to any priest who is approved for hearing the confessions of women, but only in particular cases. We have now to outline the obligations and rights contained in cc. 520–523.

No other canons of the Code have given occasion for so many controversies.[32] Thanks to them, the answers of the Commission for the Interpretation of the Code have become more and more precise, and have, as a result, resolved practically all doubts regarding this matter.

a) Ordinary Confessors

112. The Ordinary Confessors of Communities.

"To every house of religious women must be given only one ordinary confessor, who shall hear the sacramental confessions of the whole community, unless, on account of the great number of religious or for any other just reason, two or more may be found necessary" (c. 520).

Must bishops appoint ordinary confessors for communities where there are less than six professed religious?

Some particular answers given since the Code but not universally promulgated are in the affirmative, and contrary to the wider interpretation given to the Bishop of Linz on July 3, 1916.[33] Particular reasons, however, may be sufficiently grave to allow the sisters of a small community the choice of several confessors. Such would be the case if the one priest possessed of all the canonical conditions required for his appointment as confessor, would come to exercise real authority over the religious by reason of his office.

An article of constitutions approved at Rome in 1930 states that religious of small communities that have no ordinary confessors may have recourse *even habitually* to any confessor whatever who is approved for hearing the confessions of women. See *Theol. pr. Qschr.*, 1930, 603.

The presence of persons who speak different languages, the diversity of communities in the same house (the novitiate, the normal school for junior professed, etc.), are sufficient reasons for naming several ordinary confessors. The superior should inform herself whether the jurisdiction of each one of them is limited to a part of the community, as is ordinarily the case, or if each has jurisdiction over all the religious.

113. The Special Ordinary Confessor.

1. "If any particular religious, for the peace of her soul and for her greater progress in the spiritual life, requests a special confessor or spiritual director, the Ordinary shall grant the

---

[32] See S. Goyeneche, *Comm. pro rel.*, II (1921), 335 sqq., and A. Tabera, *ibid.*, X (1929), 390 sqq.

[33] Response to the Archbishop of Prague, January 10, 1920; Response to the Bishop of Osnabrück, January 18, 1921; See *Archiv f. K. KR.*, t. 97, 85; t. 100, 47; t. 101, 61. — De Sobradillo, O.M.C., *De religiosarum confessariis*, 11 sq.

request without difficulty, watchful, however, lest from this concession abuses arise; and if they do arise, he shall eliminate them carefully and prudently, while safeguarding the liberty of conscience" (c. 520, § 2).

Any antipathy, even though it is justified, and the difficulty of obtaining an ordinary confessor who gives acceptable spiritual direction, etc., are not always sufficient motives for asking this exception. A real and habitual difficulty of avowing one's faults, the impossibility of obtaining advice which frequently becomes necessary because of a special situation (scruples, grave and frequent temptations, extraordinary graces, etc.), would justify the asking of this favor from the Ordinary.

The Sovereign Pontiffs have more than once insisted that the Ordinary should readily grant the justifiable requests of this kind, and have insisted on the prudence with which he ought at the same time to eliminate abuses and to secure the liberty of conscience.

Abuses may be either individual or common: individual ones would be, for example, too frequent meetings had at times which are less suitable, etc., between the confessor and his penitent; a common abuse might arise if, for example, the requests would be multiplied beyond reason.[34]

2. The special confessor or director ought not to be appointed for a definite time, but the religious should be allowed to go to him as long as the necessity or utility which first suggested the request continues.[35]

The consent of the superiors is not required for the choice of this confessor, but they may require that they be informed of it, and if they think proper, they may submit to the Ordinary their observations on the matter

b) Extraordinary Confessors and Supplementary Confessors

114. "To every community of religious women shall be given an extraordinary confessor who, four times at least in the year, shall go to the religious house, and to whom all the religious should present themselves, at least to receive his blessing" (c. 521, § 1).

One and the same priest should be given this function for each community, and he must discharge his duty at least four times during the

---

[34] Battandier, *G.C.*, n. 253, writes: "I could cite the example of a cloistered community which consists of twelve religious women and numbers thirteen confessors, since one sister has need of two priests to direct her conscience."

[35] Response of the Congregation of Religious, April 20, 1913. — *A.A.S.*, IX (1913), 276; *Per.*, VIII, 229.

year. Still if the Ordinary thinks well, the priest who gives the annual retreat, may, on the occasion of the spiritual exercises, replace the extraordinary confessor. But in this case all the religious must present themselves at his confessional. In a number of dioceses it is forbidden to the ordinary confessor to hear confessions when the extraordinary confessor is fulfilling his ministry, and during the annual retreat.

Should the extraordinary confessor present himself to the sick members of the community? We believe that he should. The Code formally prescribes that all the religious present themselves to him. To say that, according to the text, it is not his duty to present himself to them, is to stop at the letter and to go contrary to the spirit of the law. If he did not present himself to them, one or the other of the sick members might hesitate to call him. The "reason" of the law is consequently equally applicable to the sick also.

115. "The Ordinaries of the places where religious communities of women exist, shall designate for each house some priests to whom, in particular cases, the religious may easily have recourse for the sacrament of penance, without having to apply to the Ordinary on each occasion" (c. 521, § 2).

These priests are specially approved for hearing the confessions of religious. As they do not exercise this office regularly, one may call them assistant confessors; this expression is found in the pontifical documents.[36]

It is not necessary for the Ordinary to assign particular assistant confessors to each community; it suffices that each community may have recourse, on occasion, to several priests. Local statutes grant this special jurisdiction to deans, to superiors of religious houses, to the ordinary and extraordinary confessors of some community in the deanery, city, or diocese. Superiors should, therefore, acquaint themselves with those to whom they may have recourse, and inform their subjects accordingly.

The appointment of these priests, assistants to the regular confessors of religious, has especially for its purpose the occasional hearing of confessions of individual religious. Still the superior may invite one or the other of them to hear the confession of the whole community in special cases. For example, if the ordinary confessor is absent or is temporarily unable to hear confessions.

---

[36] Instruction of the Congregation of Religious concerning the cloister, III, 2, g.

This authorization seems to us to follow practically from the following considerations: (1) the extra confessors have been specially appointed to hear the confessions of religious; (2) they are appointed "for each house"; (3) the religious may go to confession to them without applying each time to the Ordinary; (4) no term limits the use of these faculties to one or several religious in particular; (5) the superior must obtain for her community an opportunity of going to confession at least once a week, and the services of an extra confessor is not an encroachment on the office of the ordinary confessor, as he, by supposition, is hindered at the time from hearing confessions.[37]

116. "When any religious asks for one of these confessors, no superioress, either personally or through others, either directly or indirectly, may seek to know the reason for the petition, or show opposition to it by word or deed, or in any way manifest displeasure at it" (c. 521, § 3).

This paragraph applies to the extraordinary confessor as well as to the confessor mentioned in n. **115.** This is explicitly stated in the text of some Constitutions approved by the Holy See in 1930 (see *Theologische Praktische Quartalschrift*, 1930, 603).

It is the subject, and not the superior, who designates the confessor to whom she desires to go. At the same time this liberty must be reasonably understood. A religious has no right to require that a priest be summoned from a distant city when in the place itself, or not far away, confessors are to be found who have the special jurisdiction required for religious.

c) The "Occasional" Confessor

117. "If, notwithstanding the prescriptions of canons 520 and 521, any religious, for the peace of her conscience, have recourse to a confessor approved by the local Ordinary to hear the confessions of women, this confession, whether made in a church or oratory, even a semipublic oratory, is valid and lawful, every contrary privilege being revoked; nor may the superioress prohibit it or make any inquiry concerning it, even indirectly; and the religious are under no obligation to inform the superioress on the matter" (c. 522).

---

[37] In an excellent article in *Collationes Brugenses* (1923), 474, Professor J. Brys, though still maintaining that the opposite opinion is more conformable to the history of this article (see Decree *Quemadmodum*, II, 12), admits the serious probability of our interpretation which is also proposed by other commentators, for example, De Sobradillo, O.M.C., *De religiosarum confessariis*, 159.

When inquiry was made about the exact meaning of these words "confession made in any church or oratory, even semi-public, is valid and licit," the commission of interpretation replied: "C. 522 is to be understood in this sense, that confessions made by religious women for the peace of their conscience to a confessor approved by the Ordinary of the place for hearing the confessions of women, are licit and valid, provided that they are made in a church, in an oratory, even a semipublic one, or in a place lawfully set aside for hearing the confessions of women."

Another answer of the same Commission, dated December 28, 1927, has stated explicitly that the place is a condition required for validity.

118. For what reason may a religious go to confession occasionally to any confessor of women, whether abroad, or in her convent? The Code answers "for the peace of her conscience."

a) These words do not directly affect the power of the confessor, and do not lay down a condition required for validity. Hence the confessor may validly absolve a religious who has come to confession to him without a sufficient motive.[38] This interpretation is now admitted by all.

To make a sufficient motive a condition of validity, would be to impose on the penitent the necessity of judging correctly beforehand about the gravity of the reasons which she has for going to confession to an occasional confessor, and in many cases this would trouble her conscience, which may not be very enlightened or well formed. Again, if anxiety properly so called were necessary, many might hesitate to profit by this liberty of going to confession, so as not to give rise to suspicions on the part of others which would be hard to bear. Finally, if this were a condition for validity, the fact would have been declared in more formal terms.

b) The course of development which the law has taken in the direction of giving an increasingly greater liberty, shows that one must interpret the expression "for the peace of conscience" in a broad way. The natural meaning of these words in the light of the history of this legislation is that one should

---

[38] For this opinion we may cite, among others, Father Vermeersch, *Epitome,* I[7], n. 644; Augustine, *Commentary* on c. 876; Bastien, *D.C.* n. 201, 1; Fanfani, *De iure religiosorum,* 102, A; Leitner, *Handbuch,* III, p. 358.

confess with the sincere desire of purifying one's conscience, or of getting more light.

Reasons of conscience are likely to arise more frequently in the case of persons whose consciences are more delicate or more anxious, under certain circumstances of the religious life, and in communities which are not so highly favored as others in the choice or quality of their confessors.

Among the motives of this kind may be mentioned: a doubt of conscience, whether this arises from a fault committed, from a temptation, or from an obligation either imposed or freely undertaken; the facility to lay open one's conscience with greater ease to the occasional confessor than to the ordinary confessor; the involuntary failure to go to confession on the appointed day; the wish to purify oneself of a fault, even a light one, which has been more deliberate than usual; the opportunity of going to a priest who is particularly well instructed or experienced, etc.

The Code seems to exclude any purely human motive like a merely natural sympathy or a reason which arises only from convenience.

119. To what priest may the religious go to confession? To any priest who has been approved for hearing the confessions of women. In England and the United States there are very few priests, if any, approved only for the confession of men; but these restrictions are not unusual at Rome and perhaps in certain dioceses of Italy or in Spain.

It suffices, moreover, that the priest be approved for the confession of a group of women, for example, boarding-school girls, a community of religious women, etc., even if his jurisdiction is limited thereto.[39]

120. If a religious woman summons, that is, calls for a priest without special jurisdiction to come and hear her confession, would the confession be valid? Yes, it would be valid, according to an official answer of the Commission given on December 28, 1927. In effect, the answer declares that the word *"adeat"* (to go to) may be interpreted to mean that the religious may have the confessor come to her.

But may every religious hereafter have any confessor whatever, approved to hear the confessions of women, come to the convent in order to confess to him?

Since the Code retains the obligation of the bishops to appoint priests whom the religious may freely call to hear their confessions (c. 521, §§ 2

---

[39] Vermeersch-Creusen, *Epitome*, I⁷, n. 644, d.

and 3), the intention of the Holy See seems to be that they shall not be free to call on others. If the superior should refuse to grant such a wish, she would then run counter to no regulation. Evidently religious may not, unknown to their superior, invite priests to come to the convent in order to hear their confessions. Since, however, the sister may go to that priest if he comes to the convent in a legitimate way, it will suffice for superiors to call him to the convent in order that the sister may profit by his presence; under these circumstances the confession will be both valid and licit.

121. Where may the religious go to confession to a priest who has no special faculties to hear religious?

1. She may do this either outside the convent or inside the convent.

The Code has widened the concession made by the decree *Cum de sacramentalibus,* n. XIV, which authorized such confessions only outside the convent. The fact that in certain works on the subject the words "outside the convent" have been retained must, therefore, be regarded as a regrettable lapse of attention.

2. Within the convent the religious may not go to confession without permission except when the order of community exercises allows it. To quit a class, or supervision, or to leave the common work to go to confession would require permission. Such permission would not be necessary during meditation, Mass, or other exercises of piety, which are made in the chapel, or during study or free time.

The permission to go to confession in any church or oratory outside the convent changes nothing in the canons and rules concerning cloister. The greater number of nuns may, therefore, never take advantage of it. Among other religious the superior is not obliged to allow her subjects to go out of the convent contrary to the rule or to the customs of the community. It is for her to judge whether in an individual case an exception should be made.[40]

3. This confession, if it is to be valid, must be made in a place *lawfully* designated for the confession of women.

The text of the Code speaks only of a church or an oratory at least semipublic. But upon being asked regarding the exact sense of the

---

[40] In a private answer to the Bishop of Osnabrück (December 1, 1921), the Secretary of the Congregation of Religious communicated to him the opinion of the consultor, which fully confirms our interpretation. See *N.R. Th.* (1923), 491.

words: "the confession made in any church or oratory, even semi-public, is valid and licit," the Commission of Interpretation (November 20, 1920, *A.A.S.*, XII, 1920, 575) replied: "Canon 522 is to be understood in the sense that confessions made by religious women for the peace of their conscience to any confessor approved by the local Ordinary to hear the confessions of women, are licit and valid provided they be made in a church, in an oratory even semi-public, or in a place legitimately designated for hearing the confessions of women."

A subsequent reply of the same Commission (December 28, 1927) stated precisely that in this case the place is a condition for the validity of the confession. It adds, however, that the legitimate place is not only the confessional in which lay women may be heard, but also that set aside exclusively for religious women.

Finally (February 12, 1935), the Commission declared that these words are to be understood not only as applying to the place habitually designated for that purpose, but also the place designated for a particular case, or chosen according to canon 910, § 1.

Here are the provisions of the canon law regarding the place where one may hear confessions of women:

Can. 909, § 1. "The confessional where confessions of women are to be heard shall be always placed in a spot accessible to all and in full view, and generally in a church or public oratory, or in a semi-public oratory destined for the use of women."

§ 2. "The confessional shall be furnished with a fixed grating with small openings which separates the penitent from the confessor."

Can. 910, § 1. "The confessions of women are not to be heard outside the confessional except in cases of sickness or of real necessity, and then the precautions judged opportune by the Ordinary of the place must be observed."

In addition to the canons quoted above, every superior should consult the diocesan statutes or observe strictly whatever regulations the diocesan visitor may have made regarding the location of the confessional. For it is the bishop's business to decide when and where the confessional may be erected outside the church or oratory. The Code prescribes that "generally" the confessional should be located in the church or oratory (c. 909, § 1).

122. *Conclusions:* (1) in ordinary cases, a confessor without special jurisdiction cannot *validly* hear the confessions of religious women outside the place *habitually* designated for the confessions of either religious or of lay women; (2) in cases of sickness or of other real necessity the confessor can hear confessions validly outside the confessional in any suitable place, for example, in a parlor having a glass door, at the grille of a chapel not having a confessional, in a sick room; nuns (in the strict sense) can certainly make use of canon 522 in their own confessionals.

We may sum up the interpretation of this part of the canon as follows: "A confessor approved to hear the confessions of lay women but without any special jurisdiction for religious women may, nevertheless, absolve religious women validly in any place in which a confessor with special jurisdiction can absolve them licitly. (The reader who is interested in a further explanation of this point may consult: *N.R. Th.* [1921], 1 sq.; McCormick, *Confessors of Religious,* 202 sq.; De Sobradillo, O.M.C., *De religiosarum confessariis,* 189 sq.)

123. "All religious women when seriously ill, even if not in danger of death, may, as often as they wish during their serious illness, invite any priest whatever to hear their confession, provided that he be approved to hear the confessions of women, though not designated for religious women, nor can the superioress either directly or indirectly prevent them from doing so" (c. 523).

1. According to Wouters, C.SS.R.,[41] it is enough that the confessor shall have received his jurisdiction from any diocesan Ordinary. The text of c. 523, taken by itself, allows this interpretation. But the general principle that delegated jurisdiction for hearing confessions must come from the Ordinary of the place keeps us from admitting the correctness of this interpretation.

2. We may consider as serious any sickness which by its nature or by reason of special circumstances considerably lessens the strength of the sick person, all cases which, of their nature, may bring on dangerous complications; this may be the case even in otherwise slight illnesses with persons whose constitutions have been weakened by age, by privations, or by a preceding illness.

The mere fact that one is obliged to remain in one's room, for example, by reason of a sprain, is not sufficient since the Code speaks of "persons who are seriously ill."

The enjoyment of this privilege continues throughout the course of the sickness itself, even though there is no danger of death at any time. But it does not go any farther than that, and hence it ceases with the evident beginning of convalescence. One may rely on the judgment of the doctor as to when the illness is over, and one may interpret the permission granted in a rather wide sense. This is according to the spirit of the law.

---

[41] *Ned. K. St.* (1918), 200.

124. *Duties of the Superior.*

We have seen in numbers **115, 120,** and **121** how the superior, while she supports the rule and the lawful customs, ought to insure liberty of conscience to her religious whether sick or well. "If a superioress acts against the prescription of canons 521, § 3, 522, and 523, she shall be admonished by the local Ordinary; if again found delinquent, she shall be punished by removal from office, and the Sacred Congregation of Religious shall be immediately informed of the matter" (c. 2414).

At the same time, abuses on the part of subjects are always possible. If, therefore, a superior considers that the conduct of either the confessor or the penitent is imprudent or reprehensible, she must inform the Ordinary. Let us repeat that she may, of her own authority, forbid exterior and certain violations of the canons or of the rule, such as would be, for instance, going to confession at an inappropriate hour, or outside the confessional without necessity.

C. Appointment of Confessors — Their Duties

125. 1. *The Qualities Required.*

The office of confessor of religious women may be given to secular priests or, with the authorization of their superior, to regular priests (c. 524, § 1).

According to the former law, regulars could not be ordinary confessors of religious, but Msgr. Battandier remarks that in certain regions, notably at Rome, the exception had through necessity become the rule[42] long before the Code. The institute of the Society of Jesus does not allow its religious to be the ordinary confessors to a religious community, save in the absence of any other priest, as happens in missionary lands.

The confessors ought to be "priests who are known to be of blameless life and prudent; and who are at least forty years of age, except, in the judgment of the Ordinary, a just cause determine otherwise; these confessors have no authority *in foro externo* over the religious in question" (c. 524, § 1).

A vicar general, the visitor of the community, the ecclesiastical superior of the religious house, etc., may not be appointed ordinary or extraordinary confessor.

---

[42] *G.C.,* n. 252.

2. *The Appointment of Confessors.*

The Ordinary of the place is to choose the confessors, both ordinary and extraordinary, for all the houses of religious women which are not subject to a regular superior; for those dependent upon a regular superior, the superior is to present the priests to the bishop, so that he may give them jurisdiction. If necessary, the Ordinary shall supply for the negligence of the regular superior in this matter (c. 525).

It is always lawful for superiors to make known to the Ordinary their wishes concerning the choice of confessors. This is especially the case if the community wishes to have as extraordinary confessor a religious of some special institute; the superior of the community of religious women, after she has made sure that the priest in question will give his lawful consent, may ask the Ordinary of the place to give him the necessary faculties. It is hardly necessary to add that the bishop is still entirely free in the matter.

126. *The Duration of the Office of the Confessor.*

1. The extraordinary confessor may hold his office indefinitely; the ordinary confessor may not exercise his office for the same community for a term exceeding three years (c. 526). While the extraordinary confessor may always become the ordinary one, the ordinary confessor cannot be appointed extraordinary for the same community, until after the lapse of one year between the two offices (c. 524, § 2).

2. The double limit put upon the office of the ordinary confessor admits of exceptions in two cases. If the dearth of priests suitable for the office makes it impossible to provide otherwise, or if the majority of the community expresses the desire to keep their confessor, the Ordinary may confirm the ordinary confessor in his charge for a second and even a third term of three years.

The community must manifest this desire by an absolute majority of votes in secret ballot, in which all the professed, even the lay sisters, for whom the confessor is appointed must take part. The Ordinary must provide in some other way for the spiritual needs of those religious who express to him their desire for this (c. 526).

By special indult certain bishops are allowed to keep in office the ordinary confessors during six or even nine years without recurring to a vote of the community. The Holy See sometimes also gives permission to prolong this office for a fourth or even a fifth term of three years, but always requires the observance of the conditions laid down by c. 526 for the confirmation of an ordinary confessor.

One need only consult the sources of c. 526 to see how insistent the Holy See has been in this matter of changing confessors, even in communities in which the members have frequent and easy opportunities to leave the house. The contrary custom has been declared an abuse. In localities in which there are at least two communities, the law can easily be complied with by interchanging the confessors every three years.

3. The Ordinary may, at any time, for a serious reason, deprive any confessor of religious women of his office. If a monastery depends on a regular superior, the Ordinary must inform him of this removal.

He is not obliged to tell his reasons to anyone except to the Holy See, if he is required to do so. The fact that an appeal is made to the Holy See does not dispense from an immediate submission to the decision of the Ordinary (c. 527).

127. *The Duties of Confessors.*

1. "It is forbidden both to ordinary and extraordinary confessors to interfere in any manner either in the internal or external government of the community" (c. 524, § 3).

When a superior needs to ask advice regarding the removal or dismissal of a religious, she must always endeavor to seek this advice from some other priest rather than from the confessor. If she is obliged to have recourse to the confessor, she must explain the circumstances in such a manner that he may be able to form a judgment without finding out who the person in question is. Even in that case, she should not be surprised if the priest refuses to give any advice at all, and advises her to have recourse, even in writing, to some other competent priest.

If a member of the council asks him for information or advice about matters which have to be taken up by the council, the confessor should limit himself to making clear the obligations or the counsels which flow from the principles of moral theology or from the Church's legislation. He shall not try to secure the passage of disciplinary measures because they please him more by reason of his personal temperament or for merely personal views.

2. Confessors of religious must evidently be acquainted with the obligations of state of their penitents, that is to say, those which flow from the vows and the principal rules. It is very

desirable, but not always possible, that the confessors be able to direct the religious according to the special spirit of their order or congregation. No confessor may oblige his penitents to take from him direction of their conscience over and above that required as a condition for absolution. They retain their liberty of asking this direction from any other priest from whom they can obtain wise counsel and the moral support which is necessary for their progress in the spiritual life.

3. If the confessor without special jurisdiction observes that a religious is coming to confession to him without a lawful motive or because of a mere whim, it is his duty to call her attention to this and not to yield to her wishes in the matter. More than other priests he is obliged to respect and to cause others to respect the directions of the common law or the statutes regarding the place where confessions may be heard.

§ 2. THE ACCOUNT OF CONSCIENCE

128. To manifest one's conscience means to reveal one's hidden faults (with their degree of culpability), one's interior or hidden acts of virtue, one's intentions, the affections and repugnances to which one has yielded, the temptations or trials which God sends, the lights and good desires received from Him.

In a wider sense, one may call manifestation of conscience the revealing of all the acts which no one else has witnessed, of all the feelings which one has not shown exteriorly. There are feelings, dispositions, good qualities, or defects which are not apparent exteriorly and whose manifestation may, therefore, be called a revealing of one's conscience. Such are, for example, the greater or less ease with which one uses certain methods of prayer or examen, the attraction felt for some particular kind of spirituality, the sympathy or antipathy felt for certain characters, the taste or aversion for such and such an occupation. These are the sort of things of which one speaks readily with people with whom one has some bond of friendship. In ordinary speech we would not call such a communication an opening up or manifesting of our conscience, in the strict sense, because this expression always supposes the revealing of things which we would not care to tell anyone except under seal of secrecy.

As soon as they can be noticed by others, our neglect or our fidelity to the obligations of the Christian or religious life, the way we fulfill an office, even the movements of the passions, are no longer confined to the domain of our own conscience. From then on they become the natural object of exterior government, and it becomes lawful and often a duty of obligation for the superior to put questions about them.

129. 1. As was the case in the very beginning of the cenobitic life, the abbot in monastic orders was at the same time the superior and the spiritual father of the religious who had voluntarily placed themselves under his authority and direction. The vow of stability, and the uniformity of life which existed among the monks gave hardly any occasion for using in government the knowledge acquired in an intimate manifestation of conscience. But St. Ignatius of Loyola sought in this complete manifestation the means of securing a very supernatural and, at the same time, a very paternal government in an order devoted to the most diverse kinds of apostolic work. Was it not of as much importance for the good of the subjects as for that of the faithful that the distribution of employments and of ministries should be adapted to the moral and spiritual strength and weakness of each one? The candidate for admission was, of course, informed about this conception of religious government. He found in the priestly character and the theological knowledge of his superior sufficient guarantees that his direction would be sound. Besides, the holy founder expressly authorizes the subject to make known in confession only, if he wishes, those faults which are subject matter of sacramental confession. In this case the superior can give to his subordinate the necessary advice, but he must strictly abstain from using these communications in making his decisions about administrative and disciplinary matters.[43] Though the principle of government which is grounded on entire and mutual confidence has its application in every religious family, still the practice of manifestation of conscience, especially when it is of obligation, does not find in lay communities all the necessary safeguards. Grave abuses arose from its practice as might have been expected. In the decree *Quemadmodum* (December 17, 1890), Leo XIII mentioned three of these abuses: Lay superiors required, directly or indirectly, avowals which by their nature belonged only to the tribunal of penance; they restricted too much the freedom of going to confession, and they reserved to themselves, where there was question of receiving Holy Communion, a direction which belongs for the most part to the confessor.

2. To remedy these grave abuses Pope Leo XIII ordered

---

[43] Later on the liberty to use facts learned in the manifestation of conscience for exterior government, even where there was no danger of revelation, was restricted to very narrow limits.

struck out of the constitutions, directories, and custom books of all the lay orders and congregations everything which had the semblance of manifestation of conscience to the superiors, and he severely forbade them to try to make their subordinates give this intimate manifestation of their conscience in any manner whatsoever. In the *Normae* (a. 79), we find this prohibition extended to the masters and mistresses of novices.

There is no denying that we live in an age where the spirit of independence, the freedom of expressing all sorts of opinions, and professing all sorts of cults — individualism, in a word — is having a profound influence on all souls. Though this spirit is open to serious objections, still it has the advantage of developing personality, reasoned convictions, a more spontaneous religious practice, and the greater need for a spiritual direction which draws its force much less from the authority of the director than from his spiritual and intellectual capacity. One must take account of this spirit in the education, the spiritual direction, and the government even of religious. No one should be surprised, therefore, to see that the legislation of the Code takes account of this mentality, and emphasizes even more than the *Normae* the distinction between disciplinary government and direction of conscience. But if the Holy See respects even sensibilities arising from the peculiar circumstances of modern life from which religious have come, still it does not forget the essential and unchangeable conditions of supernatural government of souls who profess the constant will to seek after perfection by the observance of the evangelical counsels and who wish to devote themselves, in common life, either to contemplation or to apostolic works.

These reflections will make it easier to understand the directions of c. 530, § 1, and the counsels at once precise and detailed of c. 530, § 2.

130. "All religious superiors are strictly forbidden to induce their subjects in any manner whatever to make a **manifestation of conscience** to them" (c. 530, § 1).

1. By *superiors* we must here understand those to whom the Code gives that title, that is to say, those who govern the institute, its provinces, and its individual houses, as well as those who take their place, such as visitors, vice-provincials, vice-rectors, and the prior in an abbey. Subjects are all those persons who are under the authority of the religious superior, hence, the professed, the novices, and the postulants.

2. Neither the masters or mistresses of novices, nor the masters (ministers, directors) of the junior professed are superiors in the canonical sense of the word. However, excellent

authors judge that c. 530, § 1, applies directly to them also.[44] This follows from the conformity, which is always presumed, of the new law with former legislation. We do not share this opinion; the definitions of the Code ought to be applied strictly, unless there is proof to the contrary, or we shall be in danger of falling into arbitrary judgments. The reserve of the Code offers us a real advantage and without any special prohibitions abuses can be avoided readily if the following principles are kept in mind.[45]

Even though the prohibition expressed in c. 530, § 1, is not intended for them, still it is certainly forbidden to masters of novices to demand the secret manifestation of conscience, that is to say, of anything which comes within the domain of the sacrament of penance. If they are laymen, the fact is evident, because the decree *Quemadmodum* considers such a demand a very grave abuse. Indeed, by what right, except by one's free agreement or by the obligation of the divine law, can one man ask of another such a manifestation? Not only would a layman be indiscreet in making such a demand, but he would be in danger of grave imprudence in his direction, which would not be enlightened by sufficient knowledge of moral, ascetical, or mystical theology. If the master of novices is a priest, he is forbidden to hear the confession of those in his charge except in cases which are strictly determined (c. 891); for a still stronger reason he is not allowed to ask these confidences outside of confession.

3. The same considerations apply strictly to the masters of the junior professed in lay institutes; if they are priests, it would be contrary to the manifest intention of the legislator to appoint them confessors of those over whom they have disciplinary authority (c. 891).

But the fact that the text of c. 530 does not apply to masters and mistresses of novices gives them more latitude than superiors to ask about things which belong only in a wide sense, to the domain of conscience (see n. 129).

The sense of canon 530, § 1, is explained by those words of the decree *Quemadmodum:* "His Holiness formally forbids superiors, both men and women, of whatever rank or pre-eminence, to seek, directly or indirectly, by precept, counsel, intimidation, threats, or flatteries, to

---

[44] Bastien, *D.C.,* n. 371. — Jansen, *Ordensrecht,* p. 148.
[45] See Vermeersch, *Epitome,* I[7], n. 650; Brys, *I. C. Compendium,* I, n. 627, 1°.

induce their subjects to make the said manifestation of conscience to them . . ." (decree cited in the foregoing, II).

The gravity of this offense is clear from the very terms of the canon and from the obligation which was formerly imposed by the decree to report the superiors in case they violated it.

It is no longer required to report higher superiors who violate this law. Still such a denunciation will sometimes be an act of charity, and it may even be a grave obligation, especially on the part of an assistant or the counsellors.

131. In those things which, without being strictly in the domain of conscience, are still very closely connected with it, superiors will be very reserved and careful. The devotion of superiors and the trust which they show towards their subjects will make the well-disposed religious offer them the confidences counselled in § 2. Where there is question of a soul which is not very sincere or of a character which is suspicious or too reticent, questions which appear to be indiscreet will simply not be answered.

We ought to remember, however, that it will be no indiscretion on the part of a superior delicately to inquire the motives of the sadness or trouble which he sees afflicting one of his subordinates. In fact, to make such inquiries might be an obligation of charity, but he must be careful not to insist if he sees that the subject prefers not to explain the causes of his condition.

132. "Subjects, however, are not forbidden to open their minds freely and spontaneously to their superiors; nay more, it is desirable that they approach their superiors with filial confidence, and, if the superiors be priests, expose to them their doubts and troubles of conscience also" (c. 530, § 2).

All religious are earnestly recommended to practice a great openness of heart towards their superiors, but where there is question of the subject matter of this manifestation of conscience, the Code distinguishes between the superiors who are priests and superiors who are laymen.

A brother or a religious woman need not, therefore, accuse himself of lack of confidence if he reserves the manifestation of his difficulties of conscience to his confessor or to his spiritual director. There is no obligation to act otherwise, and one is not even allowed to advise such action in a general way. On the other hand, the Code does not forbid making such manifestation to a superior, even a layman, especially if there is question less of faults than of doubts or anxieties; it sometimes happens that a superior, even though a layman, can give all the more useful counsel because he knows his subject better. If the subject comes to him entirely of his own accord, it would be imprudent and not very charitable to send him away unless there is a really sufficient reason.

The Code does not forbid religious to make a manifestation of doubts and troubles of conscience to a lay superior; nor does it state that it is generally useful to do so, as it does in the case of superiors who are priests.

If a subject has given his superior the permission to question him freely, he can always take back this authorization.

It is not contrary to the regulations of the Church to bind one's self by vow to manifest one's conscience to the superior. We cannot even say that this is contrary to the spirit of the law, providing that the object of the vow is limited by the restrictions made in c. 530, § 2. But even understood in this way, such a vow should not be advised or approved except with great discretion.

Article 3. Divine Service

§ 1. GENERAL NOTIONS

133. 1. **Divine service** of the community includes the saying of the office, preaching, the administration of the sacraments, and funerals.

In the case of religious who are clerics, the divine service is carried out by the superiors and the religious of the community; in lay institutes the Ordinary entrusts it to the parish clergy and to the chaplains. Some of these services may occasionally be carried on with the help of other priests who have no particular office in the community.

2. The **chaplain** is a priest entrusted with the divine service of a community of lay religious. He is also called director or rector.

"In the case of nonexempt lay institutes, the local Ordinary appoints the chaplain; if the institute be exempt, the regular superior appoints him, and if he neglects to do so, the Ordinary will provide" (c. 529).

The only nuns who are exempt are those who depend on a superior of men of their order. In the case of monasteries which depend directly on the Holy See, the naming of the chaplain belongs entirely to the

Ordinary of the place. Superiors may, of course, always inform the Ordinary of their preferences or their lawful wishes in this matter.

Superiors of lay communities have no need of any authorization from the bishop to allow a priest to celebrate Mass in their convent, even though he comes habitually. If the priest is not known to the chaplain or the superior, he should be requested to show the letters of recommendation from his Ordinary or from his superior, or the "celebret," that is, the formal authorization to say Mass. Even if he has no letters, one may allow him to say Mass for two or three days unless some good reason arises for distrusting him, or there are some special regulations to the contrary in the diocese. When he is thus allowed to say Mass, he must write his name, his rank, and the diocese from which he comes in the register kept for the purpose (see c. 804).

134. 1. The **powers** of the chaplain are determined by the decrees of the provincial council or the diocesan synod and by special regulations of the Ordinary.

Chaplains are not given the same powers by the common law as the rectors of churches (see c. 479).

If the Ordinary gives the chaplain charge of the church annexed to a convent and in which the community does not hold its divine service (choir; conventual Mass, etc.), he enjoys there, by the very fact, all the rights of a rector.

2. The bishop may substitute the chaplain for the pastor in everything which has to do with divine worship and the ministration of the sacraments (c. 464, § 2). Such a partial exemption, it seems to us, would put the chaplain in a position similar to that of a rector of a church. Hence he could bless objects used in divine service as well as the sacred vestments (chasubles, palls, corporals, etc.) (c. 1304, nn. 3 and 4).

In Belgium the chaplains of lay communities have charge of all the divine services; that is to say, one must obtain from them the permission to say Mass, to administer the sacraments in the chapel of the convent; they may bless objects of worship, they have the right to administer the last sacraments to members of the community (Conc. of Malines, 1920, 1937, n. 181).

3. If he has the necessary delegation, nothing prevents the chaplain from being the confessor of the community of women. He must, however, observe with care the prescriptions of the Code or any special indults which have to do with the prolongation of this office.

If he is confessor, he is strictly forbidden to interfere in the government of the community (c. 524, § 3). If the bishop has not appointed him director of the institute for things which concern the administration, he can in no way interfere in the government of the community. Msgr. Battandier even counsels him not to give advice in this matter even when it is spontaneously requested, for such advice often brings with it responsibility which he will regret having assumed.[46]

N.B. Provincial councils and diocesan synods often contain this prescription which is part of the *Normae*, n. 178;

"If the confessor or chaplain of the sisters dwells in their convent, his rooms must be provided with a separate entry and must have no communication with their dwelling."

The quinquennial report requires an answer on this point (q. 222 for pontifical institutes, q. 205 for diocesan institutes).

§ 2. DIVINE WORSHIP

In this section we shall point out a certain number of canons which are of more general interest, or are taken from the most recent legislation.

A. Churches and Oratories

135. *Definition.*

1. **Churches** and **oratories** are places consecrated to divine worship. But whereas the church is intended for the worship of all the faithful (c. 1161), the oratory is built specially or solely for a determined group of persons.

2. Oratories may be public, semipublic, or private.

Public oratories are those to which all the faithful have the right to come, at least during the hours of services (c. 188, § 2, n. 1).

The Code declares oratories to be semipublic "which are built for the benefit of a community or a group of the faithful who gather there, but where admission is not free to all the public" (c. 1188, § 2, n. 2).

All chapels of religious communities are certainly semipublic oratories; so also are the chapels of third orders, sodalities and confraternities, provided divine services are held in them. The chapels erected in the country house or villa of a religious community likewise come under the definition of a semipublic oratory, even though the community live there for only a few weeks during the year. Finally the secondary chapels erected in a religious house or in a seminary to provide facilities for

---

[46] *G.C.*, n. 296.

saying Mass on the part of a large number of priests, or in which distinct groups of religious assist at the Holy Sacrifice, are to be classed as semipublic oratories.

A chapel in the infirmary of a religious house, is, therefore, a semipublic oratory, contrary to what was the case under the former law.

An oratory is private when it is erected in a private dwelling for one family or one person (c. 1188, § 2, n. 3).

136. *The Establishment of Oratories.*

1. "In the colleges or boarding schools conducted for the education of youth, in high schools, lyceums, barracks, prisons, hospitals, etc., it is not allowed to establish, besides the principal oratory, other smaller ones, unless the Ordinary judges it necessary or useful" (c. 1192, § 4).

Father Vermeersch, arguing from the very detailed enumeration of this canon, thought that there is question here only of lay establishments or those which are directed by secular priests and that it does not refer to religious houses. The Ordinary or the higher superior of an exempt institute of clerics may, therefore, approve the erection of several semipublic oratories in the same religious house (see *Epitome*, II[7], n. 501).

2. The authorization given to religious clerics to establish a house includes that of having a church or a public oratory where they may exercise the sacred ministry (c. 497, § 2).

They must ask the consent of the Ordinary of the place to determine the location of this church or oratory (c. 1162, § 4).

This restriction is intended to protect the rights of the churches and the public oratories of the neighborhood.

3. A special permission is necessary to establish a semipublic oratory (c. 1192, § 1).

137. *Celebration of Sacred Functions.*

In oratories, even semipublic ones, which are legitimately established, it is allowed to celebrate all the **sacred functions** of the Church, unless the rubrics or some special exception made by the bishop forbid it (c. 1193).

Without a special privilege, the faithful may not choose the church or oratory of a religious congregation for their funeral. They may, however, choose the church or oratory of regulars. Lay persons authorized to live within the cloister may choose to be buried from the churches of nuns, even though the nuns have only simple vows (c. 1225).

The faithful have the right to assist at Holy Mass and other services on Sundays and feast days in any church, or public or semipublic oratory (c. 1249). Religious superiors, however, are free to admit the faithful to their chapels as they see fit. They are under no obligation to do so.

The religious superior should see to it that the celebration of divine service in a religious church does not interfere with the catechetical instruction or the explanation of the gospel which must be given in the parish church (c. 609, § 3).

The Ordinary is the judge of such possible inconvenience. If the inconvenience can be avoided in some other way, he may not forbid the faithful to assist at Sunday Mass in the churches or oratories of religious communities.

If one of the faithful should assist at Mass on Sunday in a semipublic chapel contrary to the prohibition of the bishop, he would commit a sin of disobedience, but he would satisfy his obligation of hearing Mass (c. 1249).

"Religious women, insofar as they are allowed by their constitutions, the liturgical laws, and the permission of the Ordinary to sing in their church or oratory, shall do this from a place where the public cannot see them" (c. 1264, § 2).

This term: the public (*populus*) does not include students, religious, the sick, old people, boarders, etc. If a few people are admitted from without for some special reason to assist at a religious service (Mass, profession, etc.), there is no need of interpreting c. 1264, § 2, too strictly. It would seem sufficient if the religious who do the singing are grouped at the back of the chapel.

Regarding the liturgical chant the instructions and counsels should be carefully observed which are contained in the Apostolic Constitution *Divini cultus* of December 20, 1928, in the special letter of the Cardinal Prefect of the S. Congregation of Religious, in the encyclical *Mediator Dei et hominum* of November 20, 1947, and above all in the encyclical *Musica Sacra* of December 25, 1955.

138. 1. A church which belongs to religious women may not be made a parochial church (c. 609, § 2).

2. "In the churches or oratories of religious women, the diocesan Ordinary may not permit the erection of any but associations of women or a pious union which gives itself only

to exercises of piety and has none but spiritual privileges"
(c. 712, § 3).

According to this last provision a sodality of the Blessed Virgin for
men could be established there, but not a confraternity (see *Epitome*,
I⁷, n. 862, 2).

3. The Ordinaries may not allow the celebration of a marriage
in the churches or oratories of religious women except in urgent
cases and with the necessary precautions (c. 1109).

139. 1. The **objects of worship** and the sacred vestments
intended for the churches or the oratories of a community may
be blessed:

a) in the case of religious clerics by the religious superior or
his delegate;

b) in the case of nuns who are exempt by the superior of
the regulars on whom they depend, or his delegate;

c) in the lay congregations which are not exempt by the
pastor of the parish, or if the community is not under his authority, by the chaplain, or by a priest delegated by the Ordinary
of the place (c. 1304).

2. *Altar linens* (altar cloths, corporals, palls, purificators) as
well as *amices* and *albs* should ordinarily be made of linen or
hemp. The law is particularly strict in regard to the linens which
come into immediate contact with the host or the chalice, i.e.,
corporals, palls, and purificators. For the others the Holy See
grants indults permitting the use of part linen, or even of cotton.

Maniples, stoles, and chasubles should be made of precious
materials, such as cloth of gold, silver, or silk. Custom admits,
in case of necessity, the use of silk mixed with wool, cotton,
or linen, provided the silk is used in sufficient quantity and
is apparent.

B. Eucharistic Worship

a) Holy Mass

140. In all religious or pious houses which have an oratory
with the faculty of reserving the Blessed Sacrament habitually,
one priest may celebrate the three Masses of Christmas, beginning at midnight, or only one, according to the liturgy of
the day; all who are present at this Mass satisfy the precept

of hearing Mass; and Holy Communion may be distributed (c. 821, § 3).

This is a confirmation of the privilege accorded by His Holiness, Pius X, on August 1, 1907. This permission refers only to the oratory of the community. In future it is certain that the faithful may be admitted to these Masses. In churches, only the parochial Mass or the conventual Mass, that is to say, the Mass which is of obligation for the religious who are bound to the recitation of the Divine Office, may be celebrated at midnight. Father Vermeersch[47] nevertheless held the opinion that the three Christmas Masses could also be celebrated in the church in the presence of the religious only, behind closed doors, or at least in the presence of those of the faithful who were specially permitted by the superior to assist at them.

141. 1. "On *Maundy Thursday* there must be observed that very ancient tradition of the Roman Church according to which the celebration of private Masses is forbidden and all priests and clerics assist at the Mass of the *Lord's Supper* and properly receive Holy Communion" (cf. c. 862).

However, where pastoral reasons so dictate, the local Ordinary may permit one or two low Masses in each church or public oratory; in semipublic oratories, however, only one Mass may be permitted. . . . These Masses are allowed only at the same hours assigned for the celebration of the solemn Mass of the Lord's Supper.[48]

Certain priests have a privilege whereby they may celebrate one low Mass on Maundy Thursday. This is the case, for example, of Regulars for their sick. This privilege has not been revoked. The time for this Mass is determined by the beneficiary.

2. On Holy Saturday the Mass may be celebrated only during the course of the rite of the Easter Vigil.

In all churches and in public or semipublic oratories where there is a sufficient number of sacred ministers (celebrant, deacon, subdeacon) all the rites of Holy Week may be celebrated in solemn form, that is, according to the complete rite given in the *ORDO* of November 16, 1955.

In churches and in public and semipublic oratories where a

---

[47] *Epitome,* II[7], n. 97.
[48] S.R.C. *Ordinations,* Feb. 1, 1957, n. 9.

deacon and subdeacon are lacking, the simple rite may be followed (now published in a *special revision* of the *Memoriale Rituum* of Benedict XIII *for Holy Week,* Rome, 1957). But in this case a sufficient number of ministers, whether clerics or altar boys, must be on hand: at least three for Palm Sunday and Holy Thursday, and at least four for the ceremonies of Good Friday and of the Easter Vigil. These ministers are to be diligently trained in the duties to be performed by them. This twofold requirement, namely, a sufficient number of ministers and their proper training, is absolutely necessary for the use of the simple rite. Local Ordinaries should diligently see to it that these conditions are exactly observed.

The Paschal Vigil may be celebrated even in churches and oratories in which the functions of Holy Thursday and Good Friday were not held, just as one may omit the Easter Vigil when these latter functions were held.

On Maundy Thursday *Holy Communion* may be distributed to the faithful only during the evening Masses or immediately after them. To the sick, however, it may be brought in the morning or in the afternoon. On Holy Saturday Holy Communion may be distributed only during the solemn Masses or immediately afterward; but an exception is made in favor of the sick who are in danger of death.

One may follow the opinion which allows Holy Communion to be brought to the sick in the same house after Mass on Maundy Thursday or on Holy Saturday (Vermeersch-Creusen, *Epitome,* II[7], n. 136).

On Good Friday, the commemoration of the Lord's Passion and death, Holy Communion may be distributed only during the course of the solemn liturgical service, except again to the sick who are in danger of death. As far as the eucharistic fast is concerned, the latest Apostolic Constitution *Sacram Communionem* of March 19, 1957, is to be observed.

Without any special permission, all the faithful may receive Communion and fulfill their Easter duty when the Mass is said on Holy Thursday, wherever it is celebrated. In general, it is better to receive one's Easter Communion in one's parish church and if this is not done, it is strongly recommended to tell one's pastor that one has fulfilled one's Easter duty elsewhere (see c. 859, 867). Religious ought to advise all their students to go to Communion in their own parish church during the Paschal season.

142. In a house of exempt religious, the major superior may, in an extraordinary case and by exception, allow, for a just and reasonable motive, the celebration of Mass outside of the church or oratory, but never in a place which actually serves for a bedroom. Other religious must obtain this permission from their bishop (c. 822).

This faculty may be made use of on the occasion of some extraordinary solemnity so as to give some poor sick person who has long been prevented from hearing Mass by his infirmities, the opportunity to assist at the Holy Sacrifice.

b) Reservation of the Blessed Sacrament

143. Provided that there is someone to take care of the Blessed Sacrament, and that Mass is said at least once a week in the church or chapel:

a) Exempt religious are obliged to keep the Blessed Sacrament in the church annexed to their house (c. 1265, § 1, n. 1).

Nuns who are not exempt, for instance in France and Belgium, have the same obligation.

b) It is allowed to keep the Blessed Sacrament, with permission of the diocesan Ordinary, in the principal oratory of every religious house and of ecclesiastical colleges which are in charge of the secular clergy or of religious (c. 1265, §§ 1, 2).

Regarding the manner of preserving the Blessed Sacrament in the Repository during the triduum of Holy Week, confer the Instruction of the S. Congregation of the Sacraments, November 4, 1929, and of the S. Cong. of Rites, November 16, 1955.

144. An instruction of the S. Congregation of the Sacraments for May 26, 1938, lays down exactly the steps to be taken in order that the Blessed Sacrament in the Repository be safeguarded from every profanation. The Instruction itself sums up these steps in the following words: (*a*) "The Holy Eucharist should be kept in a nonportable tabernacle, one which is securely closed up on every side; (*b*) the tabernacle should be guarded with such care that all danger of sacrilegious profanation be avoided; (*c*) the key of the tabernacle should be guarded by the priest with the greatest care."

In communities of clerics, the application of these prescriptions offers no difficulty. It would be evidently a serious fault to keep the Blessed Sacrament in a small wooden tabernacle, at the altar of a chapel to which there is ready access and without any serious precaution being taken to avoid a sacrilegious theft. In the monasteries of nuns the S.

Congregation prescribes that the key of the tabernacle be kept in a container securely closed by two different locks: one of the keys should be kept by the superioress, the other by the sister sacristan. In the houses of brothers or of religious women who have a resident chaplain, it is upon him that the obligation rests of keeping securely the tabernacle key. If the community has no chaplain or rector, we believe that it can conform itself to the prescription imposed upon nuns or adopt some other safe way of preserving the tabernacle key from all illegitimate use, provided the Ordinary of the place approve the method employed. For it is to the Ordinary, in fine, that the S. Congregation entrusts the execution of this instruction (*A.A.S.*, XXI [1938], 198 sq. — *R.C.R.* [1938], 139 sq.; 161 sq.).

145. "All privileges to the contrary being revoked, it is allowed to keep the Blessed Sacrament only in the church or the principal oratory of a pious or religious house; and in the case of nuns, it may not be kept inside the choir, or within the enclosure of the monastery" (c. 1267).

This canon forbids that the Blessed Sacrament be kept in the secondary oratories, or within the cloister. It does not forbid it to be kept in the church and in the principal oratory.

By the principal oratory must be understood the place where the community takes part in certain exercises of worship, and in general makes its spiritual exercises. If several distinct communities exist in the same house, several principal oratories may be set up there; this is the case, for example, in seminaries or colleges served by a community of religious.

The novitiate certainly forms a separate community, if it is established in a building entirely distinct from the rest of the convent. If the novices dwell in a separate quarter of the same house, opinions are divided. It is sufficiently probable that they form a distinct community and may keep the Blessed Sacrament in their chapel if they assist at Mass there. In educational establishments the oratory of the boarding students is regarded as the principal one, provided it is used for all the exercises of worship, for Mass, for meetings of the sodalities, etc.[49]

146. 1. "In the churches or oratories where it is allowed to keep the Blessed Sacrament, one can have private **exposition,** that is to say, with the ciborium, for any just reason, without permission of the Ordinary. On the Feast of Corpus Christi and during the week following, it is allowed to expose the

---

[49] Response of the Commission of Interpretation, June 8, 1918. — *A.A.S.*, X (1918), 346; *Per.*, IX, 151–154.

Blessed Sacrament publicly, that is to say, in the monstrance, during Solemn Mass and Vespers; to do so at other times, a grave reason is required and permission must be had from the Ordinary of the place, even in the case of exempt religious" (c. 1274, § 1).

In some dioceses an immemorial custom authorizes the exposition of the Blessed Sacrament at certain Masses. If the Ordinary does not feel it to be his duty to suppress this custom, religious communities may profit by it.

Private exposition consists in opening the tabernacle, and bringing the ciborium a little forward so that it can be seen by the faithful. Even where the custom is established of exposing the ciborium veiled or not veiled on the upper part of the tabernacle, permission of the Ordinary is necessary for giving benediction.

By *public exposition* is meant any exposition of the Blessed Sacrament in the monstrance, even for the time of a short benediction. Such is the official interpretation given by the Commission on March 6, 1927.

2. A deacon may expose and replace the Blessed Sacrament in the tabernacle; he may not give benediction except when he has given Viaticum to a sick person (c. 1274, § 2).

3. In certain dioceses the custom has existed for more than a century of exposing the Blessed Sacrament more often and of utilizing the ciborium for solemn exposition. Religious may profit by these customs.

§ 3. PREACHING

147. 1. The authorization of the superior is always necessary for preaching before religious men. This authorization is sufficient when the audience is composed only of exempt religious, or of persons who live day and night in the house, like students, servants, boarders, etc. The preacher, whoever he may be, must always be approved by his Ordinary or by his superior.

There is no need of asking permission of the Ordinary to request a priest who is just passing by, for example, on a visit, to give the community a short instruction.[50]

2. In the lay congregations which are not exempt, the Ordinary of the place approves the preachers.

---

[50] Bastien, *D.C.,* n. 226.

In general, superiors may freely invite priests who have been approved for preaching, either to preach a special sermon or to give the exercises of a retreat.

If the bishop reserves to himself the right to appoint the preacher of the annual retreat, Father Vermeersch thought that such a restriction, unless special reasons exist for it, would not be approved by Rome (*Epitome*, I⁷, n. 649).

3. No one is allowed to preach to exempt nuns without the authorization of the Ordinary of the place, and of their regular superior.

It is probable that in the provincial councils or synods held since 1919, the bishops will have defined how the instruction on preaching of the Consistorial Congregation (June 28, 1917) must be applied in their respective dioceses.[51]

§ 4. ADMINISTRATION OF THE SACRAMENTS
A. Baptism

148. 1. A special authorization is always needed for the **baptism** of an adult in a church which is not parochial, or in a chapel of a religious community, even though it is exempt. Except in case of necessity, the authorization is to be obtained from the local Ordinary (see cc. 744, 773, 774).

2. Neither novices nor professed religious are allowed to be sponsors, except in case of necessity. Even then the permission of the superior is required, at least of the local superior (c. 766, n. 4).

B. Holy Communion

149. 1. A priest is always allowed to distribute Holy Communion during his Mass. At a low Mass, the celebrant may do so immediately before and after his Mass, and any priest may distribute Holy Communion outside the time of the Holy Sacrifice, in a place where he has the faculty to say Mass. Ordinarily Holy Communion may not be distributed except during the hours when Mass may be celebrated, that is regularly from one hour before dawn to one hour after midday. Nevertheless, any reasonable motive suffices for receiving at other times (see cc. 821, 867, 869). Regarding Holy Communion during the last three days of Holy Week, see n. 141 above.

---

[51] *A.A.S., IX* (1917), 328; *Per.*, **IX**, 31.

2. "The celebrant is not allowed to distribute Communion during Mass to those of the faithful who are so far away, that the priest would lose sight of the altar" (c. 868).

Often in religious houses the rooms of the infirmary are near a chapel. If the altar cannot be seen from the sickroom, however, Communion must be brought to the sick outside of the time of the Mass, according to the ordinary rite.

When the celebrant brings Communion to the sick before Mass, he must wear the surplice and not the alb. Immediately after Mass it is enough for him to take off the chasuble and the maniple.

When Holy Communion is distributed to a number of sick persons lodged in different stories or in different corridors of the same house, the recent instruction of the Congregation of Rites (January 9, 1929) should be followed.

C. Viaticum and Extreme Unction

150. 1. In every institute of clerics, the superiors have the right and the duty of administering by themselves or by others **Viaticum** and **Extreme Unction** to the sick professed, novices, and other persons who live day and night in the religious house, by reason of employment or education, hospitality or sickness.

When one of these persons becomes seriously ill outside the convent, it rests with the religious superior to administer Viaticum and Extreme Unction to the professed religious and novices; all the others (postulants, boarders, etc.) should receive these sacraments from the parish priest (Commission of Interpretation, June 16, 1931. — *A.A.S.*, XXIII [1931], 353. — *R.C.R.* [1931], 177).

2. In the case of nuns, it is the confessor's right and duty to administer the last sacraments. If he is absent, sick, or hindered, the right goes to the one who habitually or provisionally for the time being replaces him. Evidently the confessor can delegate for this purpose the chaplain of the community (see c. 514, § 2).

In lay religious institutes this function falls to the parish priest, unless the community has been withdrawn from his jurisdiction. In such a case the chaplain will be competent.

In Belgian dioceses the chaplain of all religious laymen administers the last sacraments to the professed, novices, postulants, and to all the persons who habitually live in the convent (see Council of Malines, 1937, n. 181).

3. Sometimes the Ordinary, in the document which he gives when appointing the ordinary confessor of the religious men, includes the power of administering the last sacraments.

D. Sacrament of Orders

151. We believe it helpful to point out here some prescriptions concerning the *Ordinations* of religious:

1. No religious may be promoted to holy orders during the duration of his temporary profession (every privilege to the contrary is revoked), nor may he receive the tonsure before having begun his theological studies (cc. 964, 976).

2. "Those who contract or attempt to contract marriage, even a civil one, while bound by the religious vows, even simple and temporary, or those who attempt such with a woman bound by similar vows, incur an *irregularity* ex delicto" (c. 985, 3).

3. The Bishop of the place where the Ordinandus resides may determine, even for exempt religious, the form and the matter of the theological examination required before ordination and may appoint the examiners. This right may be equally exercised by the ordaining Bishop, when the institute has the privilege of presenting its subjects to any Bishop whomsoever (cc. 996, 997).

4. Before ordination to the subdiaconate, the aptitude of the candidate will be the object of a serious inquiry. He himself must sign under oath a statement to the effect that he knows and freely accepts the obligations of ecclesiastical celibacy and that he is ready to obey faithfully his legitimate ecclesiastical and religious superiors (see Appendix II, n. 17, p. 295).

5. When a religious is ordained subdeacon, his superiors must be sure to notify the pastor of the church where the newly ordained subdeacon was baptized, that the ordination may be duly registered (c. 1011).

§ 5. FUNERALS

152. "**Ecclesiastical burial** consists in the transfer of the body of the deceased to the church, the funeral services, and in the burial in a place lawfully appointed for the interment of the faithful" (c. 1204).

1. *Exempt* religious, even nuns with simple vows, have a

canonical right to possess a private cemetery, distinct from the common cemetery used by all the faithful (c. 1208, § 2). *Nonexempt* communities must obtain permission from the Ordinary to have a place of burial distinct from the common cemetery and blessed as a cemetery (c. 1208, § 3).

2. If one of the faithful should desire to be interred in the cemetery of religious, the written permission of the superior is required and is sufficient. The constitutions will determine which superior is competent and the authority of the chapter or council in the matter (c. 1209, § 1; c. 1228, § 2).

3. The novices have the right to choose their place of burial and the church where their funeral will take place. They lose this right when they make their profession (cc. 1221, 1224). Postulants, however, do not share this privilege (cf. Commission of Interpretation, July 20, 1929, IV).

4. The superior may authorize the parents of the deceased religious to bury him in the family vault. The funeral, however, must be conducted according to the rules laid down below.

153. *In Institutes of Men.*

1. "A deceased religious must be translated for the funeral service to the church or oratory of his own religious house, or at least to a church or oratory of the institute . . . (c. 1221, § 1).

2. "If a religious dies far away from his religious house, so that the body could not be conveniently transported to the church of his house or at least of his institute, the funeral service must take place in the church of the parish where he dies . . ." (c. 1221, § 2).

The superior always has the right to bring the body of the deceased at his own expense to a house of the institute.

3. Novices are treated as the professed in this matter, unless they have made a choice of some particular church for their funeral (c. 1221, §§ 1 and 2).

4. Servants who have a domicile or quasi-domicile in a religious house are treated as novices in regard to burial if they die in the house; but if they die outside the religious house, they are buried as the rest of the faithful (c. 1221, § 3).

5. The funeral services are conducted by the religious superior if he is a priest; otherwise by the chaplain of the house,

if there be one, or by the parish priest (cf. Brys, *Compendium*, II, n. 759, v).

154. *In Institutes of Women.*

1. In exempt monasteries and in religious houses of sisters which are not under the jurisdiction of the parish priest, the *chaplain* conducts the funeral services of the religious and the novices who have died in the house (c. 1230, § 5).

2. In other convents it is the parish priest who has the right of holding the funeral services, and in the parish church, unless particular law has made some special provision.

3. If a religious woman or novice has died outside the house, the funeral service will be carried on in the place where she died, or in the church of the convent, as has been said in n. **153.**

4. Canonists are not agreed on the law which governs the funerals of the *servants* of religious houses. Father Vermeersch thought that they should be conducted by the chaplain of the religious house in the church or oratory of the community, if this was withdrawn from the authority of the parish priest; others think that the common law should be observed.[52]

5. The priest may not enter into the cloister and, therefore, the religious themselves will accompany the mortal remains of their sister to the portal of the cloister.

Article 4. Temporal Goods and Their Administration

§ 1. GENERAL NOTIONS

155. 1. Temporal goods include all material things which possess an economic value, that is to say, a value in use or exchange which can be computed in money, for example, land, a house, furniture, clothing, stocks and bonds. A manuscript will be a temporal possession if it can be sold for money, for instance, a manuscript of a book or pamphlet which could be printed and sold by publishers. On the contrary, notes intended merely for personal use are not considered as a temporal possession.

From the point of view which we are now taking, we must distinguish between two sorts of goods: those which by their

---

[52] Cf. Vermeersch-Creusen, *Epitome*, II⁷, n. 530. J. Brys, *Iuris Canonici Compendium*, II, 759, V, 5°.

nature have a durable character and are not destroyed by use, such as a field, a house, furniture, and those which perish by use, such as the natural products of the soil, the progeny of animals.

2. In our economic system money may be used in two ways: it may be consumed by donation or by exchange for other non-productive goods; it may be capitalized or converted into permanent investments of equal value and productive of revenue.

156. 1. The *administration* of goods includes all acts intended to preserve and to improve material goods according to their purpose and their nature.

2. *Alienation* of goods consists in acts which transfer the right of ownership, either wholly or in part, of personal or real property. Such acts are sale, free gift, exchange, mortgage, leasing, etc.

Alienation *under onerous title* means the exchange of property for a consideration, that is, for some other property of equivalent value, or considered as such; in alienation *under gratuitous title* the donor receives no consideration, that is, he receives no compensation equal to the property given.

A wise management of property almost always supposes alienations of property under onerous title, for example, the sale of produce for which the owner has no personal need, the renting of real property which he does not wish to use himself, etc. In ordinary legal language, acts of administration include those intended to keep up the value of the patrimony, and those only are considered acts of real alienation which lessen the value of the patrimony.

3. By the *investment of money* we mean any disposition of it which assures its preservation, at least in an equivalent form, or which makes it produce revenues or fruits (for example, the purchase of productive real estate, of stocks and bonds). Certain investments hardly differ from a *deposit*, because the investor retains almost his entire liberty of disposing of the funds invested, and the interest received is very small. Such are deposits made at a bank for a short space of time, or which can be recalled at will, or deposits in a running account, etc.

157. *To contract an obligation* means to give another the right to demand payment in kind, or the performance or omission of an act. *To contract a debt* almost always means to oblige oneself to pay a sum of money within a specified time, or to supply something of equivalent value.

The monetary unit used in the documents of the Holy See is always the franc or the lire which units in normal times are readily convertible into the money of other nations by reducing them to their gold value of 1914, at the time the Code of Canon Law was being composed.[53] Thus $6,000 gold U.S. dollars were considered the equivalent of 30,000 gold lire, and for the convenience of our readers we give all sums of money in U.S. gold dollars throughout this text.

[EDITOR'S NOTE: Two world wars within twenty-five years have disrupted the monetary systems of the world; a general remedy for this situation was provided by a decree of the S. Consistorial Congregation issued on July 13, 1951, declaring that "as long as present conditions last and subject to the will of the Holy See, recourse must be had to the same Apostolic See whenever there is question of a sum of money which exceeds ten thousand gold francs or lire."[54] On January 29, 1953, the Sacred Congregation of Religious published the present-day equivalents of 10,000 gold francs or lire for the principal countries of the world, designating 5,000 current U.S. dollars as the equivalent for all the countries of North and Central America. Since this legislation is temporary, we have left in the present text the sums mentioned in the Code of Canon Law in their equivalents of U.S. gold dollars of 1914. We wish to remind our readers, however, that the Apostolic Delegate in Washington may "permit the contraction of loans, sales, and alienations of property belonging to a religious institute, when the sum involved does not exceed a half million dollars" (Bouscaren-Ellis, *Canon Law: A Text and Commentary*, ed. 3, 1957, p. 251).

158. Canon law subjects the administration and above all the alienation of ecclesiastical property to detailed and strict prescriptions. These provisions may seem rather minute when there is question of property of religious institutes, especially of those of women. What is their purpose? It is to preserve superiors from the disastrous consequences of inexperience in these matters, to safeguard property destined for the support of the whole community, or the keeping up of good works, to avoid the despoiling of houses, of precious objects, whose value for the moment is not sufficiently appreciated, such as valuable books, objects of art, etc. The Sacred Congregation of Religious itself informs us that the necessity for limiting the contracting of debts and the borrowing of money was made necessary by the imprudence and the excesses of certain superiors. Good works undertaken without sufficient resources by means of money borrowed without security "are contrary to the spirit of the

---

[53] See Vermeersch-Creusen, *Epitome*, I⁷, n. 657; Ellis, in *Periodica*, XXVII, 348.

[54] *A.A.S.*, XXXXIII (1951), 602; *R.R.*, XI (1952), 301 sq.; XII (1953), 134, 150.

apostolic prescriptions, they cannot be agreeable to God and they will not secure for the neighbor a lasting good."[55]

In this matter, we ought rather to imitate the obedience of the saints to the prescriptions of the common law rather than to follow their extraordinary initiative justified by special inspiration of God.

§ 2. ACQUISITION AND ADMINISTRATION OF TEMPORAL GOODS

159. "Not only every institute, but every province, and every house is capable of acquiring and possessing property with fixed or founded revenues, unless the capacity to do so be excluded or restricted by its rules and constitutions" (c. 531).

Since the Council of Trent, all orders have the right to possess property in common, except the Friars Minor and the Capuchins. Certain exceptions to it are also made in the constitutions of the Society of Jesus.

The constitutions may prescribe that provincial or local superiors must contribute a part of the annual net income of the province or house to the general treasury. It would be entirely contrary to the actual practice of the Holy See to oblige these superiors to give to the mother-house all the surplus of the annual revenues. In any case, such an order would exceed the powers of a superior general except in very special circumstances.

The *Normae,* Ed. 1, paragraph 294, read as follows: "Every house which has a surplus shall send each year at the end of the year the third part of its net surplus to the provincial treasury, after having balanced its accounts and deducted all its expenses, and each province shall, in the same way, contribute the third part of its net surplus to the general treasury of the institute."

To determine what is the net surplus, not only the interest of the monies that have been borrowed, but the annual sum required for gradually paying off the debt itself must be deducted. The surplus of which a third part must be sent to the provincial or general treasury is that of the year which has just passed. It is not required, therefore, to pay another third on sums which have been left over from preceding years, and of which a third has already been paid.

To forbid local superiors to set up reserve funds, or to demand that they should give to their higher superiors all the net surplus of the year which has just passed, would be contrary: (1) to the relative independence which the common law of the Church recognizes in each religious community (cc. 531, 536, § 1); (2) to the security of local houses which would thus share all the financial risks of the motherhouse; (3) to the intention of certain benefactors who wish to help the works of the individual community; (4) even to the interest of the institute

---

[55] See Battandier, *G.C.,* n. 469.

itself which would thus do away with the precious stimulus of the foresight and the zeal of local superiors.[56]

On the other hand, it is just that the houses co-operate in the common projects of the province, and the provinces in those which pertain to the whole institute. This is especially the case in religious institutes which require a long time to train their subjects, or which have accepted work in missionary lands.

The spiritual progress of each house, and sometimes the temporal well-being also, are concerned in the maintenance and development of novitiates, juniorates, houses of study, missionary seminaries, etc.

160. "The property of the institute, of the province, and of the house is to be administered conformably to the constitutions.

"Besides superiors, those officials also who are empowered by the constitutions can, within the limits of their office, validly incur expenses and perform the juridical acts of ordinary administration" (c. 532).

This idea of "acts of ordinary administration" is not interpreted in the same way by all the authors. The best way to distinguish these from extraordinary acts of administration seems to be to weigh the specific purpose and specific procedure of an individual transaction. Anything exceeding this purpose and procedure (generally determined by particular law) is an act of "extraordinary" administration.[57]

The Holy See had emphasized even before the promulgation of the Code that superiors have a grave obligation to inform their council with all sincerity about the management of temporal affairs, and to submit such matters for deliberate vote of their council when this is prescribed; the counsellors or consultors have a grave obligation to exercise the control which is entrusted to their vigilance by the common law of the Church or by particular constitutions.[58]

161. Besides the formalities required by the constitutions, the superiors must ask the previous consent of the Ordinary for **investments of money,** and for the changes which have to be made in them, according to the following rules:

a) The superiors of nuns or of houses belonging to a diocesan institute must ask this consent for every investment.

[56] See Battandier, *G.C.,* n. 474.
[57] See Gutierrez, C.M.F., *Acta et Documenta Congr. Gen.,* 1950, I, 564. D. Huot, S.M.M., holds the same opinion in *Comm. pro. rel.,* 1955, 61.
[58] See *Normae,* Ed. 1, 2nd part, Chap. VI; Decree *Inter ea,* July 30, 1909.

In virtue of the legal principle: "a very small quantity is regarded as nothing" (*parum pro nihilo reputatur*), there is no need of having recourse to the bishop for investments which have no importance in proportion to the habitual expenses of the monastery, for example, to buy three or four bonds worth five or ten dollars each in a monastery which is fairly well off. Usually the Ordinary or his delegate will leave instructions sufficient to resolve particular cases of this kind.

b) The superior of a congregation approved by the Holy See must ask this permission when there is question of the dowry of the professed (see n. **187**).

c) The superior or the superioress of a house of a religious congregation must ask this consent if the funds have been given or left as a bequest to be applied to divine worship or to works of charity in the locality.

This would be the case in regard to funds given or left for a foundation for Masses; the capital, whose revenue is to serve for the keeping up of an oratory or an altar, belonging to a confraternity or to a pious union established in the convent; or whose revenues are to serve for the maintenance of orphans, the sick, the old. If a benefactor gives the superior a certain sum of money to spend according to his intentions, within a space of time more or less fixed, the superior should not invest it, but should keep it and devote it, without further permission, to the use assigned by the donor.

In this case the approval of the council is not required, since the superior is merely the executor of the will of the donor. If the latter has expressed no preference in the choice of the beneficiaries, the superior should conform himself to the directions of the constitutions regarding the distribution of alms.

d) Every religious, even a regular, must ask the bishop's consent to invest money which has been given to the parish, or to the mission, or to the religious for the benefit of the parish or mission (c. 533, §§ 1, 4).

In this last hypothesis, if the principal intention of the benefactor has been to help the institute or the good works of the institute, the money becomes entirely their property, and they need not obtain permission of the bishop for the use which they make of it. This would be the case, unless there is proof to the contrary, in regard to gifts made to a missionary by his friends or his relatives, or by a benefactor who is known for his sentiments of good will towards the institute. When donations are made to the rector of a church, even a church of religious, the law presumes in the donor the intention to help the church

(c. 1536). In regard to this distinction which sometimes is rather subtle, consult the dissertation of Father Vermeersch, *Per.*, VI, suppl. XVII, and Vromant, *De bonis Eccl. temp.*, n. 65 sqq.

§ 3. ALIENATION OF PROPERTY[59]

162. All alienation of ecclesiastical property requires:

a) a grave motive;

b) the appraising of the value by reputable experts;

c) the sale to the highest bidder;

d) the secure investment of the money which is thus acquired (cc. 1530, 1531).

There is question here only of alienation properly so called, i.e., of the transfer from one proprietor to another of goods which can be preserved and which are the permanent property of a moral person (parish, church, religious house, institute, etc.). *Ecclesiastical property* is that which belongs to a *moral ecclesiastical person,* such as a community, province, or institute. Property belonging to a physical person (an individual) is never classed as ecclesiastical property. Consequently, the canons (534, 1530, etc.), dealing with the alienation of property do not apply to the personal property of religious.

163. A. *The Previous Authorization of the Holy See Is Required:*

1. To alienate:

a) Noteworthy **relics,** pious images of value, or other relics and images to which the faithful have a special devotion (c. 1281).

By noteworthy relics are meant the body, the head, the arm, the forearm, the heart, the tongue, the hand, the leg, and also the part of the body in which a martyr has suffered if it is entire and quite large (*ibid.,* § 2). Precious images are those which are noteworthy for their antiquity, or their artistic value, or the veneration of which they are the object (c. 1280). Evidently, only the first of the conditions required in n. **162** is applicable to relics, since relics may not be sold.

b) **Precious objects** which can be kept.

"By precious objects is meant those which have a notable value, for artistic or historical reasons or because of the material of which they are made" (c. 1497).

---

[59] Instruction *Inter ea,* July 30, 1909, Vermeersch, *Per.,* V, pp. 1 sqq.; *N.R. Th.,* t. 41 (1909), 689; *Coll. Gand.,* II (1910), 89; *Coll. Torn.,* January, 1910 (supplement), 369.

There is question here of movable goods. Such would be, for example, collections, books, libraries, works of art, vases and ornaments, etc. Their value is notable when it amounts to $200. (See Genicot-Salsmans, *Instit. theol. mor.*, 17th ed., II, n. 958. Vermeersch, *De relig.*, I, n. 236).

It is allowed, without authorization of the Holy See, to sell for a sum less than $6,000, different objects none of which are precious. It is well to keep in mind that such objects as a complete set of volumes of a work, all the wood carving of a room or a staircase, a stamp collection, etc., would be regarded as one piece of property.

c) **Other property** the value of which exceeds $6,000.

There is question here of real estate or of a collection of movable goods that is not precious. When, by one moral act, the same ecclesiastical person alienates one or several pieces of real estate, or a collection of movable goods, the value of which exceeds $6,000, the authorization of the Holy See must be obtained. (Commission of Interpretation, July 20, 1929, *A.A.S.*, 1929, p. 573.) Thus, for example, were the superior of a religious community who needed ready money, to offer for sale three pieces of land valued at $2,000, $3,000, and $4,000 respectively, he would have to obtain the authorization of the Holy See.

2. For contracting **debts** or **obligations** the value of which exceeds $6,000 (c. 534, § 1).

B. For sums less than $6,000, it is necessary and sufficient to obtain the written permission of the superior, according to the constitutions, with the consent of the council or the chapter given by secret vote; but nuns and sisters of a diocesan congregation must have besides the written consent of the local Ordinary as well as the consent of the regular superior when the monastery of nuns is subject to regulars (c. 534, § 1).

Generally the Ordinary specifies, as do the constitutions, the amount for which special permission is necessary. Even in the absence of such a determination, this formality may be dispensed with if there is question of insignificant amounts.

164. 1. The request for authorization to contract debts must specify, under pain of nullity, the other debts or obligations with which the moral person in question is already burdened, whether it be an institute, a province, or a house.

2. The debts and loans which may be paid each year from the certain revenues do not require a special authorization. These are not regarded as obligations which burden the budget of the community, but rather they are classed among extraordinary or ordinary current expenses.

3. When a community contracts several debts or alienates several

pieces of property within a short space of time, these acts become morally one. Hence the authorization of the Holy See is required to accept two loans at short intervals, e.g., one for $4,000, the other for $2,500. But if the acts in question are sufficiently separated in time, and when in good faith one has not foreseen the need of the second loan at the time the first loan was accepted, there would seem to be no need of adding the two sums together and of considering them as one.

4. When requests are made for authorization, attention is to be paid only to the estimates made by experts and not to the most advantageous offers which might be made by the purchaser. Hence, there is no need of asking permission of the Holy See for selling at $6,200 a piece of real property estimated at $5,900. (See the answer of Card. Gasparri, *A.A.S.*, XII [1920], 577.)

§ 4. SPECIAL SANCTIONS AND PENALTIES

165. The Holy See sanctions the directions concerning the alienation of property and the contracting of debts by very severe penalties.

1. The following acts are null and void if authorization has not been received:

a) the alienation of notable relics and pious images (n. **163, 1, a**);

b) the alienation of precious objects (n. **163**, 1, b);

c) the alienation of goods exceeding $6,000 in value (n. **163, 1, c**);

d) the contracts for loans, for debts and obligations exceeding $6,000 in value (n. **163, 2**).

2. Excommunication is incurred by all those who, while knowing the law and the punishment for its violation, have failed to ask the authorization of the Holy See for disposing of any precious object or ecclesiastical goods of a value exceeding $6,000. This penalty falls on the ecclesiastical superior and the Ordinary or a visitor who authorizes the alienation, for example, the sale of a religious house; the religious superior who is responsible in the matter, and the counsellors who have decided or approved the act also fall under penalty (see c. 2347).

166. Those who make a contract are subject to its obligations. This principle must be applied to the community which acts for itself; to the superior who authorizes a regular to make any (no matter what) contract; to superiors who give a religious of simple vows authorization to act for the community; to a religious of simple vows who acts on his own account; and to every religious who acts without permission.

"In every case it is a rule that action can always be brought against him for whom the contract has been a source of profit" (c. 536, § 4). No one, in fact, is allowed to enrich himself at the expense of another.

The mediate or higher superior who has given the permission required by law to enter into a contract is not responsible to the creditor. Such permission merely renders the contract valid in the eyes of the ecclesiastical law. Thus, the Holy See does not guarantee loans obtained with its permission; the moral person making the contract (institute, province, house) alone is responsible. This should be kept in mind in those localities in which loans are readily made to communities, on the supposition that the authorization of major superiors is considered as a guarantee of payment. In such cases, unless the matter is made clear at the time of the loan, equity would impose a grave obligation of paying the debts of a bankrupt community upon the superiors who authorized the contract.

The Code wisely adds the following prescription: "Superiors must beware not to allow the contracting of debts unless it be certain that the interest on them may be met from current revenue, and that within a reasonable time the capital may be paid off by means of a lawful sinking fund" (c. 536, § 5).

§ 5. RENDERING OF ACCOUNTS TO THE ORDINARY
(c. 535)

167. 1. For every monastery of nuns, even exempt:

a) the superioress must furnish an account of her financial administration, to be exacted gratuitously, once a year, or even oftener if the constitutions so prescribe it, to the local Ordinary, as well as to the regular superior, if the monastery be subject to regulars;

b) if the Ordinary does not approve of the account of the administration furnished him, he can apply the necessary remedies, including even the removal from office, if the circumstances demand it, of the bursar and the other administrators; but if the monastery be subject to a regular superior, the Ordinary shall request him to see to it; and if the regular superior fails to do so, then the Ordinary himself must deal with the case.

2. In the other religious institutes of women, the account of

the administration of the property constituted by the dowries shall be furnished to the local Ordinary on the occasion of the visitation, and even oftener if the Ordinary considers it necessary.

This is the extent of the rights of the Ordinary concerning the management of property which belongs entirely to congregations approved by the Holy See.

3. The local Ordinary has also the right of inquiring into:

a) the economic state of every religious house with diocesan approval;

b) the administration of the funds and bequests referred to in n. 161, c, d (c. 533, § 1, nos. 3, 4; c. 535).

§ 6. ALMS AND GIFTS

168. It is severely forbidden to religious to make presents out of the goods of a house, province, or institute, but this sin is no longer reserved to the Holy See (c. 537).

Superiors evidently may, and even ought, to make alms proportionate to the resources of the community and to make certain gifts required by gratitude or which seem suitable.

169. Religious societies (n. 18), their provinces, and houses have the legal capacity to acquire and possess temporal goods. For the administration and alienation of these goods they must observe cc. 533–537 explained in the foregoing.

PART TWO

THE RELIGIOUS LIFE

SECTION I

Admission Into Religion

170. "Every Catholic who is not debarred by any legitimate impediment and is inspired by a right intention, and is fit to bear the burdens of the religious life, can be admitted into religion" (c. 538).

In these concise terms the legislator sums up the essential conditions and the sufficient signs of vocation to the religious life.[1] If this formula were proposed to the faithful, it would dispel many misunderstandings, and it would tend to encourage those souls who hesitate too much. Grace alone can inspire the thoughtful and constant will to serve God more perfectly by the practice of the evangelical counsels. This will, therefore, is a sign of the divine invitation. But the presence of an obstacle which the subject cannot do away with of his own accord, or the lack of aptitude, would suffice to show that this desire is the result of a call to a more perfect life in general, and not of a vocation to the religious life in particular.

CHAPTER IV

The Postulancy

171. The **postulancy** is a time of probation which is preliminary to the taking of the habit. It should give the superiors an opportunity to observe the candidates, and the candidates an opportunity to become acquainted with the obligations of the religious life.

This institution of the postulancy has been quite recently brought under uniform rules by the canon law.

172. "In religious institutes with perpetual vows all the women and, in institutes of men, the lay brothers must, before being

---

[1] See J. B. Raus, C.SS.R., *La vocation religieuse* in *N.R. Th.* (1924), 14 sqq., 94 sqq.

admitted to the novitiate, make a postulancy of at least six whole months; but in the religious institutes with temporary vows the prescriptions of the constitutions regarding the necessity and duration of the postulancy are to be followed" (c. 539, § 1).

The constitutions may impose for all subjects a longer time of postulancy; the higher superior may prolong the time prescribed in particular cases, but never beyond another term of six months (c. 539, § 2).

The statutes of outdoor sisters (S. Congregation of Religious, July 16, 1931) require a year of postulancy for them. It can also be prolonged six months (art. 21).[2]

The text of canon 539, § 2, says "beyond another term of six months," but "the prescribed time" seems to us to apply just as well to the time fixed in the constitutions as to the six months required by the Code.[3]

For a serious motive the time of the postulancy may be shortened by a few days. This may be done, for example, so as not to delay the taking of a habit of the postulant two or three months, when the postulant has been unavoidably detained in the world for several days after the official day for entering. If a postulant was obliged to be absent during several days, the postulancy is not considered interrupted. Where the absence is somewhat prolonged, it will suffice to add the number of lost days to the six months prescribed.

It is well to note that the Code requires *at least* six months of postulancy. Hence mere convenience does not justify its curtailment even by a few days.

173. 1. "The postulancy must be made either in the novitiate house or in some other house of the institute where the discipline prescribed by the constitutions is faithfully observed, under the special care of an experienced religious" (c. 540, § 1).

A woman postulant may thus finish her studies, or give a course of lectures in a school annexed to the motherhouse, or to another important house of the institute where observance is very regular. She ought evidently to live in the religious house and to give a certain time there, under the direction of an experienced religious, to daily religious exercises and to reading, which will give her an opportunity of becoming acquainted with her future obligations.

[2] *A.A.S.*, XXIII (1931), 380. — *R.C.R.* (1931), 180 sq.
[3] This opinion is held in common by Bastien, *D.C.*, n. 406[6]; Battandier, *G.C.*, n. 123; Vermeersch, *Epitome*, I[7], n. 666, 2; Goyeneche, *De religiosis*, n. 43; Berutti, O.P., *Inst. i. c.*, III, p. 134.

In institutes where the cloister is less strict, it is not forbidden to allow a woman postulant to go out, for example, to pass an examination. It is not advisable to allow the postulant to visit her family at the end of the postulancy. Enough proofs that her entry to the novitiate is altogether of her free choice are furnished by the ecclesiastical legislation, by the interrogation made by the bishop, and by the liberty of seeing her parents in the parlor. Far from being a consolation, this return to one's family sometimes renews in the relatives all the regrets and opposition of the first separation.

2. "The postulants are to wear a becoming dress, different, however, from that of the novices" (c. 540, § 2).

It is hardly practical to give postulants a uniform because they would use it for such a short time. In institutes of women the frequent practice is to add a bonnet or a veil to the ordinary secular costume. Sometimes it is useful to call to the attention of the women postulants that their costumes should be perfectly modest. The formula of the Code certainly authorizes superiors to give postulants a religious habit.

3. In monasteries of nuns the aspirants, during their postulancy, are bound by the law of enclosure (c. 540, § 3).

The Instruction of March 25, 1956, on the cloister of nuns repeats this obligation (n. 10). They (postulants) enter into the cloister with the sole permission of the local Ordinary (n. 34). They are not allowed to leave it on the occasion of the reception of the habit (n. 19), but only to return definitely to the world when they leave of their own accord or at the request of superiors (n. 10).

It should be noted, however, that were a postulant to leave the cloister she would not incur the excommunication which is inflicted by law on nuns who are guilty of this fault (c. 2342, 3).

Candidates who wish to be outdoor sisters make their postulancy in the house in which their professed companions live.

174. Except the constitutions or a formal agreement require the payment of a certain sum for food and clothing during the postulancy, nothing can be exacted to defray the expense of the postulancy (c. 570, § 1).

If the postulant leaves the institute without entering the novitiate, all that he brought with him and that has not been consumed by use shall be returned to him (c. 570, § 2).

175. Before beginning the novitiate the postulants must make a spiritual retreat of at least eight entire days; and, according to the discretion of the confessor, a general confession of their past life (c. 541).

Although nothing is determined with regard to the number and nature of the spiritual exercises, they should constitute a real retreat. This follows from the fact that the same words are used to designate the retreats imposed on candidates for holy orders (c. 1001), on priests (c. 126), and on religious (c. 595, § 1). Now both custom and pontifical documents on the "spiritual exercises" suppose that the retreatant put aside all other occupations and devote himself during some days to the exercises of the retreat (mental prayer, examen of conscience, spiritual reading, etc.).

Before the promulgation of the Code several responses from Rome had already censured the custom of counting among the days of retreat those days on which only one instruction was given at the beginning or the end of the retreat. For retreats preparatory to the taking of the habit and for the first profession, the text of the Code speaks in a manner which admits of no doubt: they must be at least eight entire days (cc. 541, 571). When the retreat is begun, for example, on the 10th of the month in the evening, or on the 11th in the morning, the retreat may not finish before the evening of the 18th.

176. In this chapter and in the one that follows, it is worth noting that the rather strict prescriptions imposed for some years regarding the reception of lay brothers, have been suppressed. This suppression may, without doubt, be explained in part by the extension of the temporary profession, which may last six years, to all religious men.

177. The prescriptions which relate to the postulancy do not affect the validity of the admission. Though their violation in certain cases may constitute a grave fault, it will not make the admission or the subsequent profession invalid.

CHAPTER V

The Novitiate

Article 1. Conditions of Admission

§ 1. IMPEDIMENTS

178. In the admission of subjects attention should be called to the **impediments** established by the canon law or by the constitutions. Only the Holy See can dispense from the first class of impediments. From the second class the Holy See grants dispensations for pontifical institutes, the local Ordinary for a diocesan congregation. The constitutions, however, may grant to the superior general and to his council the power to dispense from the impediments of particular law.

The impediments of the common law affect either the validity or the lawfulness of admission; those of particular law regard only lawfulness, unless the constitutions expressly state the contrary.

The Code has suppressed certain impediments, even some which are of rather recent date. Thus, it leaves much greater liberty to the judgment of superiors. This should be an additional reason for them to observe very exactly the prescriptions, which are expressed in rather severe terms, on the subject of the testimonial letters demanded for each candidate.

A. Impediments to Valid Admission

179. The following persons cannot be validly admitted to the novitiate (c. 542):

a) Those who have voluntarily **joined a non-Catholic or atheistic sect** (Commission of Interpretation, response of July 30, 1934. — *A.A.S.*, XXVI [1934], 494. — *R.C.R.* [1934], 176).

According to the official interpretation,[1] this impediment is incurred only by those who have apostatized from the Catholic Church and joined a sect. A person who is brought up in heresy or atheism, even

---

[1] Commission of Interpretation. Response of October 16, 1919. — *A.A.S.*, XI (1919), 477.

though he continued in it after the age of reason, does not incur this impediment. Secret societies, for example, the Free Masons, are not usually meant by the words "non-Catholic sect," unless they make a profession of atheism.

b) Those who have not **completed** their **fifteenth year.**

The fifteenth birthday may not be counted in these fifteen years. Thus, a candidate who was born on the 15th of January, 1926, may not be admitted to the novitiate before the 16th of January, 1941 (see n. **195**).

c) Those who enter religion under the influence of **violence, grave fear** or **fraud;** also those whom the superior receives under pressure of the same influences.

1. To be an impediment, moral constraint must have for its object entrance into religion. If a young lady should hasten her entrance into religion solely or principally so as to be able to leave people from whom she had received bad treatment, this fact alone would not make her consent invalid.

Note that entry into religion consists in the entry into the novitiate. If, therefore, a candidate had been morally constrained to enter into the postulancy, and there had decided of her own free choice to embrace the religious life, the reception into the novitiate would be valid. Evidently the superior must be certain that the applicant is acting with full liberty, and it would be prudent to keep written proof to this effect.

The fear which is called reverential, namely, that which children feel towards their parents or towards a guardian who has authority over them, is not regarded as grave of its nature. When the child is of a specially timid disposition, it may easily become grave; there is no doubt that it is grave if it results from repeated reproaches and from threats addressed to children by their parents, elders or guardians. If it is proved that one has entered religion for the sole or prevailing motive of desiring to escape from this sort of moral constraint, the admission is invalid.

The Church punishes very severely those who try to constrain the liberty of others in such a serious matter. Excommunication is at once incurred by all those who, in any manner whatever, force either a man or woman into religion, or to make profession, even though the profession were only simple and temporary (c. 2352).

Under former legislation the sanction was much less general.

2. Fraud exists when by dishonest means, by deceitful tricks, one gets another to perform a certain action. This would be the case, for example, in the present instance if parents made their child believe that they had promised to God that he would enter religion when, as a matter of fact, they had made no such promise, or if someone falsely persuaded another that he had the evident signs of a divine vocation.

If the postulant has concealed a disease or a family disgrace which he knew or suspected would certainly have caused his exclusion, his admission is invalid, and the profession would also be invalid.

d) Married persons, **as long as the marriage bonds last.**

In this case the mutual consent of the married persons would not be sufficient; a dispensation from the Holy See would be required. A wife abandoned by her husband, especially if he live in adultery, does not need his consent to enter religion. One may see in the *R.C.R.*, 1939, under what conditions her entry into religion may be obtained.

But even when a husband has committed adultery, and his wife is not bound in any way to resume married life, we believe that she must obtain a dispensation from the Holy See in order to enter religion.

e) Those who are or who have been bound by the bonds of religious profession.

Whoever has left a religious institute after having taken vows, even though only temporary vows, cannot validly re-enter the same institute, nor be admitted validly into any other institute, without an indult from the Holy See. It makes no difference whether the person in question was dismissed, or left of his own accord, during or after the time of his profession. Simple promises made in a society without vows do not have this effect.

f) Those who are menaced with **punishment** for the commission of a grave crime of which they have been or can be accused.

A civil crime which results from an unjust law or decree does not cause this impediment. Such would be the case of a priest threatened with punishment for having rightfully exercised his ministry, even against the prohibition of the law, or for having defended the rights of the Church against an unjust violation. The Code speaks of a grave crime, and these words indicate a special gravity because every crime supposes a grave fault. Hence, the danger of having to submit to a penalty for the breaking of some police regulation, for failing to pay duty, etc., would not render invalid the admission into religion. The mere *possibility* of being brought to judgment would not be enough to constitute a "menace," for a menace supposes the *probability* of the denunciation or of an unfavorable judgment. The good name of the religious state may, nevertheless, require more caution in such a case.

g) A **bishop,** whether residential or titular, even though only nominated by the Roman Pontiff.

h) Clerics who by a disposition of the Holy See are bound by oath to consecrate themselves to the service of their diocese or the missions, for the period during which their oath binds them.

When a cleric is not ordained on the title of a benefice, of a patrimony, or of a pension, he may substitute the title of the service of the diocese or of the missions in territories under the jurisdiction of the Sacred Congregation of Propaganda. In this case the candidate for orders must promise to consecrate himself to the service of the diocese or the mission (c. 981).

This impediment, however, does not seem to refer to the *general* provision of c. 981, since c. 542 makes no reference to it as a determinant. Yet such references are common in the Code. Moreover, the terms employed in the canon seem to imply a *special* provision of the Holy See which creates a transient obligation.[2]

Nevertheless those who have promised never, without special authorization of the Holy See, to leave their diocese or mission in order to enter religion, are, as is evident, bound to keep this promise.

N.B. The disabilities mentioned in the foregoing affect even those who are ignorant of them (c. 16).

B. Impediments to Licit Admission

180. 1. Though the admission would be valid, it is forbidden to admit to the novitiate (c. 542, 2):

a) Clerics in sacred orders, without the knowledge of the local Ordinary or against his will if his objection is based on the serious loss to souls that their withdrawal would impart, when that loss cannot by any means be otherwise avoided.

The terms of the Code are remarkable for their precision, and they correspond perfectly with the traditional doctrine in this matter. Secular clerics are entirely free to enter into religion before the subdiaconate. As soon as they have taken this decisive step towards the priesthood, they may not leave the diocesan clergy, even to follow a higher vocation, without having taken counsel of their bishop. It is very natural that the ecclesiastical law should oblige them to this mark of deference demanded by so many titles. But the Church affirms even here the entire liberty of everyone to follow the call to a state of perfection, and no one needs the permission of a superior to do so. Still, if the departure of a cleric who has received major orders deprives souls of help which is gravely

---

[2] Father Vermeersch held as certain that this article has to do solely with the students of certain ecclesiastical colleges, ordained with the temporary promise to consecrate themselves to the service of the diocese (*Epitome*, I^r, n. 680). This is also the opinion of Toso, *Jus Pont.*, 1929, 95, and of Berutti, O.P., *Institutiones*, III, 143. Larraona regards this opinion as really probable. Cf. *Comm. pro rel.* (1926), 232 sq.

needed, and which cannot be supplied by others, the Ordinary is certainly authorized to enjoin the prohibition which the divine law then imposes. In case of doubt the cleric ought evidently to submit himself to the prohibition laid on him by his legitimate superior.

How can this disposition of the law be reconciled with the opinion of those who see in clerics regular only clergy of a second class on the fringe of the hierarchy, and who consider the entrance of a secular priest into religion a step downward or an act of cowardice?

b) Persons who are in debt and insolvent.

c) Persons charged with the administration of temporal affairs which might cause the institute to be involved in lawsuits or other difficulties.

d) Children who are necessary for the support of their parents or grandparents who are in grave need; and parents (father and mother), whose help is needed for the support and education of their children.

e) Those who in religion would be destined for the priesthood, from which, however, they are excluded by an irregularity or other canonical impediment.

Such would be the case, for example, of illegitimate children, unless they enter an order in which solemn vows are taken before the reception of sacred orders, and are thus freed from the irregularity. For the irregularity or canonical impediment to orders does not prevent the entrance into religion, if it must cease before the admission to orders.

f) Those who belong to an Oriental rite may not enter an institute of the Latin rite without the written permission of the Sacred Congregation for the Oriental Church (c. 542).

Subjects of an Oriental rite may sometimes be received without the special authorization of the Holy See, provided that they are destined, after sufficient preparation, to become a part of a house or of a province following that Oriental rite, the founding of which is at least foreseen. These candidates must follow their rite even during this time of preparation.[3]

2. The Code does not speak of the *consent of the parents* and seems to allow everyone who is fifteen years of age, or older, to enter into a novitiate. Sometimes, however, it will be a duty of charity or obedience to wait for this consent, at

---

[3] Commission of Interpretation. Response November 10, 1925. — *A.A.S.,* XVII (1925), 583.

least until the candidate is of age; prudence almost always requires that superiors should make sure of the consent of the parents before admitting postulants who are still minors.

In making a choice of a state of life, children who have completed their fourteenth year are not subject to the authority of their parents. The latter, however, may oppose a choice which they judge to be unreasonable, and they may subject their children to a reasonable trial of a vocation about which they doubt. If the opposition of parents is not justified, superiors will have to determine in each individual case what account is to be taken of such opposition. Many states emancipate children from parental authority at the age of eighteen, and even in those states in which children reach their majority at twenty-one there is little danger of a child being forced to return to the home of his parents if he can prove that he left it of his own accord.

3. We may here call attention to the suppression of former impediments which arose from illegitimate birth, from the formal or equivalent dismissal from an educational establishment, a seminary, etc., and in the case of women from the age limit or from widowhood.

If the general chapter judge it opportune to keep certain of these impediments, they can be dispensed from by the superior general, either alone or with the approval of the council. It will undoubtedly be preferable to imitate the discretion of the Code in leaving to higher superiors the power of judging in special cases.

This power of the superior general was formally recognized by the *Normae,* n. 62. If the constitutions declare that the superior general cannot dispense from an impediment and if he wishes to do so in a special case, he should have recourse to the Holy See, unless the Ordinary has received a particular indult on this subject (see *Coll. Torn.* [1924], 189). In the diocesan congregations the bishop can grant this dispensation from impediments arising from particular legislation.

4. In the admission of candidates destined for the priesthood, one should be certain that they have both a religious and a priestly vocation. In the case of future priests one should demand with greater strictness and certainty a disposition for perfect chastity and for prolonged studies. (See S.C. of Religious, Instruction, December 1, 1931; given in our Appendix, II).

§ 2. THE COMPETENT SUPERIOR

181. "The right of admitting to the novitiate . . . belongs to the higher superiors with the vote of the council or chapter, according to the constitutions" (n. 543).

1. According to this canon it is certain that: (1) the right of admitting to the novitiate belongs to the religious superiors, not to the Ordinary. The constitutions could not grant this right to the Ordinary, since such a

prescription would be contrary to common law (see Larraona in *Commentarium pro Religiosis*, 1937, 321 sq.); (2) the admission is made by the higher superior according to the constitutions. The constitutions will determine whether the provincial superior can admit the candidates without any recourse to the superior general.

2. The text of the Code leaves some doubt as to the participation of the council or the chapter. We think that the superior *must* consult the council or the chapter. These are our reasons:

(1) C. 575, § 2, defines the part to be played by the council or the chapter in admission to profession. Since c. 543 speaks at the same time and in the same way of "admission to the novitiate and to the subsequent profession, whether temporary or perpetual," it would contradict c. 575, to take the words "according to the constitutions" as affecting the rôle of the chapter. We must conclude, therefore, that the constitutions can only determine which superior is to grant admission and the character, deliberative or consultative, of the intervention of the council or of the chapter; (2) this interpretation is in line with the former legislation and does not involve any modification in most of the constitutions.[4] Grave authorities allow, nevertheless, that constitutions may define the necessity and the extent of the intervention of a council or chapter.[5]

§ 3. TESTIMONIAL LETTERS

182. The Code requires, before admission, that certain documents be obtained (c. 544):

1. All are required to bring a certificate of baptism and of confirmation. If the applicant is morally certain of obtaining this certificate before entering the novitiate, she may be admitted at once to the postulancy.

2. For all candidates who have been in a seminary or college, or in a postulancy or novitiate of another institute, testimonial letters given, according to the circumstances, by the rector of the seminary or college, after consulting the local Ordinary, or by the higher superior of the institute, are also necessary.

Father Vermeersch thinks[6] that we ought to understand here by "colleges" only those establishments whose students are aiming at the priesthood or the religious life, such as apostolic schools, minor novitiates,

---

[4] In the same sense, see Battandier, *G.C.*, n. 136. — Goyeneche, *De religiosis*, n. 47. — Berutti, O.P., *Institutiones i. c.*, III, 150.

[5] See Vermeersch-Creusen, *Epitome*, I[7], n. 690, followed by Bastien, *D.C.*, n. 418, 2.

[6] See *Periodica*, IX, 6. This explanation has been adopted by many authorized interpreters of the Code; it is more probable than the opposite interpretation. See Goyeneche, *De religiosis*, 88, n. 47.

etc. This is the common meaning of the term as used in Rome. Moreover, used as it is between the word "seminary" and "postulancy or novitiate," this term seems to indicate an institution of the same sort. Besides, understanding it in this way, it would be easier to explain the severity of the measure.

3. Male aspirants must furnish testimonial letters from the bishop of the place where they were born, and from the bishops of the dioceses where, after completing their fourteenth year, they have resided for more than one morally continuous year, any privilege to the contrary notwithstanding.

According to a private answer of the Sacred Congregation of Religious, (July 28, 1918), no testimonial letters from the Ordinary are required for the time passed by postulants in the minor novitiates of the institute into which they wish to enter. This response may be extended also to apostolic schools (see Vermeersch, *Epitome*, I', n. 697).

The place of origin of the candidate is that where, at the moment of his birth, his father had his domicile, or in default of this, a quasi-domicile, or, if the young man is illegitimate or posthumous, where the mother had her domicile (c. 90, § 1).

Since the Code defines the place of origin (c. 90), we cannot understand why Dom Bastien, in the work already cited n. 86, 3, substitutes for this the place of domicile. The bishop of the place of origin is the one best qualified to give information about the parents and relatives of the candidate; if the candidate has long since left the place of his origin, the Ordinary of the place where he has lived more than a year will necessarily fill out the information about his character according to c. 544, § 2.

A young man whose home was in diocese A, and who has been a boarding student in diocese B need not obtain testimonial letters from the bishop of diocese B. The vacations have kept the school year from being "a year which is morally continuous."

4. Clerics must present, besides the certificates indicated in n. 2, their letters of ordination and the testimonial letters of the bishops of the dioceses in which they have lived for more than one morally continuous year after ordination (c. 544, § 4).

5. The *professed* religious who, in virtue of an apostolic indult, passes over to another religious institute, need present only the testimonial letters of the major superior of the institute which he leaves.

6. The Code judges it useful to add that the superiors, upon whom the admission of candidates depends, may demand other testimonials, if such seem necessary or opportune.

7. Women are not to be received until careful inquiry has been made regarding their character and conduct (c. 544, § 7).

These inquiries are all the more necessary because superiors are hardly ever required to ask testimonial letters for female postulants. It will rarely happen, in fact, that they have ever been in an establishment destined to prepare young women for the religious life, or in a religious institute.

183. 1. These testimonial letters must be sent within three months after they have been asked for, directly to the religious superior. They should be sealed and in the cases mentioned under **182**, n. 2, their contents must be affirmed under oath. The reason for dismissal or voluntary departure from a seminary, college, postulancy or a novitiate, must be indicated therein. There is a grave obligation to make known in these testimonial letters everything which concerns the character, conduct, reputation, and knowledge of the candidate (c. 545, §§ 1, 4).

Since the Holy See orders that the information given be confirmed by oath, the obligation to give such information becomes a grave one. Hence, one would fail seriously in performing his duty if he were to give inexact information, for form's sake, in order to avoid all responsibility.

2. Superiors who judge that they cannot give this information ought to refer the case to the Holy See. The religious superior who has received no answer to his request for testimonials should do the same. If the response is insufficient because the correspondent declares that he does not know the subject sufficiently well, the superior can supply this lack of information by making careful inquiries of sources worthy of credence (c. 545).

The same method of procedure may be followed, it seems to us, if the contents of the testimonial letters have not been communicated to the Ordinary (n. **182**, 2) or confirmed by oath.

The Congregation of Religious has declared on November 21, 1919,[7] that bishops or superiors general, according to the case, must take action against those superiors who refuse to attest under oath the testimonial letters required, and, in case of necessity, inflict canonical penalties upon them.

3. Superiors who have admitted a candidate to the novitiate without regard to the impediments enumerated in c. 542, or

---

[7] *A.A.S.,* XII (1920), 17; *N.R. Th.* (1920), 243 sq.; *Per.,* X, 193.

without having received the testimonial letters required by c. 544, must be punished according to the gravity of their fault, and may even be deprived of their office (c. 2411).

4. All those who have received the information in question are obliged to keep secret both the contents of the letters and the names of their informants (c. 546). This obligation is grave of its nature.

The superior who has received such information will be obliged to communicate it to the council charged with determining the admission of the candidate to the novitiate. Such information, however, as is not pertinent to admission must be kept secret. The superior is likewise bound to secrecy in regard to details which the candidate personally reveals under the seal of secrecy.

§ 4. DOWRY

184. Dowry is capital (personal or real property), the income of which should serve for the support of the religious in whose favor the dowry has been established.

A dowry is more strictly required and must be considerably larger in contemplative orders than in those institutes whose works, such as teaching, will certainly provide a part of their needed resources.

185. 1. In monasteries of nuns every postulant must bring a dowry, the amount of which is determined by the constitutions or by lawful custom. It must be handed over before the taking of the habit, or at least it should be guaranteed at that time by some document which is binding under civil law, and in this case, it must be delivered at least before profession (c. 547, §§ 1, 2).

2. In religious institutes of simple vows the constitutions are to be observed regarding the quality of the dowry and the manner in which it shall be made up (c. 547, § 3).

In teaching institutes, the constitutions sometimes provide that a diploma or teacher's certificate shall supply, at least in part, the lack of the dowry. Reputable authors have called attention to the difficulties which are likely to arise from such a measure if it becomes too widespread. In case the person leaves the community this diploma does not insure any immediate funds; after the death of the professed, it is of no use for supplying the needs of the community. These considerations hold likewise for religious engaged in hospital work, everything else being equal.

3. In pontifical institutes only the Holy See can dispense entirely or in part from the prescribed dowry; in the case of diocesan institutes, the Ordinary can give the dispensation (c. 547, § 4).

The superioress cannot do so even though the convent has abundant resources, or because the other postulants have brought a dowry greater than the sum which is demanded.

Frequently the constitutions of religious congregations authorize the superior general or the provincial to dispense with the dowry, either in whole or in part. In this case it is obviously not necessary to have recourse either to the Holy See or to the Ordinary. If the superioress uses this power, she should prudently inform the postulant that this dispensation is conditional; if later on the latter comes into possession of property which she is not morally bound to put to other uses, she should then pay the dowry.

A monastery or a religious institute may possess an endowment given or bequeathed for the purpose of supplying dowries of those applicants who have no means of their own. This is an excellent form of giving alms, especially on the part of persons who are entering into religion. In these cases the superioress may, therefore, receive postulants who have no personal dowry by allotting to them one of the dowries which have been thus provided by endowment.

186. During the lifetime of the religious:

a) Her dowry is absolutely untransferable and inalienable; it is not even allowed to use it for building or for paying debts (c. 549); the superioresses of religious women, even though exempt, should be punished, and may be deposed, by the Ordinary of the place, if they presume to alienate the dowries of religious (c. 2412).

b) After the first profession of the religious, the superioress with her council, and with the consent of the local Ordinary and of the regular superior, if the house be dependent on regulars, must place the dowry in a safe, lawful and productive investment (c. 549).

It is not practical, as a general rule, to invest the funds of the dowry in real estate; it would not, however, be forbidden to receive, by way of dowry, productive real estate not yet convertible into cash. The difficulty of selling real estate at its true value prevents its ready acceptance as a means of investment.

c) The dowry must be prudently and honestly administered in the monastery or at least in the house of habitual residence of the general or provincial superioress (c. 550, § 1).

The capital of dowries may be administered in two ways: Each individual dowry is made up of specifically determined funds ascribed to it either in themselves or in other titles which will eventually replace them. Or all the capital coming from dowries is invested in various titles the whole of which forms the capital of the dowries without any individual title corresponding to any specific dowry. If the latter method be employed, two ways of administration are possible: the community agrees to restore to the religious, in case of necessity, her capital either increased or diminished according to the actual value of the total capital or titles; or the community assumes merely the obligation of returning the actual sum of money (e.g., $2,000) brought by the postulant as her dowry. Of the three methods described above, the last is the most convenient, although it makes the community liable to incur some loss as well as to make some gains. It is to be recommended, nevertheless, unless the nature of the dowry and the will of the postulant enjoin the first method.

It is safer, as a rule, to let the provincial superioress have charge of the dowries, and not to overburden the general administration by accumulating the capital of the dowries.

The local Ordinaries must diligently see to it that the dowries of religious are conserved and they must exact an account on the subject, especially on the occasion of the canonical visitation (c. 550, § 2). Dowries may not be given as security for money borrowed by the religious institute or by a diocesan work.

187. 1. If, from whatever cause, a professed religious with either solemn or simple vows leaves the institute, her dowry must be returned to her intact, but not the interest already derived therefrom (c. 551, § 1).

In case of dismissal it is not allowed to keep the capital of the dowry, or any of the interest which is not yet due. If a religious has the misfortune to leave her convent without any authorization, the superioress is not obliged to send her her dowry until she has submitted to the just demands of the ecclesiastical authority. If all efforts to bring her back to her senses fail, it would be better to send her back her dowry, if only to avoid any appearance of self-interest in the condemnation of her apostasy.

2. If a religious who has been received by reason of a dowry which was founded in favor of the convent leaves after her profession, is it necessary to give her this dowry?

We do not think so. This amount, according to the intention of the founder, is destined solely for the support of a religious; before all else, it was established for the sake of the convent, and only secondarily for the beneficiary.[8] This sum has never become the property of the novice or the professed.

Evidently, the superiors must observe another prescription, independent of the dowry, that is to say, to provide for the needs of the former religious, unless she can reasonably secure for herself the resources necessary for her support.

Serious objections have been made to this solution, but in our humble opinion they are not convincing.[9] The Code, it is said, purely and simply directs that the dowry shall be given to the professed who leaves. Answer: The Code supposes that she herself has established and given the dowry, for it says: "the dowry must be returned. . . ." But the purpose of the legislator does not permit of establishing a dowry that would not become the property of the religious. Answer: The legislator wishes two things, both of which are fully safeguarded in our solution. The first is that a minimum of resources shall be assured for the support of the religious, especially of nuns. The second is that, in case they depart from the community, freely or of necessity, they may not be in need. We have described above that the convent ought to assume the risk of the second eventuality.[10]

188. If, by virtue of an apostolic indult, the professed religious joins another institute, the interest on the dowry, during her new novitiate, without prejudice to the prescription of canon 570, § 1, and, after the new profession, the dowry itself must be given to the latter institute; if the religious passes to another monastery of the same order, the dowry is due to it from the day the change takes place (c. 551, § 2).

If the new institute demands nothing for the board of the novice, the interest from the dowry need not be paid to it;[11]

---

[8] This is also the opinion of Bastien, *D.C.*, n. 430, 2, 6, and of Goyeneche, *Comm. pro rel.* (1930), 36.

[9] *N.R. Th.* (1924), 427.

[10] This solution finds real support in the answer of the Congregation of Religious, March 2, 1924. — *A.A.S.*, XVI (1924), 165; *N.R. Th.* (1924), 501.

[11] This opinion may be safely followed since it is favored by a considerable number of canonists (see Goyeneche, *De religiosis,* 93, note 74).

if it requires more than the interest on the dowry, the superiors ought to pay the interest on the dowry and the religious will pay the difference herself from her other goods.

In the first case, namely, where the new institute demands nothing for board, the interest which accrues may be kept by the first institute.[12]

189. The dowry is irrevocably acquired by the monastery or the institute on the death of the religious, even though she had made profession of only temporary vows (c. 548).

After the death of a religious to whom a founded dowry has been assigned (see n. **185, 3**), the dowry is not acquired by the institute. It must be preserved, in order that it may be given, when occasion demands, to another postulant. The person who founds the dowry may of course stipulate that upon the death of the religious the dowry shall become the property of the institute.

§ 5. CANONICAL EXAMINATION

190. The bishop must be informed at least two months in advance of the taking of the habit, and of the temporary profession and the perpetual profession of every individual who belongs to a community of women, so that he can proceed personally or by delegate to make the canonical examination, which must be made at least one month before each of these ceremonies (c. 552).

Superiors who neglect to inform the Ordinary must be punished by him, and may even be deposed (c. 2412, § 2). But if the Ordinary who was informed in good time did not come to make the examination, one may proceed to the admission without more ado.

The purpose of this examination is solely to make certain that the postulant, the novice, or the professed is acting with full knowledge of the case and with full liberty. Questions may, therefore, be asked her about the essential obligations of the three vows of religion, and the particular points of the institute, but neither the Ordinary nor his delegate is to examine as to her vocation, or to approve her admission.

It is absolutely forbidden to the Ordinary or to his delegate to demand

---

[12] There is no reason to affirm with Fanfani "that it is to be added to the capital, and will have the same destination as the capital" (see Vermeersch, *Epitome,* I[7], n. 700).

any fees for this canonical examination and the contrary custom, even where it has existed for more than one hundred years may no longer be observed.[13] It is not forbidden, however, to accept traveling expenses.

Article 2. Formation of Novices

191. 1. The probation must be made in a lawfully erected novitiate, and it must last at least an entire year. During this time, the novices depend almost exclusively on the master of novices, who alone is charged with the duty of initiating them into the religious life. This period of formation involves certain special obligations and rights which are explained in the latter part of this article.

2. All that is said in this chapter must be understood of novices in the canonical sense, that is to say, of those who are preparing for their first profession. In some institutes young religious, during the period of temporary vows, are called professed novices, or simply novices, for short. What the Code determines for the professed of temporary vows must always be applied to such religious. It would be altogether preferable to adopt the terminology of the Code.

192. "The novitiate begins with the reception of the habit, or in any other manner prescribed by the constitutions" (c. 553).

In certain institutes the novitiate commences by the giving of a habit to the postulants on the evening before the ceremony of the taking of the habit. As we shall see later on, this act permits of the making of a profession on the anniversary of the solemn taking of the habit, even where there is only one year of novitiate. The constitutions may also declare that the novitiate commences with the official notification that a postulant is to be allowed to take the habit.

If the approved constitutions define the act which determines the beginning of the novitiate, superiors may not, on their private authority, designate any other act. The *ceremony* is not at all essential to the taking of the habit; yet the giving of the habit necessarily means admission to the novitiate. Finally, the taking of the habit is not requisite for the *validity* of admission.

193. 1. The erection of a novitiate house requires the approval of the Holy See in institutes approved by the Holy See. If an institute is divided into provinces, it is not allowed to establish more than one novitiate in the same province without a grave reason and a special indult of the Holy See (c. 554).

Where several novitiates existed before May 19, 1918, we think that it is allowed to keep them without asking for an indult. In the same

---

[13] Response of the Congregation of Religious, March 20, 1922. — *A.A.S.*, XIV (1922), 352; *N.R. Th.* (1923), 101; *Per.*, XI, 79.

institutes the authorization of the Holy See is required to transfer the novitiate from one house to the other, but not for the transfer of one or the other novice.

If a novitiate changes its dwelling to another site in the same city, no indult from the Holy See is necessary, but one would be necessary to transfer the novitiate to another locality (see Ellis, in *Periodica*, 1938, 108).

2. "Superiors shall have in the novitiate houses and houses of study only religious who are exemplary in their zeal for regular observance" (c. 554, § 3).

In those institutes in which the novices are instructed in the rudiments of their future work during the second year of novitiate, superiors should place them in the care of such religious as are capable of edifying them while giving them their formation. This would not be the case if the novices were sent indiscriminately to assist in schools or in the wards of a hospital without any consideration of the virtues and character of the persons in charge.

194. *Conditions for the Validity of the Novitiate.*

(1) The novitiate may not be begun before the age of fifteen years completed; (2) it must last an entire and continuous year; (3) it must be made in a novitiate house (c. 555, § 1); (4) it must be adapted to the class of subjects which the novice will enter by his profession (c. 558).

195. *Age Required.*

The required age is fifteen years *completed.* Hence a candidate born on February 1 may not validly be given the habit until February 2. When the constitutions prescribe *two* years of novitiate, many authors used to hold that a novice might be admitted at the age of fourteen and allowed to begin the canonical year of novitiate at the age of fifteen. This interpretation, however, seems no longer tenable after the declaration of the Commission of Interpretation[14] which stated that the first year of the novitiate must be regarded as the canonical year.

196. *Duration of the Novitiate.*

The novitiate must last at least an entire year. This time of probation, which was established by the ancient monastic rules,

---

[14] Reply February 12, 1935. — *R.C.R.* (1935), 85 sq. — See also Sacred Congregation of Religious, Instruction, November 3, 1921. — *A.A.S.*, XIII (1921), 539. — *N.R. Th.* (1922), 160. — *Periodica*, X, 364. — *R.C.R.* (1925), 100.

was confirmed by the Council of Trent (S. XXV, *de Regul.*, c. 15); it is called the canonical year of novitiate. It is to this year that all the prescriptions of the Code about the duration, the interruptions and the place of a novitiate are to be strictly applied.

A large number of religious institutes require that the candidate make eighteen months or two years of novitiate. The six extra months or the second year are required for the *validity* of the novitiate only if the constitutions state this *expressly* (c. 556, § 2). In such cases it is the wish of the Holy See that the first year fulfill the prescriptions of the canonical year as stated above.

The year of the novitiate is calculated according to the calendar, but the day of entry does not count (c. 34, § 3, 3). If a novitiate were commenced on August 15, 1952, in the morning, it would be finished only on August 15, 1953, at midnight. This manner of calculating the year of the novitiate is a new feature in the Code and contrary to the decree *Cum propositae* of May 3, 1914,[15] according to which the year of novitiate was calculated from one day to the corresponding day of the next year (from August 15, 1929 to August 15, 1930). This essential modification seems to have escaped the notice of certain authors; others thought themselves free to deny it, although c. 34, § 3, 3 and the Commission of Interpretation have definitely settled the question, or rather confirmed the only possible interpretation of c. 555, § 1, 2 (Resp. November 12, 1922, ad. II).[16]

Since the Code came into force on May 19, 1918, the vows which were taken after that time on the first anniversary of the entry of the novitiate (in those places where the novitiate commences in the morning at the solemn taking of the habit) are certainly invalid. It is necessary, therefore, to take them over again, or to request the Holy See for a sanation.

Since the year of novitiate is to be taken according to the calendar, no distinction is to be made between an ordinary year and a leap year. In both cases the year is completed at midnight of the anniversary of the taking of the habit.

[15] See *A.A.S.*, VI (1914), p. 229; *Per.*, VIII, p. 32; *Coll. Gand.*, VI (1914), p. 175.
[16] *A.A.S.*, XIV (1922), 661; *Coll. Gand.*, XV (1923), 49; *Per.*, XI, 182.

197. The year of novitiate must be continuous. Now certain absences interrupt the novitiate, others simply suspend its course; others again are without any canonical effect. In the first case, it is necessary to start the novitiate over; in the second case, the time lost must be made up (c. 556, see S. Congr. of Relig., decree *Cum propositae,* May 3, 1914).

198. The novitiate is **interrupted** "if the novice is sent away by a superior and leaves the house, or, without the permission of the superior, leaves the house with the intention of not returning or, finally, even with the permission of the superior and from whatever motive if he has remained for more than thirty days, whether continuously or not outside the house" (c. 556, § 1).

The intention of not returning must be manifested either by the declaration of the interested party or by his way of acting. A novice who would leave informally with the secret intention of not coming back, but who, regretting his fault, would come back an hour or two later, could continue his novitiate.

As to the thirty days' absence, the text of the Code is explicit: the novitiate is *interrupted* and must be begun again in its entirety as soon as the novice has been absent for more than thirty days. One may not, therefore, allow the novice to reckon the canonical year from the first or second absence, and thus avoid his beginning an entirely new year. For example: A novice enters on September 1; for various reasons he is absent from the novitiate from October 7 to 20, again from March 9 to 18, and finally from August 6 to 18, a total of 31 days of absence. He certainly may not take his vows on September 2. But must he necessarily begin his novitiate anew on August 18? Yes, and he may not consider October 21 of the preceding year as the first day of the new canonical year.[17]

199. *Suspension of the Novitiate.*

"If the novice, with the permission of superiors or constrained by force, has passed more than fifteen days, but not more than thirty days even interruptedly, outside the precincts (*septa*) of the house but under the obedience of the superior, it is necessary and sufficient for the validity of the novitiate that he supply the number of days so passed outside; if for a period not exceeding fifteen days, the supplementing for this period can be

---

[17] The contrary opinion of Father Vermeersch (*Periodica,* X, 154) does not seem probable to us; it does not appear in the *Epitome.*

prescribed by the superiors, but it is not necessary for validity" (c. 556, § 2).

How are the *days* of absence to be reckoned? There are two opinions: the first holds that when the Code speaks of "days," c. 32, § 1 is to be applied. Hence there will be as many days as there are periods of twenty-four hours, counting from midnight to midnight. Parts of days are not considered (counted). Thus from 9 A.M. Monday to 8 P.M. Wednesday will count as one day. The second opinion holds that c. 34, § 2 applies in this case, since the moment of departure is neither explicitly nor implicitly indicated. Therefore the extent (time) of absence must be counted "from the moment of departure to the moment of return," and as many days will be counted as there are periods of twenty-four hours. Thus from 9 A.M. Monday to Wednesday noon will count as two days. We prefer the second opinion because the terms of c. 34, § 2 are explicit and seem to us to find their strict application here. The authority of many of our adversaries requires that we mention their opinion.[17a]

The villa or country house is not a house of novitiate canonically erected; the novices who stay there are consequently "outside the house of novitiate." Those who would stay there more than fifteen days (15 times 24 hours, counted from midnight to midnight) would have to delay their profession for that period. However, the Sacred Congregation will easily grant an indult permitting the novices to spend more than fifteen days in a villa house, under the direction of the master of novices.

200. "Superiors must not grant permission to remain outside the precincts of the novitiate except for a just and grave reason" (c. 556, § 3).

The novices may pass their vacation at the country house with their Father master of novices. The necessity of this rest and the change of air is sufficient motive, but this sojourn must not be prolonged beyond fifteen days of the canonical year for the reason indicated in the foregoing. The novice who is employed in the works of the institute in a building devoted to classes, or in a clinic or hospital, is actually outside the bounds of the novitiate, but his training requires these absences which are approved with certain restrictions by the Sacred Congregation of Religious. Hence he is not outside the novitiate *house*.

[17a] The *intrinsic* arguments for both opinions are stated clearly by Balzer, in his *Computation of Time in a Canonical Novitiate*, Washington, D. C., 1945, 162–168. *In practice, therefore,* the opinion which measures days of absence from midnight to midnight, and not from moment to moment, may certainly be followed, as long as no contrary decision is given by the Holy See [Ed.].

201. The transfer of a novice to another novitiate of the same institute does not interrupt the novitiate (c. 556, § 4).

This last paragraph of c. 556 merely sums up the old legislation which stated that the mere fact of passing from one novitiate to another (of the same institute) did not by itself interrupt the novitiate.

This paragraph says nothing about the time spent outside the novitiate house during the journey; such absence being regulated by §§ 1 and 2. Therefore the novitiate will be interrupted if this absence extends beyond thirty days, and the canonical year will have to be begun again. If the absence lasts beyond fifteen days but less than thirty, the canonical year will have to be prolonged to the extent of the days of absence. All discussion on this point has been ended by the answer of the Commission for the Interpretation of the Code, dated July 13, 1930.

202. The **habit** prescribed for novices by the constitutions must be worn throughout the whole period of novitiate, unless local circumstances determine otherwise (c. 557). The wearing of the habit, however, is not necessary for the validity of the novitiate.

203. Where there are two classes of members in an institute (choir religious, teachers, etc., and lay religious), the probation made for one class is not valid for the other (c. 558).

Should a subject, especially on account of reasons which concern his intellectual capacity, ask or agree to pass from one class to the other after having made a notable part of his novitiate, it will be expedient to apply to Rome to obtain a dispensation.

Sometimes the division into two classes does not exist in the constitutions; this is the case, for example, with the Brothers of the Christian Schools,[18] with the Sisters of Notre Dame de Namur, etc. It is foreseen nevertheless, even from the very time of the novitiate, that certain subjects cannot be given any occupations except those which are usually reserved for the lay brothers or the lay sisters. This practical division does not require two novitiates juridically distinct.

204. *The Master of Novices and His Assistant.*

1. The **master of novices** must be at least thirty-five years old and professed for at least ten years from the date of his

---

[18] The constitutions of the Brothers of the Christian Schools divide the religious into teaching brothers and brother servants. This division, with them, is not equivalent to the canonical division of choir and lay religious.

first vows. In institutes of clerics he must be a priest. If it is deemed expedient to give him an assistant (*socius*), he must be at least thirty years of age and professed five years from the date of his first profession; he must also be a priest in the case of a clerical institute (c. 559).

Both should be free from all occupations which could hinder them in the care and government of the novices (c. 559, § 3).

The master of novices is not a superior in the canonical sense of the word. In what regards the general discipline of the house, he and his novices are subject to the local superior.

The Code does not require that the master of novices shall have ten years of profession in the same monastery or institute, as it requires for higher superiors (c. 504). A religious of great virtue, who has come from another institute to follow the appeal of a manner of life which is more perfect, may in less than ten years have acquired sufficient of the spirit of his new religious family to take charge of the formation of the novices. Though this case is not entirely imaginary, still it is quite exceptional.

Several times the Sacred Congregation has declared that the charge of master of novices is incompatible with the office of assistant or of general counsellor.[19] Since the Code, however, makes no such restriction, the same person might hold both offices in a small Institute.

2. The master of novices is to be distinguished by prudence, charity, piety, and fidelity to regular observance (c. 559, § 1).

Should he not after the example of our Saviour, "practice and teach" and this especially before the young souls for whom he is the incarnate ideal of the religious life and of the particular spirit of the institute?

3. The appointment of the master of novices and his assistant shall be made according to the constitutions. The Code does not fix any limit to the duration of their charge, but forbids taking them out of office without grave cause, before the time fixed by the constitutions (c. 560).

The word *eligantur* used by the Code does not prove that the master of novices and his socius must be "elected." The term has here the general meaning of "choose."

205. 1. The formation of the novices and the direction of the novitiate belong exclusively to the master of novices and constitute his principal occupation. Other superiors may not

---

[19] Battandier, *G.C.*, n. 492.

interfere, except in cases provided for by the constitutions. This restriction evidently does not affect visitors, because they are delegates of the higher superiors (cc. 561, § 1; 562).

2. With regard to the general discipline of the house, the master of novices, his assistant and the novices are subject to the local superior (c. 561, §§ 1, 2).

This general discipline includes the exercises which are carried on outside of the novitiate or by the other parts of the community. The authority of the local superior is exercised principally by way of control. Recourse must be had to him for penances in the refectory, for the menial labors which the novices are to perform in the house, for visits to the parlor, for fixing the days of vacation or of a walk, and this especially if other religious are to have their recreation day at the same time, etc. It seems to us that the master of novices should regulate the correspondence of the novices; at most the superior may limit the quantity of correspondence.

The novice is subject to the superiors of the institute and to the Father Master, because he has agreed to be a member of that community. Since their authority (dominative power) directly touches, not his will, but his actions, they have no power to annul any private vow made by him, but they can suspend the obligation of such vows for the length of time during which it might interfere with the actual duties of the novice (see c. 1312, § 2).

3. In the course of the year of novitiate, the master of novices must give the chapter or the higher superior a report concerning the conduct of each of his novices. The constitutions may give further details about this obligation (c. 563).

This obligation, as well as the strict dependence of the novices upon their Father Master, explains the prohibition put upon the latter by the Code, not to hear the confessions of the novices, except in particular cases and for grave reasons (c. 891).

The Holy See has authorized the masters of novices in some religious institutes to hear the confessions of their novices regularly.

206. *The Separation of the Novices.*

1. The novitiate shall be, as far as possible, separated from that part of the house inhabited by the professed religious.

2. No communication may be carried on between the novices and the professed religious except for some special reason and with the permission of the superior or master of novices (c. 564, § 1).

When the novitiate is not in a separate house, the novices are usually assembled with the professed in the church or chapel for certain community exercises, and also in the refectory. The separation required by the Code is sufficient reason for keeping the Blessed Sacrament in a separate chapel of the novitiate which really forms a distinct community (see n. **145** above).

Some of the professed may be appointed to give the novices certain lessons, for example, in Latin, in sacred chant, etc.

In monasteries or congregations which are as yet very small, the communications between the novices and the professed will necessarily be more frequent. In fact, an excessive isolation in such a case might have rather serious disadvantages in regard to the formation of the character of the novice.

3. "A separate place must be assigned to the lay-brother novices" (c. 564, § 2).

The lay-brother novices may, however, have rather frequent communication with the other novices. Such relations will foster humility and charity.

207. *The Training of the Novitiate.*

1. The novitiate has for its object "the forming of the mind of the novice by means of the study of the rule and constitutions, by pious meditations and assiduous prayer, by instruction on those matters which pertain to the vows and the virtues, by suitable exercises in rooting out the germs of vice, in regulating the motives of the soul, in acquiring virtues" (c. 565, § 1).

According to the express words of the Code, this formation is to be given "under the direction of the master of novices." He is supposed, therefore, not only to explain the rule and constitutions, but to give instructions on prayer and the practice of virtues; to choose exercises which will form and strengthen character; to explain to the novices and to inspire them with the religious spirit proper to the institute.

To check the result of his teaching and his direction, he must be allowed to ask questions about these different subjects, but these questions should not consist in "an intimate examination of conscience such as is exclusively reserved to the sacrament of penance." For him to ask an intimate manifestation would be an abuse which the decree *Quemadmodum* condemns severely in the case of lay superiors. The master of novices may therefore question the novice about the ease or the difficulty which he finds in vocal or mental prayer, on the observance of the constitutions and the rules, about the outward signs of sympathy or natural antipathy which he is obliged to control or to overcome; about the difficulties which he finds in the common life, the exercises of the novitiate, and in the occupations of the institute.

The confession of faults which are purely interior, and of temptations may be left for sacramental confession. It is the part of the confessor to determine whether his penitent may or may not have the grave duty of manifesting to the master of novices or to the superior certain interior difficulties which might make his remaining in the institute difficult or harmful.

The *Normae*, § 87, 321, directed that each novice shall be given a complete copy of the constitutions. At present the Holy See requires that each novice receive a copy of the ascetical and disciplinary norms, provided that some copies of the complete text of the constitutions are available.

2. At least once a week the lay-brother novices are to receive a special **conference** on Christian doctrine (c. 565, § 2).

208. During the year of the novitiate it is forbidden to **employ** the novices in the external charges of the institute, or in the ministry or in studies properly so called; the lay-brother novices may not be occupied in important duties, except in a subordinate capacity, and only to that extent which is in accord with the requirements of their own formation (c. 565, § 3).

1. Even independently of the express law of the Church, there are two good reasons for such a course of action: the strict right of the aspirants to receive a solid formation in the religious life; and secondly, the good of the institute, which requires in its members solid virtue and a true interior spirit.

The fact that there are not enough in the community to do the work, as sometimes happens in congregations which have charge of hospitals or schools, is no excuse for violations of so important a law, and no authority except the Holy See itself can dispense from this law.

2. An Instruction of the Congregation of Religious, dated November 25, 1929, prescribes that in congregations of brothers and of religious women all postulants and novices be given courses in religion. No one shall be admitted to profession without having passed an examination showing that he understands and knows how to explain the Christian doctrine satisfactorily. Nothing is prescribed as to the number and choice of the examiners.

A serious study of our holy religion enters very naturally into the formation of the religious life. Without this study, one would be ignorant of the very foundation of the religious life, and of the meaning of its principal obligations.

3. It is evidently not forbidden, during the year of the novitiate, to keep up the literary or professional knowledge of the novices. According to the spirit of the decree *Ad explorandum animum*, August 26, 1910,[20] it is allowed to give them each day one hour of instruction in their native tongue, or in the Latin language in those institutes which teach that language or use it in the office said in choir. The care of the sick and watching at their bedside may be made excellent exercises of self-denial, but they must not be prolonged to the detriment of other necessary exercises. It seems little in accord with the spirit of the law to allow novices to teach secular branches to externs or boarding students, since the law of the Church forbids them even to have habitual communication with the professed.

209. In drawing up a program of daily order for the novitiate, one should keep in mind the requirements of the Code of Canon Law, the directives of the S. Congregation of Religious, the needs of an hygienic and pedagogical order, the purpose of the institute, and the stage of the intellectual and moral formation of the novices.

The course in religion (to be taught, in part at least, by a priest) and the explanation of the constitutions and rules should have first place. A wise distribution of the exercises of piety should be made between the morning and afternoon hours. Thus the reading of biographies tends to relaxation, while that of a spiritual treatise tends to become a study. A certain amount of time during the morning and the afternoon will be devoted to manual labor, and likewise to private study according to the abilities of the novices and the amount of learning they have already acquired. This study must never become an end in itself, nor should its principal purpose be a preparation for examinations.

Occasionally a sustained effort should be demanded of the novices in spite of the tedium which comes from the monotony of certain occupations. But a sane psychology demands that, generally speaking, variety be made an aid to sustain this effort without a lapse into the boredom or irritation caused by monotony.

In addition to the daily recreation in which games will have a part, it is very desirable that the novices should every week have the opportunity for a longer period of relaxation. Long walks, games in the open air, and the like, should be substituted for the instructions, manual labor, and study. The S. Congregation of Religious readily grants permission to send the novices to a villa or country house for three or four weeks under the direction of the novice master.

210. *The Second Year of the Novitiate.*

The Sacred Congregation of Religious has issued an instruction

---

[20] *Per.*, V, 195; *N.R. Th.*, t. 42 (1910), 791.

for the **second year of the novitiate** which is required by the constitutions of a great number of institutes, and all superiors are obliged to carry out the provisions of this instruction.[21] We shall comment briefly on its principal features:

1. "This Sacred Congregation prescribes that even during this second year of novitiate the spiritual formation shall be considered before every other duty, whatever it may be."

According to the intention of the founders, this second year ought, without question, to permit of the testing of the aptitude of the novice for the works of the institute, but above all things it ought to give them a more solid spiritual formation before they are devoted entirely to these exterior works. The unavoidable distractions of teaching, of caring for the sick, etc., offer difficulties to union with God, which difficulties can be transformed into means of sanctification only by an interior life which is solidly established and generously kept up. In the institutes which are devoted to these good works, the second year of the novitiate ought to carry on with the greatest care the formation of the spirit of prayer, the true abnegation of the will, and the earnest effort to overcome defects of character. This supposes a prudent and progressive training in uniting prayer and the striving after personal perfection with an external activity.

2. The Sacred Congregation of Religious allows the novice to be occupied in the works of the institute if the constitutions prescribe this. But the end kept in view ought always to be "the formation of the novice."

Besides, it is really worth while to exercise the novices in the works proper to the institute during the second year of novitiate. Thus they come to know the real difficulties of their life, and their own good qualities as well as their defects at a time when they have abundant means of perfecting themselves.

This purpose of these exterior occupations is explained by the definite restrictions laid down as to when such employment is allowed:

a) The novice may be employed in exterior offices only in a secondary capacity.

Thus, a novice may not be the principal professor of a class; he may not be the head prefect of a division; it is not allowed to put a novice to work as one of the ordinary nurses in a hospital; nor is it permitted to give him the post of director or head supervisor in a hospital ward,

---

[21] Congregation of Religious, Instruction of November 3, 1921; *A.A.S.*, XIII (1921), 539; *N.R. Th.* (1922), 158 sq.; *R.C.R.* (1925), 100 sq., 129 sq.

etc. It is not even allowed to entrust such offices for a time to the novices, so that they may replace a professor or a teacher who has been obliged to leave off teaching for the time. These examples are given in the text itself of the instruction.

b) An exceptional reason, and one which is serious in its nature and arises from the requirements of the novice's own training, is needed to allow the novice to carry on these activities in a house other than that of the novitiate. "Never and under no pretext is it to be considered as sufficient cause for sending the novice out of the novitiate to work, that the institute itself needs this service, or because it would be advantageous, as when, for example, the novices are needed in the works of the institute because there are not enough religious to do them" (Instr. n. III).

It suffices to read this text to recognize the uselessness of asking the Ordinary to dispense from this regulation, because Ordinaries can only dispense from the general laws of the Church when the Holy See is accustomed to give such dispensations (c. 82). When a house in which the works of the institute are carried on is joined to the novitiate or is located in the vicinity, there will scarcely be any reason to send the novices to another house.

3. Two months before the profession the novice must leave off all exterior works so as to have leisure to prepare for this great act in the novitiate house itself (art. IV).

This restriction alone, if it is well observed, will keep the novice from being given too important work to do. Its observance in such a case would, in fact, involve the turning upside down of the teaching organization or of the hospital personnel every year. These two months which are expressly required by the Sacred Congregation, should be calculated from one day of the month to the same day of the second succeeding month, according to the calendar (for instance, from June 15 to August 15; from July 8 to September 8).

4. Were it necessary, in order to observe this instruction, to give up certain works which are not absolutely indispensable, to restrict the number of students, to limit the field of action of the institute, these would be merely apparent or passing disadvantages which would not excuse the violation of the instruction. The legislator has foreseen these cases when he wrote: "Never, under any pretext, etc." This severity only applies to duties which have to be carried on in another house than that of the novitiate; the instruction uses less vigorous terms when it

speaks of occupations given to novices in an establishment annexed to the novitiate. Here again, the true and well-ordered interest of a religious congregation should lead superiors to prefer, at least for the time being, to sacrifice some exterior works for the sake of the solid religious formation of their subjects. The supernatural accomplishments of even a small number of religious who are filled with the spirit of their vocation are always superior to the results which are achieved by an even greater number of religious of less virtue, or who are insufficiently formed, and more preoccupied with external success than with the apostolic fruits of their work. The achievements of the latter may seem more brilliant, but the solid spiritual work done by the first mentioned is relatively much greater.

211. This instruction is of obligation for all *religious congregations,* including diocesan congregations, whose constitutions prescribe two years of novitiate. It does not apply to religious orders.

In diocesan institutes the local Ordinary (of the diocese in which the novitiate is situated) can dispense from the second year of the novitiate, providing the constitutions do not require the second year for the validity of the profession.[22] Hence he could also dispense from the observance of a part of this instruction. However, at a time when the need of an excellent training is insisted upon, one may hope that recourse to the Ordinary to use his power will not be had except in very special cases.

If the constitutions require eighteen months of novitiate, may the concessions allowed during the second year of the novitiate be applied to the last six months? The answer is certainly in the affirmative when there is question of those articles of the instruction which determine the obligations already imposed by the general law of the Church, or of obligations which the old law had already determined in the same sense. A further question may arise, whether, in this case, it would likewise be necessary to send the novice back to the novitiate two months before the profession. We do not think so, since the instruction is given for congregations which have *two years* of novitiate.

212. *Confessions of the Novices.*

1. In the institutes of women the novices are to be treated like the professed in this regard (see nn. **109** sq.).

---

[22] Comm. Interp., Answer, February 12, 1935, *A.A.S.*, XXVII (1935), 85. *Per.,* XXIV, 95; *R.C.R.*, 1935, 85.

2. In institutes of men the novices should have:

a) One or several ordinary confessors.

b) An extraordinary confessor to whom they are obliged to present themselves at least four times a year.

They are not obliged to go to confession to him; it suffices for them to ask his blessing. Since the ordinary confessor usually does not come during the week when the extraordinary confessor fulfills his office, the novices may be advised to make their weekly confession to this latter. Besides the benefit of absolution which they obtain, this manner of acting has the advantage of not attracting attention to the novice in question because of the shortness of the interview between the extraordinary confessor and the penitent.

c) Additional confessors should be at hand to whom they may freely go in special cases.

d) Finally, like all religious men, they are allowed to go to confession occasionally to any confessor who is approved by the Ordinary of the place (see n. **108**).

3. The master of novices and his assistant are not allowed to hear the confessions of the novices with whom they live, except in particular cases, if the novice, for an urgent and grave motive, asks of his own accord to go to confession (c. 891).

The master of the junior professed has the same position in this regard as the master of novices. This supposes always that he is obliged to render an account to the superior of the conduct of the professed and that he can give them external penances (private answer, January 9, 1921).

Observe that the Code is much less willing that novices should go to confession to their master of novices than that religious in general should confess to their superior. In the former case, the motive should not only be serious, but urgent, and the confessions must not be habitual. The legislator must have known that more than one novice would prefer to go to confession habitually to his master of novices, so as to receive from him more easily his entire spiritual direction. But we see that the desire to give everyone the most complete freedom of conscience and to remove the least cause of insincerity has prevailed over the other consideration, though important enough in itself.

The severity with which the sacramental direction is separated from disciplinary formation may perhaps be considered as being merely a necessary reaction against former abuses. Hence we may believe that, once complete freedom of conscience is preserved in the moral training, the Holy See will more easily allow novices to make their confession to the master of novices, should they freely choose to do so. It cannot be denied that such a practice is a great help to uniform training, and frequently corresponds to the wishes of the novices.

213. *Spiritual Privileges of Novices.*

The novices, like the professed, share in all the spiritual privileges of the institute, such as exemption from certain ecclesiastical laws, indulgences, etc. If they die while novices, the constitutions must give them the same suffrages as the professed receive. During the novitiate, however, they may not be promoted to sacred orders (c. 567).

The constitutions may give more abundant suffrages to those of the professed who have a special title to them, for example, to former superiors; the novices have the right to the suffrages of those professed who are least favored, and the contrary regulations of certain constitutions may no longer be observed (see the Commission of Interpretation, October 16, 1919).

214. *Profession Made in Danger of Death.*

In all religious institutes and societies of common life, a novice who is in danger of death is allowed to take his vows, or make the consecration or the promises, according to the different constitutions.

This privilege granted by St. Pius V to Dominican novices (August 23, 1570, *Bull. Rom.*, IV, III, 123), extended by Pius X (September 10, 1912) to all the religious institutes,[23] was confirmed by Pius XI, December 30, 1922, and explained by the Sacred Congregation of Religious in the declaration published on this subject on the same day.[24]

1. Must the candidate have begun his novitiate to participate in these privileges?

Yes, this is certain by reason of the text as well as on the authority of commentators (see Goyeneche, *De religiosis*, 111, note 72; Vermeersch, *Per.*, XII, 159; *Epitome*, I[7], n. 720).

2. These vows, etc., may be received by major or local superiors, or by the master of novices or their delegates.

If the novice is in a hospital, the superiors may delegate another religious, or the chaplain, or even a lay person (for example, the

---

[23] Decree *Spirituali consolationi*, September 10, 1912. — Vermeersch, *Per.*, VI, 288 sq.; *Coll. Gand.*, IV (1912), 277; *Coll. Nam.*, XII, 174; *N.R. Th.* (1912), 737; (1922), 468; Ellis, *R.R.*, I (1942), 117.

[24] *A.A.S.*, XV (1923), 156; *Per.*, XII, 39; *Coll. Brug.* (1923), 236; *Coll. Gand.* (1923), 99; *Coll. Nam.* (1923), 213; *Comm. pro rel.* (1923), 257.

superioress of the hospital), giving them power to receive the vows. For to receive the profession is not an act of jurisdiction, and, therefore, does not require that one be a cleric.

3. The formula shall be that of the first public vows, omitting any expression that indicates the duration of the promise.

4. The effect of these vows is to insure for the novice all the indulgences, suffrages, and spiritual favors, gained by the professed who die in the institute or society. He also gains besides a plenary indulgence of all his faults in the form of a jubilee.

This last privilege would not be obtained by mere vows of devotion; nor do the latter bind the novice to the institute any more than does this profession by privilege.

5. No other canonical effect results from this profession, consecration, or promise.

If the novice dies, the institute or the monastery does not acquire any right over his property. Hence the dowry must be given back to his relatives or heirs unless a special agreement has been freely made on this matter. If the novice regains his health, he is precisely in the same condition as though he had not made any promises. He may freely leave, and superiors on their part keep all their powers of sending him away.

If the novice has pronounced not a simple consecration or a promise to enter in a religious society, but a profession comprising the three vows of religion, what moral obligations has he contracted? The answer is that he has the same obligations as result from private vows of poverty, chastity, and obedience. These vows cease to oblige him if he becomes convalescent. Nothing, however, hinders the novice from keeping these obligations by renewing the same as vows of devotion if the superiors allow him to do so.

215. *Vows of Devotion.*

In certain religious institutes the novice whose vocation seems assured is allowed, after a certain time of probation, to make the three ordinary vows.

These vows called "vows of devotion" are of a strictly private character, even when they are made or renewed in the presence of witnesses. They are not a profession and do not impose any new obligation on the institute.

Since the three vows of poverty, chastity, and obedience are taken by the same act, it must be presumed, unless there is proof to the contrary, that their obligation is assumed in the same way. If, then, the novice should leave the institute, whether of his own will or because obliged to do so, even the vow of chastity would cease to have any force. It would hardly appear to be prudent to approve the taking of an obligation which would survive after the departure from the novitiate. Of course, nothing prevents the former novice from renewing his vow of chastity in the world, if he thinks it prudent to do so after taking the advice of a good counsellor.

216. *The Disposition of Property.*

1. During the course of the novitiate the novices are not allowed to give up their benefices or their property, or to burden them with obligations; any act of this kind is null and void in itself (c. 568).

Benefices is a name given to ecclesiastical offices to which is attached the right to permanent revenues.

There is question here evidently of obligations which would lessen the resources of the novices, and in this way would interfere with their full liberty, by rendering their condition more precarious. A novice, however, may give a sum of money in exchange for pecuniary advantages which are about equal, such as a life-annuity or pension for a certain number of years.

To lend money without security and without interest is contrary to the foregoing prescription. The Code, however, does not forbid novices to dispose of their revenue, hence they may remit the interest under the title of alms.

Can the novice allow his parents to dispose in favor of others of that portion of the property which would fall to him by way of inheritance? Without being contrary to the letter of the code, this renunciation seemingly is not in conformity with the spirit thereof and should be granted with great prudence.

Evidently, such a renunciation would become invalid if the novice should later leave the community. He has only made his renunciation on condition of his perseverance.

2. Before entering the novitiate those who aspire to the religious life may make any agreement which they wish about their present or future possessions. Prudence and charity will require both from parents and from children certain limitations in the renunciations which they ask or consent to.

3. Up to the end of the novitiate the novices can keep the administration of their property; they may make such use of their revenues as seems good to themselves. Still the constitutions may demand that they give up this free disposal and management of property during the time of the novitiate, on

account of the inconveniences which might result from the standpoint of their training.

217. Before the profession of simple vows the novice must cede the administration of his property to whomsoever he wishes for the whole period during which he will be bound by simple vows. Unless the constitutions make some provision to the contrary, he must dispose freely of the use and usufruct of his property (c. 569, § 1).

1. The novices who do not possess any property need not bother with making this cession. If they acquire property afterwards, they may make it as described above, notwithstanding their profession (c. 569, § 2).

2. The *administration* of their property can be turned over to the religious institute.

3. Those constitutions which restrict the liberty of the novice in the disposition of his revenues are not contrary to the Code,[25] but we believe that such a restriction would no longer be approved in the constitutions of those institutes which ask approbation from Rome.

A religious may apply his income to the upkeep of his capital, or even add it to the capital. There is no certain prohibition of this in canon law. But, while it may be prudent to expend as much of the income as is necessary to preserve the capital, it is not altogether conformable with religious poverty to invest all one's income, thus adding it to one's capital.

Nor is it forbidden to determine a sum which the religious, *with the permission of the superior,* will allocate every year to works of their choice. But such a disposition seems to be really contrary to the spirit of poverty, unless there be a very special reason for doing so. As a matter of fact it introduces among religious a clear-cut division between those who have possessions and those who do not; it exposes the religious to earnest requests for help, and to attentions which flatter their self-love; it leaves them the use of their income, a certain freedom which does not encourage complete detachment.

The disposition of one's income made at the time of the first profession may be changed later on for a good reason, either with the permission of the superior general or of one's own

---

[25] See Response of the Commission of Interpretation, October 16, 1919. — *A.A.S.,* XI (1919), p. 478.

accord if this is allowed by the constitutions (see n. **243**, 3, below).

4. The following form may be used to comply with the twofold obligation imposed upon novices by canon 569, § 1.

I, the undersigned N.N., make the following provisions to last during the time I shall be bound by simple vows in the Institute (Congregation) of N.: (1) I cede the administration of my property to N.N.; (2) My annual income is to be disposed of as follows: the sum of $.... is to be given to N.N.; the sum of $.... to N.N.; (3) I cede the use of .... properties to N.N.

Date......   (Signed) N.N.

218. "In every religious congregation the novice, before making profession of temporary vows, shall freely dispose by will of all the property which he actually possesses or may subsequently possess" (c. 569, § 3).

In the monasteries of nuns, even of those who take only simple vows, the novices are not obliged by the law of the Church to make a will.

In every *religious congregation,* each novice must make a will, even though he is still a minor or possessed of no property.

The objections brought against this interpretation seem to us to have little value, because:

1) The Code makes no distinction between novices who have attained their majority and those who have not, nor between those having property and those not having any.

2) If the novice is a minor, his will is valid according to canon law. As a consequence Catholic parents must respect it and carry out its provisions. We may note in passing that the Code does not oblige the novice to any effort to render the will valid in civil law. When he becomes of age according to civil law, he can make a new copy of the will and date it accordingly.

3) The will includes property actually possessed by the novice as well as such as will come to him in the future, and provides for the disposal of the same after the death of the testator. Hence, a person who actually possesses nothing may make a perfectly good will disposing of any property, whether real or personal, which may come into his possession later on.

4) The editors of the Code must have been aware that the majority of novices would not have any personal property as yet. A lack of knowledge of what their future fortune may amount to is not an insurmountable difficulty. If a novice knows approximately the amount of his possessions, he may dispose of them in his will and declare that he leaves the remaining part to X or Y. If he cannot determine that amount, there is no objection to his writing for example: "I leave

possessions — one third of my personal goods to X; the other part, two thirds to Y," and so forth.

5) Finally, the possibility of changing the will without having recourse to Rome, when there is an urgent reason for making such a change, will furnish a solution in more difficult cases.[26]

In our humble judgment, the opinion which exempts novices who are minors or who have no property from making their will has little foundation, and several particular answers of the Holy See have been given contrary to it. Nevertheless, one may wait to see if the Holy See modifies this law when the occasion offers, because of the difficulties often enough met with in its application. Meanwhile it does not pertain to any religious superior to grant a dispensation, and it is not advisable to criticise thoughtlessly, since this regulation is an order of the highest superior of religious.

219. Superiors can require the payment of an amount provided by the constitutions or by formal agreement to defray the expenses incurred for food and clothing while at the novitiate, but no other compensation can be demanded (c. 570).

220. *The End of the Novitiate.*

1. During the course of the novitiate the novice is free to leave the institute, that is to say, no bond as yet attaches him to it. Evidently, his departure might render him guilty before God of inconsistency or unfaithfulness. Still, since the vows are only a matter of counsel, this inconsistency would hardly ever constitute a mortal sin (c. 572, § 1).

2. The constitutions determine which superior is authorized to dismiss novices. Such a dismissal can only be made for just reasons, but the superior is not obliged to render any account to the novice of these reasons.

The major superior cannot admit novices to the first profession without the favorable vote of the majority of his council or chapter (according to the constitutions). If the vote of the chapter is against the novice, the superior may, of his own accord, prolong the time of probation. He may do so even without taking advice of his council if he has serious doubts regarding the aptitude of the novice (c. 571, § 2).

3. Superiors who doubt about the fitness of the novice may prolong the novitiate but not beyond six months (c. 571, § 2); unless there is question of the health of the novice, it is rare

---

[26] For a detailed explanation see Ellis, "The Vow of Poverty in the Code of Canon Law," *R/R.*, I (1942), 15.

that such a prolongation can result in a decision. It would be much better to test the novice more thoroughly by a somewhat more difficult proof during the time of his ordinary probation.

May the higher superior decide that the profession shall be delayed for some days for a number of novices, so as to have but one ceremony, or can he even defer the profession of all the novices because it is very difficult to have the retreat at the required time? If the delay is really short, the motive seems serious enough to avoid any violation of c. 571, § 2, and one for which the novice should allow this merely apparent derogation of his right.

221. Before pronouncing his vows the novice must make a **spiritual retreat** of at least eight entire days (c. 571, § 3. See preceding n. 175).

These spiritual exercises need not necessarily end on the very eve or on the day of the profession. If the novice had, a short time before, followed the exercises of the common retreat, it would be sufficient for him to make a day of recollection, and even this would not be obligatory. This solution seems to us to follow by analogy from what is held about the retreat previous to ordination (see c. 1001). If it is foreseen that it will frequently be difficult to have the retreat immediately precede the profession, a particular indult may be asked of the Holy See to anticipate the retreat for some time. Such an indult has been given to some congregations.

CHAPTER VI

Religious Profession

Article 1. General Ideas

222. Religious profession is the act by which a person embraces the religious state. Although, according to the existing law of the Church, religious profession always includes, explicitly or implicitly, the three vows of poverty, chastity, and obedience, it is not identical with these vows. For besides the vows, it establishes a new bond of dependence in regard to the hierarchy and includes an agreement made with the religious institute which one enters. When this agreement is accepted by the competent superior, it creates henceforth a whole group of reciprocal rights and obligations between the institute and the religious.

The theory which sees in the religious profession merely or principally a *bilateral contract* is being discarded more and more. It will rather be considered as a public act of religion whereby one promises to God the practice of the evangelical counsels of poverty, chastity, and obedience, in an approved institute, and in virtue of which one puts himself under the authority of the lawful superiors of the institute.

223. 1. A **vow** is a deliberate promise made to God to do something which is possible, and which is better than its contrary.[1]

Distinction is made between **public** vows, that is to say, those which are accepted in the name of the Church by a lawful superior, and **private** vows (c. 1308, § 1).

The word "public" is not used here in opposition to hidden or secret. This word indicates the official character of the vow which is taken. Public vows in this official sense are usually taken only in religion. Though the Church has the power to allow public vows to be taken in a secular institute, the vows usually taken are only *quasi-public* or *social*.

Since the beginning of the sixteenth century it must very seldom

---

[1] See Cotel-Jombart-McCabe, *Catechism of the Vows*, p. 17.

have happened that vows were officially received by the Church outside of a religious institute. Before that time this had been done in the case of certain hermits and recluses. We read, nevertheless, in the *Acta Apostolicae Sedis*[2] that the bishop of St.-Agatha-of-the-Goths officially received vows of poverty, chastity, and obedience taken by the Venerable Philomène-Jeanne Genovese (1825–1864), without being a member of any institute. At the present time such a thing would no longer be possible.

The Congregation of Religious has even refused the permission asked for by a number of bishops to bestow the blessing or consecration of virgins upon persons living in the world. The Holy See grants it only to nuns with solemn vows in those monasteries in which this custom has been preserved (see n. 234, 3).

2. A public vow is **solemn** when the Church recognizes it as such, otherwise it is **simple.**

The solemnity of a vow does not differ in the rites or ceremonies connected with it, but consists in a special approval of the Church which is accompanied by particular guarantees and effects.

For many centuries the Holy See has no longer granted solemn vows to new institutes. In the monastic and mendicant orders the vows of all the religious are solemn. Among the members of the Society of Jesus some pronounce solemn vows, and others simple vows.

By virtue of their rule all nuns have solemn vows. In many countries, however, since the French revolution, the Holy See allowed many of them to take simple vows only, or permitted the foundation of monasteries with simple vows. The Constitution *Sponsa Christi* of November 21, 1950, favored the taking of solemn vows, and made it the general rule for those nuns who could fulfill the conditions (art. III, § 2).

224. Dispensation from public vows is in itself reserved to the Holy See. The Holy See communicates this power in determined cases to the diocesan ordinaries, and to the superiors of orders and of clerical congregations.

The power to give an indult of secularization (cc. 638 and 640) contains indirectly (not implicitly) the power to dispense from vows. Dismissal almost always carries with it a dispensation from temporary vows (c. 648), and often from perpetual simple vows (c. 669).

225. The Code distinguishes between a simple profession of temporary vows, a simple profession of perpetual vows, and a solemn profession. Solemn vows are all perpetual.

---

[2] *A.A.S.,* XI (1919), 355.

N.B. The word "profession" was once reserved for the vows of choir religious (men or women), or sometimes it applied only to solemn vows. In reading books which were written before the Code, this former usage should be kept in mind.

Article 2. Conditions Required for the Different Kinds of Profession

226. For the **validity** of any religious profession whatsoever, it is required (c. 572):

1. That he who makes it be of the legitimate age, that is to say, sixteen years completed, for the temporary profession, and at least twenty-one years completed, for the perpetual profession (c. 573).

2. That the lawful superior according to the constitutions admit him to profession.

The council or the chapter, according to the constitutions, will have a deliberative vote for the first temporary profession, and only a consultive vote for the perpetual profession (c. 575, § 2).

When, however, there is question of profession of perpetual vows on the part of a religious who has passed to another institute while still bound by perpetual vows taken in the first institute, then the council or chapter has a deliberative vote (c. 634 and Commission for the Interpretation of the Code, July 14, 1922, VI).

This first profession in the second institute would be invalid, therefore, if the superior had allowed it contrary to the decision of the council or chapter, or without asking its advice. In certain cases the superior would not be bound to follow the *favorable* vote of his council.

The Code says nothing of the renewal of temporary professions. In their regard, therefore, one may follow the constitutions.

3. That the novitiate shall have been validly made (c. 555).

4. That the profession be free from violence, grave fear, or fraud.

This violence or fraud must be suffered by the person making the profession, as is evident from the omission of any express reference to c. 542, 1° (see above n. **179** *c*). The Code has not judged it necessary to protect the superior in the same way. As a matter of fact, the superior who has been influenced by violence or fraud will easily have the power later on to dismiss the religious in question.

5. That it shall be expressed in formal terms.

In former times the tacit profession was not declared invalid in the case of orders of men. Even now a written formula is not required by the Code, although the attestation of the act of profession should be in writing.

6. That the profession shall be received by the lawful superior according to the constitutions, acting either in his own person or by his representative.

227. "To admit to the profession" and "to receive the profession" are two different acts which should not be confused. To *receive* the profession means to accept it in the name of the Church, either by virtue of one's own power, or as representative of the lawful superior. The priest before whom the profession is usually made in lay religious institutes is not necessarily the one who receives it. This is the case only when he is delegated by the bishop, to whom the constitutions reserve the reception of the profession; if not thus delegated, the priest acts simply as assistant at the ceremony, and the vows are pronounced before him, because he is saying the Mass, or to give the ceremony a more sacred character. In general, in the institutes approved by the Holy See, the profession is received by the superioress or her delegate. In such a case it would be useful to have the constitutions declare expressly that the presence of the local Ordinary or of his delegate is not required either for the validity or for the lawfulness of the profession, but merely for the greater solemnity of the rite. The constitutions may make other arrangements as is the case with the Little Sisters of the Poor. In diocesan institutes, there is no general rule. The question is of some importance. As a matter of fact, if the profession is received, in a strict sense, by the bishop or his delegate, it belongs to him to designate who shall replace him on occasion, and a profession made before another priest would be invalid. On the contrary, if the profession is addressed to the superior general or to his delegate, it can be made in the presence of any priest.

The priest who is habitually delegated by the bishop to receive the profession, for example, the dean or the chaplain, may subdelegate in particular cases. It would be prudent to ask the Ordinary of the place to be so kind as thus to delegate the priest who celebrates the Mass at which the vows are taken, with the approbation, legitimately presumed, of the usual delegate. The superioress will preserve this episcopal document so as to be able to show it to the priest who might doubt about his powers in the matter.

It is to be desired that in lay institutes the constitutions or the formula of profession shall clearly state which superior receives the vows. The Commission of Interpretation has decided that, if the formula of the vows makes no mention of the superioress, but only mentions the bishop or his delegate, it is he who receives the vows by virtue of a lawful mandate.[3] Though the Commission speaks only of institutes approved by the Holy See, its decision may be applied with all the more reason in the case of diocesan congregations. It would not be proper to conclude, however, that it is always the superior who receives the profession when she is named in the formula. Still this interpretation may be held to, unless the constitutions or the formula of the vows clearly state the contrary.

The superior designated by the constitutions to *receive* the profession, may certainly delegate another person for this act, e.g., a prominent guest (a bishop, a secular priest, a visiting religious, etc.). This case may be practical if a religious is obliged to take his last vows outside his community, e.g., in a hospital.

228. Perpetual profession may not be validly made until at least three years after the temporary profession, except in the case of a religious professed of perpetual vows who passes to another institute (cc. 574, 634, n. **328, 2**).

In certain institutes of simple vows, the formula of profession contains this condition: "As long as I shall live in the congregation," or some other equivalent expression. Such a promise is not absolute, and the Church does not consider these truly perpetual vows. Thus, in these congregations it is not necessary to make first a strictly temporary profession to last for three years. This is the decision of the Commission of Interpretation.[4] We shall see later that when there is question of dismissal these vows are equivalent to a temporary profession. These three years are to be reckoned from day to day, but the profession of perpetual vows can be made on the anniversary day of the first vows. If it should be anticipated, even only by twenty-four hours, it would be invalid.

Even when the temporary vows have been renewed before the anniversary date (see n. **236**), the perpetual vows may not be pronounced before the third anniversary of the first vows.

229. This temporary profession is imposed by the Code on all orders and congregations in which perpetual vows are taken.

The Society of Jesus is not subject to this prescription. The Religious of the Sacred Heart have also been dispensed from it. According to the former law, the first vows in religious orders were perpetual.

The first temporary profession regularly lasts three years. If, however, the novice will not have reached within three years

---

[3] Response March 1, 1921. — *A.A.S.*, XIII (1921), 178; *N.R. Th.* (1921), 270; *Per.*, X, 325.

[4] Response, March 1, 1921. — *A.A.S.*, XIII (1921), 177; *N.R. Th.* (1921), 269; *Per.*, X, 325.

the age required for his perpetual profession, he will take his vows for the length of time which intervenes. Those constitutions may also be kept which prescribe annual professions during three years (c. 574, § 1).

230. The lawful superior may prolong the duration of the temporary profession by directing the religious to renew his profession, but this may not be done beyond a second period of three years (c 574, § 2).

1. The lengthening of the profession beyond three years depends, according to the Code, on the lawful superior. He is to be designated by the constitutions and ordinarily he will be the same person who has the right to admit to the first vows. The constitutions will direct whether and how he must take the advice of his council or chapter.

May the constitutions prescribe temporary vows for a period of five years without special authorization of the Holy See? In the case of an institute approved by the Holy See the question will be determined by Rome's approval of the constitutions. In the case of a diocesan institute, we believe that the Ordinary has no such power.

The Holy See rather readily allows these professions for three years to be immediately followed by one for two years, or it will grant permission to make the profession for five years immediately, or even for two periods of three years each.

Is the desire of the subject a sufficient reason for the superior to prolong the period of temporary vows? It may be, and such a case is explicitly provided for in certain statutes approved by the Holy See.

2. The superior who, to prove the professed, causes him to renew his profession for one, two, or three years, may always, if he judges it fitting, allow the perpetual profession to be made sooner.

The lawful superior who extends the time of temporary profession, is not obliged to do this for an entire year. In the case of such an extension, the day of the perpetual profession will, therefore, depend on this superior. Evidently the term of six years after the first vows may not be exceeded.

231. After six years of temporary vows the religious who is old enough must either be admitted to perpetual profession, or must leave the institute (c. 575).[5]

---

[5] When the period of six years has been unduly exceeded, Father Vermeersch thought that the prorogation was null (*Epitome*, I⁷, n. 726, 2, c). But the

232. When the professed of temporal vows will not have reached, at the end of the usual period, the age fixed by the Code or the constitutions for the *perpetual* profession, how does he take his vows?

If the constitutions prescribe annual professions, they will be renewed from year to year. That which precedes the date on which the professed will attain the age required for solemn profession may be made for the number of months and days required.

If the constitutions require a first profession of three years (or four or five years), a double solution is possible. The novice may immediately make profession until the required age; or he may make the ordinary profession and then renew it until the required age. The former solution seems the only one which is conformed to the text of the Code.

In this case may the lawful superior postpone the profession once more for a period of three years? According to the text of the Code this postponement is not forbidden.

To be sure, it says: "no longer than another period of three years," but the motive is to be found in the fact that the normal duration of the first profession is three years. We may reason by analogy from c. 539, § 2 (*non tamen ultra aliud semestre*) (not, however, beyond another six months); according to the opinion of the best commentators the superior may prolong postulancy for six months more, even though it has already lasted more than six months according to the constitutions. If, however, the professed had already six years of temporary vows, it would be contrary to the spirit of the Code and to the decisions of the Sacred Congregation to lengthen the time of probation still more. The more extended the time fixed by the constitutions for the perpetual profession, the stronger are the reasons for not putting off the final decision.

What is to be done if the anniversary (21 years) of the professed falls on a day on which the ceremony of profession would cause serious inconvenience? This would be a sufficient motive for the lawful superior to have the profession renewed once more for the necessary time.

233. The first profession should be made in a **novitiate** house (c. 574, § 1). The text of the Code does not indicate clearly that

Code which forbids such a prorogation does not add a nullifying clause. Hence, though acting contrary to Church law, the superior nevertheless keeps the authority necessary to admit to profession which, on this point at least, will be valid (see cc. 15 and 19).

this is to be a condition of validity. Until an official decision is given to the contrary, we may consider it a simple direction.

234. In making the religious profession, the **rite** prescribed by the constitutions must be observed (c. 576, § 1).

1. The rite comprises the essential elements and also the accidental ceremonies which go with them. It is essential that the formula should clearly express the obligations accepted and their duration. The precise meaning of the formula is determined by the rule, the constitutions, or by custom. The recitation of this formula in the presence of the competent superior, or of his delegate, suffices to assure the incorporation of the professed into the institute, with all its rights and obligations.

If the formula of the vows is inserted in the constitutions, its text and any subsequent modifications require the approbation of the same superior who approves the constitutions. If the formula is merely inserted in the Directory — which rarely happens — it may be approved in the case of diocesan congregations of nuns by the Ordinary of the place or by the regular superior.

The profession need not necessarily be made in a church or chapel. It can be made in the chapter room or in any other room, in the presence of the required witnesses. When the profession takes place during Mass, it should be made after the Communion of the priest. The profession of first vows or of perpetual vows must be made separately by each religious who immediately thereafter receives Holy Communion. For the renewal of vows the professed may pronounce the form in common; Holy Communion is given to them after all have renewed their vows (see S. Congregation of Rites, August 27, 1894 and June 5, 1896; decrees nos. 3836 and 3912).

2. In the case of nuns the rites and formulas which refer to the perpetuity of the religious state should be kept for the solemn profession. For the simple and temporary profession it is enough to make one's vows in the choir or in the chapter, in the hands of the lawful superior or his delegate. This is the decision taken by the Sacred Congregation of Religious, July 10, 1919.[6]

---

[6] This answer published in the *A.A.S.*, XI (1919), 323, annuls explicitly the responses given on the same subject by the Sacred Congregation of Bishops and Regulars July 18, 1902, and January 15, 1903. The first-mentioned document may be found in Vermeersch, *De relig.*, II, 182; the second, in the *Monitore ecclesiastico*, XV, 387.

Many of the usual ceremonies, for example, the blessing of the veil and the blessing and giving of the ring have no necessary relation to the absolute perpetuity of the religious state, but indicate simply a change in one's state of life. Thus, they may be used in the first profession since no decision forbids that it be made publicly and with a certain solemnity.[7]

The answer of the Sacred Congregation regards nuns of solemn vows. But the reason evidently holds for all the nuns, because for all the first profession is temporary.

3. In certain monasteries the special rite of the consecration of virgins has been preserved. Since the ceremonies of the Pontifical contain only the consecration of virginity, they are not sufficient as a rite of profession.

Since it is strictly forbidden to the officiating Prelate to use this consecration in the case of anyone who has not kept her virginity, it will be well to call the attention of the aspirants to this condition. We cannot enter into a discussion of the different opinions on this subject. The one point which is beyond discussion is this, that a young woman who by a grave, culpable, exterior act has lost the virginity of her soul and her corporal integrity, cannot be admitted to this consecration. She is not obliged to acknowledge those sins, even though they are grave, which have not destroyed this integrity, or to mention the violence suffered without gravely culpable consent.[8]

235. The act of profession is to be drawn up in writing, signed by the professed and at least by the superior or the delegate who has received the profession. This document is to remain in the archives. In the case of solemn profession the superior must inform the parish priest of the parish in which the professed was baptized (c. 576, § 2).

236. *Renovation of the Vows.*

There are two kinds of **renovation of vows,** one of obligation, and the other of devotion.

1. The obligatory renovation required by the law of the Church, is a new profession of vows, which have expired or shall soon expire.

No interval must be allowed to lapse between the expiration of previous vows and the renovation. The latter must be made, at the latest, on the anniversary day of the former profession,

---

[7] See *Comm. pro rel.,* I (1920), 289 sq.; *Theologie und Glaube* (1921), 355.
[8] See Pellizzari, *De Monialibus,* Chap. III, sec. III.

and not earlier than one month before that day, if there is a just reason for anticipation (c. 577).

This liberty granted by the Code allows renewing the vows for one or three years, plus the number of days by which one has anticipated the renovation. The religious who, for example, on August 2, renews his first vows made on the preceding August 15, takes his vows not merely until the following August 2, but until August 15 on the following year; for it is the date of the first profession that determines that of the perpetual profession. The vows which were taken on February 29 ought to be renewed on February 28, and not on March 1.

The perpetual profession may not be anticipated; it is to take place at the earliest on the third anniversary day of the first profession.

Those religious who renew their vows which are about to expire must pronounce the formula separately, and indicate the time for which they renew them. Otherwise who can bear witness to the exact meaning of this renovation?

To institutes in which difficulty was frequently found in renewing the temporary professions, or in making the perpetual profession on the anniversary of the first vows, the Sacred Congregation has already given an indult to count the years of the profession from retreat to retreat.

In this case the religious remains bound by his vows up to the time of *his* retreat of the following year, hence up to the time of the last of these retreats if there be several of them and he is destined for the last one. But if he wishes to leave the institute, or if his superiors refuse to allow him to renew his vows, he may leave after the first retreat, since he could have been assigned to make this retreat.

2. The renovation of devotion, prescribed by the constitutions, has for its purpose the renewal of fervor with which each one should observe the temporary or perpetual vows which are still in force. This renovation of devotion cannot prolong the time for which the vows are taken. To act otherwise would be to take away from the professed and the superiors a freedom which the Holy See has wished to give them by means of the temporary vows.

This renovation of devotion must not be confused with the renovation of the vows of devotion.

It is important to note that this renovation of devotion as such would not validate a profession that was invalid (c. 586, § 1).

237. *The Profession of Religious Who Are Obliged to Military Service.*[9]

By military service is meant the ordinary service which young religious, when first placed under military authority and discipline by civil law, are obliged to render for at least six months continuously or intermittently, either by bearing arms or by serving in any auxiliary capacity, even in that pertaining to sanitation and health.

No religious can be admitted *validly* to *perpetual* profession before he has performed his military service, or has been absolutely declared unfit for it, or for any other reason has been freed legitimately and permanently from the obligation to serve.

Ordinarily the temporary vows of a religious who has been called to the service are *suspended* when he comes under military discipline.

However, the major superior, acting with the advice of his consultors and according to his own conscience and prudence, can permit a religious called to military service who asks for the favor and is certainly worthy of it, to remain under temporary vows during such service for a definite time or *ad nutum.*

During the period of military discipline the same superior for a just and serious cause can, by a notice in writing, suspend the vows which were allowed the religious; and he can likewise grant the restoration of the same vows which were suspended either at the beginning of his military service or afterward.

238. In the United States, ministers of religion or divinity students are by law placed in class IV-D of deferred registrants which exempts them equivalently from ordinary military service. Religious living in other English-speaking countries should consult their national laws regarding military service to determine whether they are subject to these prescriptions of the S. Congregation of Religious.

Article 3. Effects of Religious Profession

239. The religious profession produces different effects, according to whether it is temporary or perpetual, simple or solemn.

---

[9] Read the Decree on Religious and Military Service issued by the S. Congregation of Religious, July 30, 1957, and printed in Appendix VI.

The first profession is always (except in case of special privilege) simple and temporary. What we have to say under these two headings must, therefore, be applied to it.

§ 1. TEMPORARY PROFESSION

240. 1. This temporary profession brings with it all the spiritual advantages which are enjoyed by the professed who have taken perpetual vows whether simple or solemn.

2. It imposes on the professed the obligation to observe the rules and constitutions. He is, however, not bound to the private recitation of the divine office, unless the constitutions expressly declare this. Of course, from the time he is ordained subdeacon, the religious is obliged to this recitation by reason of his major order.

3. It does not confer active or passive voice, unless the constitutions expressly declare the contrary. The time required to obtain these rights is calculated from the time of the first profession, unless the constitutions direct otherwise (c. 578).

"Active voice" is the right to vote in the chapter; "passive voice," the right to be elected to some office which is conferred by election.

4. "The obligation of vows made before the religious profession is suspended as long as he who made those vows remains in religion" (c. 1315).

5. The affiliation to pious associations. Those who have pronounced perpetual or temporary vows in a religious institute may not belong to a third order, even if they were members before their profession; but they can become members of other pious associations whose obligations are, in the judgment of superiors, compatible with the observance of the constitutions (cc. 693, § 4; 704).

But there is no objection to granting the privilege of aggregation to a third order with all its advantages, either to a religious institute or to a religious house; the individual members then do not become tertiaries, and do not assume the obligations of tertiaries.[10]

---

[10] Cf. the aggregation of the Company of the Daughters of St. Ursula to the Third Order of St. Francis (*A.A.S.*, IX [1917], 350; *Per.*, IX, 48). This Company is not to be confounded with the order or the different congregations of Ursuline religious.

§ 2. PERPETUAL PROFESSION

241. 1. By this profession the religious definitely becomes a member of the institute; he may thereafter be elected to all the offices, if certain conditions are fulfilled; his dismissal is subject to provisions which make it very difficult.

2. Perpetual profession separates the religious from the diocese to which he had belonged as a secular. There is question here, for all religious, of the domicile of origin, and for clerics, of the diocese in which they had been admitted to the clerical state. In other words, by the perpetual profession, clerics are "excardinated" (c. 585).[11]

3. The unlawful and definitive abandonment of the religious institute constitutes the crime of apostasy (c. 644. See n. **340**).

This crime of apostasy from religion must not be confused with the crime of apostasy from the faith.

4. Marriage becomes forbidden under pain of excommunication incurred by the act itself, and absolution from which is reserved to the Ordinary of the culpable party (see c. 2388, § 2).

§ 3. SIMPLE PROFESSION

242. The simple profession renders acts against the vows illicit, but not invalid, unless the constitutions explicitly state the contrary (c. 579).

If, therefore, the professed of simple vows disposes of his patrimony in favor of a third person, even without permission, this third person acquires a true right to it, though he sins if he knowingly co-operates with such a fault of a religious. A marriage contracted by one professed of simple vows would be valid, except in case of a member of the Society of Jesus.

"Those who contract or attempt to contract marriage, even before a civil magistrate, while they are themselves still bound by vows of religion, though these are merely simple and temporary, or who enter upon marriage with a woman who is bound by such vows, incur an irregularity[12] by reason of the crime" (c. 985, 3).

---

[11] Incardination is the definitive admission into the clergy of a diocese; by excardination one ceases to belong to that body.

[12] An irregularity is an impediment which forbids the reception or the exercise of holy orders.

243. *Disposition of Property* (cc. 580, 583).

1. A professed of simple vows keeps the **ownership** of his property and the right to acquire more property, unless the constitutions explicitly state the contrary.

In religious congregations this double right is almost always kept. It is done away with by the last profession in the Society of Jesus.

2. If one who is professed acquires new property, he must give over the **management** of it to someone else, and determine **what disposition is to be made of the revenues** and of its use, as has been explained in the foregoing (n. **217**).

Such cession and disposition of property cease to bind as soon as a subject leaves the institute.

In the formula of transfer of the management, or of the disposition of property by gratuitous title, the professed must avoid putting in a condition whose realization depends entirely on his own will, for example: "unless I leave the institute." In some countries the civil law does not recognize this sort of condition. He may write, for example, "as long as I remain in the institute," or "unless I am sent away from the institute," etc.

3. A professed may **change** the dispositions which he has made in regard to his property:

a) Freely, if the constitutions allow it.

The constitutions may authorize him to change these dispositions which he has already made, but not to use the revenues as he wishes without permission. This faculty would be directly contrary to the vow of poverty as the Church conceives it; it would be equivalent to declaring that the professed need make no disposition regarding the use of his revenues, and this would be contrary to the Code (c. 580, § 1).

b) In any case, with the express permission of the superior general. But nuns must have the authorization of the Ordinary of the place and also of the regular superior of men on whom their monastery depends.

At the moment of determining to what use his revenues are to be put, the professed may make the institute the beneficiary.

A change may never be made so as to give the institute a notable part of the property. A notable part would be, for example, a fourth, or certainly a third of the revenues.

If the religious had never disposed of the revenues before his first profession, we think that he could do it afterwards, even in favor of the institute and without the authorization of superiors.

4. It is forbidden to the professed of simple vows in religious congregations:

a) To abdicate gratuitously the dominion over their property by a voluntary deed of conveyance (*per actum inter vivos*) (c. 583, 1).

An act *inter vivos* is a juridical act in which two or more persons participate, and which becomes effective while they are still living; hence any act, except a last will or donation in case of death (*mortis causa*). One alienates gratuitously when no compensation is asked for, or at least no consideration which is about equal to what is loaned, sold, pledged, etc. One cannot say, however, that a person abdicates the dominion of his property when he gives away sums which are comparatively small in comparison with the size of his fortune or his revenues.

The Holy See wishes by this prohibition to avoid having the professed place himself in a position in which he could not live outside of the institute, in case he should be obliged to leave it.

b) The professed of simple vows are also forbidden to change the will they have made before their profession (c. 583, 2); authorization to do this must be asked of the Holy See. In urgent cases, the higher superior, or, if recourse cannot be had to him, even the local superior may give this authorization.

This prohibition has to do with the will which was drawn up conformably to the prescriptions of the Code (c. 569). The Code forbids any modification of any importance which is not made strictly necessary by the failure of the previous disposition of property. Thus, the professed may dispose anew of gifts which he had bequeathed to a person who has died before the maker of the will. If one who has been left a legacy becomes gravely unworthy of this favor, we are of the opinion that even then the will made in his favor cannot be changed, except in case that it would constitute a direct or indirect co-operation with his sins.

244. Those religious who made their profession before Pentecost (May 19), 1918:

a) Can make their will without special authorization, unless the constitutions which were in force before the Code demand this authorization for the making of a will after profession.

b) They are allowed to change their will once without special authorization, if the constitutions previous to the Code permitted it.

There is question here of an acquired right which the Code has not done away with (see c. 4). We say "once," because in making this new form of will, the religious knows that the existing law forbids him to make any further modification.

c) They are under no obligation to make their will. It is advisable, however, that all who have any property or any real expectation of acquiring property should do so.[13]

245. All **property acquired** by religious through their personal activity, or in behalf of the religious institute, becomes the property of the religious institute.

Such are the offerings given for the exercise of the holy ministry; the fees and royalties paid to authors; alms given, unless the institute is formally excluded from their enjoyment; the salaries of professors and teachers, etc.

246. Military pensions. Pensions which come to a religious because of outstanding merit or by reason of wounds received or disease contracted during military service, are turned over to the religious institute and belong to it as long as the religious remains in it. The individual acquires them for himself if he leaves.

Gratuities or gifts or any such largesses, given on account of the death of a religious during military service, go to the religious institute of which he was a member at the time of his death (see Appendix VI, Art. V).

§ 4. SOLEMN PROFESSION

247. 1. The solemn profession establishes between the order and the religious mutual bonds which **cannot be severed by** the mere consent of the parties.

2. In those orders which have the obligation of choir, the religious who have made the solemn profession, except the lay brothers, are bound to the private recitation of the **divine office,** if they have not taken part in its public recitation (**c. 610, § 3**).

---

[13] See B. Lijdsman, C.SS.R., *Der neue Kodex und das Testament der Ordensleute, Th. prakt. Q. Schrift* (1920), 336 sq.

3. The solemn profession makes **invalid** those acts **contrary** to the vows which are susceptible of nullity (c. 579).

Thus, for example, any donation or sale, made in one's own name, or a marriage contracted after the solemn profession, is void.

Furthermore, marriage contracted but not consummated is annulled by the solemn profession (c. 1119).

In this law, the Sovereign Pontiff uses the special power which he possesses, by divine right, over the matrimonial contract of the faithful, as long as this contract has not been made absolutely indissoluble by the conjugal act.

248. Unless he has obtained a special indult of the Holy See, the professed of solemn vows is **incapable** of possessing and of acquiring property.

Regulars in Belgium and Holland can, with the authorization of their superiors, possess and acquire temporal goods and, with permission, can dispose of them as real owners. This authorization has been accorded by the answer of the Sacred Penitentiary (December 1, 1820) and has been confirmed by an indult of the Sacred Congregation for Extraordinary Affairs, July 31, 1878. It allows to Regulars the "intention to possess," required by the Belgian law in those to whom property is transferred by voluntary deed of conveyance, by will, or by intestate inheritance.[14]

249. Renunciation of Property. "Except within sixty days preceding the solemn profession the professed of simple vows cannot validly renounce his property, but within this time he must, saving special indults from the Holy See, renounce in favor of whomsoever he wishes all the property which he actually possesses, on condition of his profession subsequently taking place" (c. 581, § 1).

The choice of the persons in favor of whom he renounces his property is left to the free choice of the regular. Even in Belgium and in Holland regulars, except in exceptional cases, make this renunciation of their goods.

Immediately after the solemn profession has been made all necessary measures must be taken to make the renunciation effective according to civil law (c. 581, § 2).

---

[14] See Vermeersch, *De relig.*, II, pp. 78 sqq.; *Epitome*, I^r, n. 685.

The religious may also renounce that property which may come to him after his solemn profession, especially if he already has a certain right to it, as is the case for the lawful share of a paternal inheritance. The property which he has not renounced will accrue to the order, the province, or the monastery, according to the constitutions, at the moment when the professed would acquire the title to it. If the order were incapable of acquiring such property, it would become the property of the Holy See (c. 582).

In certain orders, the institute, the province, and the houses, though all capable of acquiring property, cannot do so in the place of a professed who is made heir or universal legatee. In such cases the property left to the professed would not be acquired by the Holy See, but by those heirs to whom it would have been given, if the professed were dead.

Article 4. Validation of an Invalid Profession

250. 1. A religious profession which was null on account of some external impediment can only be made valid by an indult of the Holy See or by a new profession. This new profession must obviously fulfill all the required conditions for validity which were wanting in the former invalid profession. Hence, the impediment must have disappeared. It is required, furthermore, that a religious when renewing his vows should know that the former profession was null. If the profession was null on account of a purely internal defect of consent, it is sufficient that the internal consent be now given, provided that the institute has not revoked its own consent (c. 586).

An external impediment is not the same thing as a known impediment. External impediments would be, for example, the lack of age required for the valid beginning of a novitiate or for the profession itself, or the taking of the vows before the completion of the novitiate, or the presence of an impediment to the validity of admission.

If the constitutions state that the renovation made from devotion shall produce all the effects of profession, even in case the profession itself has been invalid, this declaration is only equivalent to the continuance of consent on the part of lawful superiors. It does not do away with the requirement that the religious should be aware of the nullity of his previous profession, in order to take his vows validly in the renovation.

2. "If there be serious arguments against the validity of the religious profession, and the religious refuses, as a measure of

precaution (*ad cautelam*), either to renew the profession or to petition for its convalidation, the matter shall be referred to the Apostolic See" (c. 586, § 3).

No religious, therefore, may leave his institute because he has serious reasons to doubt the validity of his profession. There is no question here of private vows, but of promises officially accepted by ecclesiastical authority. The latter reserves to itself the right to examine the doubt and, in case of need, to annul the effects of the doubtful obligation.

Obligations and Privileges of Religious

CHAPTER VII

Obligations of Religious

251. The obligations of religious result from their state, from their vows, from their rules and constitutions, and from the special laws of the Church (cc. 592, 593).

Article 1.   Obligations in Common With Clerics
252. Being consecrated to God, religious are subject to the common obligations of clerics, always taking account of the exceptions and modifications which are introduced into the case by the condition of persons, by the nature of things, and by the special provisions of the law (c. 592).

§ 1.   A LIFE OF PERFECTION
253. "Each and every religious, superior as well as subject, is bound not only to faithfully and integrally observe the vows of which he has made profession, but also to order his life according to the rules and constitutions of his institute, and thus tend to the perfection of his state" (c. 593).

1. Religious, like clerics (c. 124), are bound to live a more holy life than lay people. The graces they have received from God, the promises which they have made to Him, the majority of the obligations of their state, require of them a greater purity of heart and, therefore, a greater perfection. They satisfy this obligation by observing their vows and the constitutions of their institute (cc. 592, 593).

The perfection of man consists in his union with God by charity. According to the very words of Jesus Christ, this love shows itself by the doing of the divine will. Hence the striving after perfection is nothing else than the constant will to avoid all sin, even venial sin. If it is admitted that a person can, without sin, refuse to follow an inspiration, or to do a work which is merely of counsel, then we must add that to tend to perfection supposes, also, the habitual will to respond to these desires of God when they are clearly manifested. They are manifested especially and above all by the rules and by the orders and wishes of superiors. Finally, perfection depends also on fervor, that is to say, the purity and the intensity of the love with which one accomplishes the will of God.

Has a religious, because he is a religious, a special obligation to tend to perfection? In other words, has he agreed by his profession not only to keep his vows and observe the constitutions, but also to take special care to flee sin and avoid all tepidity? Does he then commit a special fault when he fails to fulfill obligations of his state, a fault of which a secular priest or a layman would not be guilty if he showed a similar negligence?

A very common opinion answers "yes." An implicit promise is given by joining a religious institute that one will strive after perfection; a new duty of state results from the profession, a duty to tend to perfection; the profession, as distinct from the vows, is an engagement to strive after perfection. Those who hold this opinion are not so well agreed as to when and how the lax religious commits a fault against this obligation. Practically they all admit that it is sufficient in the tribunal of penance to confess faults against the vows and the constitutions.

This opinion does not seem to us to be sufficiently substantiated. The religious, it seems to us, manifests the *intention* of striving after perfection; he assumes the *obligation* of employing certain *means* which Scripture and tradition present to him as most efficacious for this purpose; his state of life obliges him *indirectly* to strive after perfection, because he *must* place acts which lead to perfection. The graces included in his vocation, as well as those which the religious life is continually obtaining for him, make a religious more clear-sighted. He has freely taken upon himself obligations more numerous and more holy than those which bind ordinary Christians. If, under these circumstances, a religious is not determined to strive after perfection, he exposes himself to the danger of committing venial sins both more numerous and more serious than would be committed by ordinary Christians in a similar state of mind. This concept seems to us to follow from the following principles: every man must strive to love God with his whole heart, with his whole soul, and with all his strength; poverty, chastity, and obedience, the religious rule, are excellent means for attaining this end, which all must endeavor to obtain; the religious is *expressly* bound to employ these means. That suffices to explain his whole life.[1] Hence we may conclude that a religious

---

[1] A detailed study of these two opinions may be found in Vermeersch, *De relig.*, II, 68 sq., and P. Geerts, P.S.C., in *Rev. Asc. et Myst.*, II (1921), 213 sq.

has no *special* obligation to strive after perfection, and that he does not commit a *special* fault when he fails to fulfill the obligation of his state.

2. The *duties of his state* are, for the religious, as for every other man, the certain will of God which must be accomplished before every other work of piety, penance, and charity.

The first duty of state for every religious is the observance of the rules and constitutions of his institute. These show him how he must discharge the duties which belong to his vocation, according to the nature of the religious institute which he has entered; these duties make up the other obligations of his state of life.

Religious will, therefore, measure their perfection, that is to say, their love of God, by the constant generosity with which they give themselves to the different works of their institute, to the celebration of the divine services, to preaching, to the teaching of youth, to visiting the poor, to the care of the sick or the infirm.

To neglect, under any pretext whatever, these primary and certain obligations, would be to fall into the deplorable delusion of doing one's own will and not God's will, and perchance would cause grave scandal to the faithful and to the enemies of our holy religion.

3. Zeal for perfection should likewise inspire a very delicate concern for the virtues which go to make up the gentleman, such as justice, equity, urbanity, etc.

The Code has thought it useful to recall such principles when occasion offers, for example, the following: "All, and especially clerics, religious, and the administrators of ecclesiastical property when contracting with employees, should give workmen an honest and just salary; they should avoid imposing burdens upon them which are beyond their strength, or not compatible with their age and sex" (c. 1524).

These virtues will find room for their exercise in the scrupulous delicacy with which religious safeguard the interests, even material interests, of those parents who confide their children to their care, in the respect for agreements entered into with boarding students, with the sick or with old people, in the salaries paid lay teachers, workmen, and servants.

§ 2. EXERCISES OF PIETY

254. 1. The Holy See imposes upon superiors the obligation of providing for their subjects both time and opportunities to attend to mental and vocal prayer, as well as for the frequent reception of the sacraments of penance and of the Eucharist.

The Code imposes no new obligation on subjects beyond what is already contained in the constitutions.

The gravity of this obligation arises both from the important part which prayer plays in the religious life, and from the very nature of the religious vocation. All who enter religion must suppose that they will always be allowed to draw abundantly from these sources of the supernatural life.

2. Superiors should take care that all the religious:
1) "Make a **retreat** each year."

Nothing is determined regarding the form or the length of duration of these spiritual exercises.

In the following words His Holiness Pius XI expresses his esteem of retreats made according to the spiritual exercises of St. Ignatius of Loyola. "Among the different means of promoting piety and the perfection of Christian life, a special place belongs of right to the spiritual exercises which St. Ignatius, by truly divine inspiration, has introduced into the Church." The Sovereign Pontiff then recalls that St. Francis de Sales prepared for his episcopal consecration by making the exercises of St. Ignatius, and during their course decided on the manner of life which he observed ever afterwards; that St. Charles Borromeo, after having acquired from these exercises the zeal for perfection, promoted their use far and wide among his clergy; that St. Teresa of Avila, "that mistress of the highest contemplation," had a singular esteem for these exercises, as did St. Leonard of Port Maurice, son of the seraphic patriarch, who declared that to gain souls for God he followed in every respect the method of St. Ignatius.[2]

2) "Daily assist at **Mass,** unless legitimately impeded; make their **meditation,** and faithfully perform the other exercises of piety prescribed by the rules and constitutions."

3) "Approach the **sacrament of penance** at least once a week" (c. 595).

From all this, superiors have the obligation:
a) to give religious the time and the opportunity to go to confession at least once a week;
b) to notify the Ordinary, if the ordinary confessor or his substitute neglects or refuses to hear the confessions of the religious at least once a week;
c) without spying upon them, to remind those religious who neglect weekly confession of their obligation.

---

[2] The apostolic constitution *Summorum Pontificum* declares St. Ignatius of Loyola the heavenly patron of retreats or spiritual exercises. — *A.A.S.*, XIV (1922), 420; *N.R. Th.* (1923), 337 sq.; Encycl. *Mens nostra; A.A.S.*, XXI (1929), 589.

This canon indirectly confirms the obligation of the rule for inferiors, but it does not add any new obligation under pain of sin.

255. As the Code treats of **indulgences** immediately after the sacrament of penance, of which they perfect the fruits, we shall mention some decisions on this subject here:

1. When a visit to any church or public oratory is required for the gaining of an indulgence, and when a religious community has no church or public chapel, the religious, their boarders and domestics, can gain these indulgences by visiting the chapel of the house where they hear Mass, on condition that they fulfill the other works prescribed (c. 929).

2. If confession is prescribed for gaining any indulgence, it may be made within the eight days which precede that to which the indulgence is attached. Holy Communion may be received on the day before; both confession and Communion also are permitted during the octave, i.e., on the day itself and on the seven days following (c. 931, § 1).

For example: To gain a plenary indulgence which is attached to the Feast of the Assumption, the confession may be made from August 7 to 22. Holy Communion may be received from August 14 to 22 (see *Coll. Nam.*, XVIII [1924], 152).

The faithful who are accustomed to confess at least twice a month, or who go to Communion every day, even if they have missed once or twice during the week, may gain the indulgences even if they have not gone to confession within the prescribed time. Indulgences granted for an ordinary or extraordinary jubilee, or in the form of a jubilee, are excepted from this concession (c. 931, § 3).

3. Those who are prevented, for example, by sickness, from fulfilling the works prescribed, may ask their confessor to change them into other good works (c. 935).

4. The indulgences which are attached to beads or other objects cease only when the beads or objects are entirely destroyed or sold (c. 924, § 2).

Before the Code it was held that these indulgences were a privilege reserved to the first owner of the object, and that they ceased to have any value as soon as they passed to another person. This is no longer the case.

5. Those regulars who have the power to give the papal blessing (twice a year, on condition that there is some special solemnity), may use this privilege within the ordinary limits, in their churches and those of nuns or tertiaries who are lawfully affiliated to their order (c. 915. See *Epitome*, II⁶, n. 209).

6. Higher superiors of exempt clerics can designate and declare one altar to be daily and perpetually privileged, provided there is no other privileged altar in their church. They cannot declare an altar privileged in public or semipublic oratories, unless these are united to or subsidiaries of a parochial church (c. 916. See *Epitome*, II⁶, n. 211).

256. "Superiors should promote among their subjects the frequent, even daily, reception of **Holy Communion**; and liberty must be given to every properly disposed religious to approach frequently, even daily, the Most Holy Eucharist."

"If, however, a religious has, since his last sacramental confession, given grave scandal to the community, or committed a serious external fault, the superior can forbid him to receive Holy Communion until he shall have again approached the sacrament of penance" (c. 595, §§ 2, 3).

The number and the days of Communion fixed in the directories and custom books have now only a directive value. They may be expressed in the following manner: "Communion is especially recommended on the following days . . ." (see c. 595, §§ 2–4).

It belongs to the confessor or the director of conscience to give religious who apply to him proper advice about the frequency of Holy Communion. They are not allowed to forbid Communion to any person who is in the state of grace, but they may advise a certain abstention which they judge necessary for this particular soul, when such advice will be likely to dissipate certain illusions, or to encourage a greater care in making the proper preparation.

Religious must carefully avoid watching how often others go to Holy Communion, and must also avoid forming any judgment on their occasional abstention; above all, they should never make this the subject of conversation. If a religious who is charged with observing the exterior conduct of the community or without having tried to find out, notices that one of the members of the community is staying away from Communion frequently or for a long time, he may, and sometimes he ought to, communicate this fact to the superior. A prudent word to the confessor will often be the best means of charitably helping a soul which has grown lax or too anxious.[3]

To make it easier for those religious who occasionally may not wish to receive Holy Communion, it will be advisable to avoid having the members of the community approach the Holy Table according to seniority or any other strictly determined order (Bergh, "Safeguarding Worthy Reception in the Practice of Frequent Communion" in *R.R.*, III [1944], 252).

The obligation placed upon superiors regards religious who are sick at least as much as those who are in good health, since the sick have greater need of being strengthened by the Holy Eucharist. Superiors, then, will do all in their power to assist the sick in receiving Holy Communion daily, if such be their desire.

To limit, without serious reason, the days on which Holy Communion is to be brought to the sick, is absolutely contrary to the wishes of the Holy See.

It should likewise be made easy for the sick to omit receiving Holy Communion, if such be their wish. Hence it will be expedient each evening to give them the opportunity to express their minds in this matter.

257. Under the legislation of January 6, 1953, regarding the Eucharistic fast, all the faithful, including religious, were obliged to consult their confessor for the use of the dispensations. This is no longer the case since the *Motu Proprio* of Pope Pius XII, dated March 19, 1957, and which went into effect on March 25 of that same year. Here is the paragraph concerning the sick which all religious may follow without any consultation:

"4. Although they be not confined to bed by their illness, the sick may take non-alcoholic drinks and true and proper medicines, whether liquid or solid, before the celebration of Mass or the reception of the Holy Eucharist, without any time limit." [*Ed.*]

§ 3. STUDIES

258. 1. All religious should apply themselves with care to acquiring and retaining the knowledge required for their duties and their ministry, whether they are devoted to teaching, to the care of the sick, to social works, etc. (see cc. 129 sq.).

Teaching, the care of the sick, etc., are for religious a means of exercising apostolic zeal. They ought, therefore, to try to excel therein, so that the excellence of the service they render will give them a more extended supernatural influence. Hence they may not remain indiffer-

---

[3] See Decrees *Quemadmodum* (December 17, 1890), and *Sacra Tridentina Synodus* (December 20, 1905).

ent to progress in methods of teaching, of hospital work and administration, etc., but they must, under the direction of their superiors,
themselves try constantly to improve all their works.

2. It is common today for religious men and women to attend
universities. A number of instructions have been published by
the Holy See on this subject. Here are a few practical conclusions drawn from these instructions:

a) It is the desire of the Holy See that all institutes devoted
to teaching and hospital work should see to it that at least
a certain number of their subjects are given a truly superior
intellectual formation.

b) A religious who frequents a Catholic university should not
follow courses in a secular university which he can find in the
former.

c) Religious university students should live in a religious
house, in a seminary, or in a hostel directed by priests or religious
and approved by ecclesiastical authority.

d) Superiors should be very careful in their choice of those
whom they send to follow courses in a university, especially if
it be a secular university, and they must see to it that such
students are supplied, especially during the school term, with
all the religious helps they may need (see Creusen, *La frequenta-
tion des universités,* in *R.C.R.* [1932], 194 sq. — *Sacred Congregation of Propaganda,* Instruction, February 11, 1936. — *R.C.R.*
[1936], 81 sq. — Ellis, in *Periodica,* XXVII [1938], 106 sq.).

259. The pontifical constitution *Sedes Sapientiae* of May 31,
1956, has prescribed what is necessary for the complete formation of religious clerics, and has promulgated *General Statutes*
regarding this matter. These statutes are of obligation for all
clerics belonging to the three states of perfection: religious,
societies of common life, and secular institutes. The statutes
give a detailed application of canons 587–591 of the Code which
deal with the studies undertaken in clerical religious institutes.

1. These studies have a public character, like those made in
diocesan seminaries (General Statutes, art. 41).

2. Each institute of clerics shall have its determined houses
of studies, provided with a qualified staff and the necessary
instruments for work (library, and the like) (General Statutes,
art. 23).

"If an autonomous monastery or an institute or province cannot fulfill these conditions, the students should be sent to another monastery or to a house of formation of another province, or to an inter-province or general house, or even to a house of another religious institute, or to a diocesan seminary or a Catholic university" (c. 587, § 3; G. S., art. 23, § 3).

3. In houses of studies perfect common life must be observed; otherwise the students may not be promoted to orders (c. 587).

The nature and obligations of common life are explained below in n. 275.

If parents or friends are allowed to offer the religious students necessary or useful things, such as clothing, habits or cassocks, books, and the like, these must become the property of the community. In the use which they make of such gifts, these religious depend upon their superiors just as in the use of all other objects held in common.

4. Religious who are sent outside for study are not allowed to live in private houses, but only in a house of another religious community of men, or in a seminary or a house conducted by priests and approved by ecclesiastical authority (c. 587, §4).

This provision obliges formed religious as well, since the text makes no distinction between them and those in their studies.

260. 1. The function of the *prefect* or *spiritual director* of the students consists in forming their souls to the religious life by seasonable admonitions, instructions, and exhortations, and to direct at firsthand, under the guidance of superiors, the work of their moral, religious, clerical, and apostolic formation (c. 588, § 1; G. S., are. 28, § 2, 2). This task is so important that the post of spiritual director may never be vacant in houses of studies (G. S., art. 28, § 2, 1°).

2. The prefect or spiritual director must have the qualifications that are required in the master of novices (c. 588, § 2; see n. 204).

The role and authority of the spiritual director of religious in studies vary in different orders and congregations. The Holy See respects these differences. If true disciplinary authority is granted to this person, he should not at the same time be the ordinary confessor of his subjects (G. S., art. 28, §§ 2, 9, and 11).

261. The Code (c. 589, § 1) requires that religious clerics shall be properly trained in the lower studies. The General Statutes specify in detail that the average (ordinary) classical studies should have been completed before the beginning of the novitiate, or at least of philosophy (art. 43, § 2, 3). The study of philosophy shall last for at least two years (General Statutes, art. 44, § 1, 1) and theological studies for at least four years (G. S., art. 45, § 1, 1). These are to be rounded out by a year in pastoral training (G. S., art. 48).

Any interruption in the philosophical or theological studies of more than a total of three months of the scholastic year, even though not culpable and not continuous, makes that year invalid. If such absences from the course amount to more than one month, the omitted lessons must be made up in private under the direction of an instructor (General Statutes, art. 42, § 4).

When the Holy See authorizes the ordination of a religious before the conclusion of the prescribed studies, the beneficiary of the indult must always continue his theology to the end of the fourth year. Before the conclusion of these studies, superiors are not allowed to employ him habitually either in the sacred ministry (confessions or preaching), or in the exterior works of the institute. These restrictions are always supposed, even though the dispensation was given personally by the Sovereign Pontiff, and the obligation they impose on superiors has been declared to be grave.[4]

262. During studies it is forbidden to impose on the professors or on the students occupations which would in any manner whatever form an obstacle to their studies, or to the attendance at classes (c. 589, § 2).

Superiors may even dispense them from certain common observances if they judge it necessary for the success of their studies. The Code mentions in particular the office in choir, especially during the hours of the night (*ibid.*).

Students and professors will fail in their duty if they jeopardize their philosophical and theological studies, or their teaching, by engaging in other works, no matter how apostolic these latter may seem to be. Thus, a superior cannot allow his religious who are students in philosophy or theology to be employed as professors or prefects in a college.

Regarding the important opportunity of a final formation at the end of studies (third year, year of perfection) confer the *Statuta Generalia*, art. 51–53.

---

[4] Congregation of Religious, Declaration of October 27, 1923. — *A.A.S.*, XV (1923), 549; *N.R. Th.* (1924), 56; *Per.*, XII, 154.

263. All religious priests, after having finished their studies, shall, each year, for five years at least, undergo an examination before learned and grave fathers on the different parts of theology to be assigned in advance. Those only are excepted who are professors of theology, of canon law, or of scholastic philosophy, or those whom the higher superiors may exempt for a grave reason (c. 590).

Professors of liturgy and of ecclesiastical history may certainly enjoy this exemption from examinations, but not so the professors of sciences in the faculty of philosophy.[5]

264. In every large house (*domus formata*) a discussion on moral or liturgical cases must be held at least once a month; to which the superior may add a **conference** on dogmatic or kindred subjects connected with it; all those who are studying or who have finished theology, must assist at these conferences unless the constitutions direct otherwise (c. 591). Religious who are assistant pastors, as well as chaplains who exercise pastoral functions in religious and pious houses, are bound to assist at the diocesan conferences (Commission of Interpretation, Reply of February 12, 1935. — *A.A.S.*, XXVII [1935], 92. — *R.C.R.* [1935], 81).

§ 4. THE RELIGIOUS HABIT

265. Religious must wear the **habit** proper to their institute both inside and outside the house. The higher superior or, in case of urgency, the local superior may judge whether the circumstances excuse from this obligation (c. 596).

The religious habit which indicates to all the dignity of the profession of him who wears it, is for the religious, at once an incentive to irreproachable conduct and a safeguard for his virtue.

"Laymen are not allowed to wear the clerical garb unless they are students in ecclesiastical seminaries or aspirants to holy orders" (c. 683).

The religious habit is likewise a privilege of religious; it may be allowed only to those who are members of the institute, including the novices (see cc. 540, 639, 640 and nn. **173,** 2; **202, 332**).

§ 5. OFFICES, OCCUPATIONS, RECREATION

266. Religious are not allowed to accept spiritual or temporal **offices** whose fulfillment would require the free disposal

---

[5] See *N.R. Th.* (1921), 152.

of their person or of their property. For this reason it is forbidden to novices and professed of all institutes to be sponsors in baptism, except in urgent cases, and with the express permission of at least the local superior (c. 766).

They are not allowed to go bail or to be surety even with their own property, without consulting their Ordinary (see c. 137), nor act as a notary, a procurator, or advocate, except in cases where their institute is concerned, and which are tried before an ecclesiastical tribunal (c. 139).

267. Religious must avoid recreations which are not suited to their profession (cc. 592, 138). Religious are forbidden to enter taverns except in case of necessity. This prohibition does not include hotels and restaurants; as to cafes, they must conform to approved customs or to the particular statutes of the territory where they are at the time.

They may not take part in parades, assist at shows, dances, or fetes, where their presence would be likely to cause scandal; this is the case especially in public theaters (see cc. 138 sq., and 592).

268. Religious may not practice **medicine** or surgery without an indult from the Holy See (c. 139, § 2).

The ordinary care given in hospitals and dispensaries, and especially in mission territory, even though they form in a sense a practice of medicine, are either imposed by charity or authorized by the approval of the constitutions. If the religious must devote themselves to the actual practice of medicine and surgery, and their constitutions do not explicitly either approve or authorize them to do so, they should ask the Holy See for an indult which will readily be granted, especially in missionary territories. It is the desire of the S. Congregation for the Propagation of the Faith that religious women who have been especially prepared by the study of medicine should assist women in their confinement and take care of their newborn infants (see Instruction, February 11, 1936. — *A.A.S.*, XXVIII [1936], 208–209).

269. Religious are forbidden to engage either personally or through others in any **business** or **trading,** even for the benefit of others (cc. 592 and 124).

This prohibition has recently been repeated and very severe penalties attached to its violation.[6]

---

[6] S. Cong. of the Council, March 22, 1950; *A.A.S.*, 42, 1950, 330.

There are two commercial transactions, clearly defined, which are forbidden to clerics and to religious: the first consists in buying objects (or securities) with the intention of selling them again unchanged at a higher price; the second consists in buying raw material which, after being made up by hired help, is then sold again for profit.

But religious, like other men, may live from the fruit of their labors or from the produce of their property.

270. Instead of giving a theoretical exposition on this subject, we think it preferable to substitute some practical applications. Here are some of the transactions, which, although they have a commercial aspect, are not, from this standpoint at least, forbidden to religious.

They may sell the fruits or products of their property, whether in their natural state or changed by the labor of the religious. They may sell, even for profit, objects which have become useless, for example, furniture, materials, books, etc. They may resell, even with a great but just profit, when some special occasion arises, objects which were not bought for that purpose. They may sell the produce of work that has been done under the direction or with the help of religious by apprentices who are trained by means of this work to the exercise of an art or a trade. Justice requires that the apprentices then be given a salary proportionate to their work, after the expenses of their apprenticeship have been deducted. They may sell school supplies at the current price so as to make it more convenient for the scholars to secure these things.

Two remarks must be made in regard to these different cases: one is that the prescriptions of cc. 534 and 1531 are to be observed regarding the alienation of property; the second, that the danger of scandalizing others, or of provoking attacks or suspicions, even if these are not justifiable, will at times induce religious to avoid acts which would otherwise be perfectly honest and lawful.

Article 2. Particular Obligations of Religious

§ 1. OBSERVANCE OF THE RULES
AND CONSTITUTIONS

271. 1. All religious must faithfully observe their rules and regulations (c. 593). But, with the exception of certain religious orders, these do not oblige, by themselves, under pain of sin.

The "Rule" in ecclesiastical law means the group of principles regarding the religious life proposed to their disciples by the first organizers of this kind of life. It is in this sense that we speak of the **Rule of St. Augustine**, the **Rule of St. Benedict**, etc. In contrast with the rule thus understood, the constitutions contain the laws which are characteristic of the different institutes and which regulate their organization and their principal obligations. Since the sixteenth century a great many institutes have arisen which do not follow the ancient rules; in their case the constitutions take the place of the rule. One may also understand by the term *rules* (in the plural) those prescriptions which are rather of a disciplinary character (rules of modesty, rules of the clotheskeeper, rules of the doorkeeper, etc.).

2. In the constitutions four sorts of articles may be distinguished. The first class consists of an exhortation to practice with great perfection certain virtues, as, for example, humility (the third degree of St. Ignatius), mortification (continual, in all things), obedience (to the least sign of the will of the superior, at the first sound of the bell), charity (always giving the best part to others), etc. There is question here principally of tendencies, of an habitual inclination of will. These rules are violated only by habitual neglect to cultivate such dispositions.

A second group determines the obligations of the vows; the violation of these rules is necessarily a sin, mortal or venial. A third group contains the disciplinary prescriptions, which may be divided into two series. One series merely reproduces the ecclesiastical law; its obligation is the same as that which the Holy See has attached thereto. The other series has to do with the special life of the institute (the order of the day; spiritual or corporal exercises which are obligatory; the determination of the hours and places where silence is prescribed, at least where it is to be observed in a more rigorous manner, etc.). The violation of these rules, as such, is not a sin, but an imperfection. However, because of their suitableness to the life which the religious in such an institute should live, it will happen more or less easily that a deliberate violation of them will be sinful. It will depend, of course, on the rule in question and on the capacity of the subject, whether the violation of the rule constitutes a lack of charity, or temperance, or humility, or industry, etc. If the violation is public, and especially if it is frequent, it often gives a bad example which tends to the relaxing of discipline (see Cotel-Jombart-McCabe, S.J., *Cathechism of the Vows*, n. 135).

272. Dispensation from the rule may be obtained from the religious superior who is designated by the constitutions, unless the rule in question repeats a prescription of the Code. If it does, then a dispensation must be asked from the Holy See, unless the Ordinary has general or special powers to dispense from it.

Usually the local superior may dispense in individual cases which concern domestic discipline; the provincial superior should give the dispensation when it is intended to last for some time, or when it concerns a matter which is of more general importance.

273. In religious orders the authentic interpretation of the rules or constitutions ordinarily depends on the general chapter; in congregations approved by the Holy See, it is reserved to the Holy See; the Ordinary of the motherhouse would be entirely authorized to give this interpretation for a diocesan congregation; but the approval of other Ordinaries would be necessary if the congregation has spread into several dioceses.

To interpret a law is to explain the meaning of a law which is really doubtful. The authentic or official interpretation is that which is given by a competent superior, e.g., the author of the law, his successor, or his delegate for this purpose. Such an interpretation necessarily carries authority with it. If a community observes a law constantly according to a certain interpretation, this observation creates a law, thanks to the tacit consent of the legislator. This is what we call interpretation by custom. Finally, specialists or approved authors can give a doctrinal interpretation of laws, which is worth just as much as their reasons and their authority.

Since the constitutions contain a considerable number of passages which reproduce literally or very closely the provisions of the Code, only the Holy See can give an authentic interpretation of such articles.

Superiors, however, may follow in their government the doctrinal interpretation given by those authors whose opinions carry weight. In this case the inferior who may have a different opinion must submit himself to the superior, for it is the superior who has the right to choose among several opinions the one which seems to him to offer the best guarantees of truth.

The *Normae,* nn. 251, 252, reserve to the Holy See the authentic interpretation of constitutions in congregations subject to the Holy See. These articles have been incorporated in the greater number of the constitutions of modern congregations.

§ 2. OBLIGATIONS OF VOWS[7]

274. 1. Obligations arising from the **vow of poverty**.

a) Everything which a religious acquires by his personal industry or by reason of his being a religious is acquired for the institute (see n. **245**).

b) A religious renounces the right to exercise independent proprietorship over material possessions. He can no longer dispose of property except with the general or particular authorization of his superiors, at least lawfully presumed. When the vow is solemn, the religious loses even the capacity to acquire or possess property by personal title.

It is, therefore, contrary to any vow of poverty to borrow, loan, give, receive or exchange without lawful permission, any object which has a value estimable in money. To injure or destroy an object which belongs to a third person or to the institute, is a sin against justice, and if one has knowingly disposed of the thing as his own, it is also a sin against poverty. But to destroy an object or to damage it in a fit of anger, or through carelessness, would not constitute a violation of the vow of poverty. In such a case, indeed, the thought has not even occurred of disposing of a thing unlawfully as though one were its owner. To waste one's time is a sin of laziness, but not of injustice, nor is it contrary to the vow of poverty.

2. Considering the very nature of the vow of poverty, one must hold that the matter is grave or slight according as the act of independent disposition of property is, or is not, of real importance. Hence this matter will vary according to the kind of poverty practiced in the institute.

For example: no matter what might be the resources of a Franciscan monastery or a house of the Society of Jesus, the independent disposal of the same sum of money by a Franciscan and by a Jesuit would always be more grave in the case of the former than of the latter, because the

---

[7] We here indicate only those essential obligations which result from each vow. Further explanations, which would be outside the purpose of the present work, may be found in other books, as, for example, in Cotel-Jombart-McCabe, S.J., *Catechism of the Vows*, 2nd Ed., New York, 1945; Cotel-Jombart-Bouscaren, S.J., *Principles of the Religious Life* (an explanation of the Catechism), New York, 1926; Brothers of the Sacred Heart, *Catechism of the Religious Profession*, Metuchen, 1943; Fennelly, C.S.Sp., *Follow Me* (The Three Vows of Religion Ascetically and Canonically Considered), Dublin, 1943; Gay, *Religious Life and the Vows*, Westminster, 1942; Polit, S.J., *Perfect Obedience* (Commentary on the Letter of Obedience), Westminster, 1947.

form of renunciation of property is more extensive in the Order of St. Francis than in the Society of Jesus.

In practice, it is sufficient to abide by the determinations of the constitutions or by their lawful interpretation. Most frequently the rule is given that an amount which is necessary and sufficient to constitute a grave sin against justice, is also sufficient to sin gravely against the vow of poverty. This norm depends, therefore, to a certain degree on the usual resources of the community.

In sins against justice a distinction is made between matter that is *relatively grave,* and that which is *absolutely grave.* The first is determined entirely by the seriousness of the harm done to the injured party (relative to his possessions, to his needs); the matter is absolutely grave when the theft (damage done, etc.) is a grave offense against property rights and does serious harm to society, independent of the wealth of the injured party. When the injury is done to a community, except it be small and rather poor, the sin will ordinarily not be mortal unless the matter is absolutely grave.

The application of these principles to violations of the vow of poverty must be rounded out by other considerations; e.g., it is a less grave fault to give something to a member of the community than to give it to an outsider, less grave also, though contrary to poverty, to dispose of one's own goods, than to give away the goods of the community, etc.

3. If it happens that a religious must give or receive an object, incur an expense, etc., without being able to have recourse to his superior, he can act by presuming permission, as long as he sincerely believes that the superior would approve this conduct. Generally the rule prescribes that the superior is afterwards to be informed, but the vow of poverty does not oblige one to do so. However, to keep an object which has been received with presumed permission, or to dispose of it when recourse has meanwhile become possible, the permission of the superior must be obtained.

To give or receive when lawfully presuming permission to do so is to act with a real, though not with an explicit dependence of the will upon the superior. The superior, as a matter of fact, really wishes that the subject should accept or give what in this particular institute and in these circumstances is reasonable to give or to receive, even though it is not possible to obtain his consent formally expressed. "To presume permission" is, therefore, to act conformably to the will of the superior, but the superior cannot be supposed to wish that one should keep an object and dispose of it, without asking his authorization when it is possible to do so.

275. 1. The best means of observing the essentials of poverty, and of acquiring the spirit of poverty, that is to say, a real detachment from temporal possessions and the comforts of life, is to practice life in common. In the canonical sense, community life consists in this that everyone uses the goods belonging to the community and does not possess anything as his own in the matter of food, clothing, and furniture.

The Code orders that the community life shall be carefully preserved.

"In every religious institute common life must be exactly observed by all, even in those things which pertain to food, clothing and furniture" (c. 594, § 1).

"Whatever is acquired by the religious, including the superiors, according to the terms of canon 580, § 2, and canon 582, n. I, must be incorporated in the goods of the house, or of the province, or of the institute; and all the money and titles (*tituli*) shall be deposited in the common safe" (c. 594, § 2).

2. It is not contrary to the community life, to have and to use, with the permission of the superiors, what is necessary or really useful because of particular circumstances of health, employment, or occupation.

3. The so-called *"peculium"* (pin money) is incompatible with the common life imposed on all religious by canon 594, § 1. The peculium may be defined as a thing which has a monetary value, separate from the property belonging to the convent, and which the religious can possess, administer, keep for his own use, over and above that which he needs for his present necessities (Vermeersch, *De relig.*, I, n. 273).

4. The virtue of poverty is nothing more than a form of mortification. Its object is the satisfaction procured from material possessions. Since these material possessions are only means in themselves, the use or the privation of them has no immediate moral value. But the privation of the satisfactions which they procure has, like all mortification, the value of liberating the soul and of making reparation for sin.

The vow of poverty should be only a means for arriving at the renunciation so earnestly counseled by our Lord; insofar as it is a form of obedience applied to the use of material possessions, it frees the subject greatly from less noble preoccupations which are very common obstacles to prayer and to the love for supernatural things.

276. The vow of chastity:

1. This vow forbids in virtue of a new title — that of the

virtue of religion — all acts contrary to the sixth and ninth commandments of God.

2. It imposes the obligation of observing celibacy.

The sacrilege which in the case of professed religious is added to any sin against purity will be venial or mortal just as the sin itself is venial or mortal.

In the case of solemn profession, the vow of chastity constitutes a diriment impediment to marriage.

277. The object (the matter) of the vow and of the virtue of chastity is the same according to the almost unanimous opinion of theologians. Consequently, not only words or acts, but even thoughts and desires contrary to the holy virtue constitute a violation of the vow of chastity.

It will be useful to give here the common teaching of moralists concerning the theological character of sins contrary to chastity.

The deliberate seeking of impure pleasure or the voluntary consent to it are always mortally sinful. Venial sin against the holy virtue can be committed in two ways:

1. When in the acts which are committed the person does not possess the entire use of his faculties, although he is conscious of a certain malice in the action committed.

Ex. Such are actions committed before one is fully awake; hesitation, not fully deliberate, in repelling an impure thought or desire, etc.

2. By actions in which sinful pleasure is not directly sought, but in which one exposes oneself, without sufficient reason, to the danger of consent thereto.

For instance: curious or imprudent looks, dangerous reading, unbecoming familiarities in which one experiences a certain inclination toward carnal pleasure, without exposing oneself to the *proximate* danger of giving *full* consent to it. The stronger the sensation is, the less important is the motive for the action which provokes it, and the more ought one to fear that he is deluding himself about the real motive for his conduct. This is especially the case in regard to marks of affection that are excessive or even out of place when given or received by persons who have taken a vow of chastity.

A thorough explanation of this delicate subject may be found in the *Journal of Religious Education*, 1933, p. 387.

278. In virtue of the **vow of obedience**, religious engage under pain of sin: (1) not to withdraw themselves from the legitimate authority of superiors by flight or apostasy; (2) to fulfill the orders of legitimate superiors which are conformable to the constitutions, and imposed "in the name of holy obedience," or by any other formula which is clearly equivalent to this.

That there may be a violation of the vow of obedience, the following are, therefore, necessary:

1. An order, a formal precept.

It is not an offense against the vow of obedience if one fails to follow the advice of a superior, even when it is given very urgently; this way of acting may, of course, be a sin for other reasons, for example, because of a lack of humility, of charity, of prudence, etc.

2. The order of a legitimate superior.

There is question here of those who have authority to command religious as such. The sphere of the authority of the different superiors may easily be ascertained from the general law of the Church and from the constitutions. The confessor is not a superior; by virtue of his ministry he can prescribe a penance which is in proportion to the sins committed, and he can order that those steps be taken which are necessary to avoid sin. This is the extent of his authority. In particular he cannot order any action which is contrary to the rule, or to the orders of the superiors, or to religious observances; neither can he impose public penances. Outside of confession he has only that authority which his natural and supernatural qualities merit.

3. An order which is in accordance with the constitutions.

A religious does not promise every sort of obedience. It would be very meritorious, no doubt, to fulfill even those orders which exceed the limits or the kind of obligations supposed by the constitutions; but the religious is not bound to this. In case of doubt, humility and charity demand that one should yield to the superior; the presumption is in his favor.

4. Generally, an expression is required which indicates the intention of the superior to oblige in virtue of the vow.

In certain constitutions these expressions are definitely laid down, for example, "in the name of our Lord Jesus Christ," "in virtue of holy obedience," etc. In other constitutions it is only required that there should be the formal expression of an order.

The *virtue of obedience* has for its object everything which the legitimate superior imposes, no matter how he expresses his will. The perfection of the vow of obedience consists in an entire dependence on all those who have any authority.

§ 3. CLOISTER AND RELATIONS WITH THE OUTSIDE WORLD

279. To protect religious institutes and their members from the disadvantages which free communication with persons of the world would bring about, especially communication with those of the other sex, ecclesiastical legislation, whether general or particular, has taken care to regulate the visits of externs to religious houses, as well as the going abroad of religious, and their epistolary correspondence. The most important of these deal with the cloister. The Code imposes some form of cloister on *all* religious institutes and even on religious societies (cc. 597, 604, 679, § 2). It confirms the very severe sanctions already attached by the old law to the violation of the cloister of regulars and nuns.

280. 1. The **cloister** may be understood in either the material sense or the formal sense. *In the material sense* the cloister means that part of a religious house from which certain persons from without are excluded, and which religious may not leave without authorization. *In the formal sense,* this word "cloister" signifies the ecclesiastical *laws* which have to do with this double prohibition.

2. **Papal** cloister is that cloister which for some centuries past religious with solemn vows, regulars or nuns, have been obliged to observe (cc. 597–603).

This name comes from the causes of this cloister and the nature of its obligation. It was imposed by papal constitutions; the Holy See reserves to itself the right to dispense from it; it is sanctioned by punishments imposed by the general or papal law of the Church.

3. **Common** cloister is that which members of religious *congregations,* whether pontifical or diocesan, must observe (c. 604).

This is also called **episcopal** cloister, because, being under the vigilance of the bishop, it may, under certain circumstances, be fortified by him with canonical censures (c. 604, § 3).

4. By **statutory** or **legal** cloister is meant the prescriptions contained in the constitutions of each institute regarding this matter.

A. PAPAL CLOISTER

I. *Cloister of Regulars*

281. 1. "Papal cloister must be observed in all convents of regulars . . . canonically erected, even though the Community does not count six professed members" (c. 597, § 1).

This prescription does not pertain either to the temporary house of a community, nor to secondary ones as a country house or villa.

2. All parts of the house inhabited by the community, as well as the gardens and orchard, are subject to cloister. The church, however, with its *adjoining* sacristy, is not in cloister, nor are the guest rooms and the parlor; this last should, as far as possible, be located near the main entrance of the house (c. 597, § 2).

It is the duty of the major superior or of the chapter, according to the constitutions, to determine the limits of cloister exactly, and these limits must be clearly indicated (c. 597, § 3).

The superior who has the authority to determine the limits of the cloister can also modify them, either permanently or in an exceptional case. Such modification obviously may never remove from cloister those who are absolutely obliged by the common law to be subject to it.

It is permissible, for example, on the occasion of some solemnity to permit women to pass along a corridor or a path, to enter a chapel or a room when these are quite near the outer door and are regularly included within the limits of the cloister.

3. When a school or a place for some other work of the institute is annexed to a house of an order of men (regulars), a separate part of the house should, if possible, be reserved exclusively for the occupancy of the religious. Likewise, without a just reason and the permission of the superior, persons of the opposite sex are not to be admitted to places, even outside cloister, which are reserved for boarding students or externs or for works proper to the institute (c. 599).

Hence a religious house should be arranged in such a way that the living rooms of the religious do not open onto the stairs or corridors which are a necessary approach, for example, to the parlors or to the infirmary of the pupils.

4. Under pain of excommunication incurred *ipso facto* and reserved to the Holy See, it is forbidden to women of any age

or relationship or condition to enter into the cloister of male regulars under any pretext whatsoever. Those who so introduce them or permit them to enter incur the same penalty. The wives of rulers of states with their retinues are excepted. This holds also for wives of governors of different states in a federated country (cc. 598, 2342, 2°).

N.B. There is no *special* prescription in the common law regarding the *leaving* of cloister on the part of male regulars. By reason of c. 606 superiors are obliged to see to the observance of the constitutions on this point.

II. *Cloister of Nuns*

282. In the Constitution *Sponsa Christi* of November 21, 1951 (art. IV), and in the complementary Instruction *Inter praeclara* of November 23, 1951 (art. IV–XVI), papal cloister characteristic of their juridical status was retained and even strengthened for all nuns. More ample provision, however, was made for dispensations; and the distinction between major and minor papal cloister was introduced in connection with either purely contemplative nuns or those who are also engaged in certain apostolic works.

A new Instruction *Inter cetera,* of March 25, 1956, has revised this entire matter (c. 22), and thus has suppressed the Instruction *Nuper edito* of February 6, 1924, regarding cloister. It will be sufficient to analyze this new Instruction in order to give a complete idea of the cloister imposed on nuns at present.

(N.B. In the text the numbers in parentheses refer to the 73 articles of this Instruction; see Appendix IV.)

1. Nuns who wish to retain their title and their juridical status, even though by way of temporary exception they still take only simple vows, and even though their number has been reduced, must observe at least minor papal cloister (4, 6).

2. When there is question of establishing a monastery, or of restoring cloister in a monastery which should have it, the nuns will be strictly obliged to observe the prescriptions regarding entering and leaving, beginning with the time mentioned in the decree of the local Ordinary. He will also determine the exact limits of the cloister (5).

A. MAJOR PAPAL CLOISTER

283. *Nature and Extension.*

1. Major papal cloister is that which is referred to in the Code (cc. 597, 600–602).

2. This is the rule for monasteries in which the nuns take solemn vows and lead only the contemplative life (8, a).

Nevertheless, two exceptions are possible: 1. Nuns who for the time being take only simple vows even though they live the contemplative life; the Holy See may permit them to have the minor cloister (8, b). 2. The Holy See may grant major cloister even though some of the nuns are engaged in apostolic works either imposed or authorized (9).

3. All nuns (c. 601), novices, and postulants (c. 540, § 3), are subject to the prescriptions of cloister.

At the expiration of their vows the professed who have temporary vows, and novices and postulants at any time, may leave the cloister provided that they wish to leave the monastery definitely (10).

4. Cloister must of obligation include not only the monastery building and any annex in which the nuns live, but also the gardens and orchards and all places to which they have access. The following places are outside the cloister: parlors, the section intended for visitors; the church or chapel, *but not the choir of the nuns;* the sacristy together with adjacent rooms to which the clergy and their assistants have access; the place in which the priest hears the confessions of the nuns; the part of the house inhabited by the extern sisters and the apartments destined for the use of the chaplain and guests (11).

The local Ordinaries may temporarily extend the cloister to the church, the sacristy, and the neighboring rooms, to the parlors and other such places adjacent to the monastery, in case the nuns are obliged to go there to work, for example, because of a lack of extern sisters (12).

5. The parts of the house under cloister should be so arranged that no one can enter them from outside. It is also necessary as far as possible to use effective means to prevent outsiders from being able to see into cloister and the nuns from having a view to the outside.

Cloistered gardens and grounds must be enclosed by a sufficiently high wall, wooden fence, iron lattice work, or a thick and stiff hedge.
The windows should have opaque glass and fixed shutters or lattices. If the roof has a terrace, which the nuns use, it should be surrounded by screens or other effective means of protection (13, 14).
The law of cloister should never prevent the nuns from seeing the altar, unless there is a more strict regulation from particular law. They, however, may never be exposed to the view of the faithful (15).

6. In the parlor two grilles, securely fixed and slightly separated, or some other truly effective means, should make any contact with visitors impossible (16).

At the door of the monastery, in the parlor, in the sacristy, and the like, a turnstile or revolving wheel may be placed (17).

284. *On the Nuns Leaving Cloister.*

An informed reader will notice here also a certain change in the law, especially regarding its mitigation or the solution of some doubt.

1. The law of major cloister obliges the nuns to remain perpetually within the confines of the monastery, as these have been determined by ecclesiastical authority. The nuns are forbidden to depart from them under any pretext, even for a very short time, except in cases provided by law or by permissions lawfully granted (18).

It is not permitted to leave cloister on the occasion of a clothing, or a profession, of a communion, or for any other similar motive (19).

Nuns may not pass from one monastery to another even of the same order, not even for a very short time, without the permission of the Holy See or in virtue of a particular law approved for a federation of nuns (20).

2. The Instruction mentions as a legitimate reason for leaving the *danger of death* or of *very serious injury,* which will first be interpreted as under the old law (fire, floods, earthquakes, an invasion of soldiers, air raids, demands of the public authorities); but the Instruction adds examples of a less strict danger, for instance, if the illness of a nun presents a real danger to the community (21, a, b).

Attention may be called again to the social-mindedness of the Instruction from the fact that it is permissible for a superior or another nun to go with a companion to help an extern sister or some other person performing the same duties, if these, in case of grave and urgent necessity, cannot otherwise be assisted (21, c).

It is also considered legitimate to leave the cloister when an obligation arises to use one's civil rights or to fulfill one's civil duties (22).

These various cases must be submitted to the Ordinary if time permits. If not, he should be informed afterwards (21, d).

3. The Instruction then enumerates the *grave circumstances,* as well as *cases of great utility,* which may create a just motive

for asking a dispensation or, on the part of the Ordinaries or the religious Assistants, for obtaining habitual faculties from the Holy See (25).

Such circumstances are:

1) Care of health which must be undertaken outside the monastery;

2) Consulting a doctor, particularly a specialist, e.g., for the eyes, the teeth, for radiation-therapy, for medical observation;

3) To accompany or to visit a nun who is sick outside;

4) To supply for absent extern sisters or the persons who are performing that duty;

5) To exercise supervision over fields, property, buildings, or the quarters inhabited by the extern sisters;

6) To perform administrative acts or financial transactions of great importance which otherwise might not be done or be done badly;

7) Monastic labor both apostolic and manual;

8) The undertaking of an office in another monastery, and other similar things (24).

4. A nun who has legitimately gone out of cloister is obliged to go by a direct route to the place for which permission was given, nor may she use the opportunity to make other visits (23).

If there is question of going to confession, it seems that a nun could make a slight detour for this purpose; in this case her companion should not inform the superior.

284 bis. *Entrance of Strangers.*

1. "No person of whatever class, condition, sex, or age, may be admitted to the cloister of nuns without the permission of the Holy See . . ." (c. 600).

It is obvious that this cloister is much more rigorous than that of male regulars into whose monasteries men who have habitual or special authorization of superiors are allowed to enter.

2. The Code makes certain exceptions which the Instruction makes more precise.

The local Ordinary or the regular superior, if the monastery is subject to him, or one delegated by either of these or by the Holy See, may enter the cloister on the occasion of the canonical visitation, but only to inspect the premises in accordance with the law (cc. 512, 600), care being taken that the visitor is accompanied continuously from his entry to his departure by at least one cleric or one religious, even a lay brother, of mature age. The stay should not be extended beyond the time necessary for the inspection; nor should other business be transacted at the same time or other acts performed which do not refer to the aforesaid inspection (26, a).

Visits should take place in the common parlor, the visitor remaining outside the cloister, unless there is question of listening to a sick nun who cannot come to the parlor.

For the discharge of other duties, namely, for the canonical examination of candidates (cf. c. 552), for presiding at elections (cf. c. 506, § 2), for the ceremonies of clothing or profession and like matters, the prelate or delegate may not enter the cloister; all these things must be done from without (26, b and c).

It is difficult to admit with Berutti, o.c. n. 115, 1, 13, that every cleric or religious who is twenty-four years old is "of mature age," since the Code demands that a candidate for ordination to the priesthood must be twenty-four years of age and a confessor of religious women at least forty years old.

The Instruction of the S. Congregation does not authorize receiving into cloister nuns who are traveling, even though they be members of the same order. Nevertheless, certain constitutions permit an exception in this case, granted by privilege. The Sacred Congregation grants this favor by particular indult. One must also take into consideration faculties contained in the Statutes of Federations (see number 289 below).

3. The confessor of the community or any other priest within the prescriptions of the law may, while observing the prescribed precautions, enter the cloister in order to administer the sacraments of Penance, the Eucharist, and Extreme Unction to the sick; to assist the dying; and finally, where it is the custom, to bury the dead; in that case, he may be accompanied inside cloister by the ministers required by the rubrics. Priests are not permitted to enter the cloister to perform other ministries (27, a).

This holds not only for the ordinary confessor (c. 520), the extraordinary and supplementary confessors (c. 521), but also for the approved priest whom a seriously ill woman religious during the entire duration of her illness may select and have summoned to her (c. 523). Only the occasional confessor is excluded (c. 522).

For hearing confessions, two nuns are to conduct the priest to the cell of the sick nun and, after the confession, conduct him immediately to the door leading out of cloister. The same is to be done for the administration of Extreme Unction and for the assistance of the dying.

For the administration of Holy Communion the priest should be accompanied, from his entry up to his leaving the cloister, by at least two nuns. Nothing, however, prevents the entire community from escorting the Blessed Sacrament in procession, if that is the custom (27 b).

4. The preaching of the word of God should be done at the grille of the choir or of the parlor.

If this cannot be done conveniently, the Holy See may be petitioned for permission to have the sermons in the choir itself or in the chapter-hall. Under similar circumstances the local Ordinary may permit sermons to be given to the nuns in the church to which cloister is then extended, the doors of the church being closed (28).

5. The following persons may enter the cloister of nuns:

a) Those who actually hold supreme power in some state, even in a federated one, whatever their title may be, together with their wives and respective retinue.

b) Cardinals of the Holy Roman Church who may take with them as companions one or other cleric, or a lay member of their household.

c) Physicians, surgeons, and other persons qualified to care for the sick; architects, craftsmen, workmen, and other persons of this kind whose work the superior judges necessary for the monastery.

The superior should obtain at least general approval for the above from the local Ordinary. She may do so at the beginning of each year, showing the Ordinary a list of such persons.

Persons who must frequently be admitted into cloister should be of irreproachable reputation and of excellent morals.

In case of urgent necessity, when time does not permit applying for a required approval, it may be lawfully persumed (29).

6. Without prejudice to the Constitutions and the Statutes which prescribe more severe regulations, persons who lawfully enter the cloister must be escorted by two nuns while they are passing through the living quarters of the community.

No matter what the reason may be, persons authorized to enter the monastery may not remain there beyond the time really necessary to accomplish the purpose for which permission was granted.

Aside from those who must do so by reason of their office, no nun should converse with outsiders admitted to the monastery (31, 32).

7. Without special permission of the Holy See young girls or women may not be admitted inside cloister for the purpose of receiving an education, nor for testing their vocation for a while, nor for any other reasons of piety or the apostolate. An exception for nuns engaged in the apostolate is provided for in the

Constitution *Sponsa Christi* (IX, § 2, 1 and 2). Similarly recourse must be had to the Holy See to obtain for extern sisters special permissions which are not contained in the approved Statutes (33).

According to the Statutes for extern sisters promulgated in 1931, in monasteries which have such sisters either by general or particular grant of the Holy See, these sisters should make the canonical year of novitiate within the cloister and re-enter it for the two months preceding their first profession. They may also be permitted to enter with the authorization, at least habitual, of the Ordinary in order to help with urgent work. Finally, they may likewise be admitted within the cloister of the monastery in case of illness when it would be inconvenient to take care of them outside cloister, and when by reason of the infirmities of old age they are no longer able to perform their duties.

It may be noted that a number of monasteries have asked and obtained dispensations for their extern sisters to enter the cloister.

For postulants (c. 540) to enter the cloister permission from the local Ordinary suffices (34).

284 ter. *Custody of the Cloister.*

1. It is the right and the duty of the local Ordinary to supervise the observance of cloister in all the monasteries of his diocese, even if a regular superior exercises the same right (c. 603, §§ 1 and 2) (35).

Within the monastery the custody of the cloister pertains immediately to the superioress. She should see to it that the keys of the doors are returned to her every day, and she should entrust them only to nuns whose duties require them (36).

2. Regarding visits to the parlor (their duration, their frequency, the quality of the persons, and the like), and the manner of conducting one's self while there, the Constitutions are to be observed.

The legislator may perhaps be alluding to modifications in this matter when he declares that recourse must be had to the Holy See for any adaptation (37).

3. Nuns (cf. *Sponsa Christi*, General Statutes, Art. 1, § 1), but not novices or postulants, who unlawfully leave the major cloister in violation of the prescription of c. 601 are punished by excommunication incurred *ipso facto* and reserved simply to the Holy See (c. 2342, 3°) (38).

After the Code good canonists claimed that the penalties would not be incurred *ipso facto* by nuns with temporary vows. It seems to us that the text itself is perfectly clear on this point. It explicitly excludes novices and postulants and speaks of nuns without any distinction.

4. The same penalty falls on any person, man or woman, of whatever class or condition, who violates the major cloister either by entering it unlawfully, or by introducing or admitting other persons into it unlawfully (c. 2342, 1°) (39).

B. MINOR PAPAL CLOISTER

285. *Nature of Minor Papal Cloister.*

1. Minor papal cloister has the following qualities:

a) Being *pontifical* no less than major cloister, it protects and fosters the observance and custody of the public, solemn vow of chastity, and of the monastery's contemplative life;

b) Being *minor,* although it is truly far more severe than the cloister of congregations (c. 604) and even than that of orders of men (cc. 598–599), it affords, nevertheless, a suitable opportunity and facility for the fruitful exercise of certain ministries by the nuns (Instr. *Inter praeclara,* XI) (40).

2. These ministries, determined by the Constitutions or by legitimate permission or even by prescription of the Church because the needs of souls are constantly growing, must, nevertheless, be such as will truly promote a genuinely contemplative life (Const. *Sponsa Christi,* IX) (41, a, b).

The Instruction gives examples of this kind of work: catechetical instruction, especially for children; also the education of young girls; and likewise the care of the sick. From these examples it is not difficult to determine the kind of works to which the nuns may devote themselves. Besides, indults granted to certain monasteries show that the text is to be interpreted broadly; otherwise many monasteries would not be able in any way to take solemn vows and also have minor cloister.

3. Two things are to be noted regarding nuns who are engaged in such works: where the majority of the nuns are thus engaged, only minor cloister may be established; on the contrary, if only a few of the nuns are thus occupied, the Holy See may grant even major cloister (42).

285 bis. *Division of a Monastery.*

1. The precincts of a monastery comprise two parts: the one

reserved for the nuns, as in major cloister, and comprising the same places (cf. above); the other destined for works of the apostolate. Into this latter part the nuns assigned to these works as well as those who direct them may go. The church or public oratory and the places adjoining them, and the parlors of the monastery must on principle be outside this secondary part of the monastery. Nevertheless, with the consent of the Ordinary some of these places may occasionally be used for apostolic works (45, b). It is not allowed, without permission of the Ordinary, to have some sections reserved, now for the community, now for the works of the apostolate (46). Even in that part of the monastery which is reserved for apostolic works view from within or without is to be obstructed. This provision, however, with the consent of the Ordinary need not be as rigorously enforced here as it must be for the quarters reserved for the nuns (47).

The rules which have been laid down regarding the doors of the major cloister are also to be applied to the doors which open upon the part of the monastery reserved for the nuns (48, b). In the part destined for apostolic works there will be special parlors without grilles where the nuns engaged in these works may go to discuss them with others (49, c).

286. *Nuns Leaving Cloister.*

1. This number requires careful reading, for it contains concessions which help very much in applying the Instruction, while at the same time sustaining the authority and the proper rights of the superioress.

The fundamental principle is that minor cloister very strictly forbids the nuns and other persons bound by this obligation to leave the precincts of the monastery (Instr. *Inter praeclara*, XII, 2).

2. Dispensations may be granted when they are really necessary for the apostolate. Permission to leave in the cases enumerated below or in the Constitutions, and for as long as the circumstances certainly remain the same, is granted by the superioress on whose conscience the matter rests. If other cases very similar to those listed in the law occur, it is necessary to have recourse to the local Ordinary who, after considering the matter before God, will give the permission himself and, if he

thinks it appropriate, he will refer the matter back to the superioress afterward. The reasons indicated in the Instruction which allow the superioress, within the limits noted above, to grant permission to leave the precincts of the monastery are as follows:

a) By reason of the ministry itself, which really demands that one leave the cloister so that it can be exercised effectively, for example, when it is necessary to accompany young girls outside the cloister for their studies, their health, their recreation and when women lay teachers or oblates or other persons who could suitably perform these tasks are not at hand.

b) By reason of preparation for various ministries: to acquire knowledge, training, degrees, and other qualifications, and which necessarily entail attendance at courses, schools, universities, lectures, and conventions. If any of these are so markedly secularistic and worldly that attendance at them would be a danger to religious virtues or a cause of scandal, the local Ordinary should always be consulted previously. In any case the Instructions given by the Holy See must always be observed.

c) By reason of business, litigation, or problems connected with their works, which must be discussed and settled with either civil or ecclesiastical authorities, or with official bureaus or private concerns, and which cannot be safely or conveniently dealt with by others than the nuns themselves (51, a, b, c).

287. *Entrance of Externs.*

1. The laws for major cloister are applied to monasteries with minor cloister in regard to the part of the monastery reserved for the nuns (52).

2. All the beneficiaries of the works, namely, women, young girls, and small boys, may enter the part of the monastery assigned to apostolic works. Pupils, therefore, may also be boarders. The same holds for women who are needed for the works, such as teachers, nurses, servants, and other workers (53).

Parents and benefactors (54), and obviously both ecclesiastical and civil inspectors (55), and others who are authorized to enter the precincts of the monastery reserved to the nuns (56) may be admitted for a rather short time.

3. For urgent cases different from those already enumerated, the decision belongs to the local Ordinary (57); to him is entrusted the custody of the cloister in the places destined for apostolic works (58).

288. *Custody of the Cloister.*

1. The immediate custody of this cloister belongs to the superioress, who shall retain the keys of the door leading from one part of the monastery to the other, or she may prudently entrust them to the nuns assigned to the apostolic works (59, a, b).

2. Nuns who unlawfully leave the confines of the monastery are punished with excommunication incurred *ipso facto* and reserved simply to the Holy See, according to c. 2342, 3° or, by an express grant of the Holy See reserved to the local Ordinary (Instr. *Inter praeclara* XV, 1) (60).

3. Nuns who unlawfully go from those parts of the monastery reserved for the community to other places reserved for apostolic works are to be punished by the superioress or by the Ordinary according to the gravity of the fault (61, a).

"Those who enter the cloister of nuns unlawfully and those who introduce or admit them to the part of the monastery reserved for the community incur *ipso facto* excommunication reserved to the Holy See" (c. 2342, 1°) (62). Those who unlawfully enter and those who introduce or admit them to the parts of the monastery not reserved to the community are to be punished by the local Ordinary (63).

C. PAPAL CLOISTER AND FEDERATIONS

289. 1. The Statutes of federations may make such enactments regarding the cloister, whether major or minor, of the federated monasteries as are considered necessary to realize the purposes of the federation. With regard to *government,* permission may be given to a nun to leave her own monastery in order to go to another on the occasion of chapters or council meetings, or of visitations made by the Federation-Authority or by its delegates, or of transfers of superiors or nuns. *In order to promote fraternal collaboration* a nun may go to another monastery to assume an office there, to give help, or even for her own personal benefit. *For the better training of the nuns* common houses may be established; conditions for going to those houses and for remaining in them should be clearly determined

(64–67). The Statutes can decide which works may be under-taken, and which persons may be admitted into the places devoted to these works (69).

Superioresses will undoubtedly find great help for their government in these provisions.

III. *Establishing Papal Cloister*

290. 1. All monasteries must observe one or other cloister according to the regulations given above.

Unless provision has already been made by the Holy See after the promulgation of the Constitution *Sponsa Christi,* it will be the duty of the local Ordinary to erect minor papal cloister for those monasteries of nuns who, though desirous of leading a purely contemplative life, are engaged in apostolic works.

In doubtful cases the matter should be referred to the Holy See.

For the future, recourse must be had to the Holy See for a monastery to transfer from major papal cloister to minor papal cloister (70).

It is the duty of the local Ordinary, when minor papal cloister is erected, to set the exact limits of the cloister (c. 597, § 3), and to indicate clearly the parts destined for the community and those destined for apostolic works, and to approve the separation between them (71).

2. Statutes, indults, privileges, and dispensations, by virtue of which certain monasteries, while retaining their juridical status, were exempted from pontifical or papal cloister, are revoked (Reply, March 1, 1921; *A.A.S.,* XIII, 1921, p. 178).

Consequently the cloister which is called "episcopal" cannot in the future be admitted for nuns (73, a).

3. Particular Statutes by which minor papal cloister is speci-fied and adapted for orders of nuns given to works of the apostolate remain unchanged (73, b).

4. In this brief analysis, we had no intention of giving an exhaustive commentary of this long and valuable Instruction, but merely of pointing out the obligations which the introduction of this twofold cloister entails. From the first moment it appeared, this Instruction could not be ignored; now one would not wish to lessen the importance of the commentaries already made about it.

B. COMMON OR EPISCOPAL CLOISTER

291. 1. The new canon law imposes the cloister on all religious congregations likewise. In the houses of religious congregations there must, therefore, be a part exclusively reserved to the religious. Persons of the other sex are not to be admitted there, with the exception of those who have been mentioned previously (see n. **287,** 2) and others that the superior considers may be admitted for just and reasonable motives (c. 604, § 1).

Thus, for example, it might be necessary for a sick person to go through a corridor of the cloister to enter the chapel and assist at the Holy Sacrifice.

There are certain places it seems where persons of the other sex are never to be admitted. Such are the rooms of the religious, the dormitory, the refectory, the chapter room. In special cases, superiors are to judge if it is right to make an exception, for example, so as to allow parents to visit their child who is seriously ill.

Contrary to what is laid down for nuns, superiors of religious congregations need not have the authorization of the Ordinary to allow anyone to enter the cloister in cases where they judge this opportune.

Though there is no formal prohibition in this regard, the Sacred Congregation does not approve that the constitutions should permit men professors to give lessons to religious women or to their pupils. It is easily understood that an exception was made for the course of religion which is given to higher classes; even this ought not to be entrusted to anyone except a priest of mature age. The superiors of religious women have the right and the duty to see to it that these professors shall remain strictly within the limits of their office in their dealings with the students and by their reserve shall avoid even the least suspicion which might be injurious to their sacerdotal character.

2. The classroom buildings, workshops, etc., shall be separated as much as possible from the places reserved for the religious. Permission to enter there may be given more readily than to enter the religious house, but not without a just reason.

Care must be taken to provide infirmary rooms outside of the cloister for the students and other boarders.

3. The bishop is to watch over the exact observance of this cloister. In special circumstances and for a grave motive he can

declare censures against those who violate it, "except in the case of an exempt clerical congregation" (c. 604, § 3).

C. VISITORS, PARLORS, LEAVING THE HOUSE

292. 1. All those who have charge of the cloister shall carefully see to it that useless conversations with outsiders may not relax discipline and weaken the religious spirit (c. 605).

Generally, the religious who is charged with the duty of porter has orders to inform the superiors of visitors received by the religious, and to tell him whether the rules about the parlor are violated or kept. For a stronger reason, he himself must avoid in the discharge of his duty the bad effects which c. 605 warns against. It is enough to say that the charge of porter or portress requires qualities which are rarely possessed by those who have just left the novitiate.

2. Superiors must see that the constitutions be faithfully observed regarding the going out of subjects, or their receiving visits from, or paying visits to, outsiders (c. 606, § 1).

Although a certain amount of strictness in forbidding visits to one's family may at first stir up some resistance on the part of relatives, it is usually a source of great edification, preserves religious from numerous imperfections and faults, and draws to the institute souls desirous of a truly interior life.

3. With the exception of the expeditions that are regularly made for the purpose of collecting alms, "superiors may not allow their subjects to remain outside the house of their own institute except for a just and grave cause and for as brief a period as possible according to the constitutions; but for an absence of more than six months, unless for motives of study, the permission of the Apostolic See is always required" (c. 606, § 2).

The constitutions which permit the spending of vacations with one's family are not clearly abrogated by this canon.

If the constitutions approve the exercise of the sacred ministry outside of the houses of the institute, if, in particular, they approve the accepting of the post of parish vicar or of parish priest, the religious thus employed outside the house may remain more than six months outside their convents. The approbation of such constitutions implicitly contains the necessary permission.

What has been said previously regarding the attendance at universities (see nn. 258–259) by male religious is to be applied by analogy also to religious women who follow the courses in a normal school or a university, etc.

Even though a hospital or a sanatorium is conducted by religious, the permission of the Holy See is necessary to remain there more than six months for reasons of health.

For the regulations regarding religious military chaplains, see the Instruction of the S. Congregation of Religious, dated February 2, 1955, *Acta*, 47, 1955, 93; *Digest, Suppl.* 1953 under canon 451.

4. C. 607 orders the local Ordinaries and the superiors "to see to it that religious do not go out alone, except in case of necessity." This does not apply to sisters who are authorized by their constitutions to take care of the sick in private homes.

293. What fault does a religious commit who goes out without the necessary permission?

If there is question of a nun with solemn vows, this action is always a grave sin, because it is gravely forbidden by an ecclesiastical law.

Other religious, by going out without permission, first of all violate their rule. If the absence is prolonged, it withdraws the religious from the authority of the superior and is contrary to the vow of obedience; an unlawful absence of two or three days is a grave matter. Finally, if the religious goes out at night, it will nearly always be, even independently of the motives which inspire his action, a serious sin by reason of the scandal which it causes.

If the unlawful absence is equivalent to the crime of "flight," it subjects the guilty person to very severe ecclesiastical penalties (see n. **342**).

D.   CORRESPONDENCE

294. The constitutions of all religious institutes impose on their members the duty of not sending or receiving letters without general or special permission. The majority of religious institutes grant superiors the right to read the correspondence of their subjects. The abuses and the dangers which may result from such correspondence are a sufficient reason for this discipline.

There are two ways in which the superior may satisfy his obligation and may use his right in this matter. The first consists in destroying the correspondence received or sent; this would not be licit, except in very special circumstances. The second method consists in reading the letters before sending them or giving them to the one to whom they are addressed.

295. This right of control over correspondence has its limits. The principal exceptions to it are as follows:

1. All religious may freely send letters, exempt from all control, to the Holy See; to the legate of their country (the Apostolic Delegate); to their cardinal protector; to their higher superiors; to their local superior when he is absent; to the Ordinary of the place to whom they are subject; and to the regular superior on whom they depend.

Conversely, the letters of all these persons, when addressed to religious, must be given to the persons to whom they are addressed and may not be opened.

In the cases in which they are subject to the local Ordinary exempt religious have the right, according to c. 611, freely to send to the said Ordinary and to receive from him letters subject to no inspection (Commission of Interpretation, Response, November 27, 1947. — *A.A.S.*, XL [1948], 301).

2. If the superior authorizes the sending or receiving of letters of "conscience," he is not allowed to read them.[8]

3. Charity may demand that the superior shall not acquaint himself with certain family secrets which the correspondent — the father or the mother, for example — does not wish to communicate except to the person to whom the letter is addressed. We may observe, however, that relatives and friends of religious generally know that their correspondence may be opened, and that they have confidence in the discretion of the superiors. If, nevertheless, they put "personal" on the letter, we think that the superior should not inform himself of the contents of the letter. But the superior may, if he suspects an abuse, refuse to give the letters to the one to whom they are addressed, with or without previously informing the subject.

296. It is hardly necessary to add that the superior is rigorously bound to keep the contents of letters secret. In this matter he shall follow the ordinary rules relative to professional secrets.

---

[8] Cf. E. Jombart, *"Les lettres de conscience,"* R.C.R. (1925), 122.

230 OBLIGATIONS AND PRIVILEGES

§ 4. DIVINE OFFICE AND CONVENTUAL MASS

297. The obligation of the *public* recitation of the divine office *in common* exists, by virtue of the Rule or of the constitutions, in all religious orders, with the exception of the Society of Jesus, and in some congregations of men and women.

In the Order of the Visitation the canonical office is replaced by the little Office of the Blessed Virgin.

The Code speaks only of the divine or canonical office, and lays down the conditions for its public recitation in common in the institutes where it is prescribed by the constitutions. The divine or canonical office is different from other offices, even those approved by the Church, but which are not imposed by her. It is also called the "great Office" to distinguish it from the little Office of the Blessed Virgin.

The public recitation of the office in common is distinguished from the private recitation of it. The former does not depend upon the number of persons nor upon the manner in which they recite the office —e.g., in a loud voice and in alternating choirs; it indicates rather the juridical character of the recitation. The public recitation of the office in common is the official fulfillment by a certain number of religious of a duty imposed on the community to recite the office in choir. The recitation of the divine office on the part of one or of several religious to satisfy the obligation of holy orders or of religious profession is an official (public) recitation, but not a recitation in common, even though they pray together in a church. The recitation of the Little Office of the Blessed Virgin by a community is a recitation in common, but it is of a private character and not official.

298. 1. "In the institutes, whether of men or women, in which the choral obligation exists, the divine office conformably to the constitutions, must be recited in common in every house in which there are at least four religious who are bound to choir and who are not lawfully impeded, and even in those houses where there are fewer, if the constitutions so prescribe it" (c. 610, § 1).

This prescription has been explicitly repeated for nuns in the Constitution *Sponsa Christi,* of November 21, 1950; Article 5:

"§ 1. Among women consecrated to God the Church deputes only nuns to offer public prayer to God in her name, in choir (c. 610, § 1) or privately (c. 610, § 3): and she places upon

them a grave obligation by law to carry out this public prayer daily at the canonical hours according to the norm of their constitutions.

"§ 2. All monasteries of nuns as well as individual nuns, whether professed of simple or solemn vows, are everywhere obliged to recite the Divine Office in choir according to c. 610, 1 and the norms of their constitutions."

The novices and the lay religious are not obliged to choir. The obligation is incumbent not on the religious as individuals, but on the community. The superior, who represents the community, has the grave duty of seeing to it that the office is said. Absence from the choir does not in itself constitute a grave fault; it would be so if this negligence would hinder the recitation in common, or if its public repetition would cause grave scandal, etc. The study of philosophy and theology, preparatory to the priesthood, is a legitimate motive for dispensation from choir (see c. 589, § 2).

The prescriptions mentioned above bind also congregations of women whose constitutions, approved by the Holy See, prescribe the recitation of the *canonical office*. This canon does not apply to any of the communities which are bound merely to the recitation of the Little Office of the Blessed Virgin, even though this is to be recited in common.

2. "The Mass corresponding to the office of the day according to the rubrics must also be celebrated in the institutes of men and even, where possible, in the institutes of women" (c. 610, § 2).

The conventual Mass is prescribed here for all religious men who are obliged to say the divine office.[9] In adding the words "where possible," the Code contents itself in the case of religious women with giving a pressing invitation and does not add any obligation to that contained in their constitutions. The nuns will follow the calendar of the order to which they belong.

If the nuns have only one Mass, this will be celebrated according to the rubrics of the "single conventual Mass" (*Addit. et variat. in rubricis Missalis*, I, 4).

3. In the orders where the obligation of the divine office exists, the professed of solemn vows who have not been present at the choir, but not the lay brothers, are bound to recite the office privately (c. 610, § 3).

The newly professed of solemn vows is only obliged to recite that part of the divine office which is prescribed by the rubrics to be said after

---

[9] Commission of Interpretation, Response, May 20, 1923. — *A.A.S.*, XVI (1924), 118; *N.R. Th.* (1924), 303, 489 sq.; *Rev. eccl. Liége*, XV, 386.

the hour of his profession, that is to say, practically speaking, from Terce or from Sext, if he has made his vows before nine o'clock in the morning or between nine o'clock and noon. When the recitation has been antici- pated, especially in choir with the community, one may admit that this is sufficient.

299. *The Little Office of the Blessed Virgin.*

In some congregations of men and in the greater number of the congregations of women, the constitutions prescribe the common recitation of the Little Office of the Blessed Virgin. The Code orders superiors to see that this exercise of piety is carried out (c. 595, § 1, n. 2). The Code neither specifies nor increases the obligation of the rule. The Holy See has even forbidden several times that this recitation should be imposed under pain of sin. To omit it, therefore, will not be a sin, except by reason of the motive or the circumstances of this negligence.

§ 5. RELATIONS WITH THE DIOCESAN CLERGY

300. Charity and the good of souls require that religious and the secular clergy should fraternally unite their efforts. There- fore, religious should willingly lend their aid in the sacred ministry, and the diocesan clergy should willingly invite them to do so, especially in the matter of hearing confessions (c. 608).

301. 1. If the church of a religious community is at the same time a parish church, the rights and obligations of the religious who exercise the office of pastor and those of the religious supe- riors should be carefully defined (c. 609, § 1). The Code here refers back to canon 415 which determines accurately the duties and obligations of the pastor as well as those of the chapter in regard to cathedral or collegiate churches which are also parish churches.

It will be very helpful to determine in writing the rights or obligations that could give occasion for controversy, for example, the celebration of certain religious offices, the administration of property, the co-operation which the religious should give the pastor, etc.

2. A parish may not be established in a church or a public oratory belonging to a community of women (c. 609, § 2).

302. Superiors are to be on their guard that the celebration of divine offices in their church offer no obstacle to the catechetical instruction or to the homily which is given in the parish church. It is the right of the local Ordinary to decide in case of doubt whether this inconvenience exists (c. 609, § 3).

The simplest way of obviating this inconvenience is for the religious to give a catechetical instruction and a homily during the Sunday and feast-day services, as is done in the parish churches. In certain dioceses the Ordinary himself prescribes that on those days a catechetical instruction be given at all the Masses which the faithful attend. The local Ordinary may not forbid religious to say Mass on feast days in their churches when the faithful are present, in order to force the faithful to go to their own parish churches.

CHAPTER VIII

Privileges of Religious

In this chapter we will treat, according to the Code, the general privileges and the special privileges of religious institutes, especially the privileges of exemption and the right to collect alms.

Article 1. General Ideas

303. A privilege is a particular law, granting a favor to an individual or to a community.

A privilege either accords an exemption from a common law (a privilege against the law) or it adds to the common law a special favor (a privilege outside the law).

304. *The Acquisition of Privileges.*

Privileges may be acquired either by a direct grant on the part of the competent superior, or by communication, or by legitimate custom, or by prescription (c. 63, § 1).

1. The direct grant of a privilege is an act of a superior according a special favor by spontaneous indult (*motu proprio*), by rescript, at the request of those interested, or by word of mouth (*vivae vocis oraculo*).

Canon 613 does not declare that privileges acquired by custom or prescription are revoked. Therefore, they remain in force (c. 4). Besides, they are implicitly contained in the Code by virtue of c. 4 and by the canons on custom and prescription.

2. The communication of a privilege is the extension of a privilege to one, other than the principal beneficiary. It is made in two ways in a form equally principal, or in an accessory form.

In the first case the enjoyment of the privilege communicated becomes independent of the grant made to the principal beneficiary; in the second case it shares in all the vicissitudes of the grant made to the principal beneficiary.

Before the Code, the majority of privileges accorded to a mendicant order passed to the other mendicant orders by communication in a form equally principal; the confraternities participate in an accessory manner in the privileges conceded to the archconfraternities to which they are affiliated.

3. What are we to think of the privileges acquired by communication before the Code came into force? Canon 613, § 1, is worded in this way: "Each institute enjoys only those privileges which are contained in this Code, or may have been directly conceded to it by the Apostolic See; every communication of privileges is henceforth excluded."

Canonists were divided in their interpretation of this text. Some said that it suppressed all privileges already acquired by communication; others maintained that it suppressed only the future acquisition of privileges by communication, leaving the privileges acquired before the Code intact. The Commission of Interpretation declared in favor of the latter interpretation.[1]

4. "The privileges which a regular order enjoys belong also to the nuns of the same order, insofar as they are capable of enjoying them" (c. 613, § 2).

Nuns being strictly a part of the religious order, the extension to them of the privileges accorded to the first order is not a communication in the proper sense of the term. On the other hand, these privileges being only those of the first order, any change in the extent of the concession made to the regular order of men, immediately affects the second order.

305. Religious cannot renounce the privileges which they enjoy in virtue of the general law of the Church, or of a papal grant made to their order or congregation. In fact, these privileges are not granted for the particular advantage of the individual, but for the honor of the Church and the general good or advantage of the order or of the congregation.

A superior of regulars may not, therefore, allow the diocesan Ordinary to make a canonical visitation of his convent; in a congregation approved by the Holy See, a superior of women is not allowed to submit to the Ordinary the accounts of the temporal administration, except in cases specially provided for by the law (see c. 618, § 2, 1). But the nonuse of a positive privilege does not constitute a renunciation of this privilege, and will sometimes be advisable for the sake of peace.

---

[1] Response of December 30, 1937. — *A.A.S.,* XXX (1938), 73. See Ellis in *Periodica,* XXVII (1938), 157 sq.

Article 2. Privileges Common to Religious and Clerics

306. Religious, even lay religious, and novices, enjoy the following privileges of clerics (c. 614):

1. Every action which is seriously injurious to their person is punished with excommunication incurred by the very act, and reserved to the delinquent's own Ordinary; and the Ordinaries can add other punishments to this excommunication (cc. 119, 2343).

One would render himself guilty of this offense, for example, if he inflicted blows or wounds on a religious, cast him into prison unjustly, etc.

This privilege was formulated for the first time in favor of clerics by Pope Innocent II, at the Second Council of the Lateran in 1139.

2. The privilege of court. Without the permission of the legitimate superior one may not oblige religious to appear before a lay judge either as defendant or as culprit.

a) Permission should be asked from the Ordinary of the place in which the trial occurs.

b) If the delinquent has cited a superior general in a court of justice, he incurs excommunication reserved to the Sovereign Pontiff; in other cases if the culpable person is a cleric, he is suspended from his office; others must be punished by the local Ordinary (cc. 120, 2341).

c) In a great number of countries agreements between the Holy See, or legitimate custom, have greatly narrowed this privilege. The obligation still remains, however, to avoid the scandal which certain citations in the court of justice would stir up.

In Belgium, in France, in Germany, in Italy, etc., the use of this privilege has been limited in a concordat and no longer exists where there is question of civil cases. Some diocesan statutes counsel the laity and order the clergy to ask permission before beginning such a case, and this permission is never refused them if the cleric or religious who is culpable does not, of his own accord, make good the wrong.

The danger of scandal will counsel religious never to bring suit against a clergyman or religious without having obtained permission from competent ecclesiastical authority.

3. The privilege of personal immunity. The Church claims

for her religious exemption from military service and from civil offices incompatible with their training or their vocation (c. 121).

307. All the members, including the lay members of a society which imitates the religious life (see n. 17), also enjoy these three privileges, but unless they have a special indult, they do not enjoy the privileges which are proper to religious (c. 680).

Article 3. Exemption

[See O'Brien, Joseph, S.J., *The Exemption of Religious in Church Law,* Milwaukee, 1943. — Ed.]

§ 1. GENERAL IDEAS

308. 1. The word "exemption" in ecclesiastical law means a privilege in virtue of which an individual or a community is withdrawn from the authority of his or its immediate superior and is put directly under the authority of a higher superior or of his representative.

Exemption comprises very different degrees and may be taken in a more or less strict sense. Thus, the general law of the Church exempts seminaries from parochial jurisdiction except in matters which concern marriage (c. 1368); a bishop may entrust the exercise of parochial powers (usually reserved to the parish priest) to the chaplain of a religious community or of a hospital, etc. (c. 464, § 2); institutes approved by the Holy See are almost entirely withdrawn from episcopal jurisdiction in their internal government (c. 618, § 2); in all orders of clerics the religious depend on their own superiors, even for the observation of the general laws of the Church (c. 615); superiors of exempt clerics exercise over the lay people who live in the same house with the religious certain powers which are reserved to bishops or to parish priests in the case of other lay people (cc. 514, 1245, § 3, etc.); the abbots or prelates of some monasteries are the Ordinaries of the clerics and of the faithful who live in a certain number of parishes situated in the neighborhood of the monastery[2] (c. 319 sq.) and which are attached to it.

2. Exemption is divided into personal, local, and mixed.

Personal exemption is a privilege which a person enjoys wherever he may be, but which does not extend to the place itself in which he resides (in other words, it is not local). By local exemption a territory,

---

[2] They are called abbots or prelates *nullius,* that is to say, "of no diocese," which means that the abbey and its dependents are not within the territory of any diocese.

or a church, or a monastery is withdrawn from the authority of the Ordinary who, in consequence, cannot exercise his authority over any persons as long as they are within the exempted territory or place (even though these persons do not enjoy personal exemption). Mixed exemption combines at one and the same time the privileges of both the preceding cases.

Exemption is said to be *active* when the superior who is exempt exercises his jurisdiction over other persons besides his religious subjects; it is called *passive* when the religious (together with their house) are partially independent of the Ordinary although they are in the diocese. All religious enjoy a certain degree of exemption; in the strict sense, however, the word exemption means the exemption of regulars.

3. Religious are subject to two kinds of obligations: those which the Church imposes on all the faithful, and those which result from the particular rules of their institute.

As religious, they depend on their superiors alone, save in the exceptions mentioned in the law; as members of the faithful the nonexempt religious depend on the local Ordinary.

Even in diocesan Institutes religious depend, as such, almost exclusively on their superiors. The constitutions, in fact, limit to a great extent the intervention which the Ordinary would strictly have the right to exercise.

Religious who enjoy exemption depend, even in regard to the common obligations, on their superiors alone, and through these, on the Sovereign Pontiff. This is what constitutes exemption in the strict sense of the word.

309. Exemption must always have a just and important reason, because it restricts the authority regularly confided to a determined superior and legitimately exercised by him. The most common motive is to make more easy the interior government of a community which is more or less extended and whose special obligations and needs require a direction which is more immediate, more constant, more uniform, and based on a more intimate knowledge of individuals and of their condition in the Church. Besides, it would be impossible, or very difficult, for this or that superior to meet all the needs of the faithful who would be subject, according to the general rules, to his care; finally, when there is question of religious orders, we must take into account the wish of the Holy See to keep the aid of their ministry more immediately under its own direction and to render it more fruitful both by the liberty of action and by other privileges granted to different orders. If they were under the immediate authority of the superiors put over a certain territory, religious could not consecrate themselves as they do to the evangelization of mission countries, nor could they give to their works of teaching or to the apostolate the unity which they now give and that strength which comes from the freedom to appoint or change the subjects, to undertake, to continue, or to suppress apostolic works, with the sole purpose of securing the most universal good.

On the other hand, no community established in a diocese is entirely withdrawn from the authority of the Ordinary; in the teaching of religion, in matters of public worship, and in the exercise of the sacred ministry, etc., a real and considerable dependence on the bishop is strictly safeguarded (see cc. 612, 874, 1261, 703, etc.).

Though exemption withdraws a community partially from the authority of a more immediate superior, it does not, for all that, withdraw them from the Catholic hierarchy. By divine commission the Sovereign Pontiff may exercise his jurisdiction immediately upon all the faithful. Hence regulars, even the most exempt, are lawfully bound to our Lord by their full submission to His Vicar on earth. They are also joined to the Church through the bishops to whom they remain subject for a part, often a very important part, of their activity. Since the office of parish priest is an institution which is purely ecclesiastical, the Holy See can freely determine the extent of the power of parish priests. By the will of the Holy See the greater number of the faithful must depend on the parish priest for a determined part of their Christian life; the parish is the first form in which their religious activity ordinarily develops; each time that the Sovereign Pontiff or the bishops decide otherwise, certain members of the faithful may or ought to have recourse to another priest, and their religious life as well as their charitable or apostolic action will thus develop for greater good in another ecclesiastical form outside the parochial territory.

These few ideas will be very useful to anyone who wishes to understand and explain, without doing any injury to Catholic teaching, the institutions created in our holy Church which are so different one from the other; these ideas also help to gain the respect, obedience, and devotion which are due to all those who are clothed with authority, and at the same time to insure the liberty of views and of religious action which are approved and directed by the Vicar of Jesus Christ and the successors of the Apostles.

§ 2. EXEMPTION OF REGULARS

310. *The Principle of Exemption.*

"Regulars, both men and women, including novices, except those nuns who are not subject to regular superiors, are exempt, together with their houses and churches, from the jurisdiction of the local Ordinary, excepting in the cases provided for by law" (c. 615).

For regulars, exemption, therefore, is the rule, and exceptions have to be proved. By regulars is to be understood all religious who take solemn vows. Nuns who only pronounce simple vows ordinarily do not enjoy exemption. The same thing is true of nuns who are not under the jurisdiction of a regular superior; they depend on the bishop who acts as representative of the Holy See. The constitution *Sponsa Christi* has changed nothing in this regard (art. VI, § 3).

Postulants do not enjoy the privilege of exemption. First of all, it is to be noted that they are not mentioned in canon 615. This would not suffice to exclude them from the privilege, since the postulate is a true stage of the religious life and the Code treats of it explicitly in the section *De Religiosis*. But several replies of the Holy See restrict to the professed and novices the exercise of the power of superiors, and place the postulants on the same footing as lay people who live habitually with the religious.[3]

We do not think that exemption makes the house of regulars a particular territory; in other words, the subjects of the bishop are not withdrawn from his jurisdiction when they happen to be in a monastery. Thus, a layman would not be allowed, for example, when in the monastery, to read a newspaper or book forbidden by the Ordinary of the place; a marriage could be celebrated in a church or oratory of regulars in the presence of the parish priest or his delegate. The contrary opinion seems to us to have no serious probability (see Vermeersch-Creusen, *Epitome*, I⁷, n. 774, 2).

311. *Exceptions.*

Exceptions to the privilege of exemption have to do principally with the erection of houses (cc. 497, 1162), the exercise of public worship (cc. 612, 1261), the administration of the sacraments to the laity (c. 874), and, in orders of women, the cloister (c. 603, § 1) and the management of temporal goods (c. 533, § 1, 1).

312. 1. Regulars who are unlawfully absent from their house do not enjoy exemption. They may be punished by the bishop for every notorious fault committed outside the convent if the superior, duly informed, does not correct them himself (c. 616).

2. The local Ordinary has the right to watch over every house which is not formed (n. 11) and, in case of abuse which would be a source of scandal to the faithful, he may take provisional measures (c. 617, § 2).

This right of watching over the situation has taken the place of the privation of exemption which usually held in regard to these houses.

---

[3] Commission of Interpretation, Reply July 20, 1929, 4. — *A.A.S.*, XXI, 573. *R.C.R.* (1929), 178. — Reply June 16, 1931. — *A.A.S.*, XXIII, 353. — *R.C.R.* (1931), 177.

Good order requires that except in urgent cases the bishop should inform superiors before intervening. The provisional character of the measures to be taken is indicated by the text of the Code itself (c. 617, § 2).

The Ordinary has no duty of watching over the formed houses, but if abuses occur, whether in the house or in the church, he must inform the superior. He may not, however, intervene directly, even to make good the negligence of the superior. In such a case, he has only the right and the duty to inform the Sacred Congregation as soon as possible (c. 617, § 1).

3. Publications of **Regulars** are subject to the control and **the** authorization of the local Ordinaries of the place (see n. **316**).

4. We have mentioned in n. **94** the right of the bishop to watch over, or even to visit, the schools, hospices, etc., directed by regulars.

§ 3. EXEMPTION IN RELIGIOUS CONGREGATIONS

313. *The Principle of Nonexemption.*

"Institutes with simple vows do not enjoy the privilege of exemption unless it has been specially conceded to them" (c. 618, § 1).

This concession is very rarely granted. The Redemptorists and the Passionists enjoy such a concession, as do also under a very special form, the Daughters of Charity of St. Vincent de Paul.[4]

314. *The Limits of the Ordinary's Jurisdiction.*

"In institutes approved by the Holy See, the local Ordinary may not:

"1. Make any change in the constitutions or inquire into the temporal administration, saving the dispositions of canons 533–535 (see nn. **161–167**).

"2. Interfere in the internal government and discipline, except in the cases expressed by law; nevertheless, in regard to lay institutes, the local Ordinary can and must inquire: whether discipline is maintained conformably to the constitutions, whether sound doctrine and good morals have suffered in any way, whether there have been breaches of the law of enclosure, whether the reception of the sacraments is regular and frequent; and, if superiors having been warned of the existence of grave abuses have failed to duly remedy them, the Ordinary himself shall provide; if, however, something of greater importance, which will

---

[4] Bastien, *D.C.,* p. 403.

not suffer delay, occur, the Ordinary shall decide immediately; but he must report his decision to the Holy See" (c. 618, § 2).

The Code entrusts to the Ordinary a great number of decisions which specially concern the clerical life. In the case of regulars and congregations of exempt clerics, these decisions are the business of the higher superiors who are the ordinaries of their subjects. In the congregations of clerics who are not exempt, these decisions must be made by the local Ordinary. But in some cases it would seem that he cannot do this without concerning himself with the interior government, contrary to the principle of c. 618, § 2, 2. An attempt has been made[5] to prove that in such cases, by reason of canon 20, it is necessary to supply for the silence of the Code and make the superiors of nonexempt clerics Ordinaries by analogy. Father Vermeersch[6] rightly criticizes this conclusion which does not take the special character of the Ordinary into account: the Ordinary is distinguished from other superiors, most of all, by the nature of his jurisdiction. We may grant, however, that in certain cases the superior of nonexempt clerics must perform this or that action assigned by the text of the Code to Ordinaries. This partial exemption must evidently be proved in each case.

§ 4. GENERAL EXCEPTIONS TO ALL EXEMPTION

315. 1. It is desirable that the Gospel or some point of Christian doctrine shall be explained at the Masses at which the faithful assist on holydays of obligation in all churches or public oratories. If the local Ordinary issues a statute on the subject, regarding these instructions, this statute obliges not only the secular clergy, but even also all religious, including those who are exempt (c. 1345).

In the countries where the Ordinaries have taken this wise measure which ensures for all the faithful who assist at the Holy Sacrifice a minimum of religious instruction, it is not permitted to religious to celebrate in the church, at altars which the public can see, Masses which are not interrupted by instruction. If they judge it opportune to provide a very early Mass or one which is very late so as to enable people who are in a special hurry to assist at the Holy Sacrifice, they must not do this except after they have received the authorization of the local Ordinary. Communities of religious women should endeavor to have the priest who says Mass on these days in their public chapel give the homily or the prescribed instruction. In case of need, the superior should inform the Ordinary of grave neglect in a matter of such great importance.

---

[5] *Comm. pro rel.,* IV, 115.
[6] *Per.,* XIII, 1 sq.

2. "If the Ordinary prescribes, from a motive of public utility, the ringing of bells, certain prayers or sacred solemnities, all religious, even the exempt, must obey, without prejudice to the constitutions and privileges of each institute" (c. 612).

316. Without the permission of the local Ordinary no religious may publish a book on any subject whatsoever, even on a profane subject, or direct newspapers and periodicals, or even collaborate in such direction (c. 1386, § 1).

What is said about books applies equally to any writing which is published, that is to say, which is given to the public.

1. Multigraphed copies distributed by a professor to his students to avoid dictation and the work of transcribing are not published. The same thing is true of writings, whether they are printed or not, which are solely for the religious of the institute.

It is doubtful whether permission must be asked for the publication of a prospectus or of a circular in which the program of studies, the list of expenses, or other information of this sort is given.

2. To write one or two articles occasionally in a paper or review which is not hostile to religion, a religious need not ask the permission of the local Ordinary, but he should do so if he is to collaborate, that is to say, to write more or less regularly.

3. The authorization or permission of the Ordinary, necessary for the publication of a folder which is not religious, need not be mentioned in the work.

This permission must not be confused with the permission to publish which is granted after the censoring or the examination of the work required for every publication on any religious subject (explanation of religion; pious biographies; a manual of prayers or of piety, etc.), or which treats of the natural law. These writings must be submitted to the Ordinary of the place where the author, or the editor, or even the printer resides. The formula which expresses his favorable judgment must be printed with date and signature at the beginning or the end of the work. This is what is called the *imprimatur* (cc. 1385, 1386, 1394).

317. "In all matters in which religious are subject to the local Ordinary, he may coerce them, even by penalties" (c. 619).

It should be observed that this canon does not revoke the privileges to the contrary, such as those possessed by mendicant orders.

318. Another exception to the law of exemption, but in favor of religious: "every **indult** lawfully granted by the local Ordinary dispensing from the obligation of the common law (for example, a dispensation from the ecclesiastical fast) avails likewise for all religious living in the diocese, without prejudice to the vows and particular constitutions of their own institute" (c. 620).

This canon solves a double doubt. It is now plain that their exemption does not prevent religious from profiting from indults given by bishops to the members of their dioceses. But these dispensations do not suspend the obligations of the rules and constitutions (the fast ordered by the rule, for example).

Article 4. The Privilege of Mendicants and the Right to Beg

319. In this article (cc. 621–624) there is question of begging properly so called, of collecting from house to house and from persons other than the special benefactors of an individual religious or of a community. Appeals for help made in writing are not included. But that does not mean that these latter sort of appeals may be made without discretion; for the Ordinaries may forbid them to a certain extent.

The Code here distinguishes three classes of religious: regulars who are mendicants in the strict sense of the term, religious of congregations approved by the Holy See, and those who belong to a diocesan congregation. The Code does not speak of regulars who still bear the title of mendicants, although they are allowed to possess revenues, e.g., the Order of Preachers. Save in exceptional cases, it is not likely that they will have to have recourse to begging from door to door in order to obtain the resources they need. We believe that in contrast to "mendicants in name and in fact" they should follow the rules laid down for nonexempt religious approved by the Holy See.

320. 1. Regulars who "by their institute bear the name of mendicants and who are so in fact" may beg from door to door in the diocese where their religious house is established, without special authorization of the bishop; elsewhere they need the written permission of the local Ordinary (c. 621, § 1).

Those regulars are "mendicants in name and in fact," whose rule forbids not only individual property, but also the holding of property in common. Since the Council of Trent (*Sess. XXV, c. 3, de Regul. et Monial.*), only the Friars Minor of the strict observance and the Capuchins are in this condition. By reason of its professed houses and its residences which are compared to the professed houses, the Society of Jesus is also, in the strict sense, a mendicant order. This qualification, as a matter of fact, does not suppose that one actually lives from alms collected from door to door.[7]

2. Members of congregations approved by the Holy See, in order to beg must have a special privilege of the Holy See and the written permission of their Ordinary; and only a special clause in the indult can dispense them from this. Diocesan congregations depend solely on the different Ordinaries in this matter (c. 622, §§ 1, 2).

3. The Code recommends to bishops to show themselves rather indulgent to the regular mendicants, but to fix strict limits to the permissions granted to other religious (cc. 621, 622).

321. To avoid the grave dangers to which all religious are exposed when occupied in the collection of alms, the Holy See renews the orders formulated in previous decrees on this matter.[8]

The collection of alms, especially in the case of women, must not be entrusted to any except professed of mature age and of approved virtue, and students must never be so employed (c. 623).

Those who seek alms, at least in the case of religious women, must always go two by two, except in case of grave necessity. They must, of their own accord, show their testimonial letters to the parish priest. In certain dioceses, that of Liége, for example, these testimonial letters must be renewed each year. When outside the place where they have a convent, they must dwell either with a priest or in a religious house or, if this is not possible, with a worthy benefactor.

Modesty, humility, and a great fidelity to their spiritual exercises are recommended to them.

Their absence must not exceed one or two months, according as they beg in their own diocese or in another; one or two months' interval must elapse after the previous absence, before setting out again to beg (c. 624).

Repeated and strict decisions of the Holy See forbid bishops of the Latin Church to authorize Orientals of whatever rank to seek alms in

---

[7] Vermeersch, *Epitome*, I[7], n. 782.

[8] Decree *Singulari quidem*, March 27, 1896; Vermeersch, *De relig.*, II, pp. 401–403; *Coll. Brug.*, I (1896), 317; *N.R. Th.*, t. 28 (1896), 277; Decree *De eleemosynis colligendis*, November 21, 1908; Vermeersch, *De relig.*, II, p. 404; *Coll. Gand.*, I (1909), 166; *Coll. Nam.*, IX, 115; *N.R. Th.*, t. 41 (1909), 113.

their diocese, unless they have obtained a *special* and *recent* authorization from the Sacred Congregation of the Oriental Church, or from the Sacred Congregation for Extraordinary Affairs.

Religious should be very careful not to give Mass stipends to such strangers; otherwise they will burden their conscience with a heavy responsibility. Before giving them other alms, they should demand a recommendation of the local Ordinary written in the *vernacular*.

Article 5. Privileges of Regular Abbots

322. "Regular Abbots who have been legitimately elected must, within three months after their election, receive the benediction of the bishop of the diocese in which the monastery is situated. After having received his benediction, they enjoy the following privileges . . ." (c. 625).

1. They may confer the tonsure and minor orders on those religious who are subject to them, at least by reason of simple profession (c. 964, 1).

Ordination conferred on another lay person or cleric would be null by the very fact. The Holy See may establish this nullity because tonsure and the minor orders are purely of an ecclesiastical institution.

2. Even though they have not the episcopal character, in their monastery they enjoy the use of the pontifical insignia, with a throne and the baldachin, but without the *zuchetta*, (violet skullcap); they may also pontificate at the sacred offices.

The *pontifical insignia* which abbots may use are, among others: colored stockings, sandals, silk gloves, the dalmatic, the short tunic, the ring with one facet, the pectoral cross, the simple mitre or the mitre with bands of red silk or threads of gold, etc.

3. Even outside their monastery they may wear the pectoral cross and the ring with the precious stone.

CHAPTER IX

Religious Promoted to Ecclesiastical Dignities or to Parishes

323. The religious state, with its obligations, in practice prohibits religious from accepting certain ecclesiastical offices, and demands in every case that the religious receive the authorization of his superiors in order to accept honors and particular offices, unless the Holy See itself imposes such offices upon the religious (c. 626).

A religious elected to an office by a chapter other than one of his own institute or monastery, should have the permission of his superior in order that he may accept the position that is offered him.

324. The religious promoted to the cardinalate or the episcopate remains a member of his institute. He keeps all the privileges, therefore, and also the obligations which are compatible with his dignity and his office. He is withdrawn from the jurisdiction of his superior and he is subject to the Sovereign Pontiff alone by reason of his vow of obedience (c. 627).

He always has the administration and use of the goods which thereafter come to him; he acquires the ownership of such goods, or not, according to the nature of his profession (c. 628).

If he renounces his dignity or his office, he must return to some house of his institute, whichever one he chooses, but he is no longer eligible for office, and has no voice in chapter (c. 629).

325. 1. The religious who is assigned to the duty of a parish, either as a parish priest or vicar, keeps the obligations of his vows and the constitutions insofar as they are compatible with his office. He is subject at the same time to the local Ordinary in regard to his parochial charge, and to his superiors in everything which concerns his religious obligations. The bishop appoints him on the presentation of his superior; either one or the other can remove him from office, and neither the bishop nor the superior is obliged to communicate to the other the reason for the removal (cc. 630, 631).

2. Whatever comes to him in behalf of the parish is acquired by the parish. Other goods he acquires like other religious of his institute (c. 630, § 3).

Consequently: 1) everything which is given to him for the purpose of divine worship becomes the property of the church;

2) the offerings for Masses and occasional offerings become the property of the religious house. The same thing is true of his salary as parish priest;

3) gifts which are purely personal are added to the patrimony of the parish priest, if the constitutions allow this, or if the general law of the Church requires him to keep his patrimony.

PART THREE

SEPARATION FROM THE INSTITUTE

326. Titles XIV, XV, and XVI of the Code (Book II, part 2) have this in common, that they deal with the separation of a religious from his institute. But this separation may take one of three forms, very different from one another. A religious may leave his institute to continue the religious life in another institute, or to return to the world. In the latter case his departure may be voluntary or forced, legitimate, or culpable. These subjects will be treated in this third part.

CHAPTER X

On Passing to Another Institute

327. To pass from one institute to another, even to one of more strict observance, or from one independent monastery to another, requires the authorization of the Holy See, except in the case where special privileges exist (c. 632).

This article applies to diocesan congregations as well. But the members of a diocesan religious society (n. **18**) may pass to another institute with the permission of the bishop. In societies whose members do not make any promise of perseverance, there is no obstacle to the passage of a member into an entirely different religious group.[1]

Even the nuns of monasteries where only simple vows are taken may not pass into another independent monastery of the same order without permission of the Holy See. This permission is required even for a temporary passage.[2]

328. 1. Religious who pass to another institute must begin their **novitiate** over again; meantime they retain the obligations of their vows, but their other obligations and particular rights are suspended (c. 633). During the novitiate they shall wear the same habit as the other novices (see c. 557).[3]

The Code assigns to such a person as superiors not only the superiors themselves, but the master of novices of the new institute whom he must obey in virtue of his vow of obedience.

2. At the end of the novitiate, if he has already made perpetual vows, he shall immediately be admitted to perpetual profession, or else he must return to his former institute.

The duration of this new probation may, in case of need, be prolonged by the superiors, but not beyond one year (c. 634).

The vote of the chapter or of the council, necessary for admission to this perpetual profession, is *deliberative,* and not consultative, as it is in the case of such as those whom the chapter or the council has already had the obligation of determining whether they should be admitted to first profession. It is understandable that the Holy See in this

---

[1] Goyeneche, C.M.F., *Comm. pro rel.* (1920), p. 298.

[2] Congregation of Religious, Response, November 9, 1926. — *A.A.S.,* XVIII (1926), 490; *R.C.R.* (1927), 33.

[3] This conclusion, evident from cc. 557 and 633, has been confirmed by an answer of the Congregation of Religious, May 14, 1923. — *A.A.S.,* XV (1923), 289; *N.R. Th.* (1923), 543; *Per.,* XII, 67 and (16).

case gives to the chapter (or to the council) a more extensive power since it can pass judgment only once, and since its vote will be final.

3. If the religious is not admitted to the new institute and has formerly pronounced only temporary vows whose time has expired, he is free to return to the world.

4. When a religious passes to another monastery of the *same order,* he need not repeat either the novitiate or the profession (c. 633, § 3).

The same thing is to be said of the religious who pass from one independent house to another in the same congregation.

5. The institute or the monastery which the religious leaves is to keep all the property acquired through the person who is leaving. The dowry is given to the new institute, but the revenues which have accrued from it are retained by the former institute.

If a nun passes from one monastery *of the same order* to another, her dowry and her personal property should, from the day of her departure, be given to the new monastery (cc. 635, 551). The passage from one institute to another does not render void the disposition of his property previously made by the religious.

To whom do the goods acquired during his novitiate by a religious who has transferred to another institute (order or congregation) belong? The question is much debated among canonists, and good arguments can be given for both sides.

If the novice had only simple vows (which will more often be the case), certain authors impose upon him the obligation to make the dispositions required in cc. 569, 580, 583 (see above n. 217, 243); others permit him to act thus without obliging him to do so.

329. The taking of simple vows in a religious congregation, in conformity to the preceding canons, annuls, by the very fact, the solemnity of the vows previously taken unless there is an express provision to the contrary in the papal indult (c. 636).

Canon 635, which declares null all the rights acquired and obligations contracted in the monastery or order which is left, does not make an exception for the vow not to seek or to accept dignities, ecclesiastical or religious. Formerly this vow continued in force, even after the new profession.

CHAPTER XI

On Abandoning Religion

330. The Code distinguishes, under this title, three forms of lawful abandonment of the religious life, and two cases where such leaving is culpable.

Supposing that the religious has legitimate internal reasons, a point with which the Code does not concern itself, he may lawfully leave his institute in the following ways:

He may leave when the time of his temporary vows has expired; (*a*) of his own accord; or (*b*) by the wish of his superiors; (*c*) he may leave by virtue of an indult which allows him to remain temporarily or definitely outside of the institute.

His departure is culpable if he withdraws himself from the authority of the superiors by flight or by apostasy.

It may be well to recall here that a religious whose profession turns out to be invalid, certainly is also free to return to the world (c. 586; n. **250**).

§ 1. LEGITIMATE LEAVING OF RELIGIOUS

331. A professed of **temporary vows** may freely (from the standpoint of canon law) leave the institute when the time of his vows has expired.

For just reasons the superiors may also refuse to allow him to renew his profession. Lack of health, however, is not a sufficient motive, at least when the professed has not fraudulently hidden or dissimulated his state of health before his profession (c. 637).

A serious lack of the intellectual or moral qualities required to carry on the work of the institute would be a sufficient reason to forbid a person to renew the temporary profession, or to take perpetual vows. For the Code does not at all require that the motive of the superior's refusal be blameworthy faults on the part of the professed.

1. The fact that a religious is not allowed to renew his temporary vows or to make his profession of perpetual vows is in nowise to be considered the same as dismissal. Such a confused notion would lead to serious issues, since the two cases are quite distinct as regards necessary power, reasons, procedure, and recourse to the Holy See.

Superiors are not allowed to admit a religious to temporary profession as an experiment and on condition that he will be sent away later if his health is not better. Such a condition would be contrary to the Code. For the rest, it is easy to see the reason for such severity on the part of the Code. After several years passed in religion, a person in ill health might find it still more difficult than another person to establish himself in the world.

In those institutes in which only temporary vows are taken, and in those in which the perpetual profession can be indefinitely postponed, it would seem that admission to the renewal of vows after six years could not be refused except for grave culpable reasons and after proof of the subject's incorrigibility. This interpretation is suggested by canon 642, § 2, which likens nonadmission after six years of temporary vows to dismissal after perpetual vows. To allow religious who have been professed for eight or ten years or more, to be sent back into the world "for a just and reasonable motive," seems absolutely contrary to the procedure of the Code and to the most elementary justice (see d'Ambrosio, O.M.Conv., in *Apollinaris*, 1931, 125 sq.).

2. A religious who becomes afflicted with mental derangement during the period of his temporary vows *must be kept* in the religious institute. Such a person continues to be a part of the institute in the condition or state in which he was at the moment the malady manifested itself, and the institute retains in his regard the same obligations which it had before.[1]

A person who before his perpetual profession is afflicted with a strongly marked and serious hysteria will have a moral obligation to leave the institute, because his presence there will cause considerable annoyance. Still the superiors are not allowed to dismiss him on that account, despite the rather serious breaches of discipline committed under the influence of the malady.

3. The religious who wishes to leave his institute of his own accord, or who is obliged to do so at the expiration of his temporary vows, may leave at any time during the anniversary day of his temporary profession. At first sight one might be tempted to say that he should remain throughout that day, since the profession made, by its nature, obtains until midnight. But Father Vermeersch was correct in stating that the authorization which canon 34, § 3, 5°, grants to the religious to renew his vows or to make his perpetual profession at any moment whatsoever on the anniversary day, likewise grants, by analogy, the freedom to leave at any moment of the anniversary day.

If serious reasons so demand, superiors may authorize the religious to leave a day or two before the expiration of his vows, provided that, having put aside the religious habit, he observe his vows until the anniversary day.

---

[1] Response of the Congregation of Religious, February 5, 1925. — *A.A.S.*, XVII (1925), 107; *R.C.R.* (1925), 65.

332. 1. It may happen that one who is professed of temporary vows or perpetual vows has grave motives for leaving the religious institute either for a time or definitely. In the first place, he must obtain an **indult of exclaustration**[2]; in the second place an **indult of secularization.**

These indults are reserved to the Holy See in all institutes approved by the Holy See; the local Ordinary is competent to grant them to religious of diocesan institutes (c. 638).

2. Which diocesan Ordinary can grant these indults?

This right belongs exclusively to the Ordinary of the place in which the religious resides. The Ordinary of the place in which the motherhouse is located may grant such indults only for those religious who reside in a house of his diocese. This interpretation, which is self-evident, has been officially confirmed by the Commission of Interpretation (see Reply, July 24, 1939. — *A.A.S.,* XXXI [1939], 321).

The place of residence (*commoratio*) of a religious is that of the community to which he belongs, even though he be not present there at the time. However, if the religious actually dwells in another house for over six months, or if he is sent to another house with the intention that he remain there for more than six months, we believe that such a sojourn could be considered sufficient to establish a quasi-domicile, and the Ordinary of that place would be competent to grant the indult (see Vermeersch-Creusen, *Epitome,* I[7], n. 617).

3. The indult of secularization goes into effect only after it has been accepted by the person who has asked for it. If, therefore, the religious, regretting his request, refuses to take advantage of the indult, or declares to his superior, at the moment when the indult is communicated to him, that he does not accept it, he remains bound by his vows and a member of the institute.

Superiors may, however, have grave reasons for wishing or desiring the departure of a subject who perhaps has added inconstancy to other faults. In this case they will refer the matter to the Sacred Congregation.[3]

If the religious belongs to a diocesan institute, recourse must also be had to the Holy See, for the bishop cannot dispense from the vows except by an indult of secularization, and this latter, according to the response of the Sacred Congregation of Religious

---

[2] Exclaustration is the action which consists in allowing a person to leave the cloister (*ex* and *claustrum*).

[3] Congregation of Religious. Response, August 1, 1922. — *A.A.S.,* XIV (1922), 501; *N.R. Th.* (1923), 35.

(August 1, 1922), may not be imposed by the superiors on the subject against his will.

From the time when the religious fully accepts the indult, the grant produces all its effects, and the separation from the institute is perfect. Even though the person should repent a few hours afterwards, this in no way changes the juridical situation, and it is not in the power of the superiors to act as though the acceptance had not taken place.[4]

333. The **indult of exclaustration** is the permission to live temporarily outside the houses of the institute and without being subject to the authority of the religious superiors (cc. 638, 639).

As reasons for obtaining this authorization, we may mention the necessity of undertaking some business which it would be difficult to carry out with ordinary dependence on religious superiors; the necessity of attending for a time to the needs of one's parents, who cannot be taken care of in any other way, etc. If such cases seem to occur, the person interested will do well to submit them to the judgment of an adviser who is, at the same time, prudent and sincere, and who has a truly supernatural spirit.

We must clearly distinguish the indult of exclaustration from the simple permission to live for more than six months outside the institute. The effects are very different. One cannot deny that exclaustration loosens, to a certain extent, the bonds which attach a religious to his institute.

On July 10, 1955, the S. Congregation of Religious declared that religious *dispersed* by unjust laws to which they must submit and forced to live outside a religious house, are not considered as exclaustrated religious, but as lawfully dwelling outside their house. Because of their special condition, the Holy See places them under the local Ordinary of their domicile. The S. Congregation exhorts them to keep in as close contact as possible with their religious superior. They retain all the rights and obligations compatible with their situation.

334. The religious who has obtained an indult of exclaustration:

---

[4] Father Vermeersch thought that a religious can still withdraw his acceptance as long as it has not been made irrevocable by leaving the house (*Per.*, XI, 150). His argument which is drawn from the necessity of leaving the house in order to interrupt the novitiate does not seem conclusive. The act of leaving the novitiate which is necessary and sufficient to manifest complete separation is something quite different from a deliberate declaration of acceptance which gives complete effect to an indult asked for and fully granted.

a) Keeps all the obligations of the rule which are compatible with his state.

b) Must not wear the religious habit.

The Ordinary of the place who gives the indult of exclaustration may, for special motives, authorize the religious to keep the habit of the institute.[5]

c) Loses for the duration of the indult the right to vote in the Chapter and to be elected to office, but he keeps all the spiritual privileges of his institute.

By exclaustration, a religious does not cease to be a member of his institute. Hence nothing justifies us in saying that if he dies before returning, he has no right to the same suffrages as the other professed. Unquestionably this right is not a "privilege." But it is a right acquired through profession. By specifying that the religious during his exclaustration loses his right to vote and to be elected to office, the Code confirms the fact that he does not lose his other rights. An argument against this interpretation cannot be drawn from c. 567. Deceased novices have no right to the suffrages except by virtue of a special prescription of the Code; for them this is a privilege, but the same thing is not true of the professed.[6]

d) Is subject, even by virtue of his vow of obedience, to the Ordinary of the diocese in which he resides and who takes the place of his superiors (c. 639).

Before the Code, the indult of exclaustration was called "temporary secularization"; its effects were determined by the special terms of the indult.

334 bis. Recently the jurisprudence of the S. Congregation of Religious has introduced two special forms of exclaustration, to provide for exceptionally difficult cases.

1. Exclaustration *ad nutum S. Sedis* is a *precept* imposed by the Holy See on a religious to live outside a house of his institute. The purpose of this measure, which is not strictly a penalty, will more frequently be the good of the community,

---

[5] Comm. of Interpretation, Response, November 12, 1922. — *A.A.S.,* XIV (1922), 662.

[6] Dom Bastien is also of this opinion. (See *D.C.,* n. 615, 3.) We have answered in the text the arguments of Father Fanfani, *"Le Droit des Religieuses,"* n. 299, 3. Father Vermeersch, *Epitome,* I[7], n. 796, preferred the opinion which denies the right to suffrages to exclaustrated religious.

whose peace the religious is disturbing, but not to such an extent that he could be dismissed.

The effects are substantially the same as in the case of exclaustration freely asked for. Nevertheless the measure is not adopted for a determined period of time, and the return to common life may not be made without the permission of the Holy See.[7]

2. *"Qualified"* exclaustration is a provisional remedy used by the S. Congregation in the case of a religious priest who asks for reduction to the lay state. This indult, granted for one year, carries with it the usual consequences of exclaustration from the point of view of religious obligations, but, in addition, the suppression of the privileges and obligations of clerics (with the exception of celibacy) and the prohibition of any exercise of orders. After one year, recourse must be had to the Holy See which will give its final decision in the case.[8]

335. 1. **The indult of secularization** is the permission to leave the religious institute for good in order to return to secular life (cc. 638, 640).

Formerly the indult of secularization was a permission accorded to the professed of solemn vows to return to the world, where they almost always retained the obligation of their vows. The professed of simple vows who left their institute for good were generally dispensed from their vows; sometimes, however, the dispensation from the vow of chastity was excepted or limited, for example, to the licit use of a first marriage.

Secularization was sometimes advised to save the good works threatened with ruin by the dispersion of religious, as was the case in Italy and France. The Holy See has hardly shown itself favorable to this. Almost always dispensation from certain obligations, for example, that of wearing the religious habit, was sufficient. The practice of the perfect life in exile or during an apparent inaction in the midst of one's own country, imposes many sacrifices of great value in the eyes of God for the salvation of souls. Pius X in particular insisted strongly that religious should by all means prefer to persevere in the religious life, even though this demanded the sacrifice of very important works.

2. The indult of secularization does not go into effect until after it has been accepted by the subject who asked for it. If then a religious, regretting his request, refuses to pay any atten-

---

[7] CpR., 1953, 336 sq.   [8] CpR., 1955, 374 sq.

tion to the indult or declares to his superior, at the moment
the latter informs him that it has come, that he does not accept
it, he remains bound by his vows, and a member of the institute.

Superiors, however, may have grave reasons for wishing or
desiring the departure of a subject joining perhaps obvious
inconstancy to other faults. Such a case should be referred to
the S. Congregation.

If the religious is a member of a diocesan institute, recourse
must also be had to the Holy See. For a bishop has no power
to dispense from the vows of religion except by an indult of
secularization and according to an answer given by the S. Congregation of Religious (August 1, 1922) such an indult may
not be forced upon a subject against his will by his superiors.

Since 1953 the text of an indult of secularization for religious
who are not priests, contains the following clause: if this indult
which was requested is not accepted within ten days after the
religious has received the writ of execution, it loses its value.
Thus possible vacillations and waverings on the part of the religious cease in the case of secularization.

From the moment that the religious fully accepts the indult, the grant
produces all its effects and the separation from the institute is complete.
Regret following a few hours afterwards cannot change this juridical
situation in any way, and it is no longer within the power of superiors
to act as though the acceptance had not taken place.

336. 1. The indult of secularization effects an entire separation from the institute, in which the former religious has no
longer either rights or obligations, not even that of the vow of
chastity, unless, of course, this obligation is the result of
ordination.

C. 640 develops as follows the consequences of this principle:

a) The secularized religious must lay aside the religious habit.

He may wear, out of devotion, under his lay garb, the garments worn
under the habit in his former religious family, for instance, a scapular.

b) He is entirely in the position of the secular clergy in
regard to the recitation of the divine office and the celebration of
the Holy Sacrifice; and the rest of the faithful in what regards
the reception of the sacraments.

c) He is no longer obliged to observe the rules or constitutions; and he is freed from his vows. He keeps, however, the obligations attached to holy orders, if he has received them.

d) If a secularized religious re-enters religion, with a dispensation from the Holy See, he will be classed in everything with the other novices (c. 640, § 2).

2. A religious who has been secularized and who is in major orders must return to his diocese and be received by his Ordinary. If he has lost his incardination (by perpetual profession) he is forbidden to exercise holy orders until a bishop has the goodness to receive him, unless the Holy See takes some particular action in the matter (c. 641, § 1).

This reception shall be either permanent or temporary, in the nature of an experiment for three years; this period may be renewed once. Tacit renewal suffices (Commission of Interpretation, Response, July 27, 1942, art. II. — *A.A.S.*, XXXIV [1942], 241). If the bishop does not send the subject away before the end of this period of six years, he is considered, by the very fact, to have incorporated him with his clergy (c. 641).

At present the Sacred Congregation of Religious grants to the Ordinary, who is willing to receive a priest who is a professed religious, the power to grant him an indult of exclaustration. As soon as the religious priest in question has been permanently received into the diocese, the same indult effects his secularization. A copy of the form used by the Sacred Congregation may be found in *Periodica*, XVII (1929), 51*.

337. "Without a new and special indult of the Holy See, every professed who returns to the world, though he may, within the limits of canon 641, exercise his holy orders, is excluded:

"1) from any benefices in the major or minor basilicas or in cathedral churches;

"2) from all appointments as professor or to any other office in major and minor seminaries, or colleges in which clerics are educated; as well as in the universities and other educational institutions which have the apostolic privilege of conferring academic degrees;

"3) from all offices or employments in the episcopal curia and in religious houses, whether of men or of women, even though there is question of diocesan congregations" (c. 642, § 1).

1. These prohibitions apply to all religious who have left the religious life after having been dispensed from their perpetual or even temporary

vows, from the oath of perseverance or from every other special promise, provided they have been bound by these latter obligations during the space of six years. The readmission into religion puts an end to these incapacities (c. 642, § 2).

The prohibition, which was issued in 1909, from living in places where there is a house of the institute, is not renewed in the Code.[9]

2. It should be noticed that there is question here of religious or members of a religious Society who have lawfully returned to the world. The Holy See does not wish that the hope of dignities or of an honorable position among the secular clergy shall give rise to a temptation to inconstancy; it does not wish that young clerics, or religious men or women shall see in the appointment of a former religious to an important office a tacit approbation of his conduct.

The severity of the exclusions pronounced by c. 642 shows clearly the disfavor with which the Holy See regards the abandonment of the obligations undertaken by the vows of religion. The thought of the Church becomes still more evident by comparing this article with c. 542, 2. We see here that reasons of an exceptional gravity are required to refuse a cleric in major orders permission to enter religion. It is, therefore, contrary to the Catholic spirit to consider the passage from the regular to the secular clergy as an indication of progress in the understanding and the practice of the ways of perfection. Save in very special circumstances, we can only see with the Church in such a change a regrettable inconstancy in the employment of those means which all Catholic tradition declares most apt, at least in themselves, for acquiring the perfection of the Christian life.

338. Religious who leave at the expiration of their temporary profession, or by reason of an indult of secularization, are not allowed to demand any recompense for the services rendered to the institute.

If the religious woman was received without a dowry and is without resources, charity obliges the institute to furnish her with the means of returning home in a becoming manner. The institute must likewise assure her a respectable livelihood for some time.

This means is to be determined by mutual consent or, in case of disagreement, by the advice of the bishop (c. 643).

If a female religious has been received with a dowry which is insufficient to insure her support in the world, or has been admitted by reason of a dowry established in favor of the institute (see n. **185,** 3), the

[9] Decree *Cum minoris,* June 15, 1909.—Vermeersch, *Per.,* V, 41–44, 125; *Coll. Brug.,* XIX (1909), 611; *Coll. Gand.,* I (1909), 293; *Coll. Nam.,* IX, 118; *N.R. Th.,* t. 42 (1910), 573.

religious community must make up for the insufficiency of her resources, or must give her whatever she needs for the time being to live decently.[10] This help, however, need not be prolonged beyond the time required for finding employment suitable to the condition of the former religious.

If she is quite old and infirm and without resources, she must agree to enter into a suitable institution intended for persons of that condition. In any case, the help given her by her former community need never have the character of a pension for life.

339. *Dispensation From the Vows of Religion.*

1. The vows of religion are of their nature reserved to the Holy See. Those only can dispense from them directly who have received this power by way of privilege. The Ordinary can grant to religious of diocesan congregations an indult of secularization; but the Code stipulates that this includes dispensation from all vows made in religion. To restrict its effects will be contrary to the general law of the Church. The effects of dismissal are determined in the same way by the Code. The Ordinary, therefore, cannot indirectly dispense from a part of the vows of religion.

2. Do not bishops possess the power to dispense religious of diocesan congregations from the vows of religion, with the exception of the vow of perpetual chastity, in virtue of the constitution *Conditae a Christo,* n. VIII? It is certain that the question must be answered in the negative. As a matter of fact:

1) The Constitution *Conditae* granted to the Ordinaries the power to send these religious away (*dimittendi potestas est*); the consequence of this dismissal was that the vows of religion were dispensed with, except the vow of perpetual chastity. But dismissal, which includes the dispensation from the vows, is one thing, the dispensation from the vows granted because asked for and when there is no reason for dismissal is another thing.

2) If we admit — though it seems to us that it would be wrong to do so — that the bishop was once able to dispense directly, still this article may no longer be appealed to, since it has been entirely omitted in the Code and is, therefore, certainly abrogated in virtue of c. 6, 6.

We shall see further on that the dispensation from perpetual vows as a consequence of dismissal no longer depends on the Ordinaries, but on the constitutions or on special indults of the Holy See.

---

[10] See Congregation of Religious, Response, March 2, 1924. — *A.A.S.,* XV (1924), 165; *N.R. Th.* (1924), 501.

§ 2. UNLAWFUL LEAVING

340. The Code defines an **apostate** religious as "one who, having made profession of perpetual vows, whether solemn or simple, unlawfully leaves the religious house with the intention of not returning, or who with the intention of withdrawing himself from religious obedience, though he has lawfully left the house, does not return to it" (c. 644, § 1).[11]

This wrong intention is presumed if a religious has not returned within a month and has not manifested to his superior his intention of returning.

In former times the crime of apostasy supposed a solemn profession.

It is necessary to distinguish clearly between the sin of apostasy and the crime of apostasy. The sin resides in the will alone and a religious who decides to leave his institute without permission is already gravely guilty of apostasy before God. The crime, or the act punishable by the ecclesiastical law, supposes two elements: the unlawful *departure* and the *intention* of not returning.

The unlawful departure is a fact to which the superior can testify or which he can verify. Since this *intention* is a necessary element of the *crime,* it must be made known either by a clear statement in word or in writing; or by an act which can admit of no other interpretation, for example, by unconditionally accepting secular employment, or by entering into a civil marriage, etc. The prolongation of the unlawful absence beyond a month without any manifestation of an intention to return establishes a presumption of law, that is to say, that the religious may and should be treated henceforth as an apostate, unless he proves that he had the intention of returning.

341. 1. "A **fugitive** is one who, without permission of his superiors, deserts the religious house but with the intention of returning to the institute" (c. 644, § 3).

The crime of "flight" (*fuga*) implies that the religious by leaving withdraws himself from his dependence upon his superiors. This element distinguishes flight from a simple unlawful going out. The latter would consist in a brief absence, or the prolongation of a legitimate absence, during which the religious may easily be reached by his superiors. Such would be the case if a

---

[11] Apostasy from the religious life must not be confused with apostasy from the faith.

religious prolonged for a day or more, without permission, a visit allowed him to his family, or some ministerial work.

All authors are agreed in holding that *flight* supposes an absence of at least two or three days contrary to the wishes of superiors.

2. The professed with temporary vows who leaves his religious house without permission with the intention of *not returning* sins gravely against obedience and the law of the cloister. He is not, however, an "apostate" or a "fugitive" in the juridical sense of the word. His superiors must receive him if he returns; but they may find in his conduct a sufficient reason for dismissing him from the institute (see Berutti, O.P., *Institutiones*, III, n. 156).

According to Father Vermeersch, *Epitome*, I', 803, a professed with temporary vows who abandons his institute with the intention of not returning is treated juridically as a fugitive. This is also the opinion of Goyeneche in *Commentarium pro religiosis* (1933), 257.

342. 1. Both the apostate and the fugitive retain all the obligations of the rule and of the vows. They have gravely violated the vow of obedience and the law of cloister, and are obliged to return without delay (c. 645, § 1).

2. By the very fact of his apostasy the apostate incurs excommunication reserved to his higher superior or, in the case of nonexempt institutes or lay institutes, reserved to the Ordinary of the place of his residence. He loses all the privileges of his institute. If he returns, he is forever deprived of both active and passive voice (c. 2385).

3. A fugitive or an apostate religious cannot receive sacramental absolution unless he is sincerely sorry for his sin and is prepared to make fitting reparation. He must promise to return as soon as possible, or at least, to submit himself immediately to the directions of his superiors.

Since 1918, the penalties declared against an apostate religious affect not only regulars but also the members of religious congregations and nuns who are guilty of this crime.

The fugitive religious loses, by the very fact that he is a fugitive, whatever office he may have possessed in religion. If he is in orders, he incurs suspension. Other penalties must be inflicted by superiors (c. 2386).

Superiors will order the culprit to return to a house of the institute; they will secure for him, if need be, absolution from the canonical penalties incurred. If they judge that they can keep him in the community, they will impose upon him a reparation proportionate to the gravity of the fault and the scandal which he has given. If the offender considers that he can no longer fulfill the obligations of the religious life, or if the superiors desire to send him away, they will take up the procedure necessary for dispensation or dismissal. In anticipation of this, they may, if the return of the culpable person involves grave inconvenience, permit him to remain in the world until the dispensation has been obtained, or the dismissal decided on and, if need be, ratified.

4. The superiors of apostate or fugitive religious are gravely obliged to seek them out and, if it be possible, to bring them back. In the case of a nun, this duty falls upon the local Ordinary and the regular superior upon whom the monastery depends (c. 645, § 2).

CHAPTER XII

Dismissal of Religious

Article 1. Dismissal in General and by the Law

343. I. Before the Code, a distinction was made between expulsion and dismissal. Expulsion was a more solemn form of sending away which left upon the religious the obligations of his vows and which seldom took place except in the case of regulars.

1. Expulsion supposed the incorrigibility of the subject, proved by six months' severe penances. In order to pronounce sentence of expulsion, a formal process was required together with the canonical proof of the causes of expulsion, and the intervention of the general, or, at least, of the provincial. Nuns could not be expelled without the authorization of the Holy See.

2. The most simple form of dismissal was used especially in religious orders, in the case of professed of simple, perpetual vows. It was pronounced by the general, assisted by his council. For the dismissal of nuns, the intervention of the Holy See was required. The power of dismissal was granted to a certain number of religious congregations.

a) In the orders, a grave reason was required, even though this did not involve any fault on the part of the one dismissed, and judgment about the gravity of this reason was left to the competent superior. A sickness contracted after the taking of the vows, could not be given as a reason for dismissal. No legal process was required.

The dismissal included, by its very nature, dispensation from the vows.

b) In the religious congregations, the dismissal of the religious was subject to different conditions, according to the quality of the religious, cleric or lay brother, and the nature of his vows, temporary or perpetual.

A lay religious with temporary vows could be dismissed for any serious motive, and without the necessity of observing juridical forms.

Before sending away a religious bound by perpetual vows, or a cleric against his will, it was necessary to show that he had committed a serious exterior and public fault, and had shown himself incorrigible. Unless the Sacred Congregation of Religious gave special authorization to the contrary, a formal process was required.

A religious woman with perpetual vows could not be sent away unless her incorrigibility had been clearly shown. The dismissal was always to be confirmed by the Sacred Congregation of Bishops and Regulars and, after 1908, by the Sacred Congregation of Religious.

The obligation of the vows was not taken away by the dismissal, unless a privilege to that effect had been accorded to the institute. It was necessary, therefore, to obtain a dispensation.

Everything which has just been said concerns solely the institutes approved by the Holy See. Before the Code, institutes which were purely diocesan were not subject to the general decrees concerning religious unless special mention of this fact was made.

3. Before May 19, 1918, it was customary in religious orders to take simple vows, perpetual on the part of the religious, but preparatory to the solemn profession. The dismissal of religious who had made such a profession was subject to the prescriptions of the former law.[1] Since May 19, 1921, there have been no religious of this class.

344. II. 1. Since the Code, the dismissal of religious who have taken perpetual vows is subject to very strict formalities. The perpetual vows taken in institutes of exempt clerics are, in this regard, put in the same class with solemn vows. By the express revocation of privileges the new law introduces a greater uniformity among the orders and congregations.

In religious institutes where the formula of the vows contains a condition which makes them contingent (see n. **228**), the dismissal of a professed religious is regulated by cc. 646–648, and not by cc. 649 sq.[2]

In religious societies without vows cc. 646–648 or 649 sq. are to be applied, according as the bond between the society and the members is perpetual or temporary.[3]

2. All this matter is divided, in the Code, into four chapters. The first chapter deals with religious with temporary vows (cc. 647–648); chapters two and three have to do with religious with perpetual vows, first in the nonexempt institutes or lay institutes (cc. 649–653), and then in the institutes of exempt clerics (cc. 654–668); chapter four explains the condition of religious dismissed after taking perpetual vows (cc. 669–672).

A preliminary canon (c. 646) treats of the case in which dismissal is incurred *ipso facto* by law.

345. Certain very grave and scandalous crimes have *ipso facto*

---

[1] Comm. of Interpretation, Response, October 16, 1919, n. 2. — *A.A.S.,* XI (1919), 476.

[2] Comm. of Interpretation, Response, March 1, 1921. — *A.A.S.,* XIII (1921), 177; *N.R. Th.* (1921), 269.

[3] Comm. of Interpretation, Response, March 1, 1921. — *A.A.S.,* XIII (1921), 177; *N.R. Th.* (1921), 270.

the effect of expelling the culpable religious. The conditions of this penalty are defined in canon 646. The terms of this canon are to be interpreted strictly, for they have a purely penal character (c. 19).

"The following religious are *ipso facto* regarded as lawfully dismissed:

"*a*) Religious who have publicly apostatized from the Catholic faith."

Apostasy in the strict sense means the complete abandoning of the faith (c. 1325, § 2). Hence this term is not realized in the passing over to heresy, much less to schism. A number of authors admit that in these two cases defection from the Catholic faith does not entail expulsion *by law*. It is self-evident that it constitutes a serious motive for dismissal (see *Commentarium pro religiosis* [1930], 414. — Goyeneche, *De Religiosis*, n. 106). Others, arguing from the Latin text of the Code "*publici apostatae a fide catholica*" are of the opinion that the public crime of heresy or schism entails dismissal *by law*. Thus Vidal, *De Religiosis*, n. 438; Palombo, *De Dimissione Relig.*, n. 197, 1.

"*b*) A religious who has run away with a person of the opposite sex."

In order to perpetrate this crime, it is necessary that the accomplices actually leave together, the one his or her institute, the other his or her habitual residence; or that by *mutual agreement* the guilty religious go to find his accomplice after leaving religion unlawfully. The crime mentioned in the canon would not exist if a fugitive religious were to go, without previous agreement, in search of a woman and stay with her.

"*c*) Religious who attempt or contract marriage, even the so-called civil marriage."

The crime supposes the mutual giving of consent, even though it be invalid. The civil or ecclesiastical publication of the banns, if not followed by the contract, would not be sufficient.

346. "In these cases it suffices that the higher superior, with his chapter or council, according to the prescriptions of the constitutions, make a declaration of the fact; but he must take care to preserve in the register of the house the collective evidence of the fact" (c. 646).

There is question here of a simple declaration of fact, which is not required as a condition necessary for the valid dismissal by law (Commission of Interpretation, Response, July 30, 1934. — *A.A.S.*, XXVI [1934], 494. — *R.C.R.* [1934], 180).

The legalizing of this summary dismissal is intended above all to save superiors from the necessity of a process which might be impossible or useless; and afterwards to protect them against future claims on the part of the guilty person.

Once the dismissal is lawfully incurred, the obligation of the vows is taken away, if there is question of a professed with temporary vows; if the vows are perpetual, the constitutions or the privileges of the institute must be consulted as to the effects of dismissal.

Superiors are not bound in any case to readmit a religious who is clearly dismissed because of one of the crimes mentioned in canon 646. Such is the declaration of the Commission of Interpretation just referred to.

If the religious has taken perpetual vows and leaves the institute with the intention of not returning, he is excommunicated as an apostate from religion (see n. **342**).

Article 2. Dismissal of Religious Who Have Taken Temporary Vows

347. The following superiors are **competent** in the matter of dismissal:

a) In the orders and in the congregations approved by the Holy See, the superior general (or the abbot of an independent monastery) acting with the consent of his council, manifested by secret vote.

b) For nuns, the local Ordinary and the regular superior on whom they depend.

When the nuns depend on a regular superior, the consent of the Ordinary of the place and of the superior is required, according to the most common interpretation, to decide on dismissal. The causes for dismissal are to be indicated in a document signed by the sister superior and her counsellors.

No distinction is to be made here between nuns with solemn vows and those with simple vows. The profession of temporary vows is always simple.

c) In the diocesan congregations, the Ordinary of the diocese in which the convent is situated (c. 647, § 1).

The Ordinary may not act without the knowledge, or against the just opposition of superiors (c. 647, § 1), and if he should do so, the superiors will have the right and the duty to appeal to the Holy See.[4]

---

[4] See Leo XIII, Const. *Conditae a Christo,* I, § VIII.

348. Ill health may not be numbered among the grave **motives** (whether they involve a fault or not) which are absolutely required for dismissal, unless it is proved with certainty that it had been fraudulently concealed or dissimulated before profession (c. 647, § 2).

Hysteria, notwithstanding its regrettable consequences in religious life, is not, therefore, a reason for dismissal. The sick person will frequently find, however, that this disease is a sufficient reason for asking to leave religion and to try, in the world, to strive after the ideal which she was pursuing in religion.

Among the serious motives would be: the lack of the religious spirit, if this is a cause of scandal for the community and "if repeated admonition, joined to salutary penance, has produced no effect"; faults of character incompatible with religious discipline and with community life; a lack of aptitude for the work of the institute.

It would seem, however, that a well-directed probation will frequently result in the discovery of these faults during the novitiate. In this case, both the good of the subject and that of the institute demand that the responsibility be assumed immediately for a decision which, though it be painful now, is probably inevitable and which, if postponed, will only lead to very regrettable consequences.

349. A judicial **process** is not required; but the *reasons* for the dismissal must be certain. They must be made known to the religious who always enjoys full right to defend himself, and his answers must be submitted in full to the superior who is to give the final decision regarding his dismissal (c. 647, § 2, n. 3).

If the motive for dismissal be a lack of religious spirit, manifested by violations of the vows or the rules, or by insubordination, by grave negligence in essential duties, etc., the guilty religious must be given at least *two warnings*. The superior, moreover, must first of all try to bring the erring religious back to a better state of mind by imposing salutary penances upon him.

It will be expedient to give these serious warnings to the religious in question in the presence of witnesses or in writing, since, as a matter of fact, such a religious may claim that his attention has never been seriously called to his faults, or that he has never been threatened with dismissal.

It is the duty of the superiors to inform the inferior of his right of appeal, and instruct him how to make it.

350. The religious who has been dismissed has the **right to**

appeal to the Holy See and, pending the appeal, the dismissal has no juridical effect (c. 647, §§ 2, 4).

According to a decree of the Sacred Congregation of Religious,[5] the following conditions for appeal to the Holy See are laid down:

a) The religious may have recourse directly by letter to the Sacred Congregation, or through the superior who has notified him of the dismissal.

b) As evidence of the appeal it is required and sufficient to have an authentic document (e.g., a demand for appeal written and signed by the religious) or the testimony of at least two trustworthy witnesses.

c) The appeal must be made during the ten full days which follow the intimation of the decree of dismissal. If the religious is ignorant of his right, or is prevented from using it, delays are not counted.

This regulation is a protection both for superiors and subjects. If the superior, acting with sincerity and prudence, notifies or reminds a religious who has been dismissed of his right of appeal, he must make haste to use it, or he will lose it by his negligence. In either case, the superiors are freed the sooner from all uncertainty about the matter, and are protected from all future claims.

The subject, on the other hand, is protected against his own ignorance and against the negligence or the bad faith of a superior. His right of appeal is not lost by the mere fact that he is hindered from using it.

d) An appeal made within the due time suspends all the effects of the decree of dismissal. Until the decision of the Sacred Congregation is given, the religious keeps all his obligations and rights. He cannot be forced to leave the monastery or the institute temporarily, or to take off the habit, etc. Of course, if he has incurred other penalties, they evidently are not done away with by the mere fact of his appeal made against the dismissal.

351. Dismissal carries with it, *ipso facto,* **dispensation from the vows** of religion. If the religious was in minor orders, he immediately becomes a layman; if he has received major orders, he is subject to the prescriptions of cc. 641, § 1, and 642 (c. 648). (See numbers **336,** 2; **337.**)

---

[5] Congregation of Religious, Decree of July 20, 1923. — *A.A.S.,* XV (1923), 457; *N.R. Th.* (1924), 441; *Per.,* XII, 100.

352. In the dismissal of religious women, what is said in c. 643, § 2, must be observed, that is to say, necessary financial help must be given them so that they can return to their family, and so that they can meet their needs until the time when they will be able to secure other resources (see n. **338**).

Article 3. Dismissal of Religious With Perpetual Vows, in an Institute of Nonexempt Clerics or of Lay Religious

§ 1. DISMISSAL OF RELIGIOUS MEN

353. Motives.

The accused must have committed at least three offenses against the general law of the Church or against the law of religious, and these must all be of the same kind: grave, exterior, and indicative of an obstinate, bad will. One offense only would suffice, however, if it is so repeated or persisted in after frequent admonitions, that it becomes equivalent to three offenses (cc. 649, 657).

According to c. 656 the faults required as reasons for dismissal are "grave external offenses either against the universal law or against the special law of religious."

Whether the word *offense* be taken in the strict sense or not, the Code seems to wish to stress two elements in those faults which are sufficient reasons for dismissal: first, the *gravity* which results from the bad will of the guilty party and from the scandal given; second, the possibility of proving the existence of the offense (see canon 658, § 1). For external, criminal acts may exist which cannot be proven. (Such is the explanation of the best authors who have written on this subject. See Palombo, *De Dimissione*, nn. 29 and 31; Goyeneche, *De religiosis*, n. 114.) Hence the following are sufficient reasons for dismissal:

a) violations of general or particular laws of the Church to which a canonical penalty is attached;

b) violations of a formal and grave precept;

c) violations of the vows or of the constitutions which would amount to a specially grave fault or which would give rise to grave scandal either in the community or outside of it. Such offenses, however, would have to be repeated, or obstinately persisted in.

Offenses, even habitual ones, against rules which are merely disciplinary, or the frequent violation of the vows in slight matters, etc., are not sufficient reason for dismissal after the perpetual profession. These very just demands of the Holy See in regard to serious reasons for dismissal should inspire superiors with great prudence and proper severity in admitting their subjects to the first or to the last vows, and they should not forget that a passing and purely exterior amendment brought about by the threat of dismissal is a very precarious guarantee of a regular or fervent life, especially in the case of a young religious.

354. Procedure.

When the immediate higher superior has obtained certain proof of the first offense, he must, either personally or through another acting in his name, admonish the delinquent; the admonition must be repeated after the second offense; but in the case of continuous or permanent offenses, an interval of at least three whole days must elapse between the first and second admonition. To these admonitions the superior shall add exhortations and corrections, as well as penances and other penal remedies calculated to procure the amendment of the culprit. He is also bound to remove the culprit from the occasion of relapse, even to the extent of transferring him, if necessary, to another house, where the vigilance will be easier and the occasion of offending more removed. To each admonition must be added the threat of dismissal (cc. 659–661).

It is difficult to determine just what period of time must elapse after an offense for which a religious has been admonished, before a subsequent offense may no longer be counted against him as a second offense. Regardless of the nature of the offense for which he was admonished, a religious may certainly be said to have reformed if, during the period of three years, he has not relapsed into the grave and exterior fault for which he was admonished.[6]

After he has given signs and proofs of repentance, less time might be sufficient. Certain authors hold that a formal precept would no longer have any juridical effects after the lapse of a year (see Palombo, *De Dimissione*, n. 28).

355. *The Competent Superior.*

If the general council presided over by the general decides by a majority of votes that there is proper cause to dismiss a religious, a decree of dismissal shall be issued:

---

[6] See Goyeneche, *Comm. pro rel.* (1924), 21 sq.

a) in diocesan congregations, by the Ordinary of the place where the culprit has his domicile;

b) in the institutes approved by the Holy See, by the superior general; but this latter decree will have no force until it has been confirmed by the Holy See (c. 650).

§ 2. DISMISSAL OF RELIGIOUS WOMEN

356. "The dismissal of religious women who have made profession of perpetual vows requires, likewise, grave external reasons, together with incorrigibility, experience having proved, in the judgment of the superiors, that there is no hope of amendment" (c. 651, § 1).

The Code does not point out exactly the number and the nature of the offenses, nor the measures to be taken to establish the proof of incorrigibility. The formalities prescribed to establish the culpability of religious men are at least a valuable indication.

At first sight one cannot see why a sister having perpetual vows may be dismissed for faults less grave than those demanded for the dismissal of a religious brother having perpetual vows. Nevertheless, the expressions used by the Code seem less rigorous when there is question of the dismissal of sisters. But in demanding "serious external faults joined with incorrigibility" the Code, it seems to us, sufficiently excludes those faults which, despite their frequency, remain venial. Obduracy in defects regarding the vows or religious discipline which are a sufficient motive to threaten dismissal after perpetual vows have been taken, can no longer be considered a venial sin. Such obduracy would be subversive of discipline, contrary to the common good, and therefore, a grievous sin.

The superior of whom there is question here may be the local superior. Certain corrective measures, for example, the removal of the culprit may, however, require the intervention of the higher superior.

357. 1. In diocesan congregations the bishop of the place of domicile will examine the motives for dismissal and give the decision (c. 652, § 1).

2. If there is question of nuns, the Ordinary will send to the Sacred Congregation of Religious all the acts and documents with a statement of his own judgment of the case, and that of the regular superior if the monastery be subject to regulars (c. 652, § 2).

3. In the other institutes approved by the Holy See, the mother general will transmit to the Sacred Congregation the whole matter with all the acts and documents (c. 652, § 3).

In the last two cases, the Sacred Congregation will make the final decision.

Though it is prudent for superiors to consult their council in such a serious matter, still they are not obliged to do so. This great latitude is understandable since the final decision is never left to the superiors. The constitutions, however, will almost always oblige the superioress to consult her council or even to follow its decision.

The complete acts and documents of the case must contain proof that all the canonical prescriptions have been observed.

§ 3. GENERAL REQUIREMENTS FOR THE DISMISSAL OF RELIGIOUS MEN AND WOMEN

358. 1. The culpable person may defend himself freely and his answers are to be faithfully inserted in the acts of the case (cc. 650, 651).

2. If the presence of the culpable person would occasion a grave and exterior scandal or would cause a very serious damage to the community, he may be immediately dismissed and must at once put off the religious habit. The dismissal will be decreed by the higher superior or, if there is not time to consult him, by the local superior, with the consent of the diocesan Ordinary. The general or local council has in both cases a deliberative vote (c. 653).

An exterior scandal exists when the offense which causes the scandal is known outside of the convent or can no longer be hidden. To justify an immediate decree of expulsion, the harm should not only be very great, but imminent. If the dismissal is ordered by a higher superior, the consent of the diocesan Ordinary is not required.

3. It would be useless to grant to a religious who is dismissed an appeal to the Holy See. First of all, this right always exists and it may constitute the last resource of a religious of a diocesan congregation. In other institutes the sending of the acts and documents to the Holy See implicitly includes an appeal. The Sacred Congregation will not ratify a dismissal if the acts do not contain the answers, and, therefore, the defense of the religious who is sent away.

Article 4. Dismissal of Religious With Perpetual Vows in an Institute of Exempt Clerics

359. 1. The **procedure** to be followed is the legal element by which the dismissal of these religious is essentially distinguished from that of other professed bound by perpetual vows. In point of fact, except in the cases provided for in c. 646 (special offenses), and c. 653 (scandal or danger of grave and imminent harm), the formalities of the canonical process must be observed, every contrary privilege being revoked (c. 654).

The revocation of this privilege which completes the resemblance between professed with solemn vows and professed with perpetual simple vows in this matter, introduces an important modification in the government of several great orders.

2. The competent **tribunal** is made up:

a) of the superior general of the institute, or of the monastic congregation in the quality of presiding judge;

b) of the special council of this superior, composed of at least four counsellors; if one or more of these are absent, the presiding judge appoints with the approbation of the others, as many religious as are needed to make up, with himself, the tribunal;

c) the superior general names, with the consent of the tribunal, the religious who is to act as prosecutor (c. 655).

The Process

A. Preliminary Conditions

360. The process of dismissal may not be begun before the incorrigibility of the religious who is gravely culpable shall be established in a certain manner. These are the elements which go to make up this double condition:

1. The guilt of the professed consists in the threefold violation of an obligation arising from the general law of the Church, or from the special law of religious.

The essential element is "a perverse will resolved on evil." This supposes, in law, three different offenses, or a repetition of the same offense at intervals sufficiently close, or obstinacy in persisting in one offense during a determined time, in spite of warnings and penalties (c. 657).

It is understood that the offense should be such as we have described above in n. **353.**

2. Incorrigibility shows itself by the fact that warnings, penalties, and remedies prove ineffectual.

A. Warnings:

a) Each warning supposes that the offense is known in such a way that it can be proved according to legal forms. This proof may be furnished in three ways: the fault may be notorious; it may be admitted by the culpable person in the presence of his superior; it may be established by the evidence or proofs furnished by previous investigation conducted by the abbot of the monastery, the provincial, or any other immediate higher superior, or by his delegate (c. 658).

b) The warning is made by the immediate higher superior or at his order.

c) The warning is clearly to set forth: the declaration of the offense which is reprimanded, the indication of the amendment which is required, and the formal threat of dismissal.

The superior will add to these his counsel and penances calculated to procure the amendment of the culprit and the reparation of the scandal. He will efficaciously remove from the culprit the occasions of a new offense, even though he has to send him to another house.

d) The second warning supposes a new offense, known like the first, or the obstinate continuance in the same fault during three full days after the warning has been given (c. 660).

B. Proof of Incorrigibility:

The incorrigibility is presumed if the religious commits a new offense after the second warning, or if he continues obstinate in his gravely culpable fault.

We have said above, that if after one offense the religious had given proofs of his good will during at least three years, a new offense cannot be considered as a proof of incorrigibility.

B. The Instruction

361. 1. After the last warning six days must elapse before further steps be taken (c. 662).

2. When every effort to bring the culpable person to a better state of mind has proved useless, the immediate higher superior shall carefully collect all the acts and documents of the case and send them to the superior general (c. 663).

3. The promoter of justice, that is, the religious who acts as prosecutor, shall receive the documents from the general. He will decide whether it is necessary to complete the records by a

new inquiry. Then he will draw up the act of accusation (c. 664, § 1).

The accused has the right to choose his own advocate; if he does not do so, the superior general will appoint someone for this office (see c. 1655). A religious who acts as notary either habitually or by special appointment will discharge the office of secretary or recorder (see cc. 503, 1585).

4. The investigation of the judges, the defense of the religious, and the accusation of the promoter of justice must all be directed to three things: Were there three offenses or was there one offense equivalent to three? Was the warning given twice and with a threat of dismissal, and was it given after the interval of time fixed by law? Were proofs of amendment lacking?

The details of this procedure are described in Book IV of the Code; a commentary on them is to be found in Vermeersch-Creusen, *Epitome,* III[6].

C. The Sentence

362. 1. The tribunal pronounces sentence by a majority vote, that is to say, at least three out of five (c. 1577, § 1), and after having made a serious examination of the case (c. 665).

2. If the sentence is that of dismissal, this sentence and all the acts of the trial are forwarded to the Sacred Congregation of Religious. Its execution is suspended until it is confirmed by the Holy See (c. 666).

3. If any delay in dismissing the culprit after the offenses have been committed would cause a grave scandal or expose the institute to very serious harm, he may be immediately dismissed by the immediate higher superior, or in case of urgency, by the local superior. But the trial must be held at once according to the procedure indicated in the foregoing (c. 668).

Article 5. The Condition of Dismissed Religious Who Have Taken Perpetual Vows

363. The religious who has been dismissed remains bound by his religious vows, unless the constitutions or apostolic indults determine otherwise (c. 669, § 1).

If he had received the tonsure or minor orders, he is by the fact of dismissal reduced to the lay state (c. 669, § 2).

The religious who is dismissed may obtain from the Holy See a special dispensation from his vows.

364. A dismissed religious who has not been dispensed from his vows is bound to return to his institute. If he has given proofs of sincere amendment during three years, his institute is bound to take him back. If there are serious objections against his return, the matter shall be referred to the Holy See (c. 672, § 1).

The latter part of this canon does not apply to those religious who have been dismissed by the law itself because of one of the crimes listed in canon 646 (see n. **345**, above). Though such a religious is bound to reform himself and to take the steps necessary for readmission into his institute, the latter is not obliged to take him back (Commission of Interpretation, Response, July 30, 1934. — *A.A.S.*, XXVI [1934], 494. — *R.C.R.* [1934], 180).

If the religious who remains bound by his vows returns to the institute, he immediately resumes his rank among the professed; but those of his rights which depend on his seniority are counted only from the day of his return.

Commentators apply all the regulations of c. 672, § 1, to all the professed bound by perpetual vows whom dismissal has not freed from the obligations of their vows. In fact, this canon requires that the former religious should put himself once more into normal conditions for the observance of his vows.

The authorized (but not official) translation of this part of the Code, for lay religious, omits c. 672. Was it the intention to apply this only to religious clerics? As a matter of fact, special motives exist for requiring that these latter should return to their institute and that the institute should admit them once more. In practice this case will rarely occur.

In the case of lay religious the situation is best handled by obtaining a dispensation from their vows, at least from the vows of poverty and obedience.

365. The following regulations concern only those clerics who have received, at least, the subdiaconate.

A religious cleric in major orders who has committed one of the offenses mentioned in c. 646 (n. **345**), or an offense which is punished with loss of reputation or with deposition or degradation, is forever forbidden to wear the clerical garb (c. 670).

366. In less grave cases:

1. **The religious remains, *ipso facto*, suspended until he obtains absolution from the Holy See.**

Suspension is a censure by which a cleric is forbidden to exercise ecclesiastical offices or, at least, certain kinds of functions.

2. **The Sacred Congregation may allow him to stay in a specified diocese and to wear the dress of the secular clergy; in this case, the local Ordinary has charge of his amendment.**
3. **Insubordination brings with it the perpetual privation of the clerical garb, and of the right to receive any pecuniary support whatever from his religious superiors.**
4. **After serious and lasting reform, the bishop will endorse the petition of the culprit to the Holy See for the absolution and, after this has been obtained, he may employ him in the sacred ministry. If the religious is dispensed from his vows, he shall seek a bishop who is willing to receive him; if he cannot find one, the Holy See shall be notified (cc. 671, 672, § 2).**

367. In the religious societies without vows (n. **18**), the passage of the members to another society or to an institute properly so called, and the leaving or dismissal of members, are governed, due proportions being kept, by the regulations of canons 632–635 (see n. **327** sq.) ; c. 645 (n. **342**) ; 646–672 (n. **345** sq.). The regulations of the constitutions of each society must also be observed (c. 681).

APPENDIX I

A Summary of the Law Regarding Diocesan Congregations of Religious Women

(NOTE: For the convenience of Bishops and Superiors this summary presents all the matters peculiar to *Diocesan congregations of religious women.* References are given throughout to the canons of the Code and to the fuller explanation in the text of this book.)

PART I. Constitution of a Diocesan Congregation

A. *General Ideas.*

1. A Diocesan Congregation is a religious institute which has not received the *decree of praise* from the Holy See (c. 488, 3; n. **9**).

2. Such a congregation is therefore, *"a religious institute"* (*religio*), *"a religious congregation,"* and its members are *"religious"* in the proper sense of these terms (c. 488, 7; n. **14**); hence, wherever these terms occur in the Code of Canon Law they are to be applied to diocesan congregations as well (cf. c. 488, 1, 7; nn. **6, 14, 23**).

The houses of religious women in a diocesan congregation are not *monasteries* (n. **11**, 2), and their members are called *Sisters,* not Nuns (c. 488, 7; n. **14**).

3. All articles of constitutions which are *contrary* to the Code are abrogated since Pentecost (May 19, 1918), and may no longer be observed (c. 489; n. **19**).

B. *Erection and Suppression of an Institute or House.*

4. No Ordinary may *found a Congregation* without first submitting his project to the Holy See (c. 492, § 1). The authorization granted by the Holy See to proceed with the project in nowise constitutes an approval of the new institute; but once such authorization has been obtained, the Ordinary may not change the fundamentals which he has submitted to the Holy See (purpose, name, habit, etc., of the new congregation).

Should the religious of the new congregation wish to be *Tertiaries* of a regular Order, aggregation must be asked of the Superior General of that Order (c. 492, § 1; n. **25**).

5. The Ordinary should establish the congregation by a formal decree (n. **26**, 3). Once this decree is issued, the congregation *may not be suppressed* without the consent of the Holy See, even though it consist of only one house (c. 493; n. **29**).

6. Should the congregation spread to other dioceses, its juridical character is in nowise changed; it remains a diocesan congregation, entirely subject to the local Ordinaries, according to the prescriptions of law (c. 492, § 2; n. **28**). The ordinary of the motherhouse may not, either personally or through his delegate (vicar or visitor), exercise any authority over the houses situated outside his diocese (n. **28**, 2). From the moment the congregation becomes established in more than one diocese, no change may be made in any articles of the constitutions without the consent of all the Ordinaries in whose territories the congregation has houses (n. **28**, 3).

7. The Code has no provision for the establishment of *provinces* in a diocesan congregation. If circumstances should warrant such a division (or the establishment of districts in mission territory), the decision would rest with the superior general and her council. Since, however, such changes would imply a certain modification of the constitutions, they would have to receive the approval of all the Ordinaries in whose territories the congregation has established houses.

8. The foundation of a *new house* always requires the written permission of the Ordinary of the place in which it is to be established. If there is question of the *first* foundation in a *new* diocese, the consent of the Ordinary of the motherhouse is likewise required; but he should not refuse such permission without grave cause (cc. 495, § 1; 497, § 1; n. **33**). In mission territories, the permission of the S. Congregation of the Propagation of the Faith is likewise required (c. 497, § 1; n. **34**).

9. The same permissions mentioned above are required to make such *changes* in a foundation or house, which do not pertain exclusively to the internal government of the congregation (e.g., to change a school into a hospital; c. 497, § 4; n. **37**).

10. Once a community has been established in a diocese, the written permission of the Ordinary of that place suffices to open another house (school, hospital, etc.) dependent on the same community, but separated from it (c. 497, § 3; n. **36**).

11. The *suppression* of a house depends upon the local Ordinary. He should not proceed to such a measure without first consulting the superior general. The latter may always appeal to the Holy See, in which case no further step may be taken until the decision of the Holy See is received (c. 498; n. **40**, 1).

C. *Government of a Congregation.*

12. The local Ordinary exercises over all diocesan congregations an authority which is limited only by the common law and the approved constitutions of the congregation. He has the power to command the religious in virtue of the vow of obedience (cf. c. 500, § 1; n. **53**, 3).

The local Ordinary cannot dispense from the canons of the Code pertaining to religious, except under the conditions laid down in canon 81 (n. **53**, 4).

13. The *superior general is elected* according to the constitutions

(n. **68**). She may, with the consent of her council, determine the place where the general chapter is to be held, unless the constitutions determine otherwise (c. 162; n. **70,** 1).

The local Ordinary *presides at the election* of the superior general which he may ratify or annul, according to his conscience; except in the cases specified in the law, he himself may not appoint the superior general (cf. c. 506, § 4; n. **77,** 3).

D. *Administration of Temporalities.*

14. All *investments of funds* must be submitted to the approval of the local Ordinary (c. 533, § 1, 1; n. **161**); the same holds for all changes of investments (c. 533, § 2; n. **161**).

On the occasion of the canonical visitation, or oftener, the Ordinary will examine the administration of the *funds of the dowries* (c. 535; n. **197,** 2). The Ordinary likewise enjoys the right to control every act of *financial administration* (c. 535, § 3, 1; n. **167,** 3).

15. The *alienation* of precious objects, or of other goods valued at more than 30,000 francs ($6,000 or £1,200) requires the authorization of the Holy See under pain of invalidity; the same holds for the contracting of debts over the amount stated above. For all other alienations or the contracting of debts, the permission of the local Ordinary must be obtained (c. 534; n. **162**).

The Ordinary may grant habitually a general permission to make contracts within a determined sum.

PART II. Religious Life

A. *Admission to Religion.*

16. An indult of the Holy See is required to *dispense* from the *impediments to entrance* laid down by the common law in canon 542 (n. **179**); e.g., to allow a religious to re-enter a congregation, which she has left after taking vows therein.

17. The local Ordinary must *examine* each religious *three* times before final vows; a month before receiving the habit, a month before first profession, a month before final profession (c. 552; n. **190**).

18. Strictly speaking the Ordinary could demand the dismissal of a postulant or of a novice, but not the *admission* of either, since that depends upon the superiors and their council, according to the constitutions (c. 543; n. **181**).

19. The Ordinary may dispense, in whole or in part, from the *dowry* prescribed by the constitutions (c. 547, § 4; n. **185,** 3).

20. The Ordinary approves the place destined for the *novitiate house* (c. 554; n. **193**).

21. When, according to the constitutions, the Ordinary must receive the vows of the religious, it is necessary to obtain permission from him or from his *habitual delegate,* in order that some other priest may receive them (c. 572, § 1, 6; n. **227**).

APPENDIX I

B. *Obligations and Privileges.*

a) Obligations:

22. The Ordinary must see to it that in every religious house a certain part is reserved for the exclusive use of the religious (c. 604, § 1; n. **291, 1**). He will also watch over the observance of the *cloister* (c. 604, § 3; n. **291, 3**).

23. The permission of the Holy See is required for a sojourn of more than six months outside a house of the congregation, except for studies (c. 606, § 2; n. **292, 3**).

24. Superiors must transmit to the Ordinary, without reading them, all *letters* addressed to him by their subjects, and they must deliver to their subjects unread all letters addressed to them by the Ordinary (c. 611; n. **295**).

b) Privileges:

25. No diocesan congregation enjoys the privilege of *exemption* (c. 618, § 1; n. **313**).

26. Sisters may not beg from door to door without written permission from the Ordinary of the place in which their house is situated, as well as from the Ordinary of the place in which they wish to collect alms (c. 622, § 2; n. **320**).

The Ordinary shall not grant such permission without real necessity, especially in places in which mendicant regulars reside. He shall restrict the permission to beg to his own diocese, if that be sufficient (c. 622, § 3; n. **320**).

PART III. Separation From the Congregation

27. No religious may *transfer to another institute* without the permission of the Holy See (c. 632; n. **327**).

28. Ordinaries have no power directly to *dispense from the vows of religion* (n. **339**); but they can grant an indult of exclaustration and of secularization (c. 638; n. **332**).

If they grant an indult of *exclaustration,* they may, for particular reasons, allow the religious to retain the habit of the congregation during the sojourn outside the religious house (n. **334, 2**).

In virtue of the common law, an indult of *secularization* carries with it the dispensation of all the vows of religion (c. 640; n. **335**).

29. The absolution from the excommunication incurred by a religious who is an *apostate from religion* is reserved to the local Ordinary (c. 2385; n. **342, 2**).

30. When a Sister commits one of the crimes enumerated in canon 646 (n. **345**), she is dismissed by her very act; it suffices that the major superior with her council make a testification of the facts in the case.

31. The *dismissal* of a Sister with *temporary vows* depends upon the Ordinary of the place in which the Sister resides (c. 647, § 1; n. **347**). The Ordinary must be certain that grave reasons justify such an extreme

measure, and he must allow the Sister full liberty to have recourse to the Holy See within ten days after the decree of dismissal has been issued (c. 647; n. **350**). Dismissal from temporary vows carries with it dispensation from the vows by law (c. 648; n. **351**).

32. It is the local Ordinary's duty to weigh the motives for which superiors judge it necessary or opportune to *dismiss a Sister with perpetual vows;* it is the Ordinary who gives the final decision (c. 652, § 1; n. **357**).

33. When a *local* superior judges it necessary to *dismiss at once* a Sister whose presence threatens the community with grave harm, the consent of the local Ordinary is required; he shall immediately inform the S. Congregation of Religious of the fact (c. 653; n. **358**, 2).

34. Dismissal of a Sister with perpetual vows does not carry with it a dispensation from the vows of religion, unless this provision is expressly stated in the constitutions. If such be not the case, an indult must be obtained from the Holy See (c. 669, § 1; n. **363**).

APPENDIX II

Sacred Congregation of Religious

Instruction to the Superiors General of Religious Institutes and of Societies of Clerics Concerning the Clerical and Religious Training of Subjects Destined for the Priesthood, and of the Investigation Which Must Precede the Reception of Orders

1. Words can scarcely express how much all Religious Institutes and Societies are doing for the salvation of nations, whether for those already regenerated in the faith of Christ, or for those who still sit in the darkness of idolatry and in the shadow of death. Indeed, their members are they who, following the evangelical counsels and despising the world, have consecrated themselves entirely to God's service, and by virtue of their profession seek nothing else than the promotion of Christ's kingdom on earth, as our Holy Father, Pius XI, testified not so long ago: "From this great variety of religious orders, as from different trees planted in the Lord's domain, there grows and matures unto the salvation of nations a great variety of fruits; and surely nothing is more beautiful and more pleasing to behold than the entire group of these religious organizations. Although finally all strive after one and the same object, yet they each have their own field of industry and labor, distinct in some way from all the others. For Divine Providence so ordains that, as often as new needs must be met, new religious institutes likewise arise and flourish."[1]

2. In a radio address broadcast to the entire world on February 12, 1931, the same Holy Father explained in eloquent terms the sublimity and excellence of the religious state. Addressing all religious as "sons and daughters especially dear to Us," he continued: "Striving after the better gifts and observing not only the precepts but also the wishes and counsels of the

---

[1] Ep. apost., *Unigenitus Dei Filius,* 19 Martii, 1924 (*A.A.S.,* XVI, 133–134).

Divine King and Spouse by the faithful observance of your holy vows and by the religious discipline of your entire lives, you render the Church of God fragrant with the odor of virginity, you enlighten her by your contemplations, you support her by your prayers, you enrich her by your knowledge and teaching, you daily perfect and strengthen her by your ministry of the word and by the works of your apostolate. Therefore, as you are partakers of a truly heavenly and angelical vocation, the more precious the treasure you carry, the more careful watch you must keep, so that you not only make your vocation and election certain, but also that in you, as in most faithful and devoted servants, the Heart of the King and Spouse may find some consolation and reparation for the infinite offenses and negligences with which men requite His ineffable love."[2]

3. Since, then, the religious state is so excellent, it is not surprising if the enemy of man's salvation leaves no stone unturned to cast religious down from their sublime estate by perverse arguments, by the enticement of worldly pleasures and by the incitement of the passions. As a matter of fact, serious cases of defection are not lacking, both from the religious state and from the sacred army into which religious men had been enrolled by the reception of holy orders. Nor is anyone blind to the great harm such defections bring to religious and to religion itself, nor to the scandal which they give to the faithful of Christ's Church. For this reason, making use of the favorable opportunity offered by an instruction sent recently by the Sacred Congregation of the Sacraments to Local Ordinaries concerning the investigation of candidates to be made before promoting them to Orders,[3] this Sacred Congregation of Religious, with a view to discharging its duty, after consulting the Holy Father and by his special command, has decreed that the following points be again called to the attention of the Superiors General of Religious Institutes and of Societies of Clerics, and that their observance be ordered where it may be necessary.

I. The Training of Subjects Who Are to Be Promoted to Orders

4. From the very nature of things and from daily experience

---

[2] *A.A.S.,* XXIII, 67.

[3] *Instructio,* 27 Dec., 1930 (*A.A.S.,* XXIII, 120).

we learn that the well-being of Religious Institutes depends particularly upon the formation of their subjects, just as the beauty of trees depends especially upon their cultivation. Pius IX of blessed memory explained this idea as follows: "Since the condition becoming to every religious family depends largely upon a careful admission of novices and upon their efficient training, We earnestly exhort you to examine accurately beforehand the character, ability, and habits of those who intend to join your religious family, and that you carefully investigate for what purpose, in what spirit, and in what manner they are led to seek entrance into the religious life."[4]

5. After selecting youthful candidates for the religious life with prudence and at the proper time, superiors will take effective means not only of giving them such instruction in piety as is adapted to their age, but also of teaching them the subjects ordinarily taught in secondary schools.[5] "Thus the candidates will not enter the novitiate before they have completed the course in the humanities, as it is called, unless occasionally for a sufficiently grave reason superiors decide otherwise."[6] In such a case the course of humanities must be completed before the study of philosophy is begun.

6. From the first reception of candidates into the religious life, superiors must be very careful not to admit young men in crowds, nor hastily,[7] but to receive those only who show evidence of a divine vocation and give promise of persevering as useful ministers of the Church.[8] Before admitting these candidates to the novitiate, superiors shall secure additional information about them.[9] If the testimonial letters are inadequate, they shall be supplemented by careful inquiries made by trustworthy persons. Nor should superiors neglect to obtain information about the character of the candidates' families: whether their parents are free from those vices which are easily transmitted to their offspring. Indeed, in choosing candidates for the priesthood, the ordinary indications of a religious vocation are by no

---

[4] Litt. apost., *Ubi primum*, 17 Iunii, 1847.

[5] Cod. iur. can., c. 589.

[6] Pius XI, Ep. ap. cit., p. 140.

[7] Pius X, Ep., *Cum primum*, 4 Aug., 1913, ad Mag. Gen. O.P. (*A.A.S.*, V, 388. Cf. Pius XI, *ibid.*).

[8] Can. 1383, § 1.

[9] Can. 544–545.

means sufficient, but in addition special signs, proper to the clerical state, are required. For this reason the sacred canons prescribe that there be one novitiate for clerics, another for lay brothers, so that the novitiate made for one class is not valid for the other.[10]

7. After finishing the novitiate, subjects should be placed in those houses where the full observance of the rules flourishes, especially in what pertains to perfect common life[11] and to the observance of poverty; houses, moreover, where everything is so arranged that they can fruitfully pursue the prescribed course of philosophy and theology. During this time superiors will take care that the young religious do not relax in the zealous pursuit of virtue, keeping them from reading those books and newspapers which can in any way be a hindrance to solid studies. As regards relaxation of mind, superiors should not allow them to indulge in those bodily exercises which are by no means becoming to clerics, according to the most serious warning of the Council of Trent: "Wherefore clerics, called to have the Lord for their portion, ought by all means so to regulate their whole life and habits that in their dress, deportment, gait, conversation, and in all other things they may ever show themselves to be grave, well regulated, and religiously mature."[12] Superiors will likewise see to it that the spiritual directors, to whose special care these young religious are assigned during the entire course of studies, fashion their souls to the religious and clerical life by timely admonitions, by instructions and exhortations;[13] in this way and in no other, they will at length excel in sound doctrine joined with a most holy life.

8. As regards the study of the sacred sciences, religious must always bear in mind the important advice of our Holy Father, Pius XI: "Since it is necessary that the ministers of the Church esteem highly and acquire a thorough knowledge of sacred subjects, we urge, as the chief point of our admonition, that the members of Religious Institutes who have already been, or will hereafter be, raised to the priesthood assiduously cultivate the sacred sciences, without which they cannot fulfill perfectly and comprehensively the duties of their vocation. Since the one, or at least the chief, purpose of those who have consecrated them-

---

[10] Can. 588.   [12] Sess. XXII, c. I., *De reform.*
[11] Can. 587, § 2.   [13] Can. 588, § 1.

selves to God is to pray to Him and to contemplate or meditate on divine things, how can they discharge this all-important duty unless they have a thorough grasp of the doctrines of faith? We wish those who live a secluded life in the contemplation of heavenly things especially to attend to this. They err if they think that, in spite of early neglect of their theological studies or of afterwards putting them aside, they can easily occupy themselves with high and holy thoughts and be elevated to an intimate union with God, deprived as they are of that rich knowledge of God and the mysteries of faith which is drawn from the sacred studies. Will not the manifold exercises of the sacred ministry on the part of those who teach, preach, reconcile souls to God in the tribunal of penance, give missions, or deal with the people in the ordinary course of daily life, be the more powerful and effective, the more they are enlightened and strengthened by scholarly knowledge?"[14]

9. Since this intellectual training of the young religious cannot be fully carried on where dissipation is allowed, or where they are permitted at random to travel to different houses or to dwell with their parents, superiors are under grave obligation in conscience not to allow them to undertake any journey without a just and serious reason. These young religious should constantly live in houses of studies, carefully applying themselves to exercises of piety and of learning until the course of studies is completed. This holds also for those who may have been raised to the priesthood with the consent of this Sacred Congregation before they have completed the fourth year of sacred theology.

10. Since greater hazards usually occur at the beginning of the priestly life, superiors should make provision that after ordination and the completion of the course of studies, the young priests are not left to their own resources. For some time they should rather bestow special care upon them. And to facilitate this being done, let the young priests be assigned to houses where perfect observance of the rules flourishes, and where they will undergo a special sort of training adapted to their individual ability. Meanwhile, they should continue their studies and give evidence of constant progress in them, according to the norm

---

[14] Ep. ap. cit., 136, 137.

of the sacred canon which prescribes that "every year for at least five years after the completion of the course of studies, religious priests shall be examined by learned and eminent fathers in the various branches of the sacred sciences previously assigned."[15] Let superiors keep the Sacred Congregation informed on this point in their quinquennial report, at the same time stating the reasons for exemptions if they have seen fit to grant any.

11. Superiors will more easily fulfill all these duties if they exercise special care in the choice of persons to whom the training of the young religious is intrusted, so that only prudent men, outstanding for charity and religious observance, be appointed for this work. Let the spiritual directors and professors of sacred sciences see to it that they give their students from their earliest years an example of religious discipline and of priestly virtues, realizing that words to some extent, but example most of all, contribute to the formation of youthful characters.[16]

II. The Investigation Which Must Precede the Reception of Orders

12. By reason of canonical legislation, major superiors either grant dimissorial letters to the ordaining bishops for the ordination of their religious subjects,[17] or at least present their subjects together with testimonial letters for ordination.[18] In these testimonial letters the religious superior not only declares that the students belong to his religious family, but he also gives evidence that they have finished their studies and have fulfilled the other requirements of the law.[19] Hence, it is evident that the same rigorous obligation binding upon bishops in regard to the formation, examination, and selection of their own secular subjects who desire to receive holy orders, rests also upon religious superiors who have the responsibility of allowing their subjects to receive holy orders. Although Bishops, in accordance with the law,[20] need not accept the testimony of superiors, and may themselves examine religious candidates for orders, still they are not bound to do so; they may, before God and the Church, give assent to the favorable testimony of superiors

---

[15] Can. 590.

[16] Can. 559, §1; 588, §§ 1, 2.

[17] Can. 965 et 966, § 1.

[18] Can. 994, § 5.

[19] Can. 995, § 1.

[20] Can. 997, § 2.

and leave to them the entire responsibility of answering for the training and worthiness of their candidates.[21]

13. In view of these wise regulations, superiors should regard as addressed to themselves the solemn words of the Apostle, so often inculcated, by which bishops are warned of their strict obligation to test candidates repeatedly before admitting them to orders: "Impose not hands hastily upon any man, neither be partaker of other men's sins;[22] and let these [the deacons] first be proved, and so let them minister, having no crime."[23] St. John Chrysostom commented on these words as follows: "What does 'hastily' mean? Not after one trial, nor after a second, nor after a third; but only after repeated observation and careful examination."[24] The Code of Canon Law thus sums up the opinions of the Fathers and of the Councils on this subject: "A bishop should not confer holy orders upon anyone unless he is certain of the candidate's canonical fitness from positive evidence; otherwise he not only sins gravely, but also exposes himself to the danger of participating in the sins of others."[25]

14. Therefore the following points are to be observed by the Superiors General of all Religious Institutes and of Societies of Clerics. Before the profession of temporary vows, which must always precede promotion to tonsure and minor orders, novices must submit to the superior a written request in which they give evidence in explicit terms of their vocation to the religious and to the clerical state. At the same time they must declare their firm resolve to devote themselves forever to the clerical order in the religious state.[26] This request and declaration are to be kept in the archives. Superiors should allow no subject to advance to orders as long as they are not certain, after careful investigation, about his moral conduct, his piety, modesty, chastity, his inclination for the clerical state, his progress in ecclesiastical studies, and his observance of religious discipline.[27] To obtain this knowledge with greater certainty they should ask for the testimony of the spiritual director and of others who, because of their close association with the religious students, may be better acquainted with their manner of life and character. Such testi-

---

[21] Can. 970, 995, § 2.
[22] I Tim. v. 22.
[23] *Ibid.*, iii. 10.
[24] *Homil. XVI*, n. 1.

[25] Can. 973, § 3.
[26] Can. 973, § 1.
[27] Can 973, § 1.

mony is not to be regarded lightly, but is to be weighed carefully, with due regard for the prudence, sincerity, and mature judgment of those who gave it. An official document containing the testimony and the results of the investigation is to be drawn up and kept in the archives. Finally, the superior, either personally or through another learned and prudent father who enjoys the confidence of the young religious, should question them in order that he may have full assurance that they aspire to orders in the religious state freely and knowingly.

15. Religious superiors should remember that they may by no means allow their subjects to be promoted to major orders before they have made either perpetual or solemn profession.[28] In religious institutes in which perpetual vows are not taken, superiors are strictly forbidden to promote subjects to sacred orders until a three-year period of temporary vows has been completed, and in societies without vows, not before three years have elapsed from the first admission into the society after the novitiate, and if there be a perpetual or final admission, only after this has been made.

16. Before subjects are admitted to the subdiaconate, superiors must make a new inquiry on the points mentioned above.[29] For this purpose let them review the documents of the preceding inquiry which have been kept in the archives, and compare the new testimony regarding the moral conduct and spiritual qualities with the old, that they may be thoroughly informed on the showing of the young religious both in religious discipline and in progress in clerical studies since their first profession. When this has been done, and they have been found suitable and worthy, and no canonical reasons exist to prevent them from the reception of orders, superiors may grant the dimissorial letters or testimonials for their ordination, observing all the prescriptions laid down in Canon Law and in their own Constitutions.

17. In all Religious Institutes and Societies, before presenting their subjects for the diaconate, in addition to the inquiry prescribed above (n. 16), superiors must demand of each, in view of the sacred ordination to follow in due time, a statement signed by the candidate's own hand and sworn to in the presence of the superior, substantially as follows:

---

[28] Can. 964, §§ 3, 4.
[29] N. 14.

"I, the undersigned, N.N., member of the Order or Congregation N.N., having presented a request to superiors to receive the order of subdiaconate, and having carefully considered the matter in the sight of God, testify under oath: (1) That I have been urged by no force or violence, or by any fear to receive this order, but that I desire it of my own will, and with full and perfect freedom wish to receive the same, together with the burdens attached to it. (2) I acknowledge that I fully understand all the obligations arising from this sacred order, which I freely accept, and which I intend, with God's help, to keep carefully during the course of my entire life. (3) I testify that I clearly understand all that is enjoined by the vow of chastity and by the law of celibacy, and I am firmly determined, with the help of God, to observe them in their entirety to the end of my life. (4) Finally, I sincerely promise, according to the norm of the sacred canons, constant and entire obedience in all things which will be enjoined upon me by my superiors according to Church discipline, prepared as I am to give others an example of virtue both in word and deed, so that by assuming so great an obligation, I may deserve to receive the reward promised by God. Thus I testify and swear upon God's Holy Gospel which I touch with my hand.

Given this .... day, ... month, ... year.

N.N. (personal signature)."

18. It is to be noted that in orders having solemn vows, the foregoing statement must be made, signed, and sworn to before the profession of solemn vows.

19. In the dimissorial letters given for the ordination of their subjects in conformity with the requirements of the Code of Canon Law, as well as in the testimonial letters, superiors are bound in conscience to testify about all these matters to the ordaining Bishop, who may, nevertheless, according to his own good pleasure, also privately question the subjects who are to be ordained.

20. Though it is not necessary to require such extensive information and new testimonials for the reception of the diaconate and the priesthood, still superiors should be watchful to see whether, in the interval between the reception of one or

the other sacred order, anything new has happened which might disclose a doubtful vocation to the priesthood, or show that there is no vocation whatever. In this case, after a most careful investigation has been made and counsel taken with prudent men, superiors should forbid absolutely the reception of the new order, and refer the case to this Sacred Congregation which will decide in each single instance, what seems best in the Lord.

21. Our Holy Father, Pius XI, by Divine Providence Pope, having heard the contents of this Instruction in an audience granted to the undersigned Cardinal Prefect of the Sacred Congregation on December the first, 1931, has deigned to ratify and confirm them. His Holiness also ordered that the present Instruction should be made known to all the Superiors General of Religious Institutes and of Societies of Clerics, and be exactly observed by them. He further ordered that it should be read in its entirety to religious clerics at the beginning of each year, and that superiors should inform this Sacred Congregation about the faithful observance of these regulations in their quinquennial report.

Anything to the contrary notwithstanding.

Given at Rome, from the Secretariate of the Sacred Congregation of Religious, the day, month, and year as above.

FR. A. H. M. CARDINAL LÉPICIER, O.S.M., *Prefect*

L. ✠ S.   V. LA PUMA, *Secretary.*

APPENDIX III

[Institutes directly subject to the Sacred Congregation for the Propagation of the Faith must fill out instead the questionnaire published by that Sacred Congregation on June 29, 1937 (see p. 65, footnote 24 at the end). — Ed.]

The List of Questions

WHICH ARE TO BE ANSWERED BY RELIGIOUS INSTITUTES AND SOCIETIES IN THE REPORT TO BE SENT TO THE HOLY SEE EVERY FIVE YEARS ACCORDING TO THE DECREE *CUM TRANSACTIS*

(*A.A.S.*, XL [1948], 378–381)

For Congregations and Societies of Diocesan Right

POINTS TO BE NOTED

A) *Regarding the drawing up and writing of the quinquennial Report.*

a) Before the reply to each question, there should be a clear indication of the number and letter by which that question is designated in this list.

b) Whenever a pontifical document or one from the diocesan Curia is brought in, its date and Protocol number should be faithfully and uniformly given.

c) The reply is to be developed as each case may require, and is not to be dismissed with a simple affirmation or denial.

d) Clerical religious Institutes and Societies are to make out the Report in Latin; others may do it either in Latin or in one of the following modern languages: English, French, German, Spanish or Italian.

e) The Report should be typed and in clear characters. If for some just cause the Report is written by hand, the handwriting must be clear.

f) The paper to be used must not be translucent nor too thick, but durable.

g) The questions marked with an asterisk are to be answered only by religious Institutes of men; those marked with a cross, only by religious Institutes of women.

B) *Regarding the method of making this quinquennial Report to the local Ordinaries and its transmission afterward to the Sacred Congregation.*

1. According to the Code of Canon Law Congregations and Societies of diocesan right are bound by the common law for religious no less than Institutes of pontifical right, aside from exceptions expressly stated. Questions which are proposed for Institutes of pontifical right, therefore, with a few exceptions could be used also for Congregations and Societies of diocesan right.

2. Besides, there are provisions in the Code which apply only to Congregations of diocesan right; in like manner certain points are mentioned in this questionnaire as peculiar to Congregations and Societies of diocesan right.

3. The common law does not envision dividing a Congregation or Society of diocesan right into Provinces; moreover, such division could scarcely be allowed, and the mind of the Holy See is that, if there are special reasons for division into Provinces, steps should rather be taken to attain the status of a Congregation of pontifical right. Therefore, no questions about Provinces and provincial Superiors are found in the questionnaire, aside from the general inquiry in n. 9.

4. The Superiors General of Congregations and Societies of diocesan right are to send the quinquennial Report, not directly to the Holy See, but to the local Ordinary of the motherhouse (see the decree *Cum transactis*, IV, 3°).

5. The Report is to be signed by the Superior General with his Council (*ibid.*).

6. The local Ordinary of the motherhouse should see to it:

a) That a copy of the Report be sent also to the other Ordinaries in whose Dioceses exist houses of the Congregation or Society; after carefully examining the Report, these Ordinaries should send in writing to the Ordinary of the motherhouse or directly to the Sacred Congregation for Religious whatever comments they consider opportune and also their own opinion about the Congregation.

b) That a copy of the Report, signed by himself and with his own opinion about the Congregation or Society as well as the opinions of the other Ordinaries, if and as far as they were given to him, added to it, be sent to the Sacred Congregation for Religious within the year itself in which the Report is due. In giving his own opinion the Ordinary of the motherhouse should not omit matters which concern the power of all the Ordinaries regarding the government of an interdiocesan Congregation, so that namely he informs the Sacred Congregation fully and clearly of the manner in which such power is exercised, whether cumulatively by all the Ordinaries or by the Ordinary of the motherhouse even by delegation from the others.

c) That possible suggestions sent to this same Ordinary of the motherhouse by the Sacred Congregation regarding the Report be communicated as quickly as possible, if and as far as they concern them, to the Superior General and to the other Ordinaries, so that the suggestions can be faithfully put into practice (*ibid.*).

7. Along with the first quinquennial Report after the publication of this questionnaire, the local Ordinary of the motherhouse should also send to the Sacred Congregation:

a) Two well-bound, printed copies of the Constitutions.

b) A historico-juridical report of the Congregation or Society, in which are to be indicated: the founder, the year of foundation, the year of canonical establishment of the Congregation and of approbation of the Constitutions, and also which Ordinary made the establishment and gave the approbation. Likewise the principal historical events of the Congregation or Society are to be given briefly in an accurate summary. This report is to be written up clearly and bound well.

c) If the Congregation or Society according to law (c. 596) has a distinctive habit for the professed and novices, a photograph or some other faithful representation of the habit is to be sent in duplicate; two pictures of the same size as those just mentioned should also be sent, showing the habit in colors.

8. If the Superior General, by himself or with his Council, or also the individual Councillors, thinks that anything about his own Congregation or Society should be indicated directly to the Holy See, let him do this in a private letter. (See the decree *Cum transactis*, VIII.)

The Following Things Must Appear on the First Page of the Report

The name of the religious Institute or Society:
(the official title in Latin, and the common name)
Its symbols; that is, the initials or letters commonly used to designate it:
The seat of the generalate house:
(complete information: post office address, telephone number, telegraphic address)
The years which are covered by the report.

THE LIST OF QUESTIONS

CONCERNING THE PRECEDING REPORT

1. *a*) When was the last Report sent to the local Ordinary.

b) Whether the observations which may have been made by the Sacred Congregation upon the Report and which were received through the local Ordinary were faithfully carried out in practice.

2. Whether the matters of information contained in the last Report can be conscientiously considered reliable and complete, or whether anything concerning them would seem to require modification.

CHAPTER I

The Institute and Its Government

Article I. Concerning the Institute in General and Its Parts

§ 1. CONCERNING THE INSTITUTE IN GENERAL

3. What is the juridical nature of the Congregation or Society (c. 488, 4°) : clerical or lay, in only one diocese or in more (c. 495, § 1, 2°).

4. If the required conditions are existing, has a petition been sent, or is under consideration to be sent, to the Holy See for obtaining the status of a Congregation of pontifical right. In this regard what difficulties, if any, are foreseen or have already actually arisen.

Concerning the special end

5. What is the special end of the Institute.

6. Was the special end authoritatively changed during the five-year period, and by what authority.

7. In practice is this end faithfully retained, or is it in part abandoned; or are any works undertaken which do not pertain to it.

8. What are the principal works through which the special end is pursued.

§ 2. CONCERNING THE INTERNAL ORGANIZATION AND DIVISION OF THE INSTITUTE

Concerning Provinces

9. Has the Congregation perhaps been divided into Provinces; from what date; how many Provinces have been established and by what authority.

Concerning the houses

10. Which houses were modified either externally or internally during the five-year period (c. 497, §§ 1 and 4).

11. In the erection and suppression of houses, were the rules of law (cc. 497, 498) and the standards of prudence observed, among which must be numbered a written contract, clear, com-

plete, and drawn up in accordance with canon law and the Constitutions, with due regard to the civil law.

12. Whether the consent of the local Ordinary of the motherhouse was also sought for the first foundation or erection of a house in a new diocese.

13. Are all the houses provided with those things which are necessary for the common life, especially:

a) A separate cell for each person; or, if the dormitories are common, at least a separate bed for each person, properly set apart from the others.

b) A separate place fully suitable for the care and assistance of the sick.

14. Are the rooms for receiving guests sufficiently separate from the part of the house which is reserved to the community.

Article II. Concerning the Juridical Government of the Institute

Concerning the general government

15. a) Is the General Council at present up to its full membership.

b) Do all the Councillors General reside in the Curia.

c) If any are elsewhere, why is this, and where do they live (the place, Diocese).

16. What other general offices are there (Bursar, Secretary, Prefect of studies, etc.).

Concerning the General Chapter; its convocation and session

17. Within the period covered by the Report, has there been a session of the General Chapter.

18. Were the norms of the common law and of the particular law (the Constitutions, etc.) which concern the General Chapter faithfully observed; i.e.:

a) The time of the session, the designation of the place, the letter of convocation.

b) The elections of delegates to the Chapter, and of Tellers and a Secretary of the Chapter.

c) The elections of the Superior General, Consultors or Assistants and General Officials who are elected by the Chapter (e.g., Secretary, Bursar General).

19. In all these matters, even in seeking information about the

candidates, did all avoid procuring votes either directly or indirectly, for themselves or for others (c. 507, § 2).

20. Who presided at the Chapter:

a) In the election of the Superior General.

b) In the other elections and in the business meetings.

21. Were the following reports presented to the General Chapter in due time, so that they could be conveniently examined by each of the Capitulars and by a Commission elected in the Chapter if that is prescribed:

a) The report on the state of persons, discipline and works since the last General Chapter, drawn up by the Superior or Vicar General and approved by the General Council.

b) The report on the true and complete financial condition of the Institute, drawn up by the Bursar General and approved by the Superior General with his Council.

22. Was the decision on these reports read in Chapter and seriously weighed and discussed before the general elections.

Concerning promulgation and execution

23. When and how did the Superior General promulgate those decrees and decisions of the General Chapter which were to be communicated.

24. In the promulgation, were any of the provisions omitted or not faithfully reported; if so, why and by what authority.

25. What measures were taken by the Superior General with his Council and by the other Superiors and Councils to see that the prescriptions of the General Chapter be faithfully reduced to practice.

Concerning appointments to offices

26. Were the norms of the common law and of the Constitutions observed:

a) Regarding the requisites and qualifications of Superiors and Officials (cc. 504, 516).

b) Regarding the manner of appointment (cc. 506, 507).

c) Regarding the duration of offices (c. 505).

27. How many and what dispensations from the provisions of the common or particular law were granted by the Holy See or by major Superiors:

a) For appointments to positions or offices.

b) For the renewal of the same.

c) Were the conditions attached to these dispensations faithfully observed.

28. Did the Superiors of clerical Institutes duly fulfill, according to c. 1406, § 1, 9° and § 2, their obligation of making the profession of faith before the Chapter or Superior who appointed them, or before their delegate.

Concerning the duties of Superiors: Residence — Making known and observing the Decrees of the Holy See — The canonical visitation — Freedom of epistolary correspondence.

29. Did the Superior General, the Councillors General and the other Superiors, observe the law of residence according to the common law (cc. 508, 517) and the Constitutions.

30. How do Superiors see to it that the decrees of the Holy See which concern religious be known and observed by their own subjects (c. 509, § 1).

31. Is perfect freedom left to subjects, without any inspection of letters by Superiors, in their epistolary correspondence with those persons who, according to the common (c. 611) and particular law, have this right.

32. Were there any cases of secret and clandestine epistolary correspondence, either between religious or between these and secular persons, and what was done to correct these abuses.

33. *a*) Did the Superior General personally make the prescribed visitations at the proper time.

b) Did he make these visitations through delegates.

34. Were the visitations which were made according to the common law (cc. 513, 2413) and the particular law complete, so as to include:

a) All persons, as regards discipline, religious perfection, priestly life, religious and clerical training and the ministries and works of the Institute.

b) Things and property; their conservation and administration.

c) Places, especially sacred places, divine worship, pious foundations, etc.

35. Were any duly appointed extraordinary delegated Visitors sent at any time; what were the reasons and what were the results.

36. What was done to see that the decrees of the visitation be carried out in practice.

Concerning Council meetings

37. Are Council meetings held at the prescribed times and in the required cases:

a) By the Superior General.

b) By local Superiors.

38. *a*) Was the opinion of all the Councillors always asked.

b) Do absent Councillors give their opinion, and if so how.

c) Were any of the Councillors neglected; if so, what was the reason.

39. How often each year during the five-year period did the Superior General convoke his Council.

40. Are the matters in which, according to the common and particular law, Councillors have a deliberative or consultative vote, faithfully submitted to a meeting of the Council.

41. Is the proper liberty of all and each of the Councillors duly recognized in the Council meetings; and in the decisions, appointments and votes of whatever kind, were the norms of the common law (cc. 101, 105, 1°, 2°, 3°) and of the particular law always observed.

42. Are the minutes of the meetings duly drawn up and signed.

43. Are the Archives of the Institute and of individual houses properly equipped and carefully arranged.

44. Are all the offices of the general and local officials actually filled, or are any of them vacant.

Concerning corrections and the abuse of power

45. Do Superiors exercise their function of vigilance and correction either privately or publicly; by what means and in what manner do they do this.

46. Have any abuses arisen or taken root, without being corrected and without efficacious remedies being applied to prevent and remove them.

47. How often and for what reasons were canonical admonitions and penalties imposed.

48. In applying these remedies were the sacred canons and the Constitutions of the Institute observed.

49. Were there any cases of abuse of power by Superiors, or at least were any appeals or complaints on this matter received from subjects.

50. Were Superiors guilty of any grave infringements of canon law or of the Constitutions, either as regards the common obligations of religious or the obligations which concern their particular office.

51. In these cases, were the penalties either common or special, which are provided for by the common law (e.g., cc. 2389, 2411, 2413, etc.) or by the Constitutions, applied.

Concerning the exercise of authority

52. What means are taken in order that the Superior General and his Curia be constantly, fully, and sincerely informed as to the state of the Institute.

53. Are periodical reports to be made to the Superior General, and how often.

54. Is a faithful observance of the prescriptions in this matter insisted upon.

55. Are there in the Institute any firmly established means by way of internal bonds which unite the members among themselves, as for example: reports on work done, published bulletins of houses and of the whole Institute.

56. Are any other means used, as necessity may require, to promote union among the houses of the Institute; if so, what are they.

57. Is there also for each house a chronicle in which the principal events are carefully recorded.

Concerning relations with the Ordinaries of places

58. a) Are the provisions of the Code regarding the subjection of religious to the local Ordinaries faithfully observed.

b) Are good and friendly relations with the Ordinaries fostered, and do the religious, without prejudice to religious discipline, exercise priestly ministrations in favor of the diocese.

c) Have there been litigations, disputes, or difficulties with the local Ordinaries; if so, what were they.

59. What remedies have been or can be applied to restore harmony.

Article III. Concerning the Spiritual Government of the Institute

Concerning confessors

60.*[1] Are several confessors appointed for each house according to c. 518, § 1.

61.* Without prejudice to the Constitutions which may prescribe or recommend that confessions be made at stated times to fixed confessors, are the religious left free to go, in accordance with canon 519, without prejudice however to religious discipline, to a confessor approved by the local Ordinary, even though he be not among the fixed confessors.

62.†[2] Are the norms of the common law and of the Constitutions faithfully observed regarding the appointment and reappointment of the ordinary, extraordinary, special, and supplementary confessors (cc. 520, §§ 1–2, 521, 524, 526, 527).

63.† Did Superioresses faithfully observe the prescriptions made for them regarding supplementary confessors (c. 521, § 3), occasional confessors (c. 522), and confessors in case of grave illness (c. 523).

64. Do Superiors take means and exercise a prudent vigilance to see that all the religious, according to law (c. 595, § 1, 3°) and the Constitutions (c. 519), approach the sacrament of penance at least once a week.

65. Have Superiors been guilty of any abuses, and if so what were they, by which the liberty of conscience of their subjects has been restricted (cc. 518, § 3, 519, 520, § 2, 521, § 3, 522, 2414).

66. Did the Superior General and the Visitors correct these abuses.

67. Has there been, under pretext of liberty of conscience, any detriment to religious discipline on the part of subjects; did any other abuses arise; were the abuses corrected by Superiors and Visitors without prejudice to liberty.

Concerning spiritual direction

68.* How do Superiors provide for the solid training of spiritual Directors.

---

[1] Questions marked with an asterisk * concern only religious Institutes of men.

[2] Questions marked with a cross † concern only religious Institutes of women.

69.* Whether care is taken to see that in Novitiates (c. 566, § 2) and also in all clerical and religious residence-halls, the prescribed confessors and spiritual Directors be provided and chosen, and, in the case of clerical Institutes, that they reside there (c. 566, § 2, 2°).

70. Whether Superiors, in accordance with canon law (c. 530, §§ 1, 2) leave their subjects free in regard to making a strict manifestation of conscience to themselves.

71. In what ways do Superiors strive to promote spiritual direction.

Concerning the reception of the Most Blessed Eucharist

72. Whether Superiors, in accordance with c. 595, §§ 2–3, promote among their subjects frequent and even daily reception of the Most Sacred Body of Christ, always without prejudice to full liberty of conscience according to law (c. 595, § 4) and the Instructions of the Holy See.

73. Do Superiors diligently see to it that confessors be easily available before Communion, and do they allow their religious subjects a suitable time for preparation and thanksgiving.

Concerning spiritual and catechetical instructions

74. Do Superiors see to it that, according to the Constitutions and the common law, there be spiritual and catechetical instructions for the entire house (c. 509, § 2, 2°), for the novices (c. 565, § 2), for the scholastics (c. 588, § 1), for the conversi, for the domestics and servants (c. 509, § 2, 2°).

Article IV. Concerning the Financial Government of the Institute

§ 1. CONCERNING THE ACQUISITION AND LOSS OF PROPERTY

Concerning the acquisition and registration of property

75. a) What, if any, immovable property or precious movable property was acquired by the Institute and the houses; what was the value of these acquisitions.

b) Was the aforesaid property acquired by gift or other gratuitous title, or by purchase, and in this latter case was it with the funds of the Institute or house, or with borrowed money.

76. Has the Institute and each house an inventory of its movable property, especially of that which is classed as precious (by reason of workmanship, history, or material) (c. 1522, 2°) and of its immovable property.

77. When must these inventories be revised, and are they in fact revised.

78. In cases where works which are not the property of the house, such as clerical or religious residence-halls, hospitals, churches, etc., are entrusted to the religious houses, are these properties kept clearly distinct from those which belong to the religious house itself.

79. By what method or in whose name before the civil law is the religious property registered; and can this registration be regarded as safe in civil law.

80. What forms of registration have been adopted as the more secure in various localities.

81. If societies have been established for this purpose, was everything done in accordance with the civil law and is everything actually being kept in good order.

82. As regards the aforesaid societies:

a) Were all persons, to whom the administration or management of property is entrusted, chosen with due care, after making all the previous investigations which were necessary or useful.

b) Were the members of the Institute itself given the preference over outsiders for offices of administration, whenever this could prudently be done without loss.

c) What safeguards were used against dangers arising from abuses of administration.

d) Is a constant vigilance conscientiously exercised according to law, through the checking of accounts and through ordinary and other extraordinary and timely inspections of safety deposits and other properties.

Concerning expenses

83. Were extraordinary expenses paid from ordinary or extraordinary income proper, or on the contrary with borrowed funds.

Concerning contributions

84. Did the individual houses contribute to the common needs of the Institute.

85. By what authority (Chapter, Council, Superior General), on what principles, and in what proportion are the contributions to the general funds determined.

86. Were these contributions paid willingly or more or less under pressure.

87. Are the houses allowed to retain whatever is prudently foreseen to be necessary or very appropriate for their own life and growth, in view of the good of souls and the welfare of the Institute.

Concerning the alienation and diminution of property

88. What capital property, whether immovable or stable (i.e., consisting of capital funds) or precious, was alienated, and by what authority.

89. In the alienation of property, were the provisions of law (cc. 534, 1531), especially regarding the previous appraisal by experts, and the norms of the Constitutions, observed.

90. Did the Institute and the houses consume any stable or founded property or capital funds; for what reasons and by what authority.

91. Are Superiors and the general and local Bursars making serious efforts to recover this property.

92. What properties of the Institute and the houses have suffered loss; and what were the reasons.

Concerning debts and obligations

93. a) What debts were contracted, and by whom.

b) What debts are actually outstanding.

94. In contracting debts and obligations, were the following faithfully observed:

a) The provisions of c. 534.

b) The precautions mentioned in c. 536, § 5.

c) The norms of the Constitutions regarding permissions, the consent of the Council, etc.

95. Was the interest on debts and obligations faithfully paid, and is diligent care taken toward the gradual payment of a debt or the amortization of the capital (c. 536, § 5).

§ 2. CONCERNING THE CONSERVATION AND ADMINISTRATION OF PROPERTY

96. Is the administration of property conducted, not arbitrarily, but according to the common law and the Constitutions, under the direction and vigilance of Superiors and their Councils (cc. 516, § 2, 532, § 1).

97. Are there designated Bursars (c. 516, §§ 2, 3, 4) according to the common law and the Constitutions:

a) For the entire Institute.

b) For the individual houses and works.

98. Does the Superior in any case act also as Bursar (c. 516, § 3).

99. Do the Councils have their part in the administration and exercise vigilance in regard to it, even when the Superiors are acting also as Bursars (c. 516, § 1); how do they do this.

Concerning the rendering of accounts

100. How many times a year and to what Superiors and Councils must the Bursars and other Administrators render an account of their administration.

101. Was a clear and complete rendering of account demanded of all and each of the Bursars and Administrators during the five-year period.

102. Were there presented together with the accounts the documents showing the expenditures and receipts.

103. Was there regularly an inspection and checking of the safe.

104. Are the necessary directions given to the Bursars and Administrators; if so, how is this done, and what sanctions are imposed in case of necessity.

105. Have Superiors, Bursars, or Administrators, or any other religious, any money or property which they can freely use without giving a regular account of it, even though it is used for the good of the Institute or house.

Concerning the investment of money and changes of investment

106. Did Superiors, Councils, and Administrators lawfully, safely, and profitably invest (c. 533) the money which was to be invested according to law and the will of benefactors, ob-

serving the rules of law and the Constitutions.

107. Did Superiors, Bursars, and Administrators make temporary investments of surplus funds which were not required for ordinary expenses, so that they should not lie idle but might draw a reasonable interest.

Concerning the conservation of property

108. Are money, securities, contracts, precious articles carefully conserved, observing exactly the common norms and the provisions of the Constitutions.

109. On what terms, if ever:

a) Were money or precious articles received from outsiders on deposit.

b) Or conversely were such deposits made with outsiders by Superiors, Bursars, Administrators or private religious.

110. Do Superiors, Bursars, Administrators conscientiously strive that all the property of the Institute and house be religiously conserved and providently administered (c. 532, § 1).

Concerning foundations, pious causes, etc.

111. What legacies and pious foundations were accepted.

112. In accepting pious foundations and legacies, were the rules of law (c. 1544 sq.) and of the Constitutions observed.

113. Was the money of foundations and pious causes, according to law and with the consent of the local Ordinary when that was required, invested (cc. 533, §§ 1, 2, 1547) and separately and faithfully administered (cc. 535, § 3, 2°, 1546, 1549).

114. Were the obligations attached to foundations faithfully and conscientiously fulfilled (cc. 1514, 1549, § 2).

115. Did Visitors demand documentary proof of their fulfilment and an account of the administration of the property.

Concerning business and trade, etc.

116. Did any religious, Superiors or subjects, personally or through others, engage in illicit business, that is, business not permitted to religious, in violation of cc. 142, 592.

117. In cases where for just reasons the permission of the Holy See was obtained for engaging in business (give the date and Protocol number), was every semblance, not alone of fraud but also of avarice, diligently avoided.

118. What precautions were taken that religious who are occupied in business dealings may not suffer spiritual harm.

119. Whether Superiors and Councils were attentively watchful that, according to c. 1539, § 2, in the administrative exchange of securities payable to bearer, all commerce or appearance of trading be avoided.

Concerning actions or affairs which involve
financial responsibility

120. How did Superiors exercise vigilance over the actions and dealings of their subjects from which there might arise according to law a financial responsibility on the part of the Institute or house (c. 536, § 2) or of the individual religious (c. 536, § 3).

121. Did Superiors clearly and effectively, according as the circumstances required, take prompt action to clear the Institute or house of all responsibility for actions and dealings done by individual religious without observing the norms of the common or particular law.

122. Do Superiors see to it that, in all matters which concern finances, or in those generally which could give occasion to litigation in the canonical or civil courts, everything be done exactly according to law, on the basis of previous written contracts, with the guarantee of perfectly valid signed agreements, etc. (c. 1529).

123. Have any law suits or losses resulted from failure to observe the prescribed formalities of civil law according to n. 122.

124. Have Superiors and Bursars diligently seen to it that extern workmen and all persons who work for the Institute or house receive at the agreed time a just and fair compensation according to law (c. 1524), and that the provisions of law regarding the contract of hire and other matters be faithfully observed.

125. What provision is made for the spiritual welfare of those who work in the house, especially if they also reside there.

CHAPTER II

Concerning the Religious and the Religious Life and Discipline

Concerning the diversity of classes

126. What are the different classes, if any, among the members of the Institute; does harmony exist among the different classes and is fraternal charity observed among them.

127. Besides the persons who belong to the Institute or Society as members, by religious profession or lawful incorporation, are there others who are dedicated or given to it, or the like, without being members.

128. Is provision made in fairness and charity for the spiritual life of these persons and also for their material security.

129. Are there any legitimately approved Statutes for them.

Article I. Concerning the Admission, Formation, and Profession or Incorporation of Members

Concerning the postulantship in the wide sense
(Apostolic Schools)

130. Are there in the Institute any aspirantships or postulant-ships in the wide sense: apostolic schools, etc.

131. For how long a time does the instruction and education in these places last.

132. In these apostolic schools and similar houses and in the residence-halls, are the students of tender age habitually kept separate from the older ones.

Concerning the postulantship in the canonical or strict sense

133. Are the postulantships properly conducted according to law in the houses of noviceship (c. 540, § 1), or in houses where perfect religious observance exists (c. 540).

134. Was the time assigned by the common law (c. 539) or by the Constitutions for the postulantship abbreviated or pro-longed; if so, for how long a time and by what authority.

Concerning the admission of aspirants

135. What means are used to arouse and attract vocations.

136. Are there also advertisements inserted in public bulletins and papers. If so, in what bulletins or papers did they appear.

137. Taking into account the different circumstances of various localities, what causes are regarded as having an influence on the increase or diminution of vocations.

138. What are the obstacles which aspirants most frequently have to overcome in order to follow their vocation.

Concerning documents, testimonials, and informations

139. Were the documents required by the common law (c. 544) and by the Constitutions demanded before admission in the case of each aspirant.

140. At least before entrance into the novitiate, were the following testimonial letters demanded and obtained:

a)* The common testimonial letters which are to be given by the local Ordinaries and are prescribed for all (c. 544, § 2).

b) The special testimonial letters which are to be given under oath by the Rector or major Superior for those who have been in a Seminary or an equivalent ecclesiastical residence-hall, or in a postulantship or novitiate of a religious Institute (c. 544, § 3).

c) Likewise the testimonial letters which are required in the case of clerics and professed religious (c. 544, §§ 4, 5).

141. Besides the documents and testimonials which are specially prescribed by law or by the Constitutions, was further information, which it seemed necessary or useful to know in order to judge with certainty of the vocation and fitness of the aspirants, diligently sought (c. 544, § 6).

Concerning impediments and admission

142. From what impediments or defects, if any, which are imposed by the common or particular law, was a dispensation granted; how often and by what authority was this done.

143. Were the admissions of aspirants always done by the competent Superiors, observing the rules of law (c. 543).

Concerning the noviceship — The house

144. Was every novitiate house established according to the

Constitutions, or transferred after permission was obtained in advance from both Ordinaries, namely of the place [new diocese being entered] and of the motherhouse.

145. Does perfect religious observance flourish in the novitiate houses.

146. Did Superiors assign to them or permit to remain in them religious who are not exemplary in their zeal for religious observance (c. 554, § 3).

Concerning the beginning of the noviceship

147. Did all fulfill the prescribed days of spiritual exercises before entering the noviceship (c. 541).

148. Were the rite and the rules prescribed for admission to the noviceship faithfully observed (c. 553).

Concerning board and expenses for the postulantship and noviceship

149. Is the right of the Institute to demand payment for the expenses of the religious habit and board during the postulantship and noviceship, given in the Constitutions or customarily recognized by express agreement.

150. Who determines the amount to be paid.

151. Was there any instance of the grave abuse of delaying the profession because the expenses of the postulantship or noviceship had not been paid.

Concerning the discipline of the noviceship

152. Did all the novices and each of them from the beginning of the noviceship have a complete copy of the Constitutions.

153. Are the novices, according to law and the Constitutions, kept separate from the professed, and is any undue communication between them tolerated (c. 564, §§ 1, 2).

154. Did all and each of the novices before their profession perform the canonical year of noviceship complete and continuous, without counting the first day, in a house of noviceship lawfully erected, under the care and direction of a Master (cc. 555, § 1, 556, 557).

155. Was the noviceship extended or shortened beyond the limits fixed by law (c. 571, § 2) and the Constitutions; if so, for how long a time and by what authority was this done.

Concerning the government of the noviceship

156. Was there always in every novitiate a Master of novices duly appointed or elected (c. 560).

157. Have the novice Master and his Socius all the qualifications and all the requisites prescribed by the common law (c. 559, §§ 1, 2) and the Constitutions, or did dispensations have to be asked for and obtained.

158. Are the Master and Socius free from all offices and ministries, in or out of the house, which might interfere with their care and government of the novices (c. 559, § 3).

159. Do the Masters of novices, according to law (c. 561) and the Constitutions, under the vigilance and direction of Superiors and Visitors, have full possession of their proper authority and use it for the government and training of the novices.

160. Do all the Masters fulfill their office properly (c. 562) and remain constantly in the novitiate house.

161.* Do the Master of novices and his Socius abstain from hearing sacramental confessions unless the penitents of their own accord ask them to do so according to c. 891.

Concerning the spiritual training of the novices

162. Were the novices, under the guidance of the Master, during the first or canonical year of the noviceship, engaged exclusively according to law (c. 565, §§ 1, 2) in exercises of piety and other exercises proper to novices; or on the contrary were they assigned to hearing confessions, preaching, and external works or ministries; or did they apply themselves expressly to the study of literature, science, or humanities (c. 565, § 3) beyond the limited measure in which this has been approved by the Sacred Congregation.

163. During the second year of noviceship or during the time which is over and above the canonical year, were the norms which were given in the Instruction of the Sacred Congregation of Religious (Nov. 3, 1921) observed:

a) Regarding the manner of exercising the external ministries of the Institute (nos. I, II).

b) Regarding the conditions under which alone the novices may be sent outside the novitiate house (III).

c) Regarding the two months' preparation for the profession (IV).

*Concerning the documents to be drawn up
before the profession*

164. Did all the novices, according to c. 569, § 1, before the first profession of simple vows, freely cede the administration and either cede or dispose of the use and usufruct of their property.

165. In case the aforesaid cession and disposition was not duly made before the profession, or in case new property was acquired thereafter, was it made or completed after the profession (c. 569, § 2).

166. Were any changes of the aforesaid cession and disposition after the profession made always in accordance with c. 580, § 3.

167. *a*) Did the novices of the Congregation, before their first profession of temporary vows, freely make a will in due form, valid according to the civil law, regarding their present or future property (c. 569, § 3).

b) Did they afterward render this will valid according to the civil law (c. 569, § 3).

168. Were any changes which may have been made in this will after profession made according to c. 583, 2°.

169. Are the aforesaid documents, cf. n. 167 *a*), *b*), faithfully kept in the Archives.

Concerning admission to profession and the act of profession

170. Do the Superior General and the General Council carefully and constantly keep a severe watchfulness as regards admissions; have they issued any special norms in this matter.

171. Has the first profession, after eight full days of spiritual exercises, always been made validly and licitly according to law and the Constitutions (cc. 572, 573, 575) in the novitiate house itself (c. 574, § 1).

172. Was the prescribed rite observed in making the profession, and was the document attesting it duly drawn up (c. 576).

Concerning the canonical examination

173.† Did the Superioress General, or another acting in her name, two months before admission to the noviceship, to the first temporary profession and to perpetual profession, give timely notice to the local Ordinary (c. 552, § 1), so that he or his Delegate might gratuitously conduct the canonical examination regarding the free and conscious will of the postulant or candidate (c. 552, § 2).

174.† Was the prescribed examination always made.

Concerning the dowry — The obligation and delivery of the dowry

175.† According to the Constitutions, is the dowry obligatory in the Congregation, or is it on the contrary left entirely or partly optional (c. 547, § 3).

176.† Was the delivery of the dowry made according to law (c. 547, § 2) and the Constitutions.

Concerning the investment, conservation, administration, and return of the dowry

177.† Were the dowries, immediately after the first profession, invested by the Superioress General, with the deliberative vote of her Council and the consent of the Ordinary of the place where the capital of the dowries is kept (c. 549).

178.† Were the dowries spent or encumbered in any way before the death of the religious concerned; if so, by what authority was this done. Were the dowries so spent or encumbered, even though it were done after obtaining lawful permission, afterward restored or cleared of the encumbrance; what is their condition at the present time (c. 549).

179.† Where and how are the dowries administered. Are the rules of law faithfully observed regarding their administration (cc. 535, § 2, 550).

180.† Is all property which is brought in as dowry, even though it be in excess of the sum required for a dowry in the Constitutions, or even though there be in the Congregation no obligation to bring in a dowry, accepted, invested, administered, etc., with the observance of the norms which govern dowries.

181.† In case of the departure of a professed religious, for whatever cause it occurred, and in case of transfer, were the dowry and likewise the personal belongings which the novice brought with her at her entrance, in the condition in which they were when she left, restored to the religious departing or transferring, without the income which had already accrued (cc. 551, 570, § 2).

THE LIST OF QUESTIONS

182.† Is this done also with property freely contributed for increasing the dowry even beyond the sum required by the Constitutions.

183.† In case of the departure of a professed religious who had been received without a dowry or with an insufficient one, if she was unable to provide for herself out of her own property, did the Institute out of charity, according to law (c. 643, § 2), give her whatever was needed that she might safely and decently return home and be decently supported for a time.

Concerning the profession and the renewal of profession

184. What, if any, dispensations were necessary for the pronouncement of the vows.

185. How many and what sanations were afterward necessary.

186. Were the temporary vows which are prescribed by law and by the Constitutions (c. 574, § 1), when the time for which they were taken had elapsed (c. 577, § 1), always renewed according to law (c. 577, § 2), so that no one ever remained without vows.

187. How often was the temporary profession extended beyond the six-year period allowed by law, and by what authority was this done (c. 574, § 2).

188. Conversely, how often was the time of the temporary vows, which is prescribed by law (c. 574, § 1) or by the Constitutions, shortened.

Article II. Concerning the Religious Life and Discipline

Concerning the vows — Poverty and the common life

189. Is a perfect common life according to c. 594, the Rule and the Constitutions, observed everywhere, but especially in novitiates and houses of studies (cc. 554, § 3, 587, § 2).

190. What has been done and is being done positively to safeguard and promote the virtue and spirit of poverty.

191. Do Superiors and officials, out of religious charity and in order to ward off for the religious occasions of sinning against poverty, provide, within the limits of poverty, what is necessary and appropriate in the way of food, clothes, and other things.

192. Do they allow the religious to ask for or receive these things from externs.

193. Are there complaints about these things; are these complaints seriously considered, and are abuses on the part of Superiors and subjects alike corrected with equal severity.

194. Are the sick and the aged religious attended to with special care and helped in both body and soul with paternal charity, so that, within the limits of religious poverty, they lack nothing which seems necessary for the recovery of their health and for their spiritual consolation.

195. Are all the above cared for in the house; and, if in a case of peculiar necessity they have to be cared for out of the house, are they frequently visited.

196. Is there a suitable house for sick and aged members.

Concerning chastity and its safeguards

197. Did all Superiors make it a matter of conscientious duty to be attentively vigilant regarding those things, both in and out of the house, which may more easily contain dangers against religious chastity, i.e., regarding:

a) Familiarities, either in the parlors or elsewhere, with persons of the other sex, young people, and children.

b) Epistolary correspondence.

c) The reading of books and papers which are unbecoming to religious.

d) Abuses of the telephone and uncensored listening to radio programs, etc.

198. Were any rules and regulations issued by Superiors and Chapters regarding the public and private use of the radio. (Cite the documents.)

199. If, which God forbid, religious committed any offense against the Sixth Commandment with younger students entrusted to their care, did Superiors immediately remove the culprits from the occasion and punish them, and thereafter carefully watch over their life. In the more serious cases did Superiors have recourse to the local Ordinary.

200. Are the provisions of the law and the Constitutions regarding cloister (cc. 598–599, 604) faithfully observed. Did any abuses creep in.

201. Did Superiors, in violation of the norms of the Constitutions, allow visits without a companion, frequent and too protracted visits and conversations with externs, especially those

which are evidently useless or can become dangerous, which disturb silence, even that which is more strictly to be observed, which interfere with exercises of piety or other community exercises, and which are in general opposed to the religious spirit.

202. *a*) Are the parlors so arranged that what goes on in them can be seen from the outside.

b) Is the frequency of parlor visits regulated according to the Constitutions and religious prudence.

203. Do Superiors themselves diligently observe and cause others to observe all the prescriptions of the Constitutions concerning religious going out of the house and receiving visits from and making visits to externs.

204.† Except in cases of prudent necessity, do Superiors assign a companion to religious when they go out of the house, especially for the purpose of making a visit (c. 607).

205.† Do the rooms which are reserved for Chaplains and Confessors or Preachers have a separate entrance and no internal communication with the habitations of the religious.

Concerning obedience

206. Is religious discipline observed, and is the government of Superiors made easy by the docility of the subjects.

207. Was it often necessary to impose formal precepts in virtue of the vow of obedience.

208. Were such precepts given in due form according to the Constitutions, and never without grave reason.

Concerning the Rule and the Constitutions

209. Are the Rule and the Constitutions faithfully observed (c. 593).

210. Are the Rule and the Constitutions read publicly at the prescribed times (c. 509, § 2, 1°).

211. Is the private reading of the Rule and the Constitutions favored.

212. *a*) Are there any customs in effect which are contrary to the Rule and the Constitutions.

b) Do Superiors allow new ones to spring up, or on the contrary do they strive to prevent this and to eradicate the old ones.

213. In what places, if at all, since the last Report, did abuses spring up or become rooted.

Concerning the religious habit

214. Has the Institute a habit of its own (c. 596).

215. Was the habit modified or abandoned without due permission; if so, by what authority.

216. Does the habit everywhere correspond to the prescriptions of the Rule and the Constitutions, and is it uniform for all, with due allowance for the differences which may be lawfully recognized for each different class of religious.

217. Is the religious habit faithfully worn according to law (c. 596).

218. Do the excloistered religious continue to wear the habit.

Concerning exercises of piety

219. Do Superiors see to it that in all the houses the exercises of piety which are prescribed for every day, every week, every month, every year, or for other fixed times, be faithfully and worthily performed according to the Constitutions.

220. Do Superiors see to it that all the religious:

a) Make a retreat every year.

b) Be present at Mass every day if not legitimately prevented.

c) Give themselves to mental prayer every day.

d) Attend earnestly to the other offices of piety which are prescribed by the Rules and Constitutions (c. 595, § 1, 1° and 2°).

221. Do Superiors see to it that all the members are able to be present at community exercises.

222. Do they give to those religious who, either because of their particular duties or for other just cause, or even by way of abuse, are not present at community exercises, time in which they can conveniently and worthily make up the obligatory exercises.

223. Do they see to it that all these exercises are actually made up.

Concerning religious charity

224. Are the relations between the different members of the Institute, between Superiors and subjects, etc., characterized by a true spirit of charity.

225. Are defects against charity severely corrected.

Is there any special cause which is an obstacle to fraternal charity.

Concerning the reading of books

226. Are Superiors watchful that no books be used, whether in manuscript or published form, if they are not entirely safe.

227. Are the spiritual books which the religious use privately, according to law approved by the Church, conformed to the religious state and suitable for the spiritual welfare of the individual religious to whom they are permitted.

Article III. Concerning Those Who Have Departed or Been Dismissed, and Others Who Leave the Institute

Concerning those who have gone out from the Institute

228. *a*) How many in the Institute at the expiration of their vows did not renew them, either because they chose not to do so or because they were not allowed to do so.

b) How many of the professed of temporary vows were dispensed during their vows, and how many of the professed of perpetual vows were dispensed.

229. Were those who were dispensed from their vows at their own request or with their consent forced, or without serious and grave reasons and precautions permitted, to leave the religious house before the rescript was duly executed.

230. How many transfers, if any, were there to another Institute.

Concerning apostates and fugitives

231. *a*) How many apostates and fugitives, if any, were there during the five-year period.

b) Did the Society or Institute observe the provisions of law concerning apostates and fugitives, by seeking them (c. 645, § 2), and if this proved fruitless, by proceeding against them according to law, so that their juridical condition should be clearly defined. Were the provisions of law regarding those who came back observed (cc. 2385, 2386), and is watchful provision made for their spiritual good.

Concerning those dismissed by Superiors and those not admitted to profession

232. *a*) Since the last Report, how many of the professed of temporary vows and how many of the professed of perpetual vows have been dismissed.

b) In the dismissal of religious, whether of temporary or of perpetual vows, were the norms of the common law (cc. 647, § 2, 4°; 649–672) as well as those of the Constitutions observed.

c) Was the same done in regard to not admitting the professed of temporary vows to the renewal of their vows or to perpetual profession (c. 637).

233. Were the dismissed of temporary vows, while the recourse duly made within ten days was pending (c. 647, § 2; S. C. of Religious, July 20, 1923, *A.A.S.*, XV, 1923, p. 457), and the dismissed of perpetual vows, before the decree of dismissal had been confirmed by the local Ordinary (cc. 650, § 2, 1°, 652, § 1), forced to leave the Institute.

234. Are the dismissed who are not in sacred orders released from their vows by the dismissal (c. 669, § 1); and if the vows remain, does the Institute show solicitude regarding their condition (c. 672, § 1).

Concerning those dismissed by the law itself and those sent back to the world

235. What were the cases, and the causes which led to them, for both the professed of temporary and those of perpetual vows, where they were either sent back to the world on account of grave scandal or very grave harm (cc. 653, 668) or dismissed by the law itself (c. 646).

236. Were steps immediately taken according to the Code (cc. 646, § 2, 653, 668) to determine the condition of those dismissed by the law itself and of those sent back to the world.

237. Is there any such person whose condition still remains undetermined.

238.* What cases, if any, have occurred of the reduction to the lay state of religious who had received sacred orders; how many were voluntary and how many penal.

Concerning those who were excloistered

239. How many cases of exclaustration were there, if any; are

the causes carefully and conscientiously pondered in the presence of God before the petition is recommended and the rescript executed.

240. Does the Institute take care:

a) That if it seems necessary to ask for an extension of the indults, they be renewed in due time.

b) That the persons who are excloistered lead a worthy religious life and return as soon as possible to some house of the Institute.

241.* Likewise does the Institute take care regarding those who have been secularized on trial, and regarding their return to religion if at the expiration of the three-year period the indult is not renewed or they are not accepted by the Ordinary.

Concerning absences from the house

242. Do Superiors see to it that subjects remain out of the house only for a just and grave reason and for the shortest possible time, according to the Constitutions (c. 606, § 2).

243. For absences which exceed six months, except for studies or ministries according to law and the Constitutions, was the permission of the Holy See always obtained (c. 606, § 2).

244. Is it allowed by reason or under color of a vacation, that time be spent with one's parents or outside a house of the Institute.

Concerning the deceased

245. Were the prescribed suffrages faithfully and promptly performed for all the deceased.

Article IV. Concerning the Various Classes and Conditions of Religious

§ 1. CONCERNING CLERICS
(This is dealt with in the Report on formation and studies.)

§ 2. CONCERNING *CONVERSI* OR COADJUTORS

Concerning their education and training

246. Do Superiors, in accordance with c. 509, § 2, 2°, give to those religious who belong to the class of *conversi* instruction in Christian doctrine; and do Superiors, both before and after their profession but especially during the earlier years, carefully attend

to their spiritual, intellectual, civil, and technical education according to the functions which they have to fulfill.

247. Are the religious allowed to engage in works which do not seem to be suitable to the religious state.

248. Do Superiors with paternal charity diligently provide also for the bodily health of the *conversi* or coadjutors.

§ 3. CONCERNING THOSE WHO ARE APPLIED TO MILITARY SERVICE

Concerning the profession of those who are to be called for the first time to active military service

249.* Did Superiors regulate according to the decrees of the Holy See the temporary professions of those who are to be called for the first time to active military service or its equivalent.

250.* Were perpetual professions permitted before the first active military service or its equivalent, to which the young men are liable to be called.

Concerning the religious during their military service

251.* *a*) Did Superiors take care of their members in the service, watch over their life, communicate frequently with them, requiring a periodical account of their conduct, their actions and exercises of piety, etc.

b) What special means were used to secure their perseverance.

252.* In cases of dismissal for just and reasonable causes, or of voluntary separation from the Institute, did the Superior General follow the prescribed procedure and faithfully conserve all the documents in the Archives.

Concerning the renewal of temporary profession after military service and the making of perpetual profession

253.* For admission to the renewal of temporary profession, was everything done which is prescribed by the common law and in the decrees regarding this matter.

254.* Was the prescribed time of the temporary profession completed after military service, and also the time of the temporary vows which is prescribed by law and by the Constitutions before the making of the perpetual profession.

CHAPTER III

Concerning the Works and Ministries of the Institute

Article I. Concerning Ministries in General

Concerning the special end and the works of the Institute in general

255. Were the ministries proper to the Institute abandoned or neglected.

256. Were any works engaged in which are not contained in the special end of the Institute; if so, with what permission was this done.

Concerning abuses in the exercise of ministries

257. Were any abuses in the exercise of ministries introduced during this time; if so, what were they.

258. Is all appearance of avarice carefully avoided on the occasion of ministries.

259. Was begging from door to door, according to law (c. 622, §§ 2 and 3) and the Constitutions, done with the required permissions.

260. Moreover, in begging, were the rules of law (c. 623), the instructions of the Holy See (c. 624) and the norms of the Constitutions observed.

261. By reason of or under pretext of ministries, are an excessive or too worldly communication with seculars and frequent and prolonged absences from the religious house permitted.

262. What precautions are taken in this communication in order to avoid harm to the religious and scandal to seculars.

Concerning difficulties with the secular clergy or with other Institutes, etc., because of the ministries

263. On the occasion of the ministries did any friction occur with ecclesiastical Superiors, with pastors and the secular clergy, with other Institutes or with Chaplains. What were the chief instances of such difficulties and where did they occur.

264. What probable reasons can be assigned for these difficulties, and what remedies can be suggested for their avoidance.

Article II. Concerning Special Ministries

Concerning Missions among infidels and heretics

265. In the Missions, or in any one of them, did the religious life suffer any harm, and if so, what were the reasons for this.

266. What safeguards were used or should have been used so that in the apostolate the faithful observance of religious discipline and the care of one's own sanctification be better secured.

267.* In the Missions, is the internal religious Superior distinct from the ecclesiastical Superior.

268.* Did this union of offices in the same person result in advantages or rather in disadvantages.

Concerning Parishes, Churches, and Sanctuaries

269.* For the incorporation or union of parishes, was an indult of the Holy See obtained, according to cc. 452, § 1, 1423, § 2, so that there should be a union or incorporation properly effected.

270.* In what form were parishes united to the Institute: *pleno iure* (absolutely, at the will of the Holy See), *in temporalibus*, etc., and from what date. (A copy of the document should be sent if there is one.)

271.* Was an agreement made with the Ordinary of the place to accept any parish. (Send copies of the agreements made during the five-year period.)

272.* How do Superiors watch over and assist those of their subjects who are pastors (c. 631, §§ 1–2), and in case of need admonish and correct them.

273.* Was the office of local Superior ever united with that of pastor, observing c. 505; did this union give rise to difficulties, or was it on the contrary attended with good results.

274.* Did the Institute obtain from local Ordinaries that Churches or Sanctuaries should be entrusted to it; if so, with what permission and on what terms and conditions was this done.

275.* How do all Superiors see to it that religious discipline suffer no harm from the ministries engaged in by the religious in parishes or in public churches which are entrusted to them.

Concerning Colleges, Schools, and Seminaries

276.* Has the Institute entrusted to it any Seminaries of clerics, and, if so, on what terms. (Documents and agreements entered into regarding this matter during the five-year period should be attached.)

277.* In these Seminaries, are there any difficulties with the Ordinaries, concerning either the religious life and discipline or the government of the Seminary.

278.* What measures and efforts are employed toward the sound and thorough training and religious education of the students.

279. Are there houses for the residence of young people who are attending public schools.

280. In these cases is very special care taken to see that the schools are safe from the standpoint of both instruction and education; especially is a careful supervision maintained over the instruction and religious education; and, if there are any deficiencies, are they carefully remedied.

281.† Are there schools which are attended by both sexes; as regards fixing the age beyond which boys may not be admitted or retained, have the prescriptions made by the Ordinaries been observed.

282. Do Superiors strictly see to it that Rectors, Prefects, Teachers, and Professors receive adequate preparation for their work:

a) Scientifically, by acquiring knowledge which corresponds adequately to the grade of the class, and by obtaining degrees and certificates, even such as are recognized outside ecclesiastical circles.

b) Pedagogically, by the study and practice of the art of teaching.

c) Spiritually, so that they may exercise the office of teaching with a genuine zeal for souls and make it a means of sanctification for themselves and others.

283. Do Superiors carefully see to it that the work of teaching be properly harmonized with religious discipline.

284. Did they promptly remove from the office of teaching those who in practicing it make light of the religious life and are not a good example to the students.

Concerning the practice of the corporal works of mercy

285. Does the Institute practice the corporal works of mercy toward the sick, orphans, the aged, etc.

286. Are there:

a) Guest-houses and hospitals for persons indiscriminately, even for those of the other sex.

b) In this case, by what authority were these institutions accepted and what precautions are used to avoid dangers and suspicions.

287. What, if any, difficulties have arisen.

288. Do Superiors diligently see to it that all persons who are to be engaged in various capacities in these institutions be competently prepared:

a) Scientifically, by obtaining even State certificates and other equivalent credentials.

b) Practically, by a suitable period of trial.

289. In the assistance and care of the sick and in the exercise of corporal charity, are the provisions of the Constitutions and the norms which have been given in this matter by the Holy See and by the Ordinaries observed.

290.† Do the religious women who attend the sick in private houses faithfully observe the special provisions of the Constitutions; do they carefully take appropriate precautions to avoid dangers.

291. Do Superiors see to it that the bodily health of the religious who are engaged in these ministries be preserved by suitable food and sleep; that moral dangers be avoided; that the religious life and the exercise of charity be properly harmonized; that zeal be kept, both in fact and in appearance, free from any form of avarice or admixture of other human affection.

Concerning the apostolate of the press

292. Does the Institute exercise the apostolate by writing, publishing, or editing and distributing books and papers.

293. Were the publications submitted according to law to the previous censorship of the major Superiors and Ordinaries of places (c. 1385, § 2).

294. Was the necessary permission of Superiors and Ordinaries of places obtained for publishing books treating of profane

matters, and for co-operating in the production of papers, magazines, or reviews or editing them (c. 1386, § 1).

295. In the distribution and sale of books, is the appearance of excessive profit avoided, and are proper precautions used to avoid dangers.

Concerning Catholic Action

296. Do the religious strive to promote Catholic Action and to collaborate in it.

297. Have any difficulties arisen in this matter, either with the directors or with the secular clergy.

298. What remedies have been used to remove these difficulties, and what further remedies can be recommended.

Concerning priestly ministrations — The celebration of the Holy Sacrifice, and Mass stipends and obligations

299.* Do Superiors diligently see to it that the religious priests do not fail to prepare themselves by pious prayers for the Sacrifice of the Eucharist, that they celebrate worthily and devoutly, observing the rubrics faithfully and giving the proper amount of time to it; and that after the Mass they give thanks to God for so great a gift.

300. Whether each house has, according to cc. 843, § 1, 844, a book in which are marked in due order the number of Masses received, the intention, the stipend, and who has said the Mass and when.

301. How often and by what Superiors are the books of Masses of each house examined and signed.

302. Whether all the houses as regards the manual stipend of Masses observed the decrees of the local Ordinaries and the customs of the dioceses according to cc. 831, §§ 2–3, 832.

303. Whether in each of the houses the obligations of Masses, both perpetual and manual, were faithfully satisfied in due time according to cc. 834, 1517.

304. Were any special concessions made in this matter, either as regards the reduction of the stipends or intentions, or as to deferring the celebration of the Masses; if so, what were they.

305. In accepting the obligations of Masses, in collecting and in giving up or transmitting the intentions, and in fulfilling them, did Superiors conscientiously observe the provisions of law (cc.

835–840, 842), those of the Constitutions or Statutes and the terms of the Foundations.

Concerning domestic services

306.† Do the religious women perform any services in Seminaries, ecclesiastical residence-halls, Communities of clerics or of religious men, or in other Colleges or institutions destined for male students, or in parishes. How many such Seminaries, Colleges, etc., have they, and by what permission did they accept them.

307.† Were the prescribed precautions for avoiding all danger and difficulty faithfully observed.

308.† Was there any such difficulty to be deplored during this time, and what was done about it.

Conclusion. A Summary Comparative Judgment Regarding the State of the Institute

Concerning striving toward perfection

309. What is to be said about the desire for and the actual striving toward evangelical perfection on the part of the members (cc. 487, 488, 1°).

310. In this respect is there in the Institute progress or retrogression as compared with the preceding five-year period, and how is this manifested or proved; what are the reasons for the progress or retrogression.

311. What has been done by Superiors during the five-year period to promote the tendency toward perfection and to prevent relaxation.

Concerning the state of discipline

312. What is to be said summarily about the observance of the vows and of the provisions of canon law, the Rule and the Constitutions, both absolutely and in comparison with the preceding five-year period.

313. What are the points of religious discipline which are more easily and frequently violated.

314. What causes may be assigned for the progress in religious observance or, if there be any, for its decline.

315. What difference, if any, is there between the various localities in regard to religious observance.

316. What has been done by Superiors to secure faithful and complete regular observance in every locality and house.

317. What are the difficulties and the chief obstacles which obstruct the work of Superiors and impede its effectiveness.

Concerning the economic condition

318. What, in itself and in comparison with the preceding five-year period, is the condition of the Institute with regard to capital and finances.

319. To what causes is the growth or diminution of capital and income to be attributed.

Concerning the special end and works

320. In comparison with the preceding five-year period, was there an increase or a diminution in the activity of the Institute in regard to its specific end. What are the reasons for the increase or diminution.

321. Were any new means or works looking toward the attainment of the specific end introduced during the five-year period, and what concrete plans are entertained for the future.

322. What are the plans of Superiors and what provisions are needed for the good of the Institute and its members.

Given at Rome, from the Sacred Congregation of Religious, the 9th day of December, 1948.

ALOYSIUS CARDINAL LAVITRANO, *Prefect*.

† FR. L. H. PASETTO, *Secretary*.

Name of the Institute (Society) .... ANNEX TO THE QUINQUENNIAL REPORT (1)

Diocese: (2) ....

Five-year Period: (3) .... CONSPECTUS OF THE CONDITION OF THE HOUSES

I	II	III	IV									V
			MEMBERS (5)								Priests (6)	
			Nov.		Temp. vows		Perp. vows					
NATION (4)	DIOCESE	HOUSE	1 class	2 class	1 class	2 class	1 class	2 class				WORKS WHICH ARE PRACTICED (7)

TOTALS

Houses ....

Members { Priests ....
Professed of perp. vows ....
Professed of temp. vows ....
Novices .... }

(1) The annex is to be made out exactly like this model.
(2) In which the generalate house is located.
(3) The years are to be indicated so as to include in the five-year period both the first and the last years, e.g., 1949–53.
(4) The individual houses are to be listed according to nations: in the nation, the houses are to be listed according to the Diocese in which they are located, e.g., Italy (col. I), Diocese of Bergamo (col. II), and then let the individual houses of this Diocese be listed (col. III).
(5) If the Institute has only one class of members, all are to be listed in the first column under each title.
(6) How many priests, whether of perpetual or temporary vows, even though they are included in the foregoing classifications.
(7) The various works are to be listed as briefly as possible.

APPENDIX IV

Sacred Congregation of Religious

The Cloister of Nuns

This Instruction, entitled *Circa Monialium Clausuram*, is as follows:

1. Among the motives which prompted His Holiness Pius XII to promulgate the Apostolic Constitution *Sponsa Christi*,[1] he himself attached considerable importance to the difficulties occasioned by the present rather strict laws of papal cloister. And this is not to be wondered at, since he clearly perceived the changes which time and circumstances have wrought in the entire institution of Nuns. When it came to outlining the general character of the renovation and adaptation of this institution, the Apostolic Constitution wisely provided: "Accordingly, without the least prejudice to any of the native and principal elements of the venerable institution of Nuns, as to the rest, which are found to be external and adventitious, We have decided to make, with caution and prudence, certain adaptations to present times, which may not only do honor to the venerable institution but at the same time enlarge its effectiveness." His Holiness therefore, whereas in the General Statutes (art. IV) he paternally decreed some adaptations of the papal cloister of Nuns to the conditions of our time, in other respects confirmed and restored it everywhere.

For one of the peculiar and most important elements of the canonical contemplative life is that strict enclosure which, based on ancient tradition and defended in the course of the centuries, is at the same time a safeguard for the solemn profession of chastity and an excellent way of disposing the soul for a more intimate union with God. And in these days, the more violently men's minds are drawn to external things, the stronger must be

---

[1] Ap. Const., 21 Nov., 1950; *A.A.S.*, Vol. 43, p. 5 seq.; *Canon Law Digest*, 3, p. 221 seq.

the observance of the cloister, which enables Nuns to be more closely united to God.

2. The Sacred Congregation of Religious, in pursuance of the task assigned to it by the Supreme Pontiff, namely, "through instructions, declarations, responses and other documents of the kind, to do everything which concerns putting the Constitution carefully and effectively into practice and securing the faithful and prompt observance of the General Statutes," as early as the 23rd of November, 1950, published an Instruction, *Inter praeclara,* the first part of which is entirely concerned with the major and minor cloister of Nuns.[2]

3. And now after the fruitful experience of several years and after having repeatedly examined and carefully considered all the reports that have reached the Holy See on this matter, seeing that after the introduction of the minor papal cloister by the Apostolic Constitution *Sponsa Christi* of 21 November, 1950, the Instruction of the Sacred Congregation of Religious, *Nuper edito,* of 6 February, 1924,[3] is no longer in agreement with the present discipline, the same Sacred Congregation considers that it is now possible and appropriate to make some further provisions and to deal anew with the entire subject (cf. c. 22); and this it proposes to do in the present Instruction.

I. Papal Cloister in General

4. Nuns of all Monasteries, even though by way of temporary exception they still profess only simple vows (Const. *Sponsa Christi,* art. III, § 2), if they wish to retain the name and juridical status of Nuns, must necessarily accept and keep at least the minor pontifical or papal cloister (art. IV, § 5, 2°).

5. Whether there is question of founding a new Monastery where cloister is established for the first time, or of a Monastery already founded where cloister is to be restored, the Nuns will be strictly bound actually to observe the pontifical or papal cloister, which shall apply to the ingress and egress of all persons, from a precise moment to be carefully fixed and defined in writing by the competent ecclesiastical authority, that is by the Ordinary of the place.

[2] *A.A.S.,* Vol. 43, p. 31; *Canon Law Digest,* 3, p. 240.
[3] *A.A.S.,* Vol. 16, pp. 96, 192; *Canon Law Digest,* 1, p. 314.

6. The law of cloister, major or minor, affects every Monastery which is subject to the one or the other, even though the number of the Nuns who live there be diminished or small (c. 597, § 2).

II. The Major Papal Cloister

Character of the Major Papal Cloister

7. The major pontifical or papal cloister is the one which is in the Code (cc. 597, 600–602) and which is clearly and solemnly confirmed and more fully described in the Apostolic Constitution *Sponsa Christi,* and more exactly defined in the Instruction *Inter praeclara* (VI–X).

8. *a*) The major pontifical or papal cloister exists by rule and is binding in all Monasteries where solemn vows are actually taken and which profess an exclusively contemplative life (Const. *Sponsa Christi,* art. IV, § 2, 2°).

b) In Monasteries where, although the Nuns are given to an exclusively contemplative life, yet exceptionally and by indult only simple vows are taken (Const. *Sponsa Christi,* art. III, § 2), although the cloister should be the major one if that is possible (art. IV, § 2, 2°), yet, especially as regards the sanction by the Holy See, the minor cloister may be granted and is applied prudently according to the case (Const. *Sponsa Christi,* art. IV, § 3, 3°; Instr. *Inter praeclara,* V).

9. Monasteries in which according to the Rule and the Constitutions only the contemplative life is to be followed, may retain the major cloister even though for grave reasons and for their duration certain apostolic works are assigned to or allowed them by the Holy See, provided that only some of the Nuns and a part of the Monastery, carefully distinguished and separated from the part where the community lives and practices the common life, be assigned to those works.

10. The law of cloister is binding on all Nuns (c. 601), Novices, and Postulants (c. 540, § 3). The professed of temporary vows after their vows have expired, and Novices and Postulants always, may go out of the cloister only when they intend to leave the Monastery for good.

11. *a*) The cloister necessarily includes not only the Monastery building and its annexes in which the Nuns reside, but also

the yards and gardens, and whatever places they frequent.

b) Outside the cloister are: those parts of the parlors which are reserved for outsiders; the church and oratory *outside the choir reserved to the Nuns;* the sacristy and places adjacent to it which are open to the clergy and servers; the place where the priest hears the Nuns' confessions; the house where the extern Sisters live; and the places destined for the chaplains and guests.

12. *a*) Although the church and the sacristy and its annexes devoted to worship are not within the cloister, still if it is really necessary that the Nuns themselves occasionally perform some service there, local Ordinaries can on their own authority permit that, during such necessity and while the work continues, the cloister be actually extended to include these places, provided that all the prescriptions given below for the protection of the cloister be observed there during that time.

b) In the same circumstances and under the same conditions, Ordinaries can permit that the cloister be extended for the occasion to the parlors and other places annexed to the Monastery when, because of the want of extern Sisters or for some other reason, it is considered really necessary that the Nuns perform some service there also.

13. *a*) The parts of the Monastery which are subject to cloister as above must be so protected and secured that not only entrance into them be entirely prevented but also that the view inward by outsiders and outward by the Nuns be as far as possible effectively shut off.

b) Hence also the yards and gardens must be surrounded either by a high wall or by some other effective means, such as wooden boards, an iron grating, or a thick and strong hedge, according to the judgment of the Ordinary and the regular Superior, with due consideration especially of the site, the number of seculars, and so forth.

14. *a*) Windows looking out on the street and on neighboring houses, or which afford any opportunity for communication with outsiders, must be equipped with glass that is not transparent and with fixed shutters or lattices so as to cut off the view from either side.

b) If there are terraces or walks to which the Nuns have

access above the roof of the Monastery, they should be surrounded with screens or in some other effective manner.

15. Unless some stricter provision exists by particular law, the Nuns, in accordance with the general spirit of the liturgy, should not be prevented by the law of cloister from seeing the altar, but in such a way that they themselves be not seen by the faithful.

16. The part of the parlor which is reserved to the Nuns must be separated from the part destined for outsiders, by two screens securely fixed some distance apart, or in some other effective way according to the judgment of the Ordinary and the regular Superior — and this is a strict conscientious obligation for them — so that the persons on one side cannot be reached from the other.

17. Near the entrance to the Monastery and also in the parlors, the sacristy, and wherever it is needed, there should be inserted in the wall a revolving wheel or box, according to usage, for passing necessary articles through from one side to the other. It is not forbidden to have small openings, so as to see what is being put into the box.

Egress of the Nuns

18. The law of major cloister obliges the Nuns to remain perpetually within the precincts of the Monastery which are designated as within the cloister by ecclesiastical authority, and not to leave the same under any pretext even for a short time, outside the cases provided for by law or legitimate permission.

19. They may not leave the cloister on the occasion of their clothing, profession, Communion, or for any such reason.

20. The Nuns may not go from one Monastery to another even of the same Order, even for a short time, without the permission of the Holy See, except as provided by duly approved particular law for Federations of Monasteries of Nuns.

21. *a*) It is allowed to go out of the cloister in case of imminent danger of death or of any other very serious harm (c. 601, § 1). Such cases are: fire, flood, earthquake, dilapidation of the building or walls threatening to crumble, air raids, incursion of soldiers, urgent requisition of the Monastery by military or civil authorities.

b) Also, an urgent surgical operation or other urgent medical treatment to be had outside for the care of health, a disease of one person which is truly dangerous to the whole community.

c) Likewise, if a grave and urgent necessity of this sort occurs in the case of an extern Sister or of some one who is taking her place, who cannot otherwise receive the needed care, the Superioress in person or through another Nun, with a companion, may visit her.

d) These dangers (*a*), and grave and urgent necessities (*b*), (*c*), are to be acknowledged in writing by the local Ordinary if there is time (c. 601, § 2); otherwise he should be notified afterward.

22. A going out is regarded as legitimate when there is an urgent obligation to exercise some right or perform some duty of a civil nature, and the local Ordinary has previously issued a declaration to that effect.

23. Nuns who have obtained permission to go out of the cloister are bound to go directly to the place for which the permission was given, and they may not on such an occasion go elsewhere.

When Nuns are outside the Monastery they are bound to observe strictly the norms and safeguards which are prescribed for religious women in similar cases either by the Code (c. 607) or by the Holy See, or by Ordinaries (c. 607).

24. *a*) Seriously difficult circumstances or absolute or moral necessities, as well as advantages of great importance, may constitute just and canonical causes for asking appropriate dispensations or even some moderate and carefully defined habitual faculties from the Holy See.

Such circumstances are:

1) the care of health outside the Monastery;

2) to visit a doctor, particularly a specialist, e.g., for the eyes, teeth, radiotherapy, medical observation;

3) to accompany or visit a Nun who is ill outside;

4) to take the place of extern Sisters or persons similarly employed who are missing;

5) to look after fields, lands, buildings, or the house where the extern Sisters live;

6) to do important acts of administration or of economic management which otherwise could not be done at all or not be done properly;

7) monastic work, either apostolic or manual;

8) to take up an office in another Monastery— and the like.

b) In the use of these dispensations and faculties, the limits imposed and the precautions prescribed must be exactly observed.

25. Habitual faculties for a definite time or for a stated number of cases can be prudently granted to local or regular Ordinaries or to religious Assistants to permit brief exits from the cloister in necessities which occur frequently. These are always to be exercised in the name of the Holy See, and cannot be extended in any way, but must be held within their proper limits.

Ingress of Outsiders

26. *a*) The local Ordinary or the regular Superior if the Monastery is subject to him, or a Delegate of either of them or of the Holy See, may enter the cloister on the occasion of the canonical visitation, only for the purpose of inspecting the building according to law (cc. 512 and 600), taking care that the Visitor be accompanied constantly from his entrance to his exit by at least one cleric or religious, who may be a *conversus,* of mature age, and that he do not remain beyond the time needed for the inspection, nor attend on that occasion to any other business or do any other acts which have nothing to do with the visitation.

b) The visitation of persons should take place in the common parlor, the Visitor remaining outside the cloister, unless there is question of interviewing a Nun who is sick and cannot come to the parlor.

c) For exercising other functions, for example the *exploratio voluntatis* of candidates, to preside at elections, for a visitation or profession and the like, the Prelate or Delegate may not enter the cloister, but must do all these things outside.

27. *a*) The confessor of the community or, *servatis servandis,* any other priest, may with the proper precautions enter the cloister: to administer to the sick the Sacraments of Penance, the Most Holy Eucharist, and Extreme Unction; also to assist the dying, and where it is the custom, to bury the dead, in which case he may be accompanied by the servers according to the rubrics. The entrance of priests for other services is not permitted.

b) The precautions to be faithfully observed according to the case are as follows:

For administering Holy Communion, the priest should be accompanied from his entrance to his exit by at least two Nuns. But there is nothing to prevent the whole community from accompanying the Blessed Sacrament in procession, according to existing customs.

For hearing confessions, two Nuns should accompany the priest as far as the cell of the sick person, and after the confession is finished conduct him immediately to the exit. The same holds for Extreme Unction and assistance to the dying.

28. The preaching of the word of God is to be done at the screen of the choir or of the parlor; if this is not convenient, application should be made to the Holy See for the faculty to have the sermons in the choir itself or in the chapter room or, with the consent of the local Ordinary, in the church, to which in that case the cloister is extended, the doors of the church being kept closed during that time.

29. The following persons may enter the cloister:

a) Those, by whatever name they are called, who are actually at the time the heads of any State, even one of a Federal Union, and their wives and retinue.[4]

b) Cardinals of the Holy Roman Church; and these may bring with them one or two attendants, either clerical or, if they belong to the Cardinal's family, lay persons.

c) Physicians, surgeons, or other persons engaged in the care of the sick, architects, craftsmen, workmen, and other such persons whose services are necessary for the Monastery in the judgment of the Superioress, with the previous at least habitual approval of the local Ordinary. The Superioress may obtain this approval at the beginning of each year on presenting a list of the persons to the Ordinary. In case of urgent necessity when there is not time to ask for this approval, it is rightly presumed.

30. All persons who are to be admitted frequently into the cloister must be of excellent reputation and outstanding moral character.

31. Without prejudice to Constitutions and Statutes which may prescribe stricter regulations, persons legitimately entering

---

[4] Code Com., 26 March, 1952; *A.A.S.*, Vol. 44, p. 496; *Canon Law Digest*, 3, p. 220.

the cloister must, when they pass through the very house of the Community, be accompanied both coming and going by two Nuns.

32. *a*) Whatever be the reason for which entrance is permitted, those who enter may not remain in the Monastery beyond the time which is really necessary for the purpose for which the permission was given.

b) None of the Nuns, except those who must do so by reason of their office, should speak to persons from outside while they are in the Monastery.

33. *a*) Except as provided in the Constitution *Sponsa Christi*, it is not allowed without special permission of the Holy See to admit to the cloister girls or women to receive instruction, to try out their vocation for a short time, or for any other pious or apostolic purpose (Const. *Sponsa Christi*, art. IX, § 2, 1° and 2°).

b) Application must likewise be made to the Holy See for special permissions not contained in approved Statutes, in favor of extern Sisters.

34. Postulants (c. 540) may enter the cloister with only the permission of the local Ordinary.

The Custody of the Cloister

35. It is the right and duty of the local Ordinary to watch over the custody of the cloister of all the Monasteries in his territory, even those which are subject to a regular Superior, although the latter also has this right and duty in Monasteries which are subject to him (c. 603, §§ 1 and 2).

36. Within the Monastery, however, the immediate custody of the cloister belongs to the Superioress. She must keep the keys to all the doors of the cloister with her day and night, giving them only to the Nuns who have charge of various offices when they need them; without prejudice to particular law which may make further prescriptions.

37. As regards the access of the Nuns to the parlor (time, frequency, quality of persons to be admitted, and so forth) and the manner of their presence there (the veil, a companion who can hear what is said, and the like), let them observe their own Constitutions. If these seem to require some accommodation, recourse should be made to the Holy See.

38. Nuns (cfr. *Sponsa Christi*, General Statutes, art. I, § 1) (not Novices and Postulants) who unlawfully go out of the major cloister contrary to the prescription of canon 601, are *ipso facto* under excommunication simply reserved to the Holy See (c. 2342, 3°).

39. The same penalty attaches to any person of whatever class, condition, or sex, who violates the major cloister, either by illegitimately entering it or by illegitimately introducing or admitting others to it (c. 2342, 1°).

III. The Minor Papal Cloister

Character of the Minor Papal Cloister

40. The minor pontifical or papal cloister is outlined as follows:

1) Being truly pontifical no less than the major cloister, it protects and favors the observance and custody of public and solemn chastity and the contemplative life of the Monastery.

2) In as much, however, as it is minor, though far more severe than the cloister of Congregations (c. 604) or even of Orders of men (cc. 598–599), it affords the faculty and the convenient facility of duly and fruitfully practicing certain select works legitimately entrusted to Nuns (Instr. *Inter praeclara*, XI).

41. *a*) The minor cloister does not admit works of every sort, but only such as are harmoniously associated with the contemplative life of the entire Community and of the Nuns individually (Const. *Sponsa Christi*, A.A.S., Vol. 43, p. 11).

b) These works, whether they be undertaken in virtue of the Constitutions of the institute, or by legitimate permission, or by command of the Church in view of her ever increasing necessities and the needs of souls, are to be performed in such an orderly and moderate way, according to the nature and spirit of the particular Order, as not only not to disturb or affect adversely the true contemplative life, but rather to nourish and strengthen it (Const. *Sponsa Christi*, art. IX).

c) Such works are: teaching Christian doctrine, religious instruction, the education of boys and girls, retreats and exercises for women, preparation for first Communion, works of charity in relief of the sick, the poor, and so forth.

42. *a*) The minor cloister must necessarily be in effect where the majority or many of the Nuns and a notable part of the

Monastery are habitually given to works of the apostolate (General Statutes, art. IV, § 3, 2°).

b) On the other hand, if only a few Nuns are assigned to these works and if the works are confined or can practically and prudently be confined to narrow limits in the Monastery, then the major cloister may be retained according to the judgment of the Holy See, with the requisite faculties and dispensations as mentioned above (n. 9).

The Division of the Monastery

43. To begin with, the buildings of the Monastery which because of the works to be done are subject to minor cloister, should be divided into two parts, one of which is reserved to the Nuns and the other given over to the apostolic works (Instr. *Inter praeclara*, XI, 5°).

44. *a*) In the part which is reserved to the Nuns after the manner of the major cloister, should be: the cells, the choir, the chapter room and so forth, the refectory, the kitchen, places for recreation, walking, and community work, and that side of the parlors to which all the Nuns have access.

b) In this part of the house there should not be: the places inhabited by the extern Sisters, the rooms and places destined for guests; nor the church with its sacristy and annexes, except as provided in n. 12.

45. *a*) The other part of the Monastery is reserved for the apostolic works or ministries which are done by the Monastery itself. Hence this part of the building is equally open to those Religious who are legitimately engaged in the works and ministries and to other persons who direct the apostolate.

b) The church and public oratory, with the places annexed to them and the others mentioned in n. 12, *b*), should not be within, but as a rule outside this latter part of the Monastery.

In the church and the places annexed to it, exception may be made for the halls or rooms which are legitimately reserved for the works of the apostolate. Even the entire church, usually open to all the faithful, may in case of urgent necessity with the consent of the local Ordinary, be counted among the places assigned to the works, during the time that the Nuns are obliged to exercise their proper ministries there, provided the following prescriptions are faithfully observed and prudent precautions are taken.

46. *a*) There must not be places which are reserved alternately, now for the Community, now for the works of the apostolate.

b) However, the local Ordinary can for reasonable cause permit, either by way of act or for a definite time, that some places which are habitually destined for works be given over to the Community; and in such case during that time those places are subject to all the regulations and prescriptions mentioned above for the part of the Monastery which is habitually reserved to the Community.

47. Also as regards the part of the Monastery which is reserved for works, the view in and out must be precluded. If this cannot be done with the same completeness as for the part of the Monastery reserved to the Nuns, the Ordinary should provide prudently and carefully.

48. *a*) The division between the two parts of the Monastery shall be precisely defined and openly indicated, so as to be clearly known to all.

b) The doors which close the part of the Monastery which is reserved to the Nuns (n. 49, *a*) are subject to all the prescriptions established for the doors of the major cloister.

c) If the entire Monastery has only one door on the public street, to admit outsiders, there must moreover be an inside door properly guarded through which the persons to be admitted are led to the place of the works.

49. The passage of the Nuns from the part which is for the Community to the part which is for the works:

a) Must be always directly through a special door.

b) It is permitted only at the times lawfully designated and only to those Nuns who are assigned to the works by the Superioress, either by way of act or habitually according to the Constitutions or Statutes. Among these should be included the Superioress herself or a Nun designated by her, even for the sole purpose of exercising vigilance.

c) For the Nuns who are legitimately engaged in the place of the works, special parlors should be provided there, not necessarily equipped with screens, but with proper safeguards, where they may speak with outsiders in regard only to the works.

Egress of the Nuns

50. *a*) The minor cloister entails a grave prohibition, for all and each of those subject to it, from going outside the limits of the Monastery, just as the major cloister does for Nuns and other persons who are bound by it (Instr. *Inter praeclara,* XII, 2°).

b) Dispensations from this grave prescription can be given for reasons of the apostolate, if really necessary, only to those Nuns and members who are legitimately engaged in ministries as above explained (n. 49).

c) Permission to go out for the reasons acknowledged herein (n. 51) or in the Constitutions, for as long as such reasons certainly exist, can be granted by the Superioress upon her responsibility in conscience. In other cases not expressly mentioned in the law, even though they could clearly be considered as equivalent because of the similarity of the reasons, recourse should be made to the local Ordinary, so that he, after considering the matter before God, may grant the permission and, if he thinks well, leave the matter in future to the Superioress.

d) Both the local Ordinary and the regular Superior, to whom the protection of the cloister is entrusted (c. 603), have a strict obligation in conscience to watch carefully over the observance of these regulations.

51. The causes from which the required necessity from the standpoint of the works may be estimated so that a just dispensation may be given for going out (n. 50, *c*), fall under the following three heads:

a) *For the sake of the work itself,* which actually requires the going out so that it may be properly done, as for example if girls must necessarily be accompanied out of the cloister because of studies, health, or recreation, and there are not available teachers, oblates, or other persons who can do this.

b) *For the sake of preparation for the works,* namely: to acquire knowledge, culture, degrees, acknowledgments of competency, and so to attend schools, academies, universities, conferences, and congresses, as may seem necessary. In case any of these institutions are so permeated with an anticlerical and profane spirit as to create imminent danger for religious virtue or give rise to the possibility of scandal from their attendance, the local Ordinary should always be consulted in advance. In all cases the Instructions issued by the Holy See must be observed.

c) *By reason of business,* procedures, or questions concerning the works which cannot be safely or conveniently transacted and finished by other persons through ecclesiastical or civil authorities or public or private offices.

Ingress of Outsiders

52. The laws concerning entrance into major cloister apply equally to Monasteries of minor cloister as regards the part reserved to the Nuns (Instr. *Inter praeclara,* XII, and above, n. 26 *seq.*).

53. *a*) Women and girls or boys for whom the works are intended may enter that part of the Monastery which is assigned to those works, and may stay there day and night, according to the nature of the works.

b) The same holds for women who may be needed for the works, such as teachers, nurses, maids, working women.

54. *a*) By way of act or transiently, other persons may be admitted who have some special relationship with those for whom the works are conducted, e.g., parents, relatives, or benefactors who accompany the girls or boys or who wish to visit them; the persons mentioned, or others when it is called for or appropriate according to the nature of the work and the customs of the place, may be invited to certain festivities or demonstrations of a religious or scholastic nature.

b) All this should be appropriately defined in the legitimately approved Statutes or Ordinances.

55. All persons who have by ecclesiastical law or civil ordinance a legitimate right of inspection of any sort, should be admitted.

56. Into the part destined for works, no less than in that reserved to the Nuns (c. 600, 4°), as is reasonable, the physician, workmen, and the like, may in case of necessity be admitted with the permission, even habitual, of the local Ordinary (n. 29, *c*).

57. The permission of the local Ordinary is required and sufficient for other cases of necessity or real utility which are

not provided for above (nn. 54–56, *a*) or in the Statutes of the works concerned.

58. Saving all the prescriptions concerning major cloister as to the part reserved to the Nuns, also as regards the less severe cloister which affects the part destined for works, the local Ordinary, and in a proper case the regular Superior, as well as the one who exercises authority over a Federation, have the right and duty to keep a strict vigilance and if need be to prescribe appropriate safeguards, in addition to those which are contained in the Statutes, for the custody and protection of the cloister.

The Custody of the Cloister

59. *a*) The immediate custody of this cloister is entrusted to the Superioress.

b) She is to keep the keys for passage from one part of the Monastery to the other, or prudently entrust them to the Nuns who are assigned to the works.

c) She should not give the keys of other doors in the house devoted to works, except to persons who are altogether reliable.

60. Nuns who illegitimately go out of the precincts of the Monastery incur *ipso facto* an excommunication simply reserved to the Holy See according to canon 2342, 3°, or, by express grant of the Holy See, reserved to the local Ordinary (Instr. *Inter praeclara*, XV, 1°).

61. *a*) "Nuns who illicitly leave the parts of the Monastery reserved to the Community and go to other places within the precincts of the Monastery, are to be punished by the Superioress or by the local Ordinary, according to the gravity of their fault" (*ibid.*, 2°).

b) The transit is illegitimate whenever it is made without the permission, at least habitual or reasonably presumed, of the Superioress.

62. "Those who illicitly enter the parts of the Monastery reserved to the Community and those who bring them in or allow them to enter, incur an excommunication reserved simply to the Holy See" (*ibid.*, 3°).

63. "Those who illegitimately enter the parts of the Monastery not reserved to the Community, as well as those who bring them in or permit them to enter, are to be severely punished

according to the gravity of the fault by the Ordinary of the place where the Monastery is situated" (*ibid.*, 4°).

IV. Papal Cloister and Federations

64. The Statutes of Federations can make such regulations regarding the major or minor cloister of Federated Monasteries as are considered necessary to attain the ends of the Federation.

65. As to government, the faculty may be given to go out of one's own Monastery and go into another: for the purpose of assembling the Chapter, the Council, or some other such gathering; of timely visitations to be made by the Authority which governs the Federation or by its delegates; of summoning or, with all necessary observances, transferring the Superioress or another Nun.

66. In order to promote fraternal collaboration among the Monasteries, the same faculty may be decreed: for the purpose of assuming in another Monastery an office which has been conferred by election or appointment; of affording aid of any kind to another Monastery or of relieving its necessities; or even for the private benefit of some individual Nun, but within the limits prescribed in the Statutes.

67. For the better formation of the Nuns, when common houses have been established for this purpose, the faculty, to be clearly defined in the Statutes, may be given for Nuns who are legitimately assigned to such houses or recalled from them, to go there, to remain, and to return.

68. *a*) The Statutes may make some provisions to secure a uniform observance of the cloister in the Monasteries of a Federation.

b) For this same purpose, and always without prejudice to the rights of local Ordinaries and regular Superiors, also special interventions of religious Assistants or of the Superioresses of Federations may be provided for as regards petitions which may have to be presented to the Holy See concerning the cloister, e.g., for extraordinary journeys, long absences from the Monastery, and the like.

69. With regard to the Monasteries of a Federation which engage in apostolic works and are subject to the common minor cloister, the Statutes may decree: what works can be under-

taken, what persons may be admitted to the place of the works, habitually or transiently, for what reasons and with what conditions and safeguards.

V. The Establishment of Papal Cloister

70. *a*) All Monasteries of Nuns must observe the pontifical or papal cloister either major or minor, according to the regulations above stated.

b) For Monasteries of Nuns which, though they profess exclusively the contemplative life, nevertheless engage legitimately in works of the apostolate in the manner above described (n. 41, *a*), unless provision has already been made by the Holy See itself since the issuance of the Apostolic Constitution, *Sponsa Christi*,[5] it shall pertain to the local Ordinary, together with the regular Superior if the Monastery is subject to him, to introduce the minor papal cloister.

c) In doubtful cases the matter should be referred to the Holy See.

d) In future, in order to change from the major to the minor papal cloister for the reasons stated above (n. 41), applications must always be made to the Holy See.

71. It pertains to the local Ordinary when the minor papal cloister is introduced, to prescribe the limits of the cloister (c. 597, § 3) and to recognize and approve the assignment of the places of the Monastery to the Community or to the works respectively, and the necessary separation between them.

72. If special difficulties, temporary or habitual, stand in the way of the establishment of the pontifical or papal cloister, the matter should be referred to the Holy See with a faithful statement of the circumstances.

73. *a*) Statutes, Indults, Privileges, and Dispensations in virtue of which certain Monasteries, while keeping the juridical status of Nuns, were exempted from the pontifical or papal cloister, are revoked.[6]

---

[5] *A.A.S.*, Vol. 43, p. 5; *Canon Law Digest*, 3, p. 221.

[6] Cf. *A.A.S.*, Vol. 43, p. 12; *Canon Law Digest*, 3, p. 229; and reply of the Code Commission, 1 March, 1921; *A.A.S.*, Vol. 13, p. 178; *Canon Law Digest*, 1, p. 306.

Therefore the so-called "episcopal" cloister cannot in future be recognized for Nuns.

b) But special Statutes by which the minor papal cloister is more precisely regulated and adapted for Orders of Nuns which are dedicated to works of the apostolate by their Institute, remain unchanged.

All things to the contrary notwithstanding.

Given at Rome, the 25th day of March, 1956.

✚ Valerio Card. Valeri, *Prefect*

P. Arc. Larraona, *Secretary*

AAS 48, 1956, 512–526.

APPENDIX V

Apostolic Constitution Sedes Sapientiae

Principles and General Statutes for Those Called to States of Perfection.

Pius, Bishop, Servant of the Servants of God, for a perpetual memorial:

The Seat of Wisdom, Mother of God the Lord of the Sciences,[1] and Queen of the Apostles,[2] the Most Holy Virgin Mary, to whose veneration We consecrated an entire year, is truly in a special manner the Mother and Mistress of all those who embrace a state for acquiring perfection and at the same time aim to march in the apostolic militia of Christ, the Supreme High Priest. For in order to apply themselves effectively to adopting and developing properly so great and exalted a vocation, one which is both priestly and apostolic, they have great need of the guidance and assistance of her who is the Mediatrix of all the graces of sanctification and is truly called the Mother and Queen of the Catholic priesthood and apostolate. We therefore eagerly implore her favor, that she who obtained for Us the light of divine grace in decreeing these norms, may by her patronage stand by to assist those whose duty it is to put them into practice.

I

It is a great blessing of Divine Providence that right down through the centuries Christ the Redeemer has constantly breathed into souls of His choice, as if by an interior and mystical speech, that invitation which His living voice once extended to the young man inquiring about eternal life: "Come follow me."[3] A goodly number of those who by the grace of God have accepted that invitation and professed with the holy Apostles, "Behold, we have left all things and have followed thee,"[4] our Lord has likewise constantly made "fishers of men,"[5] and has

---

[1] Cf. 1 Kings 2:3.
[2] From the Litany of Loretto.
[3] Mt. 19:21.
[4] Mt. 19:27.
[5] Mt. 4:19.

chosen them as laborers,[6] sending them "into his harvest."

This is as true today as it was of old, since the conjunction of the states for acquiring perfection with the priestly dignity and the apostolic office has ever grown more frequent and more intimate. In olden days the Monks were for the most part not priests; only a few of them, compelled as it were by necessity to receive priestly orders so that the nations might be converted to Christianity, became almost separated from their proper Rule; afterward the Mendicants, although they were imbued with a wonderful apostolic spirit, were not all summoned by their Rule to the priesthood — even the saintly Father of Assisi did not receive it; the Canons Regular, on the other hand, and likewise particularly the Clerics Regular, were accustomed to receive and exercise Sacred Orders as part of their special divine vocation. Afterward a great number of Congregations and Societies of common life, likewise clerical, did the same. And now, as God always provides for the needs of successive ages, we have also some Secular Institutes which are likewise clerical.

At the present time, moreover, also in the older Orders of the Latin Church which are not formally designated as lay institutes,[7] all the members, with the exception of those who are called coadjutors or *conversi,* are destined for the priesthood, which moreover is absolutely required for those who are charged with the government of those Orders.

Accordingly in our days the Church has a great host of ministers who apply themselves at the same time to the acquirement of perfection through the evangelical counsels and to the performance of priestly functions. This multitude constitutes what is called the religious clergy, side by side with that which is called secular or diocesan, both however, thriving and flourishing in fraternal rivalry and enjoying the fruits of mutual assistance, under one and the same supreme authority of the Roman Pontiff, without prejudice, of course, to the power of the Bishops.

Now everyone knows that that religious clergy, in order to achieve its twofold purpose fittingly and securely, must have very wise regulations to govern and promote the education and the religious as well as the clerical and apostolic training of its members.

[6] Mt. 9:38.   [7] Cf. canon 488, 4°.

This need has indeed hitherto been very well fulfilled by the constitutions of the various Institutes or by their statutes on the training of youth or on the arrangement of the course of study; and certainly there are also prescriptions and recommendations of the Holy See on this matter. Nevertheless the need has long been felt of some general ordinances, well coordinated and more complete, fortified by the authority of the Holy See and to be observed everywhere by all, in order that this important activity, which concerns closely the good of souls, may be assured of a successful development and completion through continuous and well directed effort.

A work of such excellence demands the constant vigilance of the Apostolic See itself; for, just as diocesan schools for clerics, in their character of public ecclesiastical institutions, are placed under the active care and constant control of the Holy See acting through the Sacred Congregation of Seminaries and Universities,[8] so for the same reason the special schools for the states of perfection, which are recognized and sanctioned by the Church, are public and are under the authority of the Sacred Congregation of Religious.[9]

For these several reasons, as early as the year of 1944 We authorized, within the Sacred Congregation of Religious, "the erection and establishment . . . of a special Body or Commission of chosen men, which shall deal with all questions and matters pertaining in any way to the religious and clerical education and to the training in literature, science, and ministry of aspirants, novices, and junior members of all religious institutes and societies living in common without vows."[10]

This Commission, made up of learned men from various religious institutes and countries, after having examined all the extant documents on the subject and received reports in response to the Circular Letter which was sent to all Superiors General,[11]

---

[8] Cf. canon 256.

[9] Cf. canon 251; Pius XII, Ap. Const., *Provida Mater*, art. IV, § 1, 2 Feb., 1947, *A.A.S.*, Vol. 39, p. 121 (*Enchiridion de statibus perfectionis*, Rome, 1949, n. 387, p. 584; *Canon Law Digest*, 3, p. 135.

[10] S. C. Rel., Decree, *Quo efficacius*, 24 Jan., 1944; *A.A.S.*, Vol. 36, p. 213 (*Enchiridion*, n. 381, p. 560); English text, *Canon Law Digest*, 3, p. 100.

[11] S. C. Rel., Circular Letter, *Quantum conferat*, 10 June, 1944 (*Enchiridion*, n. 382, pp. 561–564); published also in *Periodica*, Vol. 33, p. 246. Cf. *Canon Law Digest*, 3, p. 101, note.

had already done a great deal of work when the general Congress of the states of perfection was convened in 1950. Thereafter the Commission, making use of various appropriate suggestions which had been presented at the Congress, reexamined and revised the plans they had already prepared and submitted them for Our approval.

Accordingly We now decree a certain number of Statutes, first, however, presenting some fundamental principles and norms concerning the religious, clerical, and apostolic training of the members, which are always to be observed by all.

II

First, We would have everyone remember that the foundation of the religious and of the sacerdotal and apostolic life, which is called a divine vocation, consists of two essential elements, one divine, the other ecclesiastical. As to the first of these, a call from God to enter the religious or the sacerdotal state is so necessary that if this is lacking the very foundation on which the whole edifice rests is wanting.

For, whom God has not called, His grace does not move nor assist. For that matter, if a true vocation to any state of life is considered in a certain sense divine, in as much as God is the principal author of all states of life and of all dispositions and gifts, natural and supernatural, how much more is this true of a religious and priestly vocation, which is of such exalted splendor and is made up of gifts so numerous and so great that they can come down only "from the Father of lights, from Whom is every best gift and every perfect gift."[12]

Passing on now to the other element of a religious and priestly vocation, let us recall the teaching of the Roman Catechism, that *"they are said to be called by God, who are called by the lawful ministers of the Church."*[13]

And this not only does not contradict what We said about a divine vocation, but is strictly consistent with it. For the divine call to the religious and clerical state, since it destines a man to lead publicly a life of sanctification and to exercise the hierarchical ministry in the Church, that is in a visible and hierarchical

[12] Cf. James 1:17.
[13] *Catech. Rom. ad Parochos,* cura Pii V editus, pars II, cap. 7.

society, has to be authoritatively approved, admitted, and controlled also by hierarchical superiors, to whom the government of the Church has been divinely entrusted.

And this must be kept in mind by whoever has charge of finding and approving these vocations. Never should they in any way coerce anyone into the sacerdotal or religious state;[14] nor should they entice or admit anyone who does not show signs of a genuine call from God; nor promote anyone to the clerical ministry if he shows that he has received from God only a religious vocation; neither should they, in the case of those who have received from God also the gift of a priestly vocation, limit them to the secular clergy or try to draw them to it; finally, let them never turn away from the priestly state one who gives reliable signs of being called to it by God.[15]

For it is evident that those who aspire to the clerical ministry in a state of perfection, and for whom these norms are intended, must unite in themselves all the elements which are needed to constitute a multiple vocation of this kind, religious, priestly, and apostolic, and hence must have all the gifts and qualities which are necessary for fulfilling such exalted divine functions.

III

It is clear that the germs of a divine vocation and the qualities needed for it, if they are present, require education and training to develop and mature them. For there is nothing that attains perfection the moment it is born; perfection is acquired through gradual progress. In regulating this development, all the conditions of the individual who has received the divine call and all the circumstances of place and time must be considered in order effectively to attain the desired end. Consequently the education and training of young members must be altogether safe, enlightened, solid, complete, wisely and courageously adapted to both the internal and external exigencies of the present day, carefully cultivated, vigilantly tested with regard not only to the perfection of the religious life but also to that of the priestly and apostolic life.

All this, as We know from experience, can be provided only by

[14] Cf. canon 971.
[15] Cf. canon 971.

well-chosen men, who are not only outstanding in learning, prudence, understanding of characters, wide experience of men and things, and in other human qualities, but who are also filled with the Holy Spirit and who will give the young men a shining example of holiness and of all virtue; for it is well known that in the whole matter of training they are more influenced by virtue and right conduct than by words.[16]

In fulfilling this most important duty, let educators have as their first rule the one which our Lord announced in the Gospel when He said: "I am the good shepherd. The good shepherd giveth his life for his sheep. . . . I am the good shepherd; and I know mine, and mine know me";[17] and which Saint Bernard expressed in these words: "Learn that you are to be mothers to your subjects, not masters; strive rather to be loved than to be feared";[18] and the Council of Trent itself, frequently exhorting ecclesiastical superiors, "considers that they should be urged first of all to remember that they are shepherds and not slave-drivers, and that they must so rule over their subjects as not to domineer over them but to love them as sons and younger brothers; they should endeavor by exhortation and admonition to deter them from wrongdoing lest they be obliged to administer due punishment after faults have been committed. Yet if through human frailty their subjects do wrong, they must observe the precept of the Apostle and reprove, entreat, rebuke them in all patience and doctrine; for sympathy is often more effective for correction than severity, exhortation better than threats of punishment, kindness better than insistence on authority. If in view of the seriousness of a crime there be need of punishment, then they must combine authority with leniency, judgment with mercy, severity with moderation, to the end that discipline, so salutary and essential to public order, be maintained without asperity, and that those who have been punished may amend their ways or, if they refuse to do so, that others may be deterred from wrongdoing by the salutary example of their punishment."[19]

All who are in any way responsible for the education of the members should also remember that this education and training

---

[16] Cf. canon 124.
[17] Jn. 10:11, 14.
[18] *In Cantica, Sermo* 23, Migne, *P.L.,* 183, 885 B.
[19] Cf. canon 2214, § 2; Conc. Trid., sess. XIII, *de ref.,* cap. 1.

must be imparted with an organic progression and making use, as occasion offers, of all appropriate resources and methods; it must embrace the whole man under all the aspects of his vocation, so as to make of him truly in all respects a "man perfect in Christ Jesus."[20] With regard to the resources and methods of education, those which nature itself supplies and those which are offered by the human ingenuity of the present age, if they are good, are clearly not to be neglected, but to be highly esteemed and wisely employed. However, there is no more fatal mistake than to rely exclusively or excessively on these natural means and to relegate supernatural aids and resources to a secondary place or in any way to neglect them. Because in order to attain religious and clerical perfection and apostolic results, the supernatural means, the sacraments, prayer, mortification, and the like, are not merely necessary but altogether primary and essential.

But, supposing that this order of methods and works is observed, absolutely nothing should be neglected which would conduce in any way to the cultivation of all the natural virtues and to the development of a well-rounded and virile human personality, so that the supernatural religious or priestly training may rest firmly on this solid foundation of natural goodness and human culture,[21] for people are brought to Christ the more easily and securely in proportion as they find in the person of the priest "the goodness and kindness of God our Saviour."[22]

Nevertheless, though all should make much of the human and natural training of the religious cleric, the supernatural sanctification of the soul undoubtedly has the first place in the entire course of his development. For if the warning of the Apostle, "For this is the will of God, your sanctification,"[23] applies to every Christian, how much more is he bound by it who not only has received the priesthood but has publicly professed the aim of attaining evangelical perfection, and is by his very office an instrument for the sanctification of others, so much so that the salvation of souls and the growth of the Kingdom of God depend in a considerable degree upon his holiness?

Let all, therefore, who belong to the states for acquiring perfection, remember and frequently consider in the presence of

---

[20] Col. 1:28.   [22] Tit. 3:4.
[21] Cf. Phil. 4:8.   [23] 1 Thess. 4:3.

God, that, to fulfill the demands of their profession, it is not enough for them to avoid grave sin or even with the aid of God's grace venial sins, nor to obey in a merely material way the orders of their Superiors or even to observe their vows or other conscientious engagements, or the constitutions of their institute, according to which, says the Church herself in the sacred Canons, "all and every religious, Superiors as well as subjects, are bound . . . to order their life, and thus tend to the perfection of their state."[24] For they must do all this with their whole soul and an ardent love, not merely through necessity, "but also for conscience' sake,"[25] because to scale the heights of sanctity and to present themselves to all men as living springs of Christian charity, they have to be inflamed with an ardent love of God and neighbor and be adorned with every virtue.

IV

Now, when this sanctification of the soul has been provided for, the intellectual and pastoral training of the religious cleric must be attended to most carefully, and on this subject, in view of the importance of the matter and the responsibility of Our supreme office, We wish to explain and recommend the principles at somewhat greater length.

How great is the need for these religious of a solid and altogether finished intellectual training and formation, is clear especially from their three-fold dignity in the Church of God, religious, sacerdotal, and apostolic.

Religious men, whose chief duty it is to seek God alone, to be united to Him in contemplation and to give the divine truths to others, must know that they cannot fulfill this most sacred duty well and fruitfully nor be raised to a sublime union with Christ if they lack that copious and deep knowledge of God and His mysteries which is drawn from sacred doctrines and must ever be perfected.[26]

The dignity of a priest, which makes him an ambassador of the Lord of all knowledge[27] and designates him as the *salt of the*

---

24 Cf. canon 593.
25 Rom. 13:5.
26 Cf. Pius XI, Ap. Letter, *Unigenitus Dei Filius,* 19 March, 1924; *A.A.S.,* Vol. 16, pp. 137–138 (*Enchiridion,* n. 348, pp. 403–404). Cf. *Canon Law Digest,* 1, pp. 265, 302, 312, 313, 661, 670.   27 Cf. 1 Kings 2:3.

earth and the *light of the world*,[28] demands a full and solid training especially in ecclesiastical subjects, such a formation as can nourish and sustain his spiritual life and preserve him from all error and the vagaries of novelty; one which will make him a faithful dispenser of the mysteries of God,[29] and a perfect man of God, *instructed for every good work*.[30]

Finally, the apostolic office which members of the states of perfection perform, each according to his vocation — by sacred sermons to the people, the Christian education of children and young people, the administration of the sacraments, especially that of confession, mission work among infidels, the spiritual direction of souls, or finally by the mere contacts of daily life with the people — can never produce abundant and permanent results unless they themselves are thoroughly grounded in the knowledge of sacred doctrine, and cultivate it by uninterrupted study.

In order to attain this solid and finished intellectual culture and formation concomitantly with the natural development of the young men and the arrangement of their studies, religious Superiors must first of all use every means to see to it that in the knowledge of literature and doctrine, religious students "be in no way inferior to young men of the laity who are studying the same subjects. For if this is securely provided for, it will be assured that the students receive a thorough mental training, and that they will be the more available for service each in his own time,"[31] and also that they will be prepared and equipped to go on to higher ecclesiastical studies.

In philosophical and theological courses, which are to be taught only by qualified and well-chosen professors, all the prescriptions of the sacred Canons and those made by Our Predecessors and Ourselves must be most faithfully observed, regarding especially the reverence which is due to the *Magisterium* of the Church and which on all occasions must be professed and instilled into the minds and hearts of the students; regarding the prudence and caution which must always accompany the careful and highly praiseworthy investigation of new questions which arise from time to time; and regarding the system, doctrine, and principles

---

[28] Cf. Mt. 5:13–14.   [29] Cf. 1 Cor. 4:1–2.   [30] Cf. 2 Tim. 3:17.

[31] Pius XII, Ap. Exhort, *Menti Nostrae*, 23 Sept., 1950; *A.A.S.*, Vol. 42, p. 687.

of the Angelic Doctor, which are to be faithfully held and are decidedly to be followed in the teaching of philosophy and theology to students.[32]

Following the guidance and authority of Aquinas, theology is to be taught according to a method which is both positive and scholastic, that is, in such a way that in the light of the authentic *Magisterium* the sources of Divine Revelation are very thoroughly examined, making use of all the appropriate aids to that study, and that the treasures of truth drawn therefrom be clearly explained and effectively defended. For, since the deposit of Revelation is entrusted for authentic interpretation to the *Magisterium* of the Church alone, it must be most faithfully explained according to the sense and mind of the Church herself, and not according to mere human reason and private judgment. Let professors of Christian philosophy and theology, therefore, take notice that they perform their function not in their own right and name but in the name and by the authority of the supreme *Magisterium,* and hence subject to its vigilance and control, having received from it, as it were, a canonical commission. Consequently, without restriction of freedom of opinion in those matters which are still open to discussion, "they must remember that they have received the authority to teach, not that they may communicate their own opinions to their students, but in order to teach them the established doctrines of the Church."[33]

Moreover, both masters and pupils should always remember that ecclesiastical studies are designed, not merely for intellectual training, but for a complete and thorough religious, or sacerdotal and apostolic formation; and hence they must be directed not merely to the successful passing of examinations, but to giving the students a stamp of character which shall never be effaced and from which, when need arises, they may ever draw light and strength for themselves and others.[34]

To this end, intellectual instruction must first of all be intimately united to a love of prayer and the contemplation of

---

[32] Pius XII, Encyclical, *Humani generis,* 12 Aug., 1950; *A.A.S.,* Vol. 42, pp. 573, 577–578; canon 1366.

[33] St. Pius X, *Motu proprio, Doctoris Angelici,* 29 June, 1914; *A.A.S.,* Vol. 6, p. 338 (*Enchiridion,* n. 284, p. 336).

[34] Cf. Pius XII, Speech to Clerical Students, 24 June, 1939; *A.A.S.,* Vol. 31, p. 246 (*Enchiridion,* n. 373, p. 531); English text, *Canon Law Digest,* 2, p. 427.

heavenly truth; it must also be complete, not omitting any of the prescribed subjects, coherent and so well arranged in its entirety that all the courses of study coalesce in one single well rounded system. It must also be very wisely adapted to refute the errors and meet the needs of our time; it must take account of the recent discoveries of scholarship and at the same time be entirely in accord with venerable tradition; finally, it must be effectively designed for the fruitful performance of every kind of pastoral ministry, so that the future priests with this training may be ready and well prepared to present and defend sound doctrine in sermons and catechetical instructions to both learned and unlearned audiences, to administer the sacraments properly, to promote vigorously the good of souls and help every one by word and work.

Though all that We have said about the spiritual and intellectual formation of students is most conducive and altogether necessary to the making of truly apostolic men, it being evident that if a priest lacks holiness and learning he lacks everything; yet it is Our solemn duty to add here that, in addition to holiness and learning, if the priest is to fulfill his apostolic ministry properly, he must have a most careful and quite perfect pastoral preparation such as to awaken and develop a genuine skill and dexterity in the due performance of the manifold works of the Christian apostolate.

For if the practice of any craft requires some previous preparation, theoretical, technical, and practical, and this latter tested by a long apprenticeship, who can deny that a similar, nay a much more careful and profound previous preparation, is needed for that profession which is truly called the art of arts?

This pastoral training of the students, which should begin at the very inception of the course of studies, develop gradually to perfection with the growing age of the student, and finally be consummated after the completion of the theology course by a special period of trial according to the particular end of the respective religious institute, must have for its primary purpose to imbue the future ministers and apostles of Christ solidly and thoroughly, after the model of Christ Himself, with the apostolic spirit and virtues, and to give them practice in them: namely, an ardent and unmixed desire for promoting the glory of God; an active and burning charity for the Church and for defending

her rights and preserving and spreading her truth; a flaming zeal
for the salvation of souls; supernatural prudence in word and
work, together with evangelical simplicity, humble self-denial,
and obedient subjection to Superiors; an unshakable trust in
God and a keen sense of duty; a virile ingenuity in starting
projects and constancy in pursuing them; unceasing fidelity in
the performance of duty; generosity in the greatest sufferings
and labors; finally, that Christian affability and kindness which
wins all hearts.

Another objective which must be aimed at in pastoral training
is that the students, according to the stage and progress of their
studies, be instructed in all those subjects which can contribute
very much to the complete development of "a good soldier of
Christ Jesus,"[35] and to providing him with suitable apostolic
weapons. Hence, besides philosophical and theological studies,
which, as We said, must also be appropriately adapted to pastoral
work, it is altogether necessary that the future shepherds of the
Lord's flock receive from learned teachers according to the norms
issued by this Apostolic See, an instruction in psychology and
pedagogy, didactics and catechetics, social science and pastoral
practice, and other such subjects, which is in step with the
progress now being made in these subjects and which will render
them fit and ready to meet the many needs of the apostolate
in our day.

This doctrinal instruction and preparation for the apostolate,
in order that it may be confirmed by use and experience, must
be accompanied also by practical exercise in well planned progressive stages and under prudent control; then after the priesthood is received We wish this practical exercise to be continued
and perfected by a special period of trial under the guidance of
men who are outstanding in doctrine, counsel, and example, and
to be constantly strengthened by uninterrupted sacred studies.

Now that We have prepared the way by giving these fundamental principles which must imbue and direct the work of
education and both the educators and those to be taught, We
proceed after mature consideration, of certain knowledge, and
in the fulness of Apostolic authority, to decree and establish
the following general norms on the various aspects of this very

---

[35] 2 Tim. 2:3.

important matter, which are to be observed by all whom they concern. Moreover, We empower the Sacred Congregation of Religious to put into practice the General Statutes which We have already approved, by ordinances, instructions, declarations, and interpretations given with Our Authority, and to take all measures which may be appropriate to secure the faithful observance of this Constitution and of the Statutes and Ordinances.

All things to the contrary notwithstanding, even though worthy of special mention.

Given at Rome, from Saint Peter's this thirty-first day of May, the Feast of the Blessed Virgin Mary, Queen of the World, in the year of Our Lord 1956, the eighteenth of Our Pontificate.

AAS 48–354; Pius XII, Ap. Const., 31 May, 1956.

APPENDIX VI

Decree of the Sacred Congregation of Religious Regarding Religious Who Are Obliged to Military Service.

Experience has shown that military service, which is imposed by the civil authority on religious and members of Societies of common life in disregard of the privilege of clerical immunity, may easily jeopardize a divine vocation and the religious spirit. To meet so serious a danger the Holy See has deemed it appropriate and necessary to establish definite regulations.

To this end the Sacred Congregation of Religious, on January 11, 1911, issued the Decree *"Inter reliquas,"*[1] which had been confirmed by the special approval of Saint Pius X, and interpreted and applied it through repeated declarations, as for example those of 1 Feb. 1912,[2] 15 July[3] and 30 Nov. 1919[4] and 16 March, 1922.[5]

Since however the actual conditions of military service have greatly changed in these most recent times and since more effective means of preservation are now available, it has been decided to reconsider the entire subject.

Accordingly, after having carefully considered the matter in the Plenary Meeting of the Most Eminent Fathers and with the approval of His Holiness Pius XII given in the Audience of 30 July 1957, this Sacred Congregation has decided to decree as follows.

Art. 1 — The Notion of Military Service

Military service in this Decree means the ordinary service which young religious, when first received in some branch of the service and placed under military authority and discipline, are by civil law obliged to render for at least six months, continuously or intermittently, either by bearing arms or by serving

---

[1] AAS 3–37; *Canon Law Digest,* 1, p. 106.
[2] AAS 4–246.
[3] AAS 11–321; *Canon Law Digest,* 1, p. 105.
[4] AAS 12–73; *Canon Law Digest,* 1, p. 109.
[5] AAS 14–196; *Canon Law Digest,* 1, p. 311.

in any auxiliary capacity, even in that pertaining to sanitation and health.

Art. 2 — Perpetual Vows and Military Service

No one can be validly admitted to perpetual profession before he has performed his military service or has been absolutely declared unfit for it, or has for any reason become legitimately and permanently free from the obligation to serve.

Art. 3 — Temporary Vows and Military Service

§ 1. The temporary vows of a religious who has been called to the service are suspended when he comes under military discipline, without prejudice to the prescription of § 2.

§ 2. However, the major Superior with the advice of his Consultors can, according to his conscience and prudence, permit a religious called to military service, who asks for the favor and is certainly worthy of it, to remain under temporary vows during such service, for a definite time or *ad nutum*.

§ 3. During the period of military discipline the same Superior for just and serious cause can, by a notice in writing, suspend the vows which were allowed to a religious according to paragraph 2; and he can likewise grant the restoration of the same vows, which were suspended either at the beginning of military service or afterward.

Art. 4 — The Juridical Condition of a Religious during Military Service

§ 1. During military service the religious is legitimately absent from the religious house, and consequently remains bound by those obligations of the religious life, which, in the judgment of the major Superior, are reconcilable with his military status.

§ 2. The time which one has spent in military service while bound by religious vows according to Art. 3, §§ 2 and 3, can be counted for the purpose of canon 574 § 1, without prejudice to Art. 6.

§ 3. A religious, although he be not bound by vows during military service, continues to be a member of his Institute and under the authority of his Superiors.

§ 4. A religious who is not bound by vows can, in accordance with canon 637, freely leave the Institute, having previously as a condition for the validity of his action, given notice thereof to his Superiors by a declaration in writing, or by an oral declaration made in the presence of witnesses. An oral declaration is effective immediately; a written one becomes effective when the religious is informed that the Superior has received it.

Similarly, and observing the same formalities, the Institute can declare the religious dismissed for just and reasonable causes according to the same canon 637.

Art. 5 — Poverty

As regards property which religious may acquire during their military service or which may afterward come to them from such service, whether they were during their service bound by their vows or freed from them, the following are to be observed:

§ 1, 1) Whatever the religious acquires through his own industry or because he is a religious, is the property of the Institute.

2) He acquires by his own industry his military pay and in general whatever comes to him because he is in the service.

§ 2, 1) A gratuity which is given to a professed of simple vows and which can accrue to his patrimony, shall be considered like a dowry, to be converted into capital whose income shall be received by the Institute as long as the individual remains in it. At his death the capital becomes the property of the Institute. If the religious for any reason leaves the Institute, it is to be restored to him in its entirety, without the interest that has already accrued. In the case of regulars canons 581 and 582 are to be observed.

2) Pensions which come to a religious because of outstanding merit or by reason of wounds received or disease contracted in military service, are turned over to the Institute and belong to it as long as he remains in it; the individual acquires them for himself if he leaves.

3) Gratuities, gifts or any such largesses given on account of the death of a religious in military service, go to the Institute if he was a member thereof at the time of death.

Art. 6 — The Probation after Military Service

Without prejudice to canon 574, a religious after finishing his military service, is to remain for some time under the regime of the common life and in temporary vows. As a rule this time should not be less than three months. The major Superior with the advice of his Council can for a grave reason shorten this period, or according to his prudent judgment extend it to a year before admitting the religious to perpetual profession.

Art. 7 — Extension of this Decree

§ 1. The prescriptions of the above Articles, with appropriate adjustments, are binding also on Societies of common life without vows.

§ 2. Without prejudice to canon 556, § 1, novices who are called to military service, unless they have been legitimately dismissed or have left of their own accord, continue to belong to the Institute and enjoy the privileges of novices.

Art. 8 — Relation to the Previous Law

All religious professions which have hitherto been made contrary to the prescriptions of the Decree *"Inter reliquas"* or of the succeeding declarations, are healed as to all canonical effects by the present Decree.

All things to the contrary notwithstanding; and all privileges and concessions hitherto given in this matter are revoked.

Given at Rome, the 30th of July 1957.

VALERIO CARD. VALERI, *Prefect*
ARCADIUS LARRAONA, C.M.F., *Secretary*

AAS 49–871; S. C. Rel., Decree, 30 July, 1957.

APPENDIX VII

Letter of the S. C. of Religious to the Superiors General of the Institutes of Perfection regarding the Use of Radio and Television.

As early as the first of January 1954, the date on which the transmission of television in Italy was inaugurated, the Holy Father in an important exhortation on television,[1] communicated to the Most Reverend Ordinaries of places his anxiety over the effects which this new and powerful means of diffusing news, facts and exhibitions from all parts of the world might have on the moral and spiritual life of the people.

This marvelous product of modern science, which within a short time has been made practically available to every one, is quite frequently to be found also in religious houses; and as we know, even in Italy where good intentions, promises and the good will of a number of persons might have encouraged the hope that the programs would be kept within the bounds of decency and morality, these limits have not always been observed.

The Supreme Pontiff has therefore felt a still greater concern regarding the use of this instrument at once precious and dangerous, especially in Institutes of Christian perfection.

In the religious life there is question of safeguarding the discipline and holiness of that life, which is imperilled not only by things that are evidently wrong but also by the infiltration of worldliness, which destroys the relish for the things of the spirit and diminishes, often insensibly, that desire of perfection which must always remain alive in a religious, dedicated to it as he is by his very profession.

In the aftermath of the Congress of the States of Perfection which was held at the close of the year 1950, this Sacred Congregation has taken a lively interest in the regulation of these modern inventions, the cinema, radio and television, in their

---

[1] AAS 46–18.

various aspects in relation to the religious life, its discipline and its apostolate.

Especially as regards radio and television, after having drawn profit from the results of the Congress itself, it has asked for and collected the opinions of religious Superiors and of other persons from various nations and of diverse temperaments, qualified by solid learning, religious piety and experience in the spiritual life, in order to prepare and send out an Instruction establishing some general norms from which the Superiors of the various religious Institutes might derive a more detailed and specific regulation of this matter on the basis of their particular spirit, the form of their discipline and their internal and external aims.

Evidently, considering the good and the evil, the usefulness as well as the dangers of television, this Sacred Congregation does not see any necessity for its indiscriminate suppression in all religious Institutes; nor does it mean to approve its full and absolute admission or toleration. The former course would run the risk of alienating too completely from social life certain religious Institutes which have to live in the midst of the world and deploy a social and religious activity there; the latter would plunge the religious back into the world which he has abandoned, to be gradually tainted with that worldly spirit which is incompatible with the religious ideal.

The Church does not thereby mean to reject whatever science and progress provide for humanity, if it can be directed to a good purpose; but she cannot and does not diverge from the principle *"salus animarum suprema lex"*; to do so would be to fail in her mission. In regard to religious — that select group in the Church — she seeks to eliminate not only serious and obvious dangers but also whatever may impede or retard the progress toward perfection which is the very purpose of religious life.

With regard to radio and television some needed distinctions have to be made. The requirements of the contemplative life are different from those of the active life; in the active life itself two considerations occur: what may be allowed by way of proper relaxation and amusement, and what is demanded by the needs of the apostolate; and even in the apostolate, one question is what may be allowed for one's own instruction and experience, another, what the religious themselves can give to the faithful whom they influence and assist.

On the basis of these considerations this Sacred Congregation has thought it well to establish some fundamental norms and also to invite the Superiors of the various Institutes, together with their respective Councils, to control this matter by somewhat more concrete regulations in keeping with their own spirit and traditions, so that a thing which can be an effective aid to the apostolate may not degenerate into a cause of spiritual ruin for religious, or worse still, of a general relaxation of religious discipline.

After having considered everything this Sacred Congregation establishes the following norms and presents them to Superiors for exact observance, *"graviter onerata eorum conscientia."*

1. There is no sufficient reason to justify introducing television apparatus in communities of contemplative life, either of men or of women. A radio apparatus can be tolerated for the sole purpose of enabling the religious to hear the words of the Pope when he speaks to the whole world and to receive his blessing, or on the occasion of some exceptional celebration of a religious character.

2. In Institutes of active life:

a) Never can individual radios, and much less individual television sets, be permitted, to be used freely and without the control of the Superior.

b) The radio and television apparatus must always be located exclusively in some community hall, in an open place, under the control of the Superior or of some one delegated by him.

c) Superiors must regulate the time given to television or to listening to the radio so that there be no interference with the occupations and duties of each one's state or office, the apostolate, practices of piety, exercises of the common life and hours of rest, according to the community's daily order.

d) Superiors should forbid showings or broadcasts which because of their moral tone or worldliness are not suitable for religious. Aside from the daily news and transmissions of an educational or religious character, all the rest should or at least may be considered as of that type in relation to the religious life,

and hence to be excluded if proposed only for the recreation of
the religious.

e) If reasons of the apostolate clearly require, in the case of
certain individual religious and in concrete cases, that some
reasonable exceptions be made, the decision as to these must
always be reserved to the Superior, who, *"graviter onerata conscientia,"* must see to it that the danger be made as remote as
possible, by making a careful choice of the religious concerned,
who should be persons of solid religious spirit and sound experience of life, and well able to discern not only what might
be harmful to the religious themselves but also what might harm
those for whom the show is intended.

P. A. LARRAONA, *Secretary*

P. PALAZZINI, *Undersecretary*

(Private); S. C. Rel., 6 Aug., 1957 (N. 01742/53); translated from the
original Italian.

Index

(Numbers Refer to Sections)

Abbot: 17, 88; privileges of, 322

Abrogation of constitutions, 19, 1; see *Privileges*

Administration, *temporal:* definition, 156, 1; rights of bishop in diocesan congregations, 161, *a;* nondiocesan, 161, *c;* 93; concerning funds for worship or for charity, 161, *d;* right of possessing temporal goods, 159; see *Alienation — Debts — Procurator — Trade*

Admission: to religion, 170; to the novitiate, 178 sq.; to the profession, 226, 2

Age: for novitiate, 179, *b;* for the profession, 226, 1; of the master of novices, 204, 1; of his assistant, 204, 1; of the local superior, 65, 3; of major superiors, 65, 2, *c*

Alienation: definition, 156, 2; acts requiring a pontifical indult, 163; conditions for obtaining, 163; censures, 165

Alms: 168; the right to collect, 320 sq.; for local worship, 161, *c;* acquired by the institute, 245

Altar, privileged, 255, 6

Apostasy from the faith, 345; from religious life, 241, 3; 340

Assistant of master of novices, 204; of the superior general, 17; 63, 2; 65, 2, *c*

Association of pious women in the Church, 138, 2; participation of religious, 240, 5

Baptism: of adults, 148; certificate required, 182, 1

Begging: privilege of, 319 sq.

Beneplacitum Apostolicum: for the erection of novitiate houses, 193; for the division of the institute into provinces, 30; for contracting a loan, 163 sq.; for the alienation of property, 163 sq.

Bishop: or *Ordinary of the diocese,* 45; 53

Blessing: papal, 255, 5; of objects for use in divine worship, 139

Books: forbidden, 61, *e;* censorship and permission to write, 316

Bursar: 99

Canon: idea and division, 2

Canonical contemplative life: 15, 3

Canons Regular: 24, 3

Cardinal protector: 52; correspondence with, 295, 1

Ceremony of profession, 234

Chaplain: 133; administration of last sacraments, 150, 2; funerals, 152

Chapter: definition, 55; powers, 56, 273; see *Consultors*

Chastity: the vow of, 276; dispensation from the vow by secularization, 336, 1; dispensation, 339

Children: necessary support of parents, 180

Christmas: Masses, 140

Churches: 135

Clerics Regular: 24, 3

Cloister: episcopal, 280, 3; 291 sq.; *papal:* of regulars, 279; of nuns, 282; major, 283; minor, 285; of federations, 289; see Appendix IV; and funerals, 154, 5; violations by flight, 342

Code: definition, 1; division, 2; 4; promulgation, 2, 3

Collections from door to door, 319; 320

College: meaning of, 182, 2

Commerce: see *Trade*

Common life: 275, 2, 3; required in a house of studies, 259

(Numbers Refer to Sections)

Communion, Holy: distribution of, 149; frequent, 256; privation of, 58, 2; 256; of the sick, 256; as viaticum, 150

Compromise: 79

Conditæ a Christo: Const. Apost., 3; 342, 2

Confession: frequency, 254, 3

Confessional: location and construction, 121, 3; 286; canonical visit of, 92, 1

Confessor: of religious men, 105 sq.; of religious women, 109 sq.; appointment, 125, 2; duration of office, 126; duties of, 127; requisite qualifications, 125, 1; exclusion of former religious, 337

Confirmation: certificate of, 182

Congregation: monastic, 8; religious; definition, 7; foundation, 25–26; origin, 24, 3; suppression, 29; Roman, notion, 51, 1; of the Bl. Virgin in a church of religious women, 138

Congregation, diocesan: subject to common law, 23; to Ordinaries, 28

Congregation, native: in missionary countries, foundation, 26, 2

Conscience: account of, 128–132; cases of, 264

Constitutions: 26, 4; 271 sq.; relation to common law, 20

Consultors: see Counsellors

Correspondence: 294 sq.

Counsellors: 97; consultative vote for perpetual profession, 226, 2; for dismissal, 346; quinquennial report, 88; for dismissal of the professed, 346; 347; deliberative vote for the alienation of property, 163; admission to the novitiate, 181; to the first temporary profession, 226, 2

Court: see Tribunal

Custom Book: approbation of, 19, 1

Daughters of Charity: exemption of, 313

Debts: authorization necessary for contracting, 163; impediment to admission, 180, b

Decree of commendation, 9

Decrees of the Holy See: to be read, 86

Delegate, Apostolic: correspondence with, 295, 1

Departure: leaving the house, 292; 293; and exemption, 312, 1

Directory: approbation of, 19, 1

Discipline: notion of, 2, 1

Dismissal: former law, 343; for special misdemeanors, 345; 346; of nuns, 347; 357; during temporary vows, 347; during perpetual vows, 353 sq.; of sisters, 356; 357; effects of, 351; 363 sq.

Disposal of goods: 216 sq.; 243

Divine Worship: 135; 137; 139

Domicile: loss of, 241, 2

Dowry: 184; in case of transfer to another institute, 188; 328, 3; investment of, 161; 186, b, e; in case of dismissal, 187; 338

Elections: in chapter, 69 sq.

Eucharist, Holy: reservation of, 143–145; public exposition, 146; private exposition, 146; see Mass and Communion

Eucharistic Fast: 287

Examination: canonical, 190; of studies, 261, 263

Excardination: 241

Exclaustration: 333

Excommunication: nature, 49; incurred by alienation of property, 165; for violation of cloister, 287, 3; 289; for apostasy from religion, 342

Exemption: 308 sq.

Exercises of piety: 204

Exhortation: to the community, 87

Expulsion: from lay colleges and admission into religion, 180, 3; of religious, 180, 1; see Dismissal

Extreme Unction: administration of, 150

Federation of Nuns: 8, 2

Fugitive: definition, 341, 1; misdemeanor punishable by dismissal, 342; 345

Funerals: 152 sq.

(Numbers Refer to Sections)

General Statutes: 259

Godparent: see *Sponsor*

Habit: clerical, 265; religious, 265; obligation, 265; of postulants, 173; of novices, 202; 328; privation of, 334; 366, 3

Health and dismissal: 331; 348

Heresy: impediment to admission, 179, *a*

Hierarchy: 50

Holy Thursday: services, 141

Hospital: erection of, 36; subject to canonical visitation, 94, 2

House: erection and suppression, 32 sq.; filial, 12; 67, 3; formed, 11

Ignorance: of law, 21; of penalty, 48, 2

Illegitimate (birth): abolished as an impediment to admission, 180, 3; impediment to office of superior, 65, 2, *b*

Illness: grave and confession, 123; and Mass, 142

Immunity: privilege of, 306, 3

Impediments: to entering religion, 178 sq.

Incorrigibility: 343, 1; 348; 354; 356

Indulgences: 255

Indult: episcopal, use of, 318

Insanity and vows: 331

Institute: religious, definition, 6; erection and suppression, 2 sq.

Instruction: catechetical, 87; 208, 2; on training of subjects destined for priesthood, see Appendix II; regarding quinquennial report to Holy See, see Appendix III

Investment of funds: 156, 3; authorization, 158

Irregularity: 242

Jurisdiction: meaning of, 43–44; of exempt superiors, 60

Lay Brothers and Sisters: catechetical instruction, 207, 2; occupation in the novitiate, 208; postulancy, 172;

special novitiate, 203; solemn profession, 229

Leaving: the house, 292; 293; and exemption, 312, 1; leaving the institute, 330 sq.

Letters: 294 sq.

Loans: 163 sq.

Marriage: forbidden to religious, 241, 4; 242; nullity, 247, 3; 276; constitutes a misdemeanor for religious, 345; impediment, admission, 179, *d*

Mass: celebration of, 140–142; assistance at, 254, 2; conventual, 140; 298, 2; Holy Thursday, 141; Midnight at Christmas, 140

Master of novices: 204 sq.; account of conscience, 130, 2; care and direction of novices, 205; his assistant, 204

Mendicant Orders: 320; precedence, 24

Military service: exemption of religious, 306, 3; effects on profession, 237; 238; Appendix IV; pensions and bonus, 246; in U. S., 238

Misdemeanor (*delictum*): definition, 48, 2; 353; necessary cause for dismissal, 353; 360; sufficient cause for dismissal, 345

Monastery: meaning, 11, 2; foundation, 34; suppressions, 40

Monetary values: 98, 1; 157

Monk: meaning, 24, 3; precedence, 24, 1

Normae: value of, 3

Novices: disposition of property, 216; confessions of, 212; dependence on superiors, 46; 205; 328; studies, 210; funerals, 152–153; habit, 202; privileges, 213; profession in danger of death, 214; private vows, 214, 2; see *Novitiate*

Novitiate: 178 sq.; age required, 195; testimonial letters, 182; examination of postulants, 190; power of admitting, 181; dismissal, 220; taking of habit, 192; duration, 196; interruption and suspension, 197 sq.;

(Numbers Refer to Sections)

place, 191; 193; erection or translation, 193; discipline and exercises, 205; oratory with Blessed Sacrament, 145; support, 219; transfer to another institute, 328

Nullity: of acts and ignorance of law, 21; of alienations, 165; of elections, 75; of novitiate, 177; 179; 196; 197; of temporary profession, 226; perpetual, 228; of acts contrary to solemn profession, 247, 3

Nuns: definition, 15; temporal administration, 167; apostasy, 340; chaplain, 133–134; cloister, 145; 173, 3; 285 sq.; occasional confessor, 120; disposal of property, 243, 3; dowry, 185 sq.; 328; elections, 69 sq.; loans, 163 sq.; and local Ordinary, 53, 1; transfer to another monastery, 328; investment of money, 161; postulants, 173, 3; preachers, 147, 3; profession (ceremonies), 226; dismissal, 352; 341, 2; 357, 2; Holy Eucharist, 145; Viaticum, 150, 2; canonical visitation, 92, 2

Obedience: vow of, 278
Office, divine: in choir, 297; private recitation, 240, 2; 247, 2; 297; 298, 1, 3; of the Bl. Virgin, 299
Oratory: public, semipublic, 135 sq.; principal and secondary, 145
Order, religious: definition, 7; apostasy, 340; constitution and rule, 271; contracts, 166; expulsion, 343, 1; right to possess property, 159; jurisdiction, 44, 3; mendicant, 320; Mass on Holy Thursday, 141; precedence, 24, 2; simple profession, 3; in danger of death, 214; solemn profession, 247 sq.; dismissal, 353 sq.; 358; secularization, 335; suppression of a house, 40, 1
Orders, Holy: 151
Ordinary: definition, 45; relation to diocesan congregations, 25; 26; 28; authority over religious, 53; rendering account to, 167
Ordinations: see Orders, Holy
Orientals: admission to religion, 180, 1, f

Origin: place of, 182, 3
Outdoor Sisters: 16

Parents: consent to enter religion, 180, 2; necessary for their children, 180, 1, d
Parish: and religious life, 301; religious as pastors, 325
Parlors: location, 282, 2; visits in, 292
Peculium: 275, 2
Penalty, canonical: 48
Perfection: obligation to strive after, 253
Postulancy: 171–173
Postulants: 173 sq.; confessor, 103; agreement for support, 174; funeral of, 153
Postulation: meaning, 81 sq.
Poverty: obligation of the vow, 274
Power, dominative: 46; of chapters, 56; of superiors, 58
Preaching: appointment of preachers, 147
Precedence: 24
Precept: 278
Privileges: nature, 303; acquisition of, 304; conservation of, 20; revocation of, 107; 109; 182, 3; common to clerics and religious, 306; for dismissal, 344, 1
Procurator: see Bursar
Procurator general: 100
Profession: definition, 222; conditions for validity, 226; ceremonies, 234; formula of, 228; temporary, 228; renovation, 236; invalidity, 250; in danger of death, 214; effects of, 239; validation of, 250
Provida Mater: 5, 1
Province: definition, 8, 2; erection, 30

Quemadmodum: reading of, abolished, 86, 2

Radio and Television: Appendix VII
Reading: of decrees of Holy See, 86
Regular: definition, 14
Relics: alienation, 163; notable, 163, 1, a

(Numbers Refer to Sections)

Religion: definition, 6; division, 9; see *Institute*

Religious: definition and division, 14

Renovation of vows: 236

Renunciation of property: during the novitiate, 216; by the professed of simple vows, 243; before solemn profession, 249

Report: on novices, 205, 3; quinquennial to Holy See, 88; see Appendix III

Residence: obligation of superiors, 85

Retreat: annual, 254; before the novitiate, 175; before profession, 221

Rota: tribunal of, 47

Sacra Tridentina synodus: reading abolished, 86, 2

Sacred Congregation of Religious: competence, 50, 2

Sacristy: and cloister, 282, 2; and visitation, 92

Salary: of workmen, 253, 3; of apprentices, 270

School: erection of, 36

Secular Institutes: 5 *bis*

Secularization: 335, 336; under the previous law, 343

Sedes Sapientiae: 259; Appendix V

Segnatura, Apostolic (tribunal of): 47

Servants: jurisdiction, 61; funerals of, 153, 4; catechetical instruction for, 87

Sister: definition, 14

Society, religious: definition, 18; erection, 25; suppression of houses, 41; administration of property, 169; obligations and privileges, 307; transfer to a religious institute, 367; dismissal, 367; vow or promises of novices in danger of death, 214

Sovereign Pontiff: authority over religious, 51, 1

Sponsa Christi: 15, 2

Sponsor: religious forbidden to act as, 266

Stocks: acquiring stocks in companies, 155, 2; 269

Studies: obligation, 258 sq.; in the postulancy, 173, 1; in the novitiate, 210

Suffrages for the dead: right of novices, 213; in case of exclaustration, 334, *c*

Superior: 58 sq.; account of conscience, 130; confession of subjects to, 107, 1; appointment of confessors by, 105; 106; designation of privileged altar, 255, 6; studies of clerics, 262; discipline of the novitiate, 205; admission to profession, 226, 2; postponement of temporary profession, 230; dismissal of religious, 355; last sacraments, 150, 1

Superior, local: administration of property, 159 sq.; conferences on dogma or kindred subject, 264; duration of office, 67; removal from office, 28, 3; relations with the master of novices, 205; dismissal of religious, 358, 2; 362, 3

Superior, major: 17; correction of culpable religious, 356; 360, 2; duration of office, 66; testimonial letters, 182, 2; celebration of Mass outside an oratory, 142; prohibition of books, 61; prolongation of postulancy, 172; of novitiate, 220, 3; qualities required, 65, 2; dismissal of religious, 346

Superioress: temporal administration, 159 sq.; confessions of religious, 124; appointment of, 68; re-election of superioress general, 81, 1; see *Superior*

Superior general: age, 65, 2, *c;* authorization for alienating property, 163, 2; election, 68, 2; dismissal of religious, 355 sq.

Suppression: of a house, province, institute, 29 sq.

Suspension of a dismissed cleric, 366

Television and Radio: Appendix VII

Testimonials (letters): 178; 182; 183

Third Orders: affiliation of religious to, 240, 5

Titles, honorary: 95

Tonsure: 151

Trade: forbidden to religious, 269

Transfer to another Institute: 327, 328

Exclaustration: 333; *ad nutum S. Sedis* 334 *bis;* "qualified," 334, 2
Trial: necessary for dismissal, 359; summary trial, 343, 2
Tribunal: meaning and division, 44, 2; privilege, 306, 2

Viaticum: administration, 150
Visitation, canonical: 90
Vocation: essential conditions, 170
Voice, active and passive: definition, 240, 3
Vote: right to vote, 324; in chapter, 57; in elections, 71, 75; deliberative or consultative; see *Counsellors*

Vows: definition, 223, 1; of dismissed religious, 346; 351; 363; 364; *of devotion,* 215; *private:* definition, 223, 1; dispensation, 61; 62; 205, 2; suspended by profession, 62; 240, 4; *public:* definition, 223, 1; dispensation, 224; *simple:* 14; 242 sq.; *solemn:* definition, 223, 2; effects, 247 sq.; history, 14; in case of transfer to a congregation, 329

Widows: 180, 3
Will: to be made by novices, 218; change of, 243, 4